HELLENIC STUDIES 14

HOMERIC CONVERSATION

Other Titles in the Hellenic Studies Series

http://chs.harvard.edu

HOMERIC CONVERSATION

Deborah Beck

CENTER FOR HELLENIC STUDIES
Trustees for Harvard University
Washington, D.C.
Distributed by Harvard University Press
Cambridge, Massachusetts, and London, England
2005

Homeric Conversation
  by Deborah Beck
Copyright © 2005 Center for Hellenic Studies, Trustees for Harvard University
All Rights Reserved.
Published by Center for Hellenic Studies, Trustees for Harvard University, Washington, D.C.
Distributed by Harvard University Press, Cambridge, Massachusetts and London, England
Volume editor: Casey Dué
Production: Kristin Murphy Romano
Printed in Baltimore, MD by Victor Graphics

EDITORIAL TEAM
Senior Advisers: W. Robert Connor, Gloria Ferrari Pinney, Albert Henrichs, James O'Donnell,
  Bernd Seidensticker
Editorial Board: Gregory Nagy (Editor-in-Chief), Christopher Blackwell, Christopher Dadian
  (Managing Editor), Casey Dué (Executive Editor), Mary Ebbott (Executive Editor), Olga
  Levaniouk, Anne Mahoney, Leonard Muellner, Ross Scaife
Production Editors: M. Zoie Lafis, Ivy Livingston, Jennifer Reilly
Web Producer: Mark Tomasko

LIBRARY OF CONGRESS CATALOGING-IN-PUBLICATION DATA:
Beck, Deborah.
  Homeric conversation / Deborah Beck.
    p. cm. -- (Hellenic studies ; 14)
  Includes bibliographical references and index.
  ISBN 0-674-01962-8 (alk. paper)
  1. Homer--Technique. 2. Conversation in literature. 3. Epic poetry, Greek--History and
criticism. 4. Greek language--Spoken Greek. 5. Speech in literature. 6. Homer--Language.
I. Title. II. Series.
PA4177.C64B43 2005
883'.01--dc22

                                                                    2005026662

To my teachers, who taught me the pleasures and privileges as well as the methods and responsibilities of scholarship.

TABLE OF CONTENTS

Homeric Conversation

Table of Contents

ACKNOWLEDGEMENTS

t is a great pleasure to acknowledge the assistance of many people who shaped his book during its maturation, and who encouraged me during my work on t in less obvious ways. *Homeric Conversation* began as a doctoral dissertation, and my first and deepest thanks go to Gregory Nagy, who advised my thesis. He has offered me unstinting encouragement, guidance, and collegiality over he years, which I have valued and enjoyed more than I can say. He stands at the head of the group of teachers to whom this book is dedicated. Carolyn Higbie has been unfailingly generous over many years with her expertise and good sense on a wide range of subjects, including but not limited to Homeric poetry. One of Richard Thomas' comments on my dissertation pointed me in the direction that eventually resulted in this book.

Several other colleagues have read the manuscript at different stages. I am glad to thank Richard Martin, Leonard Muellner, Richard Tarrant, and the anonymous readers for helpful comments. Needless to say, I am entirely responsible for the errors and shortcomings that remain. Several colleagues at the Pennsylvania State University were generous with their expertise: Philip Baldi helped me with the different disciplines of linguistics that relate to conversation, although he is not to be blamed for my failings as a linguist; Gary Knoppers provided valuable support and guidance in writing press proposals; Daniel Mack at the Pattee Library never failed to come up with exactly the right book, no matter how vague, comprehensive, or opaque my initial query to him might be. Casey Dué was extremely prompt and responsive as an editor and made the production of the manuscript for publication a painless and straightforward business. I used the TLG-D and E CDs for much of the philogical legwork, under an individual license from the TLG. I would also like to thank Jennifer Trimble, whose professional judgment and intelligent feedback is constantly indispensible to me. My final thanks go to my colleagues and students at Swarthmore College, whose interest in what I have to say about Homer helped me to bring this project to completion.

INTRODUCTION

"And what is the use of a book," thought Alice,
"without pictures or conversations?"

Lewis Carroll, *Alice's Adventures in Wonderland*

When some other good singer takes five hours to sing a tale,
I need ten. I don't know whether that's good or bad,
but that's how it is.

Avdo Međedović

THE *ILIAD* AND THE *ODYSSEY*, as readers since ancient times have realized, derive much of their force and power from the many speeches of their characters. These speeches represent a high proportion of the poems in comparison to other narrative poetry: between one-half (*Iliad*) and two-thirds (*Odyssey*) of the Homeric epics consists of direct speech, while Apollonius' *Argonautica* contains just 29% direct speech.[1] Because of the quantity and quality of direct speech in the *Iliad* and the *Odyssey*, and because the distinction between narrative and speech is one of the most basic in literature, a great deal of ink has been spilled on speech and speeches in Homeric poetry. However, virtually all of this ink has been used to write about "speech" rather than the joining of several speeches into a sequence to form a "conversation."[2]

---

[1] Laird 1999:154n3 for the Apollonius figure; the Homeric figures are mine.

[2] See recently Martin 1989 and Bakker 1997. Martin uses the speech act theory of J. L. Austin to explore in depth individual speakers and speeches in the Homeric poems, particularly Achilles. Bakker explores the language of the Homeric poems as a poetic version of oral speech rather than as an oral version of poetic speech. Kirk 1990:28-35 provides a general overview of speech as distinct from narrative.

Mackie 1996 forms a partial exception to this general tendency, in that one aspect of her inquiry into the differences between the Greeks and the Trojans as speakers focuses on their different behavior in face-to-face conversations on the battlefield (e.g. 6).

1

This is surprising, in that conversation is an inherently important phenomenon in the *Iliad* and the *Odyssey* simply because of how frequently it appears: something over three-quarters of the direct speeches in the poems either elicit a response or are themselves responding to a prior speech.[3] Therefore, we do not truly understand how direct speech works in the Homeric poems if we consider it simply as speech and not in its broader conversational contexts. Moreover, some kind of conversation appears in virtually every kind of scene in both the *Iliad* and the *Odyssey*. It therefore follows that understanding Homeric conversation will provide a broad and powerful kind of insight into the Homeric epics themselves.

My goals for this book are as follows: to establish that conversation should be considered a type; to describe the regular patterns of speech sequence and formula associated with the type; and to analyze from an aesthetic standpoint conversations that vary from typical patterns in order to better understand how types work within the poems overall, how conversation shapes the themes of the poems, and how the *Iliad* and the *Odyssey* work as traditional oral art. Finally, in the conclusion, I will explore the ramifications of these ideas for larger questions of composition and reception, although these conclusions are necessarily speculative.

The remainder of the first section of the introduction gives a very brief overview of the two major areas that underlie my perspective on conversation, type scenes and formulas, and linguistics. It also lays out in more detail my approach to aesthetics. The second section elaborates on the reasons we should consider conversation to be a type, what scholars have done when studying other kinds of type scenes, and how formulas and type scenes relate to one another (II, Types and Homeric Conversation). The third section (III, Linguistic Perspectives on Conversation) looks at the way the Homeric poems talk about conversation. It then provides an overview of the different areas of linguistics that can best complement the notion of conversation we find in the poems themselves. The fourth lays out the different sequences in which speeches occur in conversation and the kinds of full-verse formulas that link these speeches together into a conversation (IV, Repeated Speech Sequences and Formulas in Conversation).

---

[3] In Virgil, in contrast, a recent study states that only one-quarter of the speeches in the poem that are represented in direct speech receive an answer (Laird 1999:183).

Conversation as a Homeric Type

One key aim of this book is to *describe* for the first time the variety of sequences and contexts in which a series of individual speeches may be linked together to form a conversation. Essentially, this descriptive process aims to establish conversation as a Homeric type alongside more well-known types such as arrival, sacrifice, and so forth. Although conversational type scenes do not contain a series of different elements, like other types do (e.g. killing the sacrificial animal, spitting it, roasting it, eating it), they do contain regular sequences of events—speeches, sometimes accompanied by specific context-dependent actions—which are joined together into a conversation by the narrator[4] through recognizable formulas of speech introduction and conclusion associated specifically with conversation. Accordingly, they should be considered types, and they can be studied using the same approaches (both descriptive and aesthetic) that have been applied to other kinds of type scenes. This process will show us the common patterns that govern conversation in Homeric poetry. In addition, it will demonstrate the underlying connections that link together apparently dissimilar activities like athletic games and laments.

Like other type scenes, conversation can provide stimulating and fruitful material for thinking about Homeric aesthetics.[5] When we understand the common patterns for formulaic speech frames[6] and for the sequences of individual speeches in a conversation, we can profitably study the departures from these patterns from an aesthetic standpoint. A coherent and useful system of oral aesthetics for the Homeric poems has long been a desideratum of Homeric studies. Recently, a consensus about the general outlines of oral aesthetics has begun to emerge among researchers working on Homeric poetry from an oral perspective. This consensus identifies the interplay between repeated elements (which may apply to the formulas, the individual narrative elements, and the sequence of these elements that appear in a type scene) and variations on these repeated patterns as a central feature of oral

---

[4] Throughout this study I will be using the word "narrator" to refer to the controlling and arranging force in the poems. I have chosen this terminology, rather than "poet", because most readers agree that the Homeric poems do have a narrator.

[5] Fenik 1968 is a groundbreaking study on aesthetics and type scenes (focusing on battle scenes). More recent full-length examples include Reece 1993 (hospitality scenes) and Louden 1999 (on the repeating narrative patterns in the *Odyssey*).

[6] The term "speech frames" is used collectively to comprise both speech introductions and speech conclusions; this expression is also used for specific passages that contain both speech introductory and speech concluding language. Miller 1996 also uses the term "frame" for this kind of language in talking about the Hebrew Bible.

aesthetics. Well-established repeated patterns characterize both the order of speeches within Homeric conversations and the formulaic speech frames that join them together. Hence, Homeric conversations provide a very powerful and illuminating basis for a study of oral aesthetics in Homeric poetry.

Aesthetics and Homeric Poetry

What exactly do we mean by "aesthetics"? A recent survey article on the subject published in a cross-disciplinary journal devoted to aesthetics defines the problems that aesthetics is concerned with as follows:

> The nature and defining characteristics of art, the meaning works of art are said to have, how they may be judged, valued, or interpreted, the nature of imagination and of creativity, the kinds of experience offered by art, &C [sic].[7]

For Homeric studies, the nature and functioning of oral aesthetics has been a central question at least since the 1960s, when Nagler stated that "no coherent aesthetic theory has as yet emerged which would equip us to understand or appreciate the special nature of oral poetry as poetry."[8] Since then, many scholars have developed useful ideas about what this aesthetic theory might look like. Indeed, it may now be said that a general consensus about oral aesthetics has emerged.

Russo has put forward a particularly clear and concise statement of one view of oral aesthetics that is held by a number of scholars interested in the oral aspects of Homeric poetry:

> [Homer] composes in a style guided by the ear and meant to be heard, a style that pleases through verbal play based on an aesthetic of repetition and variation, and of relaxed fullness of expression whenever the context allows it.[9]

So, two elements of oral aesthetics are repetition and variation, and fullness of expression. Fullness of expression, stated another way, means that length constitutes emphasis within an oral poetic system.[10] In fact, the length of the speeches in the Homeric poems is in and of itself one of the key components of

---

[7] Diffey 1995:61.
[8] Nagler 1967:273.
[9] Russo 1994:372.
[10] Austin 1966, Martin 1989:206-230, Nagy 1996:76-77.

he epics' fullness of expression.[11] Current notions of Homeric oral aesthetics have moved away from the idea that original language is necessary in order to achieve an aesthetic effect. Instead, many scholars now find the unique artistic merit of the Homeric poems in their "individual and innovative use of traditional material"[12] rather than in their invention of entirely new or original material for particularly dramatic or important moments.

In sum, "oral aesthetics" as used in this work refers to a way of evaluating and appreciating the Homeric poems as works of art by using the following criteria: i) artistic excellence comes primarily through a gifted use of traditional materials rather than through inventing new things; ii) interplay between repeated language or story patterns and variations from these repeated patterns has a key role to play in creating the aesthetic pleasure of the poems and in emphasizing important points in the story; iii) unusual length creates emphasis. Although this consensus on the nature of oral aesthetics is now well established, there are relatively few studies that explore in depth how this actually works in the Homeric epics.[13] More studies of this kind are needed in order to work out the implications of these general ideas about aesthetics for our understanding of the specific building blocks of the poems—the words, phrases, formulas, scenes, stories, characters and so on that make up the *Iliad* and the *Odyssey*.[14]

Conversation provides a particularly apt and powerful basis for an aesthetic study of Homeric poetry for several reasons. First, the conversational type contains repeated elements of several different kinds: formulaic language of individual verses (speech introductions and conclusions); specific actions or events within a type scene (e.g. the fact that a speaker in an assembly rises before he begins speaking and sits down when he finishes); and the overall sequence of speeches in, and social context of, the conversation. Any or all of these elements may depart from common patterns in order to create aesthetic effects. Moreover, conversation appears in both poems and is ubiquitous throughout each poem. This means that any insights we gain about

---

[11] Compare the length of the speeches that Demodocus quotes to those quoted by the main narrator of the poems. The expansionist effect of the speeches in the Homeric epics becomes even clearer if they are compared to transcripts of actual conversations.

[12] Edwards 1990:323.

[13] In addition to the studies already cited, Taplin 1992 puts forward an extremely articulate and appealing vision of the aesthetics of the *Iliad* along these lines (see especially 9-43), but his specific analyses are not fully persuasive in support of it.

[14] Scholars who have called for such studies include Foley 1985:18, Edwards 1988:57, and Wright and Jones 1997:23, which specifically points to repetitive language as a fruitful area for research.

the structure and aesthetic functioning of conversation, in contrast to less widespread types, are broadly applicable to Homeric epic overall.

In connection with this exploration of the aesthetics of the variations in formulaic speech frames and in the common sequences and contexts of conversation, it may be useful to briefly survey various scholarly approaches to the notion of "traditional" language, characters, and so on in the Homeric poems. Although the opposition between traditional and original has generally been abandoned as a tool of aesthetic analysis, the concept of "traditional" features remains a useful one for understanding Homeric poetry on a number of levels as long as "traditional" is not considered to be the opposite (and artistic inferior) of "original."[15] Repeated patterns of language and narrative sequence within the *Iliad* and the *Odyssey* give us one kind of baseline against which to study variations in the poems. Traditional patterns that can be reconstructed in various ways as lying behind or before the *Iliad* and the *Odyssey* give us another kind of repetition to which the poems respond. Sometimes we can tell that repeated patterns in the poems are also traditional, but these two categories are not necessarily the same thing.

Since Milman Parry proposed in his French thèses that the epithets and formulas in the Homeric poems were traditional in nature,[16] scholars interested in oral theory have been exploring the range of uses of "traditional" language in formulas in the Homeric poems.[17] During the 1960s in particular this interest often found expression in an adversarial model of the relationship between an oral poet and the traditional language that Parry argued he had inherited from his poetic forebears.[18] An influential recent approach to the notion of "traditional" as it relates to language in oral poetry has been that of Foley. In a series of publications over the last fifteen years or so, he has developed the idea that each use of traditional language (such as an epithet) evokes the whole mass of traditional stories, phrases, and so forth that are connected to a particular character.[19] This is part of a general trend

---

[15] See Nagy 1979:1-5 for an important statement of the interrelationship of tradition, theme, and language in Homeric epic.

[16] Found in his collected works, Parry 1987.

[17] On this question, see also Lord (most influentially 1960), Nagy 1979, and the various publications of Foley during the 1990s (most recently 1999). Edwards' exhaustive bibliographies (1986a, 1988, 1992) give basically all the scholarship on formulas and type scenes that was done up to the dates of publication.

[18] An influential article written at this time has the illuminating title "Homer Against His Tradition" (Russo 1968). Segal, writing at almost the same time (1971), departs from this general tendency in an excellent study of the different ways that traditional formulas can be used that does not fall victim to the idea that "departure from traditional usage" has to mean "invent original usage."

[19] E.g. Foley 1991 passim.

n more recent studies of Homeric poetry that views the traditional language of oral poetry and its conventions not as a regrettable limitation on a gifted artist, but as the tool and the vehicle of the success of such an artist. This conception is closely linked to the aesthetic framework that oral theorists have developed in recent years for appreciating Homeric poetry specifically as *oral* poetry.

A different strain of Homeric scholarship, neoanalysis, has focused on the use and transformation of traditional materials on the level of characters and story elements. Neoanalysts often focus on surprising or inconsistent aspects of the Homeric poems, and they explore other early sources for the stories that the Homeric poems tell (such as the Epic Cycle). By doing this, neoanalysis aims to discover the traditional story motifs that lie behind the Homeric poems—in particular the *Iliad*—and to describe how the *Iliad* changes or adapts these motifs.[20] It has been pointed out from time to time by both neoanalysts and oral theorists[21] that both of these approaches to Homeric epic are based on examining traditional elements of the poems and considering how the poems change or adapt their traditional materials of formula, narrative structure, and story motif. Moreover, both neoanalysts and oral theorists tend to be unitarian in their attitude toward the Homeric epics.[22]

Linguistic Perspectives on Conversation

The concept of the type scene gives us a powerful tool for understanding the structure and aesthetics of conversation as an important but previously under-appreciated building block of the narration in the *Iliad* and the

[20] Kullmann 1984 is a useful comparison of neoanalysis and oral theory as approaches to the Homeric poems. Kullmann 1960, an exhaustive examination of the *Iliad*, is one of the most influential works of neoanalysis; see also Kakridis 1949. It is noteworthy that neoanalytic scholarship has much more helpful and interesting things to say about the *Iliad*, for the most part, than it does about the *Odyssey*.

[21] Holoka 1991 is a recent summary of the relations between these two schools of thought. Clark 1986 is a bibliographic review of neoanalysis which, like Holoka and Kullmann 1984, points out the similarities between neoanalysis and oral theory and uses these similarities to argue for more interchange between the two schools of thought. Reece 1994 is an example of a study that uses "neoanalysis . . . informed by the principles of oral theory" (158).

[22] That is, they generally believe that each poem is a successful and effective unity, rather than the work of several different composers (in contrast to their scholarly predecessors, the Analysts). This is not uniformly true: Schadewaldt, the teacher of Kullmann, believed that the *Odyssey* was the work of several hands (see e.g. 1966), but the majority of more recent neoanalyst scholarship is unitarian (see e.g. Erbse 1972 for a thorough and painstaking unitarian refutation of various theories about interpolations and inconsistencies in the *Odyssey*, and in English, see the bibliographic review of Clark 1986).

Odyssey. At the same time, this approach is limited because it tells us fairly general things that apply to a wide range of activities that characters in the Homeric poems regularly do. Linguistic theory gives us the basis for describing the elements of the type and integrating them into a cohesive whole.

A number of different areas of linguistics focus on speech exchanges between people.[23] Conversation analysis describes conversation as basically a turn-taking activity that the participants themselves understand and control. Moreover, the particular social context in which a conversation takes place affects the specific tendencies or rules that govern turn taking in that conversation.[24] Discourse analysis—a broad discipline of which conversation analysis is sometimes considered a sub-field—focuses on how speech is understood in context, or language in use.[25] Historical pragmatics applies principles developed originally for studying current or modern spoken language to texts, which in addition to being written rather than oral may also be fictional and/or in a dead language. This approach—unlike conversation analysis, which is based almost entirely on transcripts of actual conversations—assumes that it is possible to describe and understand language use even if the language in question is no longer spoken and the evidence available is entirely literary or even fictional.[26] Linguistic perspectives will appear in this book primarily to provide a context for the way in which the conversational type is described, but they also appear from time to time in the analysis of particular conversations, particularly those in group contexts (Chapters 5 and 6).

Type Scenes and Homeric Conversation

Generally speaking, scholarship on type scenes has dealt with speeches as one component of various other types (such as arrival or assembly) rather than treating speech or conversation in and of itself as a type. Insofar as speech has been considered a type, the salient feature of the speech has tended to be the context of the speech (lament, monologue) or the intention of the person giving the speech (persuasion, consolation). Speech per se has not

---

[23] These areas, mentioned briefly here, will be discussed in more detail in Section III of the introduction.

[24] Hutchby and Wooffitt 1998:1.

[25] Jaworski and Coupland 1999:xi.

[26] Jucker 1995:3-6.

been considered a type, nor does most literature on type scenes distinguish between "speech" and "conversation." [27] Although conversation has not generally been considered a type scene, in fact, it meets the definition put forward by Edwards in his recent survey of scholarly literature about type scenes. At the outset of this review, he defines a type scene as "a recurrent block of narrative with an identifiable structure." Edwards goes on to say that "in narratological terms, an amplified type-scene is not necessary to the 'story'."[28] That is to say, Edwards' definition fits Homeric depictions of conversation from both the descriptive and the aesthetic standpoints. He is perfectly right to question whether "speech" meets the definition of a type,[29] given that multiple instances of speech do not necessarily have an identifiable structure or consistent sequence. However, conversation—as distinct from speech—does consist of recurrent blocks of narrative with an identifiable structure, namely speeches joined together in a series by formulas specific to conversation. At the same time, the particular narrative blocks that recur, and the identifiable structures that order them, may vary somewhat depending on the number of speakers and the social context.

All the varieties of conversation discussed in this book share a basic similarity: their main components are an exchange of speeches and formulas linking these speeches together that appear either exclusively or predominantly between two speeches in an ongoing conversation. At the same time, a conversation in a given social context has specific characteristics that do not occur in other contexts: for example, assemblies have particular features that are not found in either informal conversations or other formal group contexts such as laments. While the content of the speeches in a conversation are generally not repeated between one conversation and another, the formulas that link the speeches together are among the most repetitive and regular parts of the Homeric epics. Conversations thus have the identifiable structure of a type scene throughout, although the lexical repetition in conversations is found much more in the formulas linking the speeches together than in the speeches themselves. In fact, as will be discussed further below, these formulaic verses are found specifically in *sequences* of speeches: they tend not to appear as introductions to speeches that either begin or fall outside of conversational exchanges. This makes it legitimate to

---

[27] See e.g. the categories in the bibliographic review of Edwards 1992 and the specific entries under "typical scenes" in Russo et al. 1992.

[28] Edwards 1992:285.

[29] Edwards 1992:316.

see conversation as a repeated sequence or block of narrative even though not all of a conversational sequence is repeated at the lexical level from one example to the next.

Previous Scholarship on Type Scenes

Arend first pointed out that the repetition in type scenes was not to be attributed to awkwardness or incompetence, but was part of the poetic vocabulary of the Homeric poems.[30] His work primarily described different types and the variations they might include without the then-usual attempt to isolate the "original" example of a Homeric repetition from a herd of imitations and interpolations.[31] The repetition in type scenes thus became an aspect of Homeric poetry worth studying, instead of something that needed to be explained away by anointing one example as the original and relegating all the others to an inferior or derivative role. Arend, not incorporating Parry's nearly contemporary work, did not discuss the structural or aesthetic implications of type scenes for specifically oral poetry, but Parry and especially Lord[32] considered type scenes to be a key component of the repeated patterns that characterize Homeric epic and other oral poetic traditions.

Lord describes an analogy between the theme (as he calls type scenes) at the level of narrative and the formula at the level of individual words.[33] In theory, then, type scenes and formulas should have received equal attention from scholars wishing to understand the Homeric epics as oral poems, but in practice, this has not been the case.[34] Fenik 1968 is deservedly the most influential of the few studies that used type scenes to explore broadly the structure and aesthetics of Homeric epic. Although, as he says, "the chief aim of this study is merely to identify and describe the recurrent, formulaic elements of the battle narrative,"[35] Fenik also shows very persuasively how time and again, the most powerful and significant battle scenes in the *Iliad* achieve their effects "not by inventing a new action or new details, but by the larger than average accumu-

---

[30] Arend 1933:6.

[31] So for example Wilamowitz 1916:75-77 on the relationship between the death scenes of Hector and Patroclus.

[32] 1960, especially 68-98.

[33] Lord 1960:69; see also Foley 1985:32.

[34] A rough and ready demonstration of this is available from comparing the total length of Edwards' review bibliographies on formulas (1986a:171-230 and 1988:11-60) with the one on type scenes (1992:285-330).

[35] Fenik 1968:165.

lation of familiar details."[36] Scholars have benefited a great deal from Fenik's work,[37] but surprisingly few people have extended his method to other types.

Fenik's approach is essentially also the approach of this book: to describe the components of a familiar and common type in the Homeric poems in order to understand both the construction and permutations of the type better and the way in which the elements of the type may be used—rather than abandoned in favor of different or unique material—to shape the important moments in the poem. One may reasonably assume that the insights of Fenik and others about the aesthetic functions of type scenes apply broadly to the poems and not simply to the particular types or poems on which their individual studies focus, but this is an inference rather than a clear result of these studies. No study has yet analyzed a type that is sufficiently widespread in both the *Iliad* and the *Odyssey* to cogently apply its conclusions to both poems overall, or to allow comparison of the two poems.[38]

Conversation, which not only appears in both poems but in basically every scene in each poem, is an example of such a type. Indeed, conversation occurs in as wide a variety of episodes as the poems themselves contain: it is a common denominator not only between the two Homeric poems, but between individuals and groups, between gods and mortals, between men and women, and between friends and enemies. This means that insights about how conversation functions aesthetically apply broadly to the Homeric poems, rather than to only one of the poems or to one particular type of scene in the poems. Indeed, any general conclusions about the aesthetics of conversation should apply to the aesthetics of the poems overall, given the frequency and ubiquity of conversation within the poems.

Formulas and Conversation Type Scenes

The most regular and repetitive part of conversation type scenes is the speech frames that link the individual speeches together. The vast majority of these formulaic verses follow the general pattern [accusative pronoun] / [verb of

---

[36] Fenik 1968:204.

[37] Edwards 1992:293 describes it as "a work of the highest importance for the understanding of the battle scenes of the *Iliad*;" while true as far as it goes, this represents the general and (in my opinion) unnecessarily limiting view of the book as a study of battle scenes in particular rather than of type scenes in general.

[38] But see Gunn 1971 for a demonstration that the *Iliad* and the *Odyssey* use the supernatural visit type in the same way. Based on this, Gunn asserts that both poems are the work of the same poet. His brief studies (1970 focuses on types in order to argue for an oral poet who dictated the *Iliad* and the *Odyssey*) do not allow for the kind of broad or overall view of the poems that I am arguing for here.

speaking/answering] / [nominative name/epithet] and mean something like "X answered him." These are among the most common and easily recognizable expressions in the Homeric poems. Although these are generally referred to as "speech" introductions, in fact, they are *reply* introductions: they are both the most common kind of speech introductory formula found in conversations and they are restricted almost entirely to replies, particularly those that occur in one-on-one conversations. The noun-epithet formulas found at the end of the verse in full-verse reply formulas provided the backbone for Milman Parry's seminal work on the traditional, formulaic nature of Homeric language. This is because these noun-epithet formulas demonstrate to a particularly high degree the qualities of economy (one expression of a given metrical shape available for a particular idea)[39] and extension (expressions of various metrical shapes available for a commonly occurring idea).[40] Parry argued in later work that built on his thèses that these features could only be explained by an oral model of composition for the Homeric poems that presupposed a body of traditional formulaic language from which an individual poet drew in composing his poem.[41]

At length, Parry's idea that this traditional language significantly diminished the role of the individual poet in creating the language of his poem[42] resulted in an intellectual position known as "hard Parryism," which saw artistry and formulas as mutually exclusive.[43] Hard Parryism, in turn, created a backlash in the 1960s and 1970s. During these decades, many scholars were engaged in refuting hard Parryism by exploring in different ways the flexibility and artistic functioning of formulas.[44] In addition, the term "formula" itself underwent careful scrutiny, with the result that various ideas of the term gained currency alongside, or sometimes instead of, Parry's widely used definition of a formula as "an expression regularly used, under the same metrical conditions, to express an essential idea. What is essential in an idea is what

---

[39] Indeed, it has recently been argued that economy is *confined* to such expressions (Foley 1999:210-211).

[40] For Parry's ideas about economy and extension, see Parry 1987:7 and passim.

[41] Parry 1987:328-329.

[42] See e.g. Parry 1987:22: "use of the fixed epithet, that is, of the ornamental as opposed to the particularized epithet, is entirely dependent on its convenience in versification [and not on the poet's choosing to use it]."

[43] Combellack 1959 is the most influential and also one of the strongest statements of this view.

[44] On flexibility, see in particular Hoekstra 1965 and Hainsworth 1968. For artistry and formulas, Holoka's Homer bibliography from 1973 gives a good overview both of the contemporary work being done and also of the assumptions and ideas about artistry that condition the debate about artistry at that time: the bibliography is entitled "Homeric Originality: A Survey."

remains after all stylistic superfluity has been taken from it."[45] Recently a persuasive argument has been made that the failure of any single definition of the term to gain the ascendancy should be seen as a productive multiplicity rather than a vitiation of the entire idea of "formula."[46]

Introductory Formulas[47] For Direct Speech   Most other types of formulas have been rehabilitated at least somewhat from the hard Parryan idea that meter in Homeric poetry determines all. Speech introductions, however, perhaps because they formed the backbone of Parry's original research, are still dismissed almost universally as lacking in meaning or artistic significance. A prominent scholar of oral poetry, who in general is a strong proponent of meaning and artistry within an oral framework, has recently called speech introductions "workaday phrases"[48] and "boiler-plate."[49]

Several article-length studies have collected examples of speech-related formulas. These generally strive to catalogue rather than analyze the formulas they discuss.[50] Edwards 1970, the most important study of Homeric speech introductions, provides some of the same data as the current study. Edwards' approach differs from mine in two respects. First, he is interested primarily in examining speech introductions as a Parryan formulaic system, and so he focuses throughout on economy and the metrical shapes of the components of a given speech introductory verse. At the same time, he is not interested in, and so does not discuss, how the conversational context of a particular speech relates to the speech introduction that introduces it. This means that differences in meaning between different formulas tend to be discussed only if the formulas in question also have different metrical shapes.

In addition, Edwards (at least in 1970) had an aesthetic stance toward Homeric epic that is fundamentally at odds with the idea of interplay of repetition and variation that underlies this book. For the most part, Edwards associates aesthetic force or interest with unique phraseology. He is interested in the "range of tone possible within the formulaic expressions", which he

---

[45] Parry 1987:13. For a recent useful survey of definitions of "formula", see Russo 1997, especially 245. Nagy 1979:272 puts forward the fascinating idea that formulas are "the selfsame words spoken by the Muses themselves." See also Nagy 1996:22-25 on what formulas are (and aren't).

[46] Russo 1997:242.

[47] Speech conclusions have thus far received almost no scholarly attention, so in this section I will be talking about "speech introductions" rather than "speech frames."

[48] Foley 1999:104.

[49] Ibid. 221.

[50] Krarup 1941; Fournier 1946; Edwards 1969 and 1970.

describes as "considerable." [51] His main interest, however, is in speech introductions that use unique or unusual language. The discussion of such verses takes up over half of the article. Indeed, Edwards concludes that the emotional peaks in the poem "draw their effectiveness not from colourful language but from the setting and content of the speeches, which are introduced by the most regular and familiar of verses."[52] In fact, this is not the case, in that many emotional scenes derive their power partly from the use of unexpected (although not necessarily nonformulaic or untraditional) speech introductory language. Moreover, this formulation does not allow for the possibility of creating emotional effects with traditional language, which also occurs in a number of emotionally heightened scenes. This study begins from the same point that Edwards began: what are the different formulas for introducing speeches in Homeric poetry? However, in this study, that question provides the basis for answering larger questions about the construction and aesthetics of Homeric poetry rather than an end in itself.

A number of articles in the last twenty years have considered verb formulas within speech introductory formulas that are doublets in meaning, metrical shape, or both; the consensus on these has been that they are equivalent in meaning.[53] More recent work has pointed out fruitful avenues for exploration,[54] but these individual studies do not add up to a cohesive line of thought about speech introductions or any kind of systematic advancement of our understanding of how speech introductions work. Indeed, there has never been a full-length study of Homeric speech introductions, in spite of their frequency in the Homeric epics and their importance in structuring the narrative.[55]

Notwithstanding the pervasive scholarly neglect of speech introductions, these expressions have a number of features that richly repay systematic study. Although the noun-epithet formulas within single-verse speech introductions have been generally abandoned as carriers of meaning, at the

---

[51] Edwards 1970:1.

[52] Ibid. 35.

[53] Janko 1981, Riggsby 1992, Olson 1994.

[54] Machacek 1994, anticipated to some extent by sections of Austin 1975 (in particular Chapter 1) and Beck 1999. The appendix to Pope 1960 points out instances of lack of economy in speech introductions for Athena, but does not explore the aesthetic possibilities of this lack of economy.

[55] Books on direct speech do not discuss the role of speech introductions in connecting speech to narrative. Lohmann's classic work on the structure of speeches (1970) has little to say about the interaction of speech and speech introduction; Martin 1989, which is centrally concerned with different ways of characterizing Homeric speech, does not discuss speech introductions per se and has no entry in its index for these expressions.

same time, the existence of several different metrically equivalent participles with obviously significant and contextually determined meanings that characterize the emotions or behavior of the speaker is widely admitted.[56] It is odd that meaning is granted to one component of speech introductory formulas and so universally denied to speech introductions in general. Indeed, speech introductions and conclusions are *so* repetitive, and so frequent, that it is tacitly assumed that they have no aesthetic contribution to make to either the construction or the understanding of the Homeric epics.

I take the opposite position: a strongly defined and frequently occurring pattern—like formulaic speech frames—presents an ideal opportunity for a poet to create aesthetic effects by playing off this pattern. That is, where the "normal" way to say something is easily identifiable, it is equally easy for the audience to identify instances where a different kind of language has been used and to ascribe importance to such departures from the norm. When expectations are as clearly defined as they are for speech introductions and conclusions, a poet would have an unparalleled opportunity to create effects by failing to meet these expectations. This need not mean that the poet uses untraditional or even nonformulaic language, although sometimes this is what happens at such moments: language that is traditional or formulaic in one context can create a moving effect if it is used in another context.[57]

Within conversation, then, speech framing formulas provide the bulk of the material for aesthetic studies based on the interplay of repetition and variation. This is because speech frames are very repetitive while the contents of the speeches themselves are much less so. This is not to say, of course, that the speeches are therefore devoid of interest, either aesthetically or otherwise. The conversation type consists of both speeches and the formulas that link them together, and the relationship between the two displays certain patterns that can either be followed or not followed in order to create aesthetic effects. Moreover, in some contexts, a conversational sequence may vary from the typical by including a speech at a particular spot where usually no speech would occur, and in these instances, the speech becomes noteworthy because it is a variation from the usual pattern.

[56] As is demonstrated, for instance, by the extensive bibliography on the meaning and linguistic origin of the participial expression ὑπόδρα ἰδών, on which see Holoka 1983 with bibliography.
[57] For a wonderfully sensitive analysis of such usage, see Segal 1971 on formulas for dying warriors applied to Andromache when she sees Hector killed before Troy.

Introduction

Oral poetry

The foregoing discussions have treated formulas and type scenes, aspects of Homeric poetry that are generally agreed to originate in an oral poetic tradition. Many readers of the poems who are quite ready to recognize that techniques of oral poetry are ubiquitous in the *Iliad* and the *Odyssey* at the level of individual verses and scenes have balked at seeing the entire poems as they have come down to us as likely or even conceivable productions of an oral poet. In fact, most of the major objections to the idea that the poems as we have them reflect oral poems that existed in substantially the same form as our texts can be countered with parallels from oral traditions of other cultures or from aspects of Greek culture itself. For example, the influence of our *Iliad* and *Odyssey* is extremely murky and unclear until sometime in the fifth century B.C.E.[58] This has often been used to suggest that the poems in their current form did not exist until the fifth century or even later. More generally, it is unclear how or why written texts of the poems would be seen as authoritative in an essentially oral culture, and thus it is hard to figure out how the poems would have come to be written down in the first place during the archaic period.

The Domesday Book, a survey of land and land owners made in early medieval England under the impetus of William the Conqueror, provides an excellent example of a written document that eventually came to have a major impact, but which lay essentially fallow and unnoticed for two hundred years after it was written down.[59] Once writing became an ingrained part of the culture of the English people, the Domesday Book was regularly consulted for legal precedents, but until then, it was used only rarely. This may have been the situation with the Homeric poems too. The assumption has been that if the poems were committed to writing, they must have immediately been a) used and b) authoritative in their written form, but the Domesday Book shows us that these assumptions need not be true. Indeed, the act of writing the poems down and the authoritative status of these written texts may well be two separate phenomena. The Domesday Book also provides a useful template for how the poems might have come to be written down in the first place, in that it was made by an outsider and not by a member of the oral culture that produced the contents.

[58] See recently Burgess 2001.
[59] Clanchy 1979:19.

The other problems with the idea that the poems came into being in substantially their current form at an early date and in an essentially oral milieu are primarily technical or logistical and have to do with the great length of the poems. From a poetic standpoint, the length of the poems, while noteworthy, is by no means unprecedented.[60] From the production standpoint, where did the writing ability and technical know-how in general come from that made it possible for poems of such length to be committed to writing? We don't know the answer to this question. This, however, should not be taken to mean that there is no possible answer: we know very little about either the state of the technology of writing in Greece in the archaic period or the extent to which members of other cultures with possibly more developed writing capabilities might have been present in Greece. We do not know that committing the *Iliad* and *Odyssey* to writing would have been definitely impossible in the archaic period.

Aristophanes' allusions to Euripides provide a useful perspective on the problems of arguing about how poems were disseminated based on the technical aspects of writing and/or book production.[61] It is patently obvious from Aristophanes' plays that he and probably his audience were very familiar with the plays of Euripides, not only those produced at the same time as Aristophanic comedies but those produced earlier. We know a lot more about Aristophanes, Euripides, the dramatic uses that Aristophanes made of Euripides, and the fifth century in general than we do about Homeric poetry. Nevertheless, our ideas about how either Aristophanes or his audience came by their specific and detailed knowledge of Euripides remain almost entirely speculative. Even so, no one would assert that, because we do not know how (or if) texts of Euripides were circulating at this time, the allusions did not occur. That being the case, it seems to me impossible to use writing technology as cogent proof either for or against any particular view of the transmission of the Homeric poems. Concerns about the length of the Homeric epics being incompatible with the technology of writing or the limits of oral composition cannot be either supported or disproved by our knowledge about archaic Greece or about oral poetry.

---

[60] Besides the comparatively well known poetry of Avdo Međedović in Yugoslavia (in Lord and Bynum 1974), lengthy oral compositions are known from (e.g.) the Philippines, where a poem of over 10,000 verses requiring 18 hours to chant has been documented (Maquiso 1977:38 and 47).

[61] See Harriott 1962 on the nature and possible mechanisms of allusions to Euripides in Aristophanes.

More positively, Avdo and other living oral poets who have been studied by experts share a set of characteristics that seem to fit the *Iliad* and the *Odyssey* as we have them. Avdo, quoted in the epigraph of this book, told the same stories as other poets, but he took much more time to do so and dwelled at length on the emotions and thoughts of the characters in the story. This produced a song recognized by both field workers and the members of Avdo's community for its outstanding quality. Field work in Africa produced a particularly long, detailed, and engrossing song from a well known singer who was stimulated by an engaged audience and a field worker recording his song.[62] A number of outstanding singers in modern Scotland responded to the presence of a worker recording their songs by lengthening and elaborating on the usual patterns for that particular tale without decreasing the quality of the song.[63] Niles, indeed, highlights the role of the individual in developing and maintaining traditional poetry based on his experiences in documenting the traditional songs and singers of Scotland: "it is through active, self-conscious, intelligent tradition-bearers like Međedović and Williamson that an oral culture realizes its full potential."[64] This book does not aim to prove one way or the other that the *Iliad* and *Odyssey* were orally composed in archaic Greece in essentially their current form. At the same time, the overall picture of the construction and aesthetics that emerges from these pages is consistent with such an origin for the poems, and as the previous discussion suggests, the usual objections to the Homeric poems as oral compositions of the archaic period should be strongly questioned.

Linguistic Perspectives on Conversation

The Homeric Perspective

The basic vocabulary used to refer to conversation tells us something important about what kind of activity the Homeric poems imagine conversation to be. The most common verb root used for "answer, reply" by both the main narrator and the characters who report the conversations of other characters

---

[62] West 1990:46-47.

[63] Niles 1999:104-107. He suggests that oral performance that is recorded, rather than being an adulterated version of a "true" oral performance, should be studied and valued as a distinct type of performance in its own right. He goes on to say (224n33) that the theory of oral dictation and Nagy's evolutionary theory can be reconciled if the date of oral dictation is moved later than it is posited by e.g. Janko.

[64] Ibid. 128.

is ἀμειβ-, which means "exchange."[65] Nearly one-half of all full-verse reply formulas used by the main narrator that mean something like "he answered" contain a form of ἀμείβομαι.[66] A number of other reply introductions that are not full-verse formulas also use this root. Similarly, the most common formulas that Odysseus and Menelaus use when they report conversations in the course of their storytelling all contain a form of ἀμείβομαι.[67] Occasionally, we see individual characters in the Homeric epics explicitly referring to this notion of conversation. For example, the disguised Odysseus—as one might expect from such a skilled and self-aware conversationalist—excuses himself when he speaks to Telemachus without having been spoken to first by saying "ὦ φίλ', ἐπεί θήν μοι καὶ <u>ἀμείψασθαι θέμις ἐστίν</u>"[68] ("Dear friend, since in truth <u>it is right</u> for me <u>to take an answering turn</u> as well", my translation of *Odyssey* 16.91). In fact, these are the first words in the poem that Odysseus addresses to his son. Similarly, Nestor refers to two speakers as ἀμειβομένω (*Odyssey* 3.148). So, ἀμείβομαι and its compound are used for the idea "answer, reply" at a number of different levels of Homeric discourse: the main narrator and the characters both use it when quoting the speech of other characters, and characters occasionally use it when talking about conversation.

It seems, therefore, that the Homeric poems consistently view conversation as one manifestation of a more general notion of societal exchange of commodities of value. This conception of exchange also includes the reciprocal giving of gifts.[69] The middle voice, which is used for "reply", shows the strongly reciprocal nature of conversational exchange: conversation involves essentially a simultaneous, interdependent exchange of turns at

---

[65] Chantraine 1990.

[66] 85 full-verse reply formulas with ἀμειβ- in them out of 188 reply formulas in the *Iliad*; 99 of 235 in the *Odyssey*.

[67] These two characters are the only ones who regularly quote directly the conversation of other characters. Their formulaic repertoire includes ὣς ἔφατ', αὐτὰρ ἐγώ μιν <u>ἀμειβόμενος</u> προσέειπον (So s/he spoke, and I in turn spoke up and <u>made answer</u>; 14x *Odyssey*); ὣς ἐφάμην, ἡ δ' αὐτίκ' <u>ἀμείβετο</u> δῖα θεάων (So I spoke, and she, shining among the goddesses, <u>answered</u>; 5x *Odyssey*); ὣς ἐφάμην, ὁ δέ μ' αὐτίκ' <u>ἀμειβόμενος</u> προσέειπεν (So I spoke, and he in turn spoke up and <u>made answer</u>; 3x *Odyssey*).

[68] Greek quotations are from Allen unless otherwise noted. Translations are generally from Lattimore 1951 and 1965, but some are my own where Lattimore's rendering obscures some aspect of the Greek that is important for my point. I have retained Lattimore's spelling, even where it is inconsistent with mine, to remind the reader that translation is an interpretation.

[69] See Viechnicki 1994 for a linguistic and anthropological discussion of the etymology of ἀμείβω in terms of its connection to gift-exchange and its cognates in other Indo-European languages. He proposes to define ἀμείβω as "social reciprocity" (120) or "balanced reciprocity" (122) rather than simply "exchange", which fits well with its conversational use.

speaking.[70] Gift-giving, in contrast, which uses the active voice of ἀμείβω, entails a more discrete and separable pair of actions between the parties involved. One cannot have a conversation without exchange, whereas one can give a gift without gift exchange.[71] The distribution of ἀμειβ- words for "answer" reinforces the idea that exchange is associated specifically with conversation, rather than with speech. ἀμειβ- is the only root commonly found in formulas that introduce replies that is *restricted* to replies: unlike other common verbs of answering,[72] there is only one example in over 200 instances of ἀμειβ- in speech introductions (in both simple and compound forms) where the verb appears to introduce a speech that is not a reply.[73] We may understand the verb as meaning "take one's turn [by speaking]" rather than "reply in turn", as it is often translated: a reply *is* a turn, one piece of a give-and-take structure between people that is based on speaking rather than on physical, material goods.

Modern Linguistic Perspectives

The linguistic discipline of conversation analysis takes essentially the same view of conversation (sometimes called "talk in interaction" by linguists working on conversation analysis). The most influential statement of the principles of conversation analysis[74] starts out by locating conversation within a broader spectrum of "speech-exchange systems;" it also notes that

---

[70] The middle voice is also used in a set of compounds that denote movement from one place to another, a sense which Viechnicki links to the original Indo-European stem's intransitive meaning. Over time, this meaning was supplanted in Greek by the "answer" meaning (130-131).

[71] Viechnicki interprets this differently: he attributes the difference in voice to a supposed intransitive sense of "answer" (124) and connects this to the tendency of Indo-European verbs to have transitive meanings in the active forms and intransitive ones in the middle or passive. I think that explanation is unsatisfactory, given that forms of ἀμείβομαι are almost always found with accusative pronouns.

[72] Verbs commonly found in formulas to introduce replies that also occur in non-reply contexts include the participle φωνήσας (spoke) as well as the finite verb forms προσέειπε(ν), προσηύδα or ἀντίον ηὔδα, and προσεφώνεε(ν) (all of which essentially mean "addressed"). Most of these occur predominantly in replies, but all occur regularly to introduce speeches that are not replies.

[73] *Odyssey* 5.96: καὶ τότε δή μιν ἔπεσσιν ἀμειβόμενος προσέειπεν (then he began to speak, answering what she had asked him).

In this speech, Hermes is addressing Calypso at the beginning of a conversation. Before this point, he has arrived at her island to give her the message that she must let Odysseus go (75-80) and she asks him what his business with her is (87-91). Hermes answers this question (97-115) but not until after Calypso has served him a meal (92-95). As a result, his speech both begins a conversation and answers a previous question. In fact, this single example of ἀμείβεσθαι to introduce an initial speech is the exception that proves the rule.

[74] Sacks et al. 1974.

a system of exchange regulated by turn-taking "suggests an economy, with turns for something being valued."[75] Thus, conversation analysis shares with the etymology of Homeric vocabulary a basic conception of conversation as a medium in which a commodity of value is exchanged in a social context. Conversation analysis tells us that conversation is governed by rules for taking turns among the participants. These rules, which are followed by speakers in the Homeric poems, include most basically the notions that one speaker speaks at a time, and that change of speaker is a recurring phenomenon.[76] Conversely, although only one person should speak at once (and not more than one), if no one speaks for any extended period of time, this may be perceived by the people in the conversation as some kind of mistake or problem in the conversation that needs to be rectified or otherwise addressed.[77] Moreover, the particular social context in which a conversation takes place affects the specific tendencies or rules that govern turn taking in that conversation.[78] Methodologically, conversation analysis stipulates that if a given rule or principle is to be meaningful as a tool of analysis, one must be able to demonstrate that speakers are actively oriented toward the rule in their conversational behavior.[79] As we will see, Homeric characters do behave in regular ways when they talk that are dependent on—and may be said to define—the specific context in which the conversation occurs, and they sometimes violate or adapt these rules. Moreover, they speak one at a time, and if one speaker interrupts another or no one responds after someone has finished speaking, that is cause for surprise or even chagrin.

This similarity of outlook between conversation analysis and the Homeric epics suggests that conversation analysis may have ideas about how to conceptualize and study conversation that can be usefully applied to Homeric poetry, at least at the level of the broad, context-independent insights it has reached about how conversation works. At the same time, the research methods of conversation analysis depend almost entirely on analyzing transcripts of tapes of actual conversations. Clearly, this data is very different from what we find in the Homeric epics, and the methods and conclusions that depend closely on

---

[75] Sacks et al. 1974:696.

[76] Sacks 1992 v. 2:32. 1992 v. 2:32-43 provides an extremely helpful overview of the question of "what is a conversation?" from the standpoint of conversation analysis.

[77] Sacks et al. 1974:714-715.

[78] See e.g. Drew and Heritage 1992 on features of conversations that take place in an institutional environment.

[79] E.g. Silverman 1998:30; Searle 1992 (with response in the same volume by Goffman) critiques the idea that conversationalists are following a rule.

specific conversations, rather than on the aggregate observations about many different specific conversations,[80] will not be applicable to literary texts.

Discourse analysis is a wide-ranging umbrella term for a number of different approaches to studying language use in context. In contrast to conversation analysis, which is a very specific methodological approach to studying conversation, a recent overview of discourse analysis explicitly disavows the idea of discourse analysis as a research method.[81] So, the study of language use in context may include conversation analysis, but it also includes other approaches that are less closely tied to live utterances as data. Some scholars working in discourse analysis focus on how language use (or, more generally, social relations) may be produced or represented in one context for an audience who is somehow separated or distant from the original production. This approach offers us two useful insights: first, one may legitimately apply linguistic principles to an utterance or representation that is produced in one context to be received or understood in another (in contrast to a conversation recorded by a researcher in conversation analysis, whose participants are all present in the same place and time);[82] and second, it is reasonable to assume that, in such a situation, "whether or not we identify with the way we are addressed, we do understand how we are addressed, because we do understand the way images represent social interactions and social relations."[83] That is, a representation of a conversation draws on the same kinds of ideas about how conversations work as a live conversation does. This is true for both the person creating the representation and the audience to whom the representation is addressed. Although the specific research methods that conversation analysis uses are not appropriate for Homeric poetry, work in discourse analysis suggests that we can nevertheless apply the basic ideas that conversation analysis has developed to representations of conversations as well as to actual recorded conversations.

When these representations are found in literary texts recorded in a dead language, our interpretive problems multiply, because we lack a clearly identifiable social and/or cultural context within which to place either the Homeric poems' representation of conversation or the way in which an audience might have responded to these representations. No scholarly discipline has yet come up with a scheme that will resolve the myriad problems that arise because we

---

[80] Sacks et al. 1974:699-700 note the simultaneous context-specificity and context-independence of conversation analysis.

[81] Jaworski 1999:xi.

[82] Kress, G. and T. van Leeuwen 1999:379.

[83] Ibid. 380.

lack definitive information about the context of performance, the manner of composition, the time of composition, the manner of transmission, the nature of the audience(s), and the time and manner in which the Homeric poems were committed to writing. However, historical pragmatics does give us a basis on which to apply linguistic ideas not simply to a representation of a conversation rather than an actual conversation, but to a representation contained in a text in a dead language, a literary text, or both.

Historical pragmatics combines the disciplines of historical linguistics, which studies language change over time, and pragmatics, which studies certain features of language use that affect how language is perceived by the people who hear it.[84] Some scholars working in this field emphasize the historical over the pragmatic, and aim to understand language evolution by tracing specific pragmatic features like politeness markers in a given language over time. Others emphasize the pragmatic more than the historical, in order to describe and understand "conventions of language use in communities that once existed and that are no longer accessible for direct observation."[85] In other words, historical pragmatics gives us a basis for studying language products of vanished cultures as though they are amenable to the same kinds of analysis and explanation as we use to explain language use in cultures that still exist.[86]

In sum, then, this study draws on conversation analysis for its basic model of conversation as a turn-taking activity whose structure both responds to and depends on the social context in which the conversation takes place. Discourse analysis shows us that we can apply the basic insights of conversation analysis about how conversation works to representations of conversation as well as to oral conversations. Historical pragmatics offers a parallel methodological transfer of a linguistics discipline originally developed for use in analyzing oral speech to texts from the past. Indeed, a recent overview of historical analysis includes conversation analysis as one area of linguistics that may be used to analyze texts from the past.[87]

Perhaps the most significant difference between a represented conversation and an oral conversation is the presence of the representer as a mediator

---

[84] For a recent survey of the language features studied in pragmatics, see Levinson 1983. Miller 1996, although she does not use the term "historical pragmatics", is an example of a study that applies linguistic principles that are primarily pragmatic in orientation to an ancient literary text (the Hebrew Bible).

[85] Jucker 1995:6.

[86] Lloyd 2004 performs such an analysis of the root κερτομ- in Homer.

[87] Jucker 1995:10.

between the represented conversation and the audience to whom the conversation is represented. A Homeric conversation essentially has three participants where an oral conversation would have two: besides the two speaking characters, the narrator also plays a role in the conversation. Indeed, it is the narrator rather than the character who performs many of the conversational activities that conversation analysis focuses on. Accordingly, we must look to the information contained in speech frames at least as much as to the speeches themselves for information about how (for instance) repair is effected in a Homeric conversation when no speaker takes the next turn after one speaker has finished his turn. When silence falls in the middle of a conversation, the characters themselves generally do not comment explicitly on the fact that no one has spoken. They may indirectly allude to it in their response, but it is the narrator who reports this silence and is the source of the audience's knowledge of and attitude toward it. Similarly, we usually do not see characters speaking about the social factors that affect the way they behave when they talk and the order in which they talk. Nevertheless, we can see from the comments contained in speech frames that these things do matter, and how they matter, in Homeric conversation.

From a linguistic perspective, then, the speech frames provide us with some of the information we need in order to understand how Homeric conversation works. Speech frames convey many of the non-verbal aspects of conversational interaction that conversation analysis studies. From a narratological standpoint, the directly quoted speeches in a conversation exist in both the story and the text. [88] The speech frames, on the other hand, represent verbally for the external audience of the text things that are not verbal for the characters in the story. And, from an aesthetic point of view, their extremely regular and formulaic language offers an effective basis for creating artistic effects through variation on repeated language. It is for all of these reasons that speech frames take precedence in this analysis over the speeches themselves. The next section gives an in-depth explanation of the methodology that was used to describe and classify the data on conversational sequences and formulaic speech frames that underlies this book.

---

[88] Using the word "story" in the narratological sense to refer to the "signified or narrative content" (Genette 1980:27) or "the narrated events and participants in abstraction from the text" (Rimmon-Kenan 1983:6) in contrast to the specific version of these contained in the text.

Repeated Speech Sequences and Formulas in Conversation

In the remainder of the introduction, the conversational terminology and data that underlie this study will be discussed. First, I will describe the different ways that individual speeches can relate to other speeches within a conversational sequence. The bulk of this section lists the formulas for introducing and concluding speeches, organized with reference to two features: where in a conversation the speech being introduced falls; and whether it is addressed to one person or many people.

How to Have a Homeric Conversation

A key component of the research that underlies this study is a catalog of each speech in the *Iliad* and *Odyssey* with respect both to its position relative to adjacent speeches (if any) and the type of formula (if any) that introduces the speech.[89] Any given speech may take a conversational "turn" in one of three basic ways: it may not participate in a conversation at all; it may be the first turn in a conversation; or it may respond in various ways to a previous turn in an ongoing conversation. Depending on several factors like the number of speakers involved, the social context for the speech, and others to be discussed further below, many different sequences exist for joining together a series of turns to form a conversation. Let us now turn to an elaboration of these basic categories and the various combinations in which they occur to form conversations.

Methodology   Before giving the results of this data collection, I will describe the criteria that I used to classify these speeches. My primary goals for this data collection were, first, to explore and describe the range of organizational turn-taking structures that can govern Homeric conversation, and second, to evaluate the preponderance and types of formulas for organizing different varieties of conversational turn-taking. For both of these goals, it is preferable to overestimate rather than underestimate the proportion of Homeric speech that occurs in conversation.

From the standpoint of describing turn-taking, overestimating the preponderance of conversation is preferable because describing a limited and very regular group of conversational types is easier than describing

---

[89] These results are given in table form in Appendix I.

a more wide-ranging and varied group of conversations. Hence, a model that can successfully describe a broad range of conversations is more powerful and more useful than one that applies to a more limited set of data. Similarly, from the standpoint of the preponderance of formulas that introduce and conclude speech, a more wide-ranging group of conversational types yields a more heterogeneous group of speeches; these in turn are likely to be framed by a more rather than less heterogeneous group of framing expressions. So, overestimating the proportion of speeches in Homer that appear in conversation will result in a conservative conclusion rather than an excessive one of how common and how regular formulas are for introducing and concluding speeches in conversation.

Types of Turns in Homeric Conversation   The most basic distinction in this data set is between speeches that appear alone ("single" speeches)[90] and those that appear as part of a conversation (those that are either preceded or followed by another speech). A speech like *Iliad* 5.714-718, in which Hera speaks briefly to Athena as a result of her distress at events on the battlefield before Troy, demonstrates many common features of a single speech. First of all, it is separate from the speeches on either side of it. The last speech before this one is clearly unconnected to it for several reasons: first, it appears thirty verses earlier (5.684-688) and events involving many different characters as well as a lapse of time intervene between the two; no speaker is common between the two speeches (at 684-688, Sarpedon addresses Hector); and the location is different (the battlefield in the former, as distinct from Olympus in the latter). The speech that follows most closely after Hera's address of Athena occurs some forty verses later (757-763) after Hera and Athena have equipped their chariot and driven it some distance away from where they started.

The speech itself also displays several features common to single speeches. First of all, Hera is giving Athena a command (couched as a hortatory subjunctive: ἀλλ᾽ ἄγε δὴ καὶ νῶι μεδώμεθα θούριδος ἀλκῆς [Come then, let us rather think of our own stark courage], 5.718). Commands, instructions to messengers, prayers, vaunts, and other kinds of boasts are among the most common kinds of non-conversational speeches. All of these forms of speech are inherently hierarchical in some way, and involve an imbalance of power between the speaker and the addressee. While these types of speeches by definition do not lead to replies,

---

[90] Goffman 1981:79n2 uses the word "single" to mean "a party of one present among other parties", in contrast to a solitary person who is all alone. This is usually the situation of a speaker who makes a single speech in Homeric poetry.

they may lead to non-verbal responses of various kinds. At the end of Hera's speech, the narrator says, ὣς ἔφατ', οὐδ' ἀπίθησε θεὰ γλαυκῶπις Ἀθήνη (So she spoke, nor did the goddess grey-eyed Athene disobey her, 719). This full-verse formula frequently occurs in the Homeric poems and it generally indicates that a particular speech will not receive a reply, whether the speech itself is a single speech or the last one in a conversation.[91]

Clearly, then, Hera's speech to Athena has no conversational links to the speeches immediately preceding or following it. Some or all of the following criteria apply to the speeches that I have classified as single speeches: in relation to preceding and following speeches, single speeches display a change of subject or theme; a change of both participants (speaker and addressee); a change of physical location; a significant lapse of story time; and/or single speeches are separated by passages of narrative from adjacent direct speeches. Not all of these criteria may apply in any given case. For instance, in *Iliad* 2, Agamemnon prays to Zeus (412-418); in the next speech, Nestor addresses Agamemnon (434-440). Both of these speeches are single speeches, although Agamemnon participates in both, insofar as 1) the first speech is a prayer and the second a command (to order the heralds to assemble the Greeks), both of which are types of speech that usually lack a reply and 2) a meal and a lapse of time occur between the two speeches. The two speeches are not about the same topic, nor does Nestor's reply respond to anything that Agamemnon said in his prayer.

Occasionally, a particular speech occurs while a conversation is in progress, but does not involve the main participants in the conversation. Such speeches are classified as "simultaneous single" speeches. These often involve anonymous speakers, as speeches introduced with the formula ὧδε δέ τις εἴπεσκεν ἰδὼν ἐς πλησίον ἄλλον (and thus a man would speak, looking at another fellow next to him [my translation], *Iliad* 2.271 and eight other places in the Homeric poems). One function of such anonymous speeches, indeed, is to dramatize the feelings or views of a multitude by using one speech as a representative sample of what the various members of the group were saying.[92] Such speeches are separate from conversational turn structures, although they accompany such a structure. Hence they are considered single speeches even though they accompany a conversation.

At the other end of the conversational spectrum we find an episode like the conversation of Penelope and the disguised Odysseus in *Odyssey* 19,

---

[91] 23 times in the Homeric epics, 22 of which occur after a single speech or at the end of a conversation.

[92] See de Jong 1987b: 80-84 on the function of τις-speeches.

which extends for over 250 verses (103-360) and includes 11 speeches in an unbroken alternating turn sequence between the two characters. This turn-taking sequence pauses briefly on two occasions to give details of Penelope's emotional response to things that Odysseus has been saying (after Odysseus' second and third speeches Penelope bursts into tears), but with the exception of these details, no elaboration, event, or passage of time occurs between the speeches. Moreover, a regular and consistent turn-taking structure governs the order of speeches, with Penelope and Odysseus speaking alternately. Just as these speeches follow one another, the content of each speech responds to or develops the content of the previous speech. One of the concerns of this book is the analysis of narrative digressions like "Penelope wept" that occur between one speech and another within an extended turn-taking sequence that is strongly oriented toward an alternative turn-taking organizational model. These digressions represent a variation of the normal pattern in the one-on-one conversational type of minimal narrative presence between speeches, and as such, merit our attention.

Conversational turn-taking structures vary in their length, the way they are organized, how closely one speech follows another, and the extent to which events as well as speeches form part of the turn-taking structure. To accommodate this variety, I have adopted a general, negative definition of the connections between speeches that constitute a "conversation": any speech that is not a single speech is considered to be part of a conversation. In practical terms, although the *degree* of linkage between speeches in different conversations varies significantly, single speeches tend to stand out clearly from their contexts because they display features of single speech described above. Thus, when one is in doubt about the nature of the linkage between a speech and its neighbor, the question is usually how strong the link is rather than whether it exists at all. In the few cases when I was unsure whether a particular speech was a single speech or was loosely connected to an ongoing conversation, I took unity of theme as the deciding consideration: if the speech was responding to an ongoing theme of the conversation and was addressed to or spoken by one of the participants in the conversation, I included it in the conversation. If it was not about the same topic as the rest of the conversation, I classified it as a single speech, even if it was spoken by one of the participants in the conversation or was spoken at the same time as the conversation.

Within the general category of "speeches that appear in conversation," I have distinguished three different kinds of conversational speeches: initial speeches (those that appear first in a conversation), replies (those preceded by another speech spoken by a different person), and successive speeches (like replies, preceded by another speech, but a speech spoken by the same person as the immediately preceding speech). Of these types, the reply is the most common in Homeric epic: 299 of 678 speeches in the *Iliad* are replies (44% of speeches) and 340 of 545 speeches in the *Odyssey* are replies (62% of speeches). Initial speeches can only be distinguished retroactively from single speeches. When a speech begins that is not preceded by another speech, the audience does not know until the speech is over and a reply either does or doesn't follow whether a conversation is in progress. Thus, initial speeches resemble single speeches in that they themselves are not responding to any other speech, but they also resemble replies insofar as they do participate in turn-taking conversational structures. Both the *Iliad* and the *Odyssey* contain few successive speeches, which violate normal conversational turn-taking structures at a very basic level because one person takes two speaking turns in a row: 37 of 678 speeches (5%) in the *Iliad* are successive speeches and 17 of 545 speeches (3%) in the *Odyssey*. Most successive speeches occur in group contexts, where the turn-taking structures are more fluid than they are for conversations between two people. Alternatively, an entire sequence may consist of one character giving two successive speeches without receiving a response from any of the people to whom he is speaking. Such successive speeches are basically two single speeches back to back rather than a conversation proper: with only one speaker, there is no real sense of turn-taking.

Formulaic Speech Frames for Different Kinds of Conversational Turns

Having examined the various sequences of turn-taking that organize the speeches in Homeric conversations, we now turn to the formulaic speech frames that both establish and display these forms of organization. This section gives an overview of the different types of full-verse speech introductions and conclusions, examining both their structure and content and their relationship to the conversational turn sequences in which they occur. The overall goal here is to introduce the reader to the range of full-verse formulaic speech frames that appear at various points in conversational types, with reference to the kinds of information they tend to include, the language they use to convey this information, and the types of contexts in which they generally occur. This will provide the reader with an understanding of the general characteristics of commonly found speech introductions and conclusions that will be necessary in order to appreciate the variations that these formulas may display. For the most part, more detailed discussions of how these verses are distributed throughout the Homeric poems and how they function in particular contexts will occur in the chapters of the book. I will begin with a brief discussion of the term "formula." The bulk of this section gives examples of the most common formulaic speech frames. It starts with those that precede a speech replying to another speech, goes on to the formulas that precede speeches of other sorts, and ends with an overview of speech concluding formulas.

Definition of "Formula"　For the purposes of this study, I will be using a fairly narrow definition of "formula": an expression of at least two words that is repeated at least three times with regard to the words that are used,[93] the order and syntactical relationship in which the individual words stand to one another, and the spot in the verse in which the expression is located. Not all of the words in a formula need be adjacent to one another: many speech framing formulas consist of several words that always occur in the same parts of the verse, with a gap or gaps left in between for a proper name or title. For instance, within verses that have the form καὶ τότ(ε) [accusative, addressee] προσέφη [nominative, subject], the fixed elements of the formula alternate with flexible slots for the name of the addressee and of the speaker. That is to say, <u>καὶ τότ' ἄρ'</u> Ἰδαῖον <u>προσέφη</u> κρείων Ἀγαμέμνων (<u>then</u> powerful Agamemnon <u>spoke to</u> Idaios,[94] *Iliad* 7.405) and <u>καὶ τότε</u> κήρυκα <u>προσέφη</u> μένος Ἀλκινόοιο (<u>then</u> the hallowed prince Alkinoös <u>spoke to</u> his herald, *Odyssey* 13.49) are considered to be examples of the same formula. τότε may be elided or followed by an additional particle.[95]

　I have excluded repetitions that are only attested twice,[96] with one exception, because there are a number of repeated expressions that appear only twice in contexts that are thematically linked. It seems to me an open question whether such repetitions should be considered "formulas" or not, and so I am excluding them from my definition. As many scholars have observed (including Parry), not all repetitions are formulas.[97] I have considered one expression that only appears twice, λιποῦσ' ἀνδροτῆτα καὶ ἥβην (leaving

---

[93] Although not the exact form of words: elision and nu-movable are not considered to change a formula to a different formula when such phenomena occur in order to accommodate proper names that begin with consonants versus vowels.

[94] Slightly adapted from Lattimore. One of the areas in which even Lattimore, the most exact translator of Homer, departs from the Greek is in the different translations he gives for repeated expressions like καὶ τότε, which at different times he renders as "at this" (*Iliad* 1.92), "then" (*Iliad* 4.444), and "now" (*Odyssey* 2.389), to name just three examples.

[95] Edwards 1970 uses the same criteria in relation to the flexibility of particles and the names of addressees for classifying speech introductions (4).

[96] Cf. Fenik 1968:5, which defines language that appears twice or more in the *Iliad* as "typical."

[97] Some repetitions, as Strasser 1984:45 points out, are not even intentional.

youth and manhood behind), to be a formula because linguistic evidence shows that it is an extremely old expression. Therefore, it may be considered traditional as well as repeated, and for this reason is unlikely to be a new invention. Although my definition of "formula" specifies a minimum length of two words, most of the formulaic expressions I will discuss are a full verse in length. This is because the vast majority of formulaic reply introductions are a full verse long. Therefore, six feet of dactylic hexameter was adopted as a uniform standard of length for all the formulas to be compared to one another in order to avoid the possibility that a difference in metrical shape affects the distribution or usage of two different expressions. Partial-verse formulas do appear in this study, but primarily as components of full-verse formulas.

My definition of the term "formula" should not be taken to mean that I believe that no language which does not meet it is therefore "nonformulaic"—quite the contrary. I have adopted this definition because it is one of my goals in the following pages to demonstrate that even highly formulaic language is compatible with aesthetic significance and meaning. The assumption that originality and artistry must go hand in hand in Homeric poetry, although less true than formerly, is not as dead as one might think. A recent statement on the subject of Homeric style and oral poetics asserts: "it must be remembered that Homer always has (and often avails himself of) the option of not taking advantage of the opportunities offered by the formulaic diction but of substituting something fitting the context and quite untraditional."[98] This statement implies that "untraditional" language is required in order to fit the context, when in fact this is not the case, as Fenik and others have demonstrated. This is not to say that nonformulaic language has no role in creating aesthetic effects, or that this study will not have anything to say about aesthetic effects of nonformulaic language. Rather, the focus of most research on the artistic possibilities of nonformulaic language has obscured the complementary importance of formulas as aesthetic devices.

Alongside my definition of "formula," I will be using the term "traditional." This expression will refer to language, characters, themes, and so forth which can reasonably be supposed to have had an independent existence before their use in the Iliad or the Odyssey.[99] Now, since we are distressingly lacking in any kind of context for the production of the Homeric epics, identifying traditional features is to some extent a matter of guesswork. Nevertheless, it seems

---

[98] Edwards 1997:274.

[99] For the importance of "pre-existing" as a criterion for discussing formulaic language, see Hainsworth 1993, especially 16.

safe to assume (for instance) that Achilles is a traditional character, and that the noun-epithet formula πόδας ὠκὺς Ἀχιλλεύς (swift footed Achilles) is also traditional. Such identifications will be made where they seem indicated by linguistic features or by frequency. Although "traditional" and "formulaic" are not equivalent expressions, the definition of "formula" adopted for this study is intended to maximize the likelihood that formulaic expressions are also traditional. Consequently, if it can be demonstrated that formulaic speech frames have aesthetic functions and that such formulas are likely to be traditional, this will to some extent uncouple the ideas of "invention" and "aesthetics" in the context of Homeric poetry. It will mean that traditional language—and thus the traditional art form of oral epic poetry—is compatible with the aesthetic system I will propose.

Speech Introductory Formulas The proportion of a particular type of speech (reply, initial, single, or successive) that is introduced by a full-verse formula roughly corresponds to the level of involvement that type of speech has in a turn-taking conversational structure. Successive speeches, which most markedly violate basic principles of turn-taking, are not only uncommon in Homeric poetry but are also the least likely to be introduced with a full-verse formula. There are 37 successive speeches in the *Iliad*, of which only seven (19%) are preceded by a full-verse formulaic speech introduction. In the *Odyssey*, there are 17 successive speeches and five of these are introduced by a full-verse formulaic speech introduction (29%). At the other end of the spectrum, 232 of 299 replies in the *Iliad* are introduced by a full-verse formula (78%); in the *Odyssey*, 288 of 340 replies have a full-verse formula introducing them (85%). Initial speeches and single speeches are similar to each other in the percentage of full-verse formulas that introduce such speeches: in the *Iliad*, 67 of 155 initial speeches are preceded by a full-verse formula (43%) and 82 of 187 single speeches have a full-verse formulaic introduction (44%); in the *Odyssey*, we find 61 of 115 initial speeches introduced by a full-verse formula (53%) and 35 of 73 single speeches so introduced (48%).[100]

What do these numbers tell us? Replies exemplify conversational turn-taking and they are almost always preceded by full-verse formulas. Successive

---

[100] In these figures and throughout this study, Odysseus' retelling of his adventures to the Phaeacians is considered one long speech insofar as it represents one turn at speaking by a character within a conversation organized according to recognizable turn-taking structures. Hence, formulas and conversational structures that Odysseus uses in his narration in Books 9-12 are not counted in my data. Similarly, direct speech in the second song of Demodocus is not counted, because it too is reported by a character and not by the primary narrator of the poem. I am currently at work on a study of speech representation by characters in the Homeric epics, in which I will deal with this language and related phenomena.

speeches, in contrast, violate turn-taking organizational principles of conversation and are seldom introduced by full-verse formulas. Both initial speeches and single speeches are neither participating in an established turn-taking conversational structure nor violating such a structure; these two types of speeches are preceded by a full-verse speech introductory formula more often than successive speeches and less often than replies. Full-verse formulas are very likely to introduce a speech that is highly involved in a regular turn-taking conversational structure, and correspondingly less likely to introduce a speech that is uninvolved in or violating such a structure. Put another way, the most typical and regular way to talk in Homeric poetry is to have a conversation.

Introductory Formulas: Replies[101]   Reply formulas, which are from the standpoint of sheer numbers by far the most common type of formulaic speech introduction, state in one self-contained verse that the next turn in a conversational sequence occurred. There are not very many different reply formulas. They all share the essential meaning and structure "X [name, often with some kind of descriptive epithet] answered Y [pronoun]", and most occur over 50 times in the Homeric epics. The following formulas are listed according to the main verb of speaking, from the most common verb to the least common.

1. reply formulas with προσέφη
   a. [accusative pronoun, addressee] δ᾽ ἀπαμειβόμενος προσέφη [nominative name/epithet, speaker]
   "Then in answer to [him/her] spoke [speaker]," 106 times in the Homeric poems (36x *Iliad*, 70x *Odyssey*)[102]
   Example: τὸν δ᾽ ἀπαμειβόμενος προσέφη πόδας ὠκὺς Ἀχιλλεύς, *Iliad* 1.84
              Then in answer to him spoke Achilleus of the swift feet[103]

---

[101] The data in the pages that follow and in the Appendices was obtained through Pandora scans of the TLG Disk D. These scans were checked and corrected against concordances and against the texts of the poems (Allen's Oxford Classical Texts, primarily, with reference to van Thiel, Leaf, and West where conflicts arose among the readings of Pandora, concordances, and Allen). The verses to be scanned were identified through multiple readings of the entire text of both poems, readings during which each speech introduction and speech conclusion and its main verb (or expression) of speaking were separately scanned with Pandora to determine how frequently the language appeared.

[102] Includes two instances with ἀπαμειβόμενον (neuter participle instead of masculine) and 13 with προσέφης ("you spoke", vocative addresses to Eumaeus). The expression ἀπαμειβομένη προσέφη (participle of feminine gender) never appears in Homeric epic. In the compound form ἀπαμείβομαι, the reciprocity already inherent in the verb ἀμείβομαι is enhanced further by the reciprocal prefix ἀπ-, "back again" (LSJ def. D4).

[103] Adapted from Lattimore; nearly all of the translations in this section are adapted in order to bring out as literally as possible the small differences in meaning that distinguish one formula from another. Translations that depart significantly from Lattimore's are marked as my own.

b. Various other participles may occur instead of ἀπαμειβόμενος, of which the most frequently occurring is ὑπόδρα ἰδών, "looking darkly, glaring" (20 times).[104]

Example: τὸν δ' ἄρ' ὑπόδρα ἰδὼν προσέφη πόδας ὠκὺς Ἀχιλλεύς, *Iliad* 1.148
Then looking darkly at him Achilleus of the swift feet spoke

c. Sometimes the name of the speaker is split up within a reply formula whose main verb of speaking is προσέφη, as in
[accusative pronoun, addressee] δ' αὖτ' [nominative, speaker] προσέφη [additional nominative(s) referring to the speaker, usually a patronymic]
"Then [speaker, son of so-and-so] addressed [him/her]," once in the *Iliad* and five times in the *Odyssey*

Example: τὴν δ' αὖτ' Ἀντίνοος προσέφη, Εὐπείθεος υἱός, *Odyssey* 1.383
Then Antinoös the son of Eupeithes addressed her

II. reply formulas with προσέειπε(ν)

a. [accusative pronoun, addressee] δ' αὖτε προσέειπε(ν) [nominative name/ epithet, subject]
[speaker] spoke to [addressee], 95 times in the Homeric epics (42x *Iliad*, 53x *Odyssey*)

Example: τὸν δ' αὖτε προσέειπε θεὰ γλαυκῶπις Ἀθήνη, *Iliad* 1.206
Then in answer the goddess grey-eyed Athene spoke to him

b. [nominative, speaker] δέ μιν οἶος ἀμειβόμενος προσέειπε
[speaker] alone, taking an answering turn, spoke to [him/her], three times in *Odyssey*

Example: Ἀντίνοος δέ μιν οἶος ἀμειβόμενος προσέειπε, *Odyssey* 2.84
Antinoös alone, taking an answering turn, spoke to him

III. reply formulas with ἠμείβετ'
[accusative pronoun, addressee] δ' ἠμείβετ' ἔπειτα [nominative name/ epithet, speaker]
Then [speaker] took an answering turn respecting [addressee], 68 times in the Homeric epics (47x *Iliad*, 21x *Odyssey*)

Example: τὸν δ' ἠμείβετ' ἔπειτα ἄναξ ἀνδρῶν Ἀγαμέμνων, *Iliad* 1.172
Then the lord of men Agamemnon took an answering turn respecting him

---

[104] A complete list of participles that occur in this verse is given in Appendix II.

V. reply formulas with ἀντίον ηὔδα
    [accusative pronoun, addressee] δ' αὖ [nominative name/epithet, speaker] <u>ἀντίον ηὔδα</u>
    Then [speaker] <u>said to</u> [addressee] <u>in answer</u>, 68 times in the Homeric epics (14x *Iliad*, 54x *Odyssey*[105])
    Example: τὴν δ' αὖ Τηλέμαχος πεπνυμένος ἀντίον ηὔδα, *Odyssey* 1.213
              Then the thoughtful Telemachos said to her in answer

√. reply formulas with ἀπαμείβετο φώνησέν
    [accusative pronoun, addressee] δ' αὖ(τ') [nominative proper name, speaker] <u>ἀπαμείβετο φώνησέν τε</u>
    Then [speaker] <u>took an answering turn and addressed</u> [addressee], once in the *Iliad* and ten times in the *Odyssey*[106]
    Example: τὸν δ' αὖτ' Αἰνείας ἀπαμείβετο φώνησέν τε, *Iliad* 20.199
              Then in turn Aineias took an answering turn and addressed him

VI. reply formulas with προσεφώνεε
    [accusative pronoun, addressee] δ' ἀπαμειβόμενος <u>προσεφώνεε</u> [nominative name/epithet, subject]
    Then in answer to [him/her] <u>spoke</u> [speaker], twice in the *Iliad* and twice in the *Odyssey*
    Example: τὸν δ' ἀπαμειβόμενος προσεφώνεε Τεῦκρος ἀμύμων, *Iliad* 8.292
              Then in answer to him spoke Teucer the blameless

VII. reply formulas with πρὸς μῦθον ἔειπεν
     [accusative pronoun, addressee] δ' αὖτε [nominative, subject] πρὸς μῦθον <u>ἔειπεν</u>,
     Then [speaker] <u>spoke</u> a word to [addressee], once in the *Iliad* and twice in the *Odyssey*
     Example: τὴν δ' αὖτ' Εὐρυνόμη ταμίη πρὸς μῦθον ἔειπεν, *Odyssey* 17.495
               Then the housekeeper, Eurynome, spoke a word to her

---

[105] This appears much more often in the *Odyssey* than it does in the *Iliad* (14x *Iliad*, 54x *Odyssey*) due almost entirely to the frequent appearance in the *Odyssey* of the Telemachus verse quoted here.
[106] Several MSS. have this verse for *Odyssey* 17.405, but it is not included here (although it is the reading preferred in Dunbar's concordance) because it is printed by neither Allen nor van Thiel.

Introductory Formulas: Group Replies   The same basic elements found in all reply formulas, "[name] addressed [object pronoun]", also characterizes formulas that introduce speeches made to or in a group (which I have called "group reply" formulas) as well as those that introduce a speech explicitly identified as the first in a series ("initial" formulas). Group reply formulas have basically the same form as simple reply formulas, except that the object pronoun is dative plural instead of accusative singular and the main verb of speaking has a prefix μετ- "[spoke] among" instead of προσ- "[spoke] to addressed." Group reply formulas occur much less frequently than simple reply formulas, and there are fewer of them.

I. group reply formulas with μετέειπε
   a. τοῖσι δὲ καὶ <u>μετέειπε</u> [nominative name/epithet, speaker]
      And [speaker] <u>spoke to/among</u> them, 19 times in the Homeric poems (8x Iliad, 11x Odyssey)
      Example: τοῖσι δὲ καὶ μετέειπε Γερήνιος ἱππότα Νέστωρ, Iliad 2.336
                  And among them spoke the Gerenian horseman, Nestor

   b. τοῖς αὖτις μετέειπε [nominative name/epithet, speaker]
      Now [speaker] spoke to/among them, twice in the Iliad and twice in the Odyssey
      Example: τοῖς αὖτις μετέειφ' ἱερὴ ἲς Τηλεμάχοιο, Odyssey 18.60
                  The hallowed prince Telemachus now spoke among them

   c. ὀψὲ δὲ δὴ μετέειπε [nominative name/epithet, speaker]
      At long last, [speaker] spoke to/among them, 7 times in the Homeric poems (5x Iliad, 2x Odyssey)
      Example: ὀψὲ δὲ δὴ μετέειπε βοὴν ἀγαθὸς Διομήδης, Iliad 7.399
                  At long last, Diomedes of the great war cry spoke to them

This formula demonstrates indirectly that the normal expectation is that speakers talk one right after another, without gaps. This, in fact, reflects one of the principles of conversation analysis, which has documented that if silence rather than talk occurs at a point when talk is expected, silence will be perceived by the participants in the conversation as a lapse.[107] Thus, this formula says not simply that a silence intervenes between one speaker and the next, but—more importantly—it implies that this is neither the usual nor

---

[107] Sacks et al. 1974:714.

the appropriate state of affairs. ὀψὲ δὲ δὴ μετέειπε [name/epithet], by itself, does not have all three of the basic features usually found in a reply formula, namely a pronoun indicating the addressee, a verb of speaking, and a nominative form of the speaker's name. So, it cannot stand alone to introduce a group reply. However, it is always found after the formulaic speech conclusion ὣς ἔφαθ', οἳ δ' ἄρα πάντες ἀκὴν ἐγένοντο σιωπῇ (So he spoke, and all of them stayed quiet in silence, 15 times in the Homeric poems including *Iliad* 7.398). Hence, these two verses together convey all the information that customarily occurs in formulaic group reply formulas. However, the group being addressed, instead of being represented by a dative pronoun within a single-verse formula, appears in a separate verse as a silent audience for the belated words of the speaker.

The close relationship between these two full-verse formulas points to a feature specific to group speech contexts: group reply formulas occur with accompanying verses of various kinds much more regularly than simple reply formulas do. Often two (or more) verses make the transition between one speech and the next in a group context. For example, person A speaks; then the reaction of the group is described; then a formula introduces the response of B; then B speaks in response to A. In a speech between two individuals, in contrast, the response of the audience is identical to the response of the next speaker, and so narrating the audience's response separately is not necessary. Indeed, in some kinds of group conversational contexts, describing the audience's behavior after one speech is as necessary to the structure of the conversation as the formulaic introduction to the next speech.[108]

II. group reply formulas with μετέφη

    a. τοῖσι δὲ [participle] μετέφη [nominative name/epithet, speaker]
      [Having done X], [speaker] spoke to/among them, six times in the Homeric poems (4x *Iliad*, 2x *Odyssey*)
      Example: τοῖσι δ' ἀνιστάμενος μετέφη πόδας ὠκὺς Ἀχιλλεύς, *Iliad* 1.58
               Achilles of the swift feet stood up among them and spoke

This verse is analogous to the individual reply formulas grouped together in I (b) pp. 33–34, although there is no group reply formula that uses a participle

[108] These group contexts are the subject of Chapters 5 and 6.

37

that simply means "answered." The participle in such a verse always conveys some additional sense besides "spoke among them." [109]

b. τοῖσι δὲ [name in nominative, speaker] <u>μετέφη</u> [nominative patronymic], "[speaker, son of so-and-so] <u>spoke to/among</u> them", six times in the *Odyssey*
   Example: τοῖσιν δ' Ἀντίνοος μετέφη, Εὐπείθεος υἱός, *Odyssey* 4.660
   Antinous the son of Eupeithes spoke to them

Introductory Formulas: Initial Speech to a Group A small group of formulas exist that show this same basic pattern of [pronoun referring to addressee] [verb of speaking] [nominative name/epithet, speaker] but with some kind of language that specifies that the speech is the first in a series. I have termed these "initial" formulas. As with reply formulas, different initial formulas exist depending on whether the audience of an initial speech is a group or an individual. Initial formulas, however, differ from reply formulas in that there are more different full-verse formulas for initial speeches in a group than for initial speeches to just one person. Group initial formulas include the following:

I. group initial formulas with μύθων ἦρχε
   a. τοῖσι δὲ <u>μύθων ἦρχε</u> (or ἄρχε) [nominative name/epithet, speaker]
      And [speaker] <u>began the talk to/among</u> them, 16 times in the Homeric poems (7x *Iliad*, 9x *Odyssey*)
      Example: τοῖσι δὲ μύθων ἦρχε θεὰ γλαυκῶπις Ἀθήνη, *Iliad* 5.420
               And the goddess grey-eyed Athene began the talk among them

   b. τοῖς ἄρα μύθων ἦρχε (or ἄρχε) [nominative name/epithet, speaker]
      [speaker] then began the talk to/among them, five times in the Homeric poems (1x *Iliad*, 4x *Odyssey*)
      Example: τοῖς ἄρα μύθων ἦρχε Γερήνιος ἱππότα Νέστωρ, *Iliad* 2.433
               Gerenian horseman Nestor then began the talk among them

   c. τοῖσι(ν) δ(ὲ) [nominative name/epithet, speaker] ἤρχετο (or ἄρχετο, as printed by Allen against the manuscripts) μύθων
      [speaker] began the talk to them, five times in the *Odyssey*
      Example: τοῖσι δὲ Τηλέμαχος πεπνυμένος ἤρχετο μύθων, *Odyssey* 1.367
               Then the thoughtful Telemachus began the talk among them

---

[109] In addition to *Iliad* 1.58, also 2.411 (εὐχόμενος "praying"), 4.153 (βαρὺ στενάχων "groaning heavily") and 19.55 (=1.59); *Odyssey* 18.51 and 21.274 (both of these are τοῖς δὲ δολοφρονέων μετέφη πολύμητις Ὀδυσσεύς [But now resourceful Odysseus, with crafty thoughts, said to them]).

These verses appear for speeches that begin a sequence of talk that occurs in a group, whether or not the particular speech being introduced is to an individual member of the group or to the group as a whole.[110] This demonstrates that in a group context, both the addressee and the audience of a particular speech are seen as the "objects" of that speech.

II. group initial formulas with ἦρχ' ἀγορεύειν
   τοῖσιν δ' [nominative name/epithet, speaker] <u>ἦρχ' ἀγορεύειν</u>
   [speaker] <u>began speaking publicly</u> to them, eight times in the Homeric epics (3x *Iliad*, 5x *Odyssey*)
   Example: τοῖσιν δ' Ἀντήνωρ πεπνυμένος ἦρχ' ἀγορεύειν, *Iliad* 7.347
   Antenor the thoughtful began speaking publicly to them[111]

III. group initial formulas with ἀγορήσατο καὶ μετέειπε
   τοῖσιν δὲ [name, speaker] <u>ἀγορήσατο καὶ μετέειπε</u>
   [speaker] <u>spoke publicly and addressed</u> them, seven times in the *Odyssey*
   Example: τοῖσιν δ' Ἀντίνοος ἀγορήσατο καὶ μετέειπε, *Odyssey* 4.773
   Antinous spoke publicly and addressed them[112]

All of the initial formulas that contain the verb ἀγορεύειν, "speak in public", introduce a speech to a group rather than to an individual in the presence of a group. Most of the time they introduce a speech that occurs in the context of a formal assembly as well. Although there is no character whose name appears in both II and III, the names that are used in each are of the same metrical shape: — ⌣ ⌣ —. However, names that appear in (II) above are modified with an epithet, so that the name plus the epithet of the speaker has the metrical shape — ⌣ ⌣ — ⌣ ⌣ — ⌣ ⌣. In contrast, names that appear in (III) do not have such an epithet available, and the name appears alone. Hence, it is not clear whether these two verses should be considered alternate formulas for the same idea "spoke to a group" where the use of an epithet with the speaker's name is the distinguishing feature; or whether there is a subtle difference in meaning between the verb portions of these two formulas and the use of an epithet is secondary to this verbal difference.

---

[110] On four puzzling occasions, however, a group initial verse introduces a speech to Odysseus when no one but he and the speaker are present: *Odyssey* 5.202 (Calypso addresses him), 7.47 (Athena), and 13.374 (also Athena), and 17.184 (Eumaeus). Edwards 1970:8n16 includes two occurrences in the conversation between Penelope and Odysseus in *Odyssey* 19 in his list of non-group contexts (103 and 508). In fact, this conversation takes place in the palace hall in the presence of other people, a fact that contributes at times to the drama of the scene.

[111] My translation.

[112] My translation.

Introductory Formulas: Initial Speech by One Individual to Another   The formulas that introduce an initial speech by one individual to another individual both imply that the speaker took the initiative in speaking in relation to his addressee.

I.   individual initial formulas with πρότερος/η προσέειπε
      [accusative pronoun, addressee] <u>πρότερος/η προσέειπε</u> [nominative name/epithet, speaker]
      [speaker] <u>spoke first</u> to [him], eleven times in the Homeric poems (10x *Iliad*, 1x *Odyssey*)
      Example: τὸν πρότερος προσέειπε βοὴν ἀγαθὸς Διομήδης, *Iliad* 6.122
                        Diomedes of the great war cry spoke first to him

II.   individual initial formulas with πρότερος πρὸς μῦθον ἔειπε
      [accusative pronoun, addressee] καὶ [name, speaker] <u>πρότερος πρὸς</u>
      <u>μῦθον ἔειπε</u>
      And [speaker] <u>first spoke a word to</u> [him], four times in the Homeric poems (2x *Iliad*, 2x *Odyssey*)
      Example: τὸν καὶ Τληπόλεμος πρότερος πρὸς μῦθον ἔειπε, *Iliad* 5.632
                        Tlepolemus first spoke a word to him[113]

Being the first to speak often has a competitive connotation in Iliadic battle scenes.[114]

Introductory Formulas: Context-Specific   Reply, group reply, and initial speech introductory formulas all share the same basic structure. They prepare for a speech by mentioning only three essential features that all speeches have (name of speaker, sometimes with epithet; action of speaking; pronominal reference to addressee). The main verb of speaking in such formulas generally identifies the type of speech (what kind of turn is it? is the audience one person or a group?). Another group of full-verse speech introductory formulas exists that describes some aspect of the conversational context other than the kind of turn and the name of the speaker. Such verses often omit one or more of the three basic pieces of information that occur in the different kinds of reply and initial formulas (most often the name of the addressee). I have termed this group "context-specific" formulas.

One example of such a formula is ὅ σφιν ἐϋφρονέων ἀγορήσατο καὶ μετέειπεν (he in kind intention toward all spoke out and addressed them), which appears 15 times in the Homeric poems to introduce a speech by an individual to an assem-

---

[113] My translation.
[114] See Chapter 4 on the relationship between speaking and attacking in battle scenes.

led group of his allies or comrades. From the structural standpoint, this verse annot stand alone to introduce a speech, because it does not name the speaker. Many context-specific speech introductions require an additional verse or verses in order to supply enough information to introduce the following speech clearly. Such verses do not appear as often as reply formulas, since their content restricts them to a particular context. For the same reason, there are many more different context-specific full-verse formulas than there are reply, group reply, or initial formulas. In addition, they have less in common with one another in terms of both structure and content than reply or initial formulas do. Context-specific formulas are found regularly with all types of speeches, including successive ones. In light of the rather eclectic nature of this group of formulas, a complete list of context-specific formulas is provided in Appendix III rather than here in the introduction. What follows is an overview of the kinds of contextual information that may be provided in a context-specific speech introductory formula.

Some context-specific speech introductory formulas identify by name not the speaker, as is commonly done in other kinds of formulaic speech introductions, but either the addressee or both the addressee and the speaker. Others specify the place that the speaker is standing (near the addressee, by the head of the addressee) or the mental state of the speaker (reproaching the addressee, grief-stricken). On the battlefield, several different full-verse formulas may characterize a speech as a shout. Occasionally, characters speak to themselves, and context-specific formulas introduce speeches "to one's own heart." A formula even exists to introduce a speech by an anonymous speaker. Speeches that occur in particular social contexts—laments, assembly speeches, battlefield vaunts, and announcements in athletic games—may be introduced by context-specific speech introductions related to the genre of the speech rather than the identity of the participants or the mental state or location of the speaker. Patterns that govern individual examples of this varied group will be discussed in more detail as relevant for specific conversational types.

An Anomalous Speech Introductory Formula: ἔπεα πτερόεντα   The verse καί μιν φωνήσας (or φωνήσασ', for a feminine subject) ἔπεα πτερόεντα προσηύδα is a unique anomaly among these various categories of full-verse speech introductions (s/he uttered winged words and addressed him, 37 times in the Homeric epics).[115] This verse has a unique distribution in that it appears

---

[115] The total figures in Appendix I for "variable formula" vary slightly from these because they include variations like καί σφεας (them; occurs four times) for καί μιν (him/her) and ἀμειβόμενος (taking a turn; occurs twice) for φωνήσας (addressing). Also, the figures I have given above do not include the few instances of this formula used by characters rather than the primary narrator.

approximately equally often before replies, initial speeches, and single speeches. Only this formula appears to lack an association with a particular type of turn in conversation (i.e. reply or initial speech). In the *Iliad*, there are 8 examples of this verse in reply introductions (3% of replies), 5 examples in initial introductions (3% of initial speeches) and 4 examples in single introductions (2% of single speeches). For the *Odyssey*, the figures are 8 reply introductions (2% of replies), 9 initial introductions 8% of initial speeches) and 2 single introductions (3% of single introductions).[116] All other types of speech introductions are specific to one type of turn and appear by far most frequently with this turn type, although they can and do appear with other turn types.

Moreover, the construction of this verse resembles a context-specific formula in that, because it does not name the speaker, it cannot stand alone to introduce a speech. And yet, it neither conveys context-specific information nor is limited to an identifiable kind of conversational or social context. καί μιν φωνήσας ἔπεα πτερόεντα προσηύδα is constructed like a context-specific formula but lacks clear links to any identifiable context. This lack of a clear contextual reference is emphasized by the existence of several context-specific formulas that end in the half-verse ἔπεα πτερόεντα προσηύδα (he spoke winged words) but have clearly context-related beginnings.[117] In fact, the formulaic half-verse ἔπεα πτερόεντα προσηύδα is itself unique: no other partial verse speech introductory formula appears with a range of different context-specific initial half-verses to make various full-verse context-specific speech introductions, in addition to a full-verse formula that is *not* contextually specific. In addition to these peculiar features, σφεας (them) appears four times instead of μιν (him/her) to introduce a speech to a group. There is no other formulaic speech introduction for a speech to an individual that can be transformed into a group reply formula without changing both the verb of speaking and the object pronoun to reflect a group addressee. This is also the only speech introductory language that is used by both the primary narrator of the *Odyssey* and by Odysseus in Books 9-12.

In sum, we can see that the half-verse ἔπεα πτερόεντα προσηύδα appears in a uniquely broad range of speech introductory contexts. Similarly, the most commonly found full verse formula in which it is found does not behave like any other full verse speech introductory formula. The verse καί μιν φωνήσας

---

[116] One such verse in the *Odyssey* introduces a successive speech.

[117] The most common of these is ἀγχοῦ δ' ἱστάμενος/η ἔπεα πτερόεντα προσηύδα (he came and stood close beside him and addressed him in winged words, 13 times); a complete list of context-specific formulas that end with ἔπεα πτερόεντα προσηύδα can be found in Appendix IV.

πεα πτερόεντα προσηύδα, indeed, essentially constitutes its own category f speech introductory formulas, a category that might be called "variable." 'aken together, these facts argue against any one meaning of the much-bela-ored phrase ἔπεα πτερόεντα[118] or any attempt to link together the verses in which this phrase appears. Rather, in order to evaluate the nature and context f a speech introduced by this phrase, it is most important to look at the rest f the language in the verse containing the phrase ἔπεα πτερόεντα.[119]

When the full-verse formula καί μιν φωνήσας (or -ασ') ἔπεα πτερόεντα ροσηύδα precedes a reply, approximately half the time, the immediate ontext contains some description of the emotional state of the person who s about to speak. Of the 38 instances of this full-verse formula, 18 precede reply. 11 of these reply contexts also include a verse or verses describing he emotions of the person about to speak, such as the following formulaic ouplet:[120]

> ὣς φάτο, ῥίγησεν δὲ πολύτλας δῖος Ὀδυσσεύς,
> καί μιν φωνήσας ἔπεα πτερόεντα προσηύδα

> So she [Calypso] spoke to him, but long-suffering great
>   Odysseus
> shuddered, and spoke again in winged words and addressed her
> > *Odyssey* 5.171–172

An additional five instances of this full-verse formula are associated with a description of the speaker's emotion but do not precede a reply. We can say hat the association of the full-verse formula καί μιν φωνήσας ἔπεα πτερόεντα ροσηύδα with describing the speaker's emotions is particularly strong in the :ase of replies, but that it also exists for speeches introduced with this verse hat are not replies.

Speech Conclusions   Speech conclusions, separate verses that say something ike "thus s/he spoke, and [something else happened next]", generally occur it the end of a conversation or after a single speech. They are almost never found during one-on-one conversations. Although they do sometimes appear

---

[118] See Létoublon 1999 for a recent overview of the various interpretations and interpreters of this formula.

[119] Here I differ from Martin 1989, who sees ἔπεα πτερόεντα as introducing a "highly marked" speech (30). Rather, I agree with Latacz 1968, who argues that πτερόεντα is a generalized epithet referring via an implied comparison with arrows to the fact that words, once spoken, cannot be unspoken.

[120] Three times in the Homeric poems, with various names at the end of the first verse.

in the middle of group conversations, there are particular speech concluding formulas that tend to be used during conversations and these usually show up in specific kinds of contexts.

The six formulaic speech conclusions that appear more than ten times in the Homeric poems provide a representative overview of this kind of formulaic speech frame. One of these verses, ὣς ἔφαθ', οἳ δ' ἄρα πάντες ἀκὴν ἐγένοντο σιωπῇ (So he spoke, and all of them stayed stricken to silence, 15 times in the Homeric epics), appears almost exclusively in the middle of group conversations. Sometimes a speech introduction immediately follows; sometimes a longer passage describes the emotions of the audience as a result of what they have heard. It emphasizes the amazement or consternation of the group at what person A has said before person B at length replies, and it reminds us indirectly that normally, emotions do not run high enough to intervene between speeches and no gaps intervene between one speech and the next. This emphasizes the startling effect of the speech of person A. This formula marks a high point of emotion in a particular conversation: we do not find more than one of these in any one conversation. Formal group contexts are distinguished from other kinds of conversational situations by (among other things) the consistent or repeated appearance of formulaic speech conclusions in between one speech and the next during an ongoing conversation.[121]

The other five most common speech concluding formulas, which appear a total of 81 times, appear only seven times in the middle of a conversation rather than after speech is finished. The verse ὣς οἳ μὲν τοιαῦτα πρὸς ἀλλήλους ἀγόρευον (Now as these were speaking things like this to each other), which generally concludes a conversation, is responsible for five of these mid-conversation speech conclusions. This is not surprising, since this verse—unlike most speech conclusions—is associated specifically with conversation rather than with speech in general. Moreover, speech conclusions appear more often in the *Iliad*, which has a greater proportion of single speech than they do in the *Odyssey*: of our six most common speech conclusions, 64 of 96 examples (67%) occur in the *Iliad*.

The six chapters are grouped into two parts of three chapters each. Part I focuses on one-on-one conversations (Chapters 1 and 2 on the *Odyssey* and Chapter 3 in the *Iliad*). In both poems, conversation consistently dramatizes a particular view of human relationships that is central to the poem's overall themes and concerns. Part II considers other kinds of conversations. Chapter 4 discusses single genres of speech that commonly appear on the battlefield

---

[121] See Chapters 5 and 6.

These single genres have a central role in depicting the characters of the main characters in the *Iliad*; by relying heavily on speech genres and contexts that are usually found in battle, the poem implicitly underlines its view that human relationships are essentially hostile and adversarial. Chapters 5 (assemblies) and 6 (games and laments) focus on various kinds of formal group contexts. These genres have a number of characteristics in common with each other because of the common features that occur in formal contexts of various kinds. Moreover, the specific formal genres that the *Iliad* emphasizes both shape and depict its vision of the events it narrates, particularly the quarrel between Agamemnon and Achilles and the death of Hector.

Alongside this grouping into two parts of three chapters each, the book also falls into three parts of two chapters each: Chapters 1 and 2 focus on the *Odyssey*; Chapters 3 and 4 on one-on-one conversations in the *Iliad*; and Chapters 5 and 6 on formal group conversations in the *Iliad*. These pairs of chapters complement each other and usually come to similar conclusions; this arrangement also calls attention to the significant differences between the *Iliad* and the *Odyssey* in terms of which specific genres of conversation most prominently appear. Despite these differences, as we will see, the poems display broad and comprehensive similarities in the way that conversations vary from typical patterns and in the aesthetic and poetic significance of these variations.

PART 1

ONE-ON-ONE CONVERSATIONS

1

ONE-ON-ONE CONVERSATIONS (ODYSSEY)

CHAPTERS 1-3 FOCUS ON ONE-ON-ONE CONVERSATIONS. In the most basic form of one-on-one conversation, two speakers alternate without either events in the story or comments from the narrator intervening between one speech and the next. All the conversations that appear in these chapters depart from that model. I will be focusing on conversations that depart from this pattern in that they contain elaborations on this basic one-on-one alternating sequence. By "elaboration," I mean some kind of variation within a single verse speech introduction or speech conclusion that goes beyond the normal range of structures and meanings for such formulaic verses,[1] or an extension of a single formulaic verse into a multi-verse speech frame. Occasionally, the basic alternating turn structure even disappears in order to show the emotions of speakers in a conversation. The most common type of variation involves one or both characters in a conversation feeling unusually strong emotions about the conflicting pressures of skeptical concealment and self-revealing honesty, which the narrator then describes for the audience. Although many individual conversations will be discussed in these chapters, they all create their effects in basically similar ways, and most of them are aimed at depicting emotions of characters. This provides one demonstration of the basically unified and consistent aesthetics we find in the Homeric poems.

One-on-one conversation, as distinct from other forms of speech exchange systems,[2] tends to take place between characters who are in some

---

[1] Such as the context-specific participles found in Appendix II.

[2] Such as prayer, orders, assembly and athletic games; Part II treats several regularly occurring kinds of speech exchange that are not one-on-one conversation.

sense peers, at least while the conversation is in progress. Regardless of their relative social status or ethnic affiliation in general, two people in a conversation have an equal role to play insofar as each is equally entitled to speak and equally expected to listen to what is said to him and to say something in reply. Indeed, one-on-one conversation both presupposes and establishes a kind of parity between the speakers that does not exist for other genres of speech and that is largely independent of differences in status between the two speakers. Athena and Odysseus (*Odyssey* 13), Penelope and Euryclea (*Odyssey* 23), and Achilles and Priam (*Iliad* 24) all have one-on-one conversations that are dealt with in Part I even though in each of these cases, there are clear differences of status between the two participants. In each of these scenes, the characters might have interacted through other speech exchange systems that are based on a hierarchical, unbalanced power relationship, but instead, they converse. So, in *Odyssey* 13, Odysseus converses with Athena; he does not pray to her; Penelope does not give Eurycleia orders in *Odyssey* 23 but questions her in a conversational way; and Achilles does not vaunt over or (mostly) threaten Priam in their memorable meeting in *Iliad* 24. Indeed, the possibility of conversing with a god or an enemy or a servant shows that there is some elasticity in social relations and power dynamics, at least at the level of speech. A character can be peers with someone in one context and his underling or superior or enemy in a different one. How characters talk to each other, or don't talk to each other, both expresses and shapes their relationship at any given time.

The next several chapters discuss conversations that have both i) an above average number of turns and ii) elaboration or variation of some kind in between the individual speeches. These chapters focus primarily on elaborations in typical speech framing language, rather than on changes to the turn structures, in the conversations to be discussed. Hence they will contain a greater quantity of detailed close readings of specific passages from Homeric poetry than the chapters in Part II, all of which are centrally concerned with changes in turn sequences in common conversational patterns. Chapters 1 and 2 focus on the *Odyssey* (Chapter 1 on conversations involving various different characters, Chapter 2 on conversations between Odysseus and Penelope), while Chapter 3 focuses on elaborate conversations in the *Iliad*. Chapter 3 is much shorter than Chapters 1 and 2, because the *Odyssey* contains a greater number of elaborate one-on-one conversations than the *Iliad* does. In addition, the elaborations to these conversations tend to be more extensive.

Conversation in the Odyssey

The *Odyssey*, as is well known,[3] is much interested in how characters conceal things from each other. Odysseus in particular is distinguished for the zest and skill with which he lies to virtually everyone he encounters in his travels. At the same time, he yearns for human connections and above all to resume his relationship with his wife. The *Odyssey* creates much of its dramatic interest from the conflict that arises between the desire to conceal as much as possible and the often incompatible need to connect to and have relationships with other human beings. Characters who feel this conflict are often aware as a result of the possibility that others are concealing information at the same time as they may appear to reveal it, and of the potential gap between what is revealed and what remains unspoken. Conversation is the primary vehicle through which the *Odyssey* dramatizes this tension.

Specific elaborations that occur within conversations in the *Odyssey* tend to highlight this tension or its effects on the characters. These elaborations generally depict one of two things: they show either the dynamics of this conflict as it plays out over the course of a particular interaction, or several interactions; or they highlight moments when the tension is finally resolved in favor of establishing a relationship and abandoning concealment. Conversely, situations in which concealment does not conflict with an urgent desire to establish a connection (as with Odysseus and Eumaeus when Odysseus first returns to Ithaca) do not result in conversational elaborations. The *Odyssey* is interested in the tension between concealment and relationships, not in concealment per se. The *Iliad*, as we will see, uses one-on-one conversation rather differently.

In fact, the *Odyssey* makes more extensive use of the one-on-one conversation than the *Iliad* does at a number of different levels. Not only is the average conversation in the *Odyssey* longer than the average conversation in the *Iliad*,[4] but conversation is much more widely used in the *Odyssey*. That is to say, there are fewer single speeches as a percentage of the whole in the *Odyssey* than there are in the *Iliad* (13% vs. 28%). People talk to each other more in the *Odyssey* than in the *Iliad*, and they talk for longer periods.[5] This chapter will discuss the elaborate conversations between Odysseus and various characters he meets on Ithaca. Through these conversations, we see how Odysseus

---

[3] See e.g. Murnaghan 1987.
[4] See Chapter 3, note 1.
[5] I will explore the possible reasons for this in Chapter 3.

negotiates the conflicting impulses he feels between revealing himself ar concealing his identity when those impulses are the strongest, namely, whe he is at home on Ithaca among the people he loves most. Indeed, the conve sations between Odysseus and Penelope (discussed in Chapter 2) depict the impulses at the greatest length and in the most detail.

Athena and Odysseus: Book 13

The only one of these elaborate one-on-one conversations that does n involve a member of Odysseus' family is his meeting with Athena in Book 1 which shows Odysseus' impulse toward concealment struggling against h desire for straightforward interaction. This particular conversation is not on one of the few occasions when a mortal and a god converse in the *Odyssey*, it also the longest such conversation in Homer.[6] Everyone agrees that Odysseu landing on Ithaca and his encounter with Athena marks a transition in th narrative, but different scholars have had different opinions of the scene quality. Older Analyst interpreters found much to criticize in this conversatio but Erbse's analysis has largely rehabilitated this episode from the disgrace i which earlier commentators left it.[7] He has argued persuasively that becaus the gods are necessary for Odysseus to succeed in his homecoming, they pla a prominent role in the point of transition when Odysseus returns to Ithac from the fantastic adventure-land he has been living in for the last ten years. [8]

Not only Athena herself marks this transition, in that she begins Odysseu homecoming and re-entry into a basically realistic environment by being th first person he meets on Ithaca and providing his disguise. Poseidon, too, put an end to the fabulous story-world of the first half of the *Odyssey*, not onl for our poem but for good, by sealing off the Phaeacians on their island an preventing them from playing host to any more refugees. Starting from th general observation that Athena appears here at the beginning of Odysseu homecoming because she helps to make it possible, this investigation will focu on the specific ways that the meeting between Athena and Odysseus sets th stage for the reunions that occur later in the poem. More particularly, throug manipulations of the sequences and formulas of one-on-one conversation, i

---

[6] Clay 1983:188.

[7] See more recently Clay 1983 (Chapter IV). Clay asserts that the scene is simply a difficult on and that "neither minor nor major surgery can remedy all the difficulties it presents" (189 Her ultimate goal is to argue that the scene shows that Athena was angry with Odysseu because his excessive cleverness calls into question the superiority of gods over men (209).

[8] 1972:144-145.

highlights the conflict that Odysseus feels between telling the truth and being circumspect and cautious, and it depicts his self-control and cleverness in being able to subdue his impulse to reveal himself inadvisedly. Athena, as a master of cunning herself, provides a particularly effective interlocutor for Odysseus here. If Odysseus can converse with a god and hold his own in deception while doing so, his deceptive abilities are outstanding indeed.

Odysseus recognizes Athena in Book 13 for the first time in the *Odyssey*;[9] after the meeting, Athena remains on Ithaca with Odysseus for the remainder of the poem. In this scene, Odysseus and Athena have a long conversation that consists of eight turns in its first section and five more turns after a narrative interlude in which they collect the treasure that Odysseus got from the Phaeacians. Not only is this conversation unusually long, but it contains several elaborations in place of single-verse reply formulas. These elaborations occur in connection with speeches that reveal to Odysseus that he has in fact returned to Ithaca. Taken in conjunction with the speeches they introduce, these narrative asides depict Odysseus' unusual ability to dissemble that helps make this return possible.

Most of the speeches in this conversation are preceded by single-verse reply formulas.[10] However, we also find several speech frames during this conversation that describe someone's emotion in a multi-verse passage that includes the ἔπεα πτερόεντα introductory verse. The ἔπεα πτερόεντα verse appears in one passage preceding an initial speech (13.226-227) and in two extended passages that precede replies (250-255, 287-290).[11] These extended speech frames and the speeches with which they are associated stand out in the conversation partly by contrast, given the preponderance of single-verse reply formulas. Moreover, the specific ideas that these extended passages describe provide non-verbal details of Odysseus' thoughts and feelings that complement the proficient verbal sparring between him and Athena. The things Odysseus says show his ability to conceal; the things he feels, or refrains from saying, show his strong desire to simply tell the truth at once. Together, they show the conflict he feels between the two. The conversation overall highlights this conflict as a key aspect of Odysseus' experience upon returning home.

---

[9] The question of whether he really does recognize her, which is controversial, will be discussed in more detail below.

[10] For Athena: τὸν δ' αὖτε προσέειπε [or τὸν δ' ἠμείβετ' ἔπειτα] θεὰ γλαυκῶπις Ἀθήνη (then in turn the gray-eyed goddess Athene answered): 236, 329, 361, 392, 420. For Odysseus: τὴν δ' ἀπαμειβόμενος προσέφη πολύμητις Ὀδυσσεύς (then in turn resourceful Odysseus spoke to her in answer): 311, 382, 416.

[11] All of these citations, in spite of their length, refer to the speech frames, not to the speeches themselves.

After Odysseus arrives on the island and awakes from his slumber, the first person he meets is Athena in disguise. Upon seeing her, he beseeches her to tell him where he is and who lives on the island (228-235). His speech to her is introduced as follows:

> τὴν δ' Ὀδυσεὺς γήθησεν ἰδὼν καὶ ἐναντίος ἦλθε,
> καί μιν φωνήσας ἔπεα πτερόεντα προσηύδα·
>
> Odysseus, in joy at the sight, came up to meet her,
> and spoke aloud to her and addressed her in winged words,
>   saying:

13.226-227

Athena's name, mentioned in verse 221, is the antecedent of the pronoun τήν (her) in 226.[12] So, from the structural standpoint, it would possible to substitute the unattested but unexceptionable verse *καὶ τότ' Ἀθηναίην προσέφη πολύμητις Ὀδυσσεύς[13] for 13.226-227 as a transition from narrative to Odysseus' first speech, without any loss of clarity about the identity of either the speaker or the addressee. However, the information contained in our couplet emphasizes Odysseus' pleasure in seeing another person and his eagerness to physically approach this person after he had initially thought that the Phaeacians marooned him on an unknown island (200-216).

Although our passage is ambiguous about whether Odysseus recognizes Athena when he first addresses her,[14] what he says in his speech itself may imply that he does. He tells Athena that he is praying to her "as to a god" to tell him where he is (σοὶ . . . εὔχομαι ὥς τε θεῷ, 230-231). Either this is an ironic reference to the gap between the audience's awareness of Athena's identity and Odysseus' ignorance of it, or else Odysseus himself is being disingenuous and ironic. Evidence for the latter position comes from speech framing language in Book 22, where Odysseus addresses Athena during his attack on the suitors. The language that introduces his speech there closely resembles that which precedes his initial speech to Athena in our passage: τὴν δ' Ὀδυσεὺς γήθησεν ἰδὼν καὶ μῦθον ἔειπε (Odysseus was happy when he saw her, and hailed her, saying, 22.207). In Book 22, the narrator goes on to state

---

[12] Verses 222-225 describe Athena and her disguise as a young herdsman.

[13] Compare *Odyssey* 23.247, καὶ τότ' ἄρ' ἦν ἄλοχον προσέφη πολύμητις Ὀδυσσεύς (then resourceful Odysseus spoke to his wife).

[14] Muellner 1976:51 believes that Odysseus does recognize her here. Those who take the opposite position include Clay 1983, whose analysis of the scene seems to assume that Odysseus does not recognize Athena (see e.g. 196-199) but does not explicitly say this. Austin 1975 thinks that Athena is hurt by Odysseus' failure to recognize "the goddess who is his Olympian alter ego" (203).

xplicitly in the speech conclusion that Odysseus suspected he was addressing
thena, even though he gives no indication of the fact in what he says to her
ὣς φάτ', ὀϊόμενος λαοσσόον ἔμμεν' Ἀθήνην [he spoke so, but thought it was
thene, leader of armies], 210). This similar passage from Book 22 suggests
nat Odysseus may smile in Book 13 not only because he is happy to see anyone
t all when he had thought that he was on an uninhabited island, but because
e is happy to know that Athena is with him. If so, he shows his capacity to
onceal important information right from the beginning of the conversation.

The structure of Athena's speech contributes to the atmosphere of conceal-
nent and skepticism that pervades the scene. First, she calls Odysseus a fool for
ot knowing where he is (νήπιός εἰς, 237). This is a piece of concealment in itself,
ince she knows who he is and therefore that he is anything but a fool, and she
lso knows that he doesn't recognize Ithaca because she herself has disguised
:. She gives a long description of the place and its good qualities (238-247),
rolonging Odysseus' uncertainty and confusion as long as possible and thereby
esting his self-control; only at the end does she finally give its name as "Ithaca"
248).[15] The speech frame that precedes Odysseus' reply dwells on his emotional
esponse to her words, at great length and in exhaustive detail.

> ὣς φάτο, <u>γήθησεν</u> δὲ πολύτλας δῖος Ὀδυσσεύς,
> <u>χαίρων</u> ᾗ γαίῃ πατρωΐῃ, ὥς οἱ ἔειπε
> Παλλὰς Ἀθηναίη, κούρη Διὸς αἰγιόχοιο,
> καί μιν φωνήσας ἔπεα πτερόεντα προσηύδα·
> οὐδ' ὅ γ' ἀληθέα εἶπε, πάλιν δ' ὅ γε λάζετο μῦθον,
> αἰεὶ ἐνὶ στήθεσσι νόον πολυκερδέα νωμῶν·

> So she spoke, and long-suffering[16] great Odysseus <u>was happy</u>,
> <u>rejoicing</u> in the land of his fathers when Pallas Athene
> daughter of Zeus of the aegis told him the truth of it,
> and so he answered her again and addressed her in winged
>   words;
> but he did not tell her the truth, but checked the word from
>   the outset,
> forever using to every advantage the mind that was in him:

> 13.250-255

---

[15] Lloyd 2004:86 suggests that Odysseus views this speech as a joke at his expense, but as will
become clear, my reading of the scene is that if it is a joke, Odysseus is certainly in on it.

[16] Lattimore translates this epithet "resourceful," as though it were the more common Odysseus
epithet πολύμητις. In fact, these two epithets are used differently in the *Odyssey*, as I will discuss
later in this chapter, and so I have changed the translation to reflect the actual epithet.

One of the single-verse reply formulas for Odysseus could easily hav substituted for this longer description of Odysseus' state of mind: a mor concise way to introduce Odysseus' next speech using the same Odysseu epithet found in verse 250 would be τὸν δ' αὖτε προσέειπε <u>πολύτλας δῖο</u> Ὀδυσσεύς (then <u>long-suffering great</u> Odysseus spoke to him in answer, Alternatively, we might expect the more common Odysseus speech introduction that appears three times in this scene (τὴν δ' ἀπαμειβόμενο προσέφη <u>πολύμητις</u> Ὀδυσσεύς [then in turn <u>resourceful</u> Odysseus spoke to he in answer], 311, 382, 416).

Instead, at this deeply moving moment for the poem's hero—when he firs knows for certain that he is on Ithacan soil at last after so many years of wanderin, and misery—the narrative describes his pleasure both generally (γήθησεν [wa happy], 250[17]) and with reference to the land itself, which has been the subject c the previous speech and is to some degree the subject of the entire conversatio (χαίρων ᾗ γαίη πατρωίη [rejoicing in the land of his fathers], 251). In place of th passage that appears here, we can recombine the various formulas that appear i verses 250-255 in a number of shorter and less emphatic combinations. By doin; so, we can see a series of different ways to create a speech frame here that ar all formulaic, but that provide different levels of detail, emphasis, and poignanc For this kind of analysis, we can divide the passage into two pieces. The first thre verses (250-252) focus on Odysseus' response to what he has just heard. Normall as we have seen, this is not described separately in a one-on-one conversatio but sometimes the emotion of one participant in a one-on-one conversation i represented by (e.g.) a single verse in combination with the ἔπεα πτερόεντα verse The second three verses of this speech frame (253-255) introduce his speech an describe his mental state in relation to what he is about to say.

Beginning with the first three verses describing Odysseus' emotions the two verses that follow the formula in 250 could both be omitted withou loss of clarity. In this version, we would simply know that Odysseus smiled but would get no further details about why he did this. Alternatively, 13.250 251 without 252 would emphasize Odysseus' return home and his joy at thi without bringing forward the divine power of Odysseus' protector, who ha enabled him to reach his home and whom he has not met face to face in th poem before. Following the actual speech introductory formula at 13.253 the couplet at 254-255 describes the hero's mental state: even at this momen of great joy, he is sufficiently self-possessed not to burst out with his tru

---

[17] This same verse appears at *Odyssey* 7.329, 8.199, 18.281; with μείδησεν for γήθησεν, 23.111.

dentity.[18] From the structural standpoint, this is perhaps the most remarkable feature of the speech framing passage, as there is only one occasion besides this one in approximately 125 occurrences of the formula ἔπεα πτερόεντα προσηύδα/ ων that the following verse does not begin a direct speech.[19] The construction of the second half of this passage, which joins together several syntactically separate verses, parallels the first: we can omit verse 255 to form a shorter and so less emphatic couplet. 13.253-254 alone, without verse 255, would still emphasize Odysseus' trickiness, but 255 reminds us of Odysseus' consistent circumspection and restraint during the long process of reaching home.

Thus, this six-verse passage is equivalent, from the purely structural standpoint, to a formulaic single-verse reply introduction. In addition, we can imagine several shorter versions of this passage by omitting various verses to make different combinations of various lengths: a couplet with just 250 and 253, both formulaic although not found together elsewhere; a three-verse passage omitting both the second verse of either 251-252 or 254-255 and all of the other couplet; four verses composed of 250-251 and 253-254. All of these permutations are entirely or predominantly formulaic. As a group, they represent a system of progressively longer, more detailed, and therefore more emphatic and more effective ways to introduce Odysseus' reply to Athena. Our passage as a whole draws out the ideas of homecoming, divine protection, and concealment. These may be said to be three of the most important motifs concerning not only Odysseus' return to Ithaca but his character in the story as a whole. These are highlighted by a speech introduction at the point of Odysseus' return; that is, at the moment in his meeting with Athena when he knows that he *has* returned.[20]

---

[18] Higbie 1995 notes that this is the only time in the Homeric poems that the narrator states in a speech introduction that the speaker is lying (72).

[19] The other exception to this rule appears at *Odyssey* 17.591-592. It includes only one verse after the formula ἔπεα πτερόεντα προσηύδα rather than our passage's three: αἶψα δὲ Τηλέμαχον ἔπεα πτερόεντα προσηύδα [sc. Eumaeus] / ἄγχι σχὼν κεφαλήν, ἵνα μὴ πευθοίαθ' οἱ ἄλλοι (at once he spoke his winged words to Telemachos, leaning / his head close to him, so that none of the others might hear him).

[20] Martin 1989:69-70 argues that μῦθος (word, speech) and ἔπεα πτερόεντα (winged words) are equivalent. He supports this by pointing out that although the phrase πάλιν δ' ὅ γε λάζετο μῦθον (he checked that word from the outset) introduces Agamemnon's retraction of his rebuke of Odysseus in the Epipolesis of *Iliad* 4, the phrase ἔπεα πτερόεντα introduces most of Agamemnon's other speeches in this scene. It will be clear from my arguments here that I concur with the general idea that both introduce marked speech. However, I disagree with the idea that they are synonyms.

In particular, in the quotation given above as well as in the *Iliad* 4 passage (4.356-357), I disagree with the suggestion that πάλιν δ' ὅ γε λάζετο μῦθον demonstrates that μῦθος and ἔπεα πτερόεντα are synonymous: it seems to me that in both passages, μῦθον refers to what the speaker did *not* say in contrast to ἔπεα πτερόεντα, which refers to what *is* said. This is particularly true in our passage in *Odyssey* 13, which in the same speech introduction distinguishes what Odysseus decides to omit (οὐδ' ὅ γ' ἀληθέα εἶπε, πάλιν δ' ὅ γε λάζετο μῦθον, 254) from what he says (ἔπεα πτερόεντα προσηύδα, 253).

Odysseus' reply, however, shows no signs of the emotions that the speech frame preceding it depicts. Despite the strength of his joy at learning where he is, his capacity for concealment asserts itself almost immediately. The strength of the two opposing impulses—toward happy reunion with his home, and toward concealing himself—and the rapidity with which one follows the other very effectively highlight the conflict between them. Not only does Odysseus not admit that he is Odysseus come home, but he reinforces his silence on this point with a fluent and elaborate false identification for himself (256-286). Athena replies admiringly to this cool-headed deception by saying that anyone, even a god, would have difficulty surpassing him in resourcefulness (ἐν πάντεσσι δόλοισι [in any contriving], 292), and reveals her identity to him. In a sense, the narrator depicts Athena as less tricky than Odysseus has been: the introduction to her speech reflects and reinforces the content of it instead of creating a complement or contrast with it.

> ὣς φάτο, <u>μείδησεν</u> δὲ θεὰ γλαυκῶπις Ἀθήνη,
> <u>χειρί τέ μιν κατέρεξε</u>· δέμας δ' ἤϊκτο γυναικὶ
> καλῇ τε μεγάλῃ τε καὶ ἀγλαὰ ἔργα ἰδυίῃ,
> καί μιν φωνήσασ' ἔπεα πτερόεντα προσηύδα·

> So he spoke. The goddess, gray-eyed Athene, <u>smiled on him,</u>
> <u>and stroked him with her hand,</u> and took on the shape of
>   a woman
> both beautiful and tall, and well versed in glorious handiworks,
> and spoke aloud and addressed him in winged words, saying:

> 13.287-290

This introduction includes language which mentions Athena's amusement at the duplicity of her protégé (μείδησεν, 287), her affection for him (χειρί τέ μιν κατέρεξε, 288), and her transformation into goddess form.

This passage as a whole is functionally equivalent to the formulaic single verse τὸν δ' αὖτε προσέειπε θεὰ γλαυκῶπις Ἀθήνη (then in turn the gray-eyed goddess Athene answered), which appears repeatedly elsewhere in this conversation (see note 10 above). The details that appear here highlight from Athena's point of view Odysseus' skill in putting the need to conceal ahead of the desire to reveal himself: his behavior both amuses the goddess and causes her to decide to reveal herself to him. Insofar as there is a veiled contest of concealment taking place in the context of this conversation, Odysseus wins. All the language that this passage contains is ormulaic and appears in other speech frames. We can construct different hypothetical versions of this particular passage that would refer to Athena's amusement, but not her transformation (287, 290); a shorter and therefore less emphatic version could be formed by omitting verse 289. The passage as we have it effectively depicts Athena's affection for Odysseus, which the sequence of speeches up to this point implies is based on his capacity to conceal himself. This indirectly highlights that capacity and shows how effectively he has managed the conflict he feels here between concealment and revealing himself.

It is striking that when Athena names herself in the speech, which she does in the context of saying that Odysseus failed to recognize her (οὐδὲ σύ μ' ἔγνως / Παλλάδ' Ἀθηναίην, κούρην Διός, 300-301), this does not lead to an extended or unusual speech introduction for Odysseus' next speech: τὴν δ' ἀπαμειβόμενος προσέφη πολύμητις Ὀδυσσεύς (then in turn resourceful Odysseus spoke to her in answer), 311. This implies that Odysseus is, in fact, not surprised to find out who Athena is, but that could either be because of her physical transformation immediately before her speech, or because he has known who she was all along. As noted, there have been subtle signals before this that Odysseus may recognize Athena. Moreover, in the speech he now makes to her in her own persona (312-328), he says only that it is difficult to recognize gods in general (ἀργαλέον σε, θεά, γνῶναι βροτῷ ἀντιάσαντι [it is hard, O goddess, for even a man of good understanding / to recognize you on meeting], 312). He does not say that he did not recognize her on this particular occasion. Given Odysseus' facility with language, his ambiguity here suggests that he has already recognized Athena but does not want to say so, particularly since her own remarks suggest that she thinks he did not recognize her.[21] After this, he and Athena converse further, and once Odysseus is repeatedly reassured that he is indeed on Ithaca at last, Athena tells him that she will remove the cloaking mist from the island so that he can see it clearly.

Here again, an elaborate speech frame falls between Athena's speech (330-351) and Odysseus' response (356-360), but this passage differs from the two discussed above: although it falls between two speeches in an ongoing

---

[21] Hoekstra (writing in Heubeck et al. 1990b) 183 has an extensive note on Athena's various disguises when in contact with Odysseus, and more generally on the portrayal of their relationship by the "tradition" vs. "poetical elaboration." He strongly implies in his discussion that Odysseus is, indeed, surprised by Athena's metamorphosis here.

conversation, it is not structurally equivalent to a single verse reply formula. This is because Odysseus is not replying to Athena in his speech, but praying to a group of Naiads, which means that it is necessary to identify both the addressees and the special nature of his utterance.

> ὣς εἰποῦσα θεὰ σκέδασ' ἠέρα, εἴσατο δὲ χθών·
> γήθησέν τ' ἄρ' ἔπειτα πολύτλας δῖος Ὀδυσσεὺς
> χαίρων ᾗ γαίῃ, κύσε δὲ ζείδωρον ἄρουραν.
> αὐτίκα δὲ νύμφῃς ἠρήσατο χεῖρας ἀνασχών·
> "νύμφαι νηϊάδες ... "

> So speaking the goddess scattered the mist, and the land
>   was visible.
> Long-suffering great Odysseus was gladdened then, rejoicing
>   in the sight of his country, and kissed the grain-giving
>   ground, then
> raised his hands in the air and spoke to the nymphs, praying:
> "Naiad nymphs ... "

13.352-356

In this passage, unlike the previous two elaborate speech frames, only one verse of the four contains detail unnecessary for avoiding confusion. Verse 352 describes the action of Athena that results in the unveiling of the island of Ithaca. Odysseus is named in the following verse, which is necessary to identify him as the speaker of the following speech since the alternating turn structure of one-on-one conversation is disrupted here. Finally, verse 355 tells us the kind of speech Odysseus made and the identity of those to whom he made it. However, verse 354 is not necessary to make the situation clear to the audience: while κύσε δὲ ζείδωρον ἄρουραν (kissed the grain-giving ground) describes a physical act and not a purely emotional response, this behavior enacts Odysseus' emotion rather than clarifying the plot.

Let us consider how the passage would work if verse 354 were removed.

> ὣς εἰποῦσα θεὰ σκέδασ' ἠέρα, εἴσατο δὲ χθών·
> γήθησέν τ' ἄρ' ἔπειτα πολύτλας δῖος Ὀδυσσεύς.
> αὐτίκα δὲ νύμφῃς ἠρήσατο χεῖρας ἀνασχών·
> "νύμφαι νηιάδες ... "

> So speaking the goddess scattered the mist, and the land
>   was visible;
> Long-suffering great Odysseus was gladdened then, rejoicing.

> At once he raised his hands in the air and spoke to the
>   nymphs, praying:
> "Naiad nymphs ... "

This abbreviated passage makes sense in the context. We do not lose any crucial information without 354, but the evocative picture of Odysseus' joyful reunion with the soil of his home vanishes, as does the contrast between his purely internal response to the disguised Athena's verbal identification of Ithaca 250ff.) and his outward demonstrations here when the goddess *shows* him the land. For Odysseus, seeing is believing, in relation to both Athena and his home. In contrast, nothing in their subsequent discussion of the situation in the palace of Ithaca, or their plans for the future and the suitors, calls forth this kind of elaborate emphasis. The way this conversation is depicted highlights the deceptions of both Odysseus and Athena surrounding his arrival on Ithaca, his "reunion" with the land itself, and Odysseus' response to these deceptions.

This meeting between Athena and Odysseus is the only time in the poem that the two spend a significant amount of time together. As Odysseus effects several more reunions and recognitions and dispatches the suitors, Athena lends her aid in various ways. She speaks to Odysseus again on several occasions, often in her own persona (e.g. before his reunion with Telemachus in Book 16). Moreover, an intervention by her closes the poem, insofar as she prevents renewed warfare from breaking out among the bereaved families of dead suitors and has (literally) the last word in the poem (24.542-544). But once Odysseus meets mortals from his family and household, it is his relations with them that assume center stage. He and Athena do not meet again in the extended and expansive manner that they do here, when Odysseus has just arrived on Ithaca and has not yet started the process of reintegrating himself into the society of Ithaca. At the point in the poem when Odysseus is between the fabulous and the familiar, he has his most developed meeting with the one figure who has been or will be with him (in some way) in both settings. It is to Odysseus' relationships with the members of his family that we now turn.

Telemachus and Odysseus: Book 16

After Odysseus meets Athena, learns that he has reached Ithaca, and is assured of the goddess' support, he sets off in disguise to test the loyalty of various servants and relatives. Before Odysseus meets Penelope in Book 19, he comes across his son Telemachus at the hut of Eumaeus in Book 16. For some readers, their reunion here is subsumed within a larger question of what Telemachus'

role in the poem is or should be. Previous generations of scholars asserte
quite energetically that the first four books of the *Odyssey*, which focus o
Telemachus and his wanderings in search of news about Odysseus, should i
fact be a separate poem (the *Telemachia*), and moreover that various infelicitie
at the beginning of Book 5, particularly the second divine assembly, betra
the inexpert joining of two different works.[22] The contrary opinion, that th
story of Telemachus dovetails with and reinforces that of his father, and tha
recognizable conventions of Homeric poetry explain the aspects of Boo
5 that Analysts have found so problematic, has been recently put forwar
convincingly by Danek[23] and de Jong,[24] among others.[25] If Telemachus and hi
exploits form a legitimate part of the opening of the *Odyssey* and its overa
structure, then his reunion with his father becomes one of the main point
toward which the poem is leading. This reunion, like the earlier one wit
Athena and the upcoming one with Penelope, uses conversation to depic
the struggles of both characters to negotiate their desires on the one han
to bridge the gulf between them, and on the other hand to keep a safe an
skeptical distance. Although these tensions characterize each of the importan
reunions Odysseus has, they manifest themselves in a unique way for him an
Telemachus because Telemachus is a youth without a relationship to Odysseu
that predates his absence during the Trojan War. The conversation betwee
them that ultimately leads to their reunion dramatizes these feelings.

Odysseus' first human encounter is with Eumaeus (Books 14-15). Odysseu
actively conceals his identity from Eumaeus, insofar as he invents a detaile
false history of himself (14.192-359) and furthers the illusion by telling a fals
story about himself and "Odysseus" (14.462-506). However, this concealmen
does not seem to struggle with any opposing desire for honesty, perhaps becaus
Odysseus does not love Eumaeus in the way he loves his home and his famil
Indeed, speeches in the conversation between Eumaeus and the disguise
Odysseus both in Book 14 and in the second part of their conversation in Boo
15 (301-494) are introduced almost exclusively by single-verse reply formulas. I
contrast to this first meeting with Eumaeus, which is *not* a recognition scene an
which uses reply formulas almost exclusively in its speech frames, the reunio
of Odysseus and Telemachus in Book 16 consistently shows unusual patterns o

---

[22] Page 1955:52-73 summarizes the positions of previous proponents of the Analyst view of th
beginning of the *Odyssey* and puts forward his own case for it.

[23] 1998:32-33.

[24] 2001:3-5, with extensive bibliography.

[25] Also Lesky 1968:810.

peech-related formulas.[26] These differ from the speech framing language that appears for either of these two characters in the period before Odysseus' return o his family (in Books 1-15) and from those that are used for each during the continuing processes of reunion and restoration in Books 17-24.

In the first section of the poem, Odysseus and Telemachus have not ret been reunited (Books 1-15, although Telemachus appears almost exclusively in Books 1-4 and Book 15). Telemachus and the long-lost Odysseus are reunited in Book 16; in the remainder of the poem (Books 17-24), father and son take revenge on the suitors and Odysseus makes himself known to the other members of his family. Thus, the reunion of Book 16 is a turning point not only for Telemachus, but also for Odysseus, who in the course of Book 16 first reveals his identity to an inhabitant of Ithaca (as opposed to Athena) and begins to re-establish himself as the rightful ruler of the island. The reunion of Odysseus and Telemachus in Book 16 contains a large number of unusual speech frames where a more common formulaic expression could have been used. These variations tend to appear at moments when one or both characters are struggling particularly hard with the conflict between being forthright and being skeptical, and their content depicts this conflict or its results. Moreover, such variations are generally equivalent—from the functional standpoint—to a single-verse reply formula, and keeping this fact in mind allows us to imagine a less moving version of the same scene that did not focus on the same way on this tension.[27]

The conversation between Telemachus and Odysseus during which their mutual recognition and acceptance takes place is eleven turns long. This in itself gives the conversation prominence simply because of its great length. Six of eleven reply formulas for Telemachus in Book 16 are the most regular reply formula for him: τὸν δ' αὖ Τηλέμαχος πεπνυμένος ἀντίον ηὔδα (then the thoughtful Telemachos said to him in answer).[28] We also find two multi-verse speech frames preceding speeches of Telemachus in Book 16 (190-193, 213-221), one initial formula,[29] and two unusual single verses introducing replies of Telemachus'.[30] In Book 17, on the other hand, there are five reply formulas to

---

[26] The following discussion is an adaptation of Beck 1999.

[27] For tables that summarize the speech introductory language for Odysseus and Telemachus in the *Odyssey*, see Beck 1999:140-141.

[28] 30, 68, 112, 146, 240, 262.

[29] 460.

[30] 43, 308.

introduce Telemachus' speeches[31] of seven total, along with one expanded intro-
duction mentioning the addressee (342-344) and one unusual verse (396). We also
find the group reply formulas τοῖσι δὲ καὶ μετέειφ' ἱερὴ ἲς Τηλεμάχοιο and τοῖ
δ' αὖτις μετέειφ' (now the hallowed prince Telemachos spoke a word to them)[32]
regularly in the last third of the poem, but not in either Book 16 or Book 17.

This periphrasis for "Telemachus" is used only for him, while
πεπνυμένος (thoughtful) is a generic epithet modifying many other Homeric
characters. It has been suggested that πεπνυμένος is "a regular description
of youthful or subordinate characters."[33] In fact this formulation is much
less suited to the *Odyssey* than it is to the *Iliad*, where the epithet appears
infrequently and primarily in speech introductions for various peripheral
young men.[34] The *Odyssey* uses πεπνυμένος in speech introductions only for
Telemachus, with the exceptions of Laertes (24.375) and Medon the herald
(4.711, 22.361, 24.442) who is described not as πεπνυμένος himself but as
πεπνυμένα εἰδώς (knowing prudent thoughts). Outside of speech introduc-
tions, πεπνυμένος in the *Odyssey* modifies a group of characters that is both
more central and older than those so described in the *Iliad*: Nestor, neither
young nor peripheral, is called πεπνυμένος by Athena (3.20, 3.52). Menelaus
(4.190) and Odysseus (8.388) are each described in this way as well. This
suggests that the usage of πεπνυμένος in the *Odyssey* is more complex and
less clearly generic than it is in the *Iliad*.[35]

In Book 16, speeches by Odysseus have six formulaic reply introduc-
tions, of which five contain the epithet πολύτλας (long-suffering)[36] and one

---

[31] 45, 77, 107, 392, 598.

[32] A more literal translation of ἱερὴ ἲς Τηλεμάχοιο might be "holy strength of Telemachus," but
"hallowed prince Telemachos" is much more graceful and does not obscure any aspect of this
formula that is important for the following discussion. For a historical discussion of the expres-
sion ἱερὴ ἲς Τηλεμάχοιο and related naming expressions using the phrase ἱερὸν μένος (holy
strength), see Schmitt 1967:109-115 and Nagy 1974:86-89.

[33] Hainsworth in Heubeck et al. 1990a on *Odyssey* 8.388. Austin 1975:77-78 suggests that the dual
association of πεπνυμένος with both young men and heralds indicates that a young man so
designated is viewed as "a man of promise" (77). This is a satisfactory formulation for its appli-
cation to Telemachus, but does not explain why the narrator should use this word for Nestor,
Menelaus, and Odysseus.

[34] 3.203 (Antenor), 7.347 (also Antenor, with different verbs of speaking), 13.254 and 13.266 (both
Meriones), 18.249 (Polydamas), 23.586 (Antilochus). The other uses of πεπνυμένος appear
either in speech introductions or descriptions of heralds (7.276, 7.278, 9.689) or in reference to
young men (3.148, 9.58, 23.570).

[35] For a more elaborate and detailed presentation of this idea, see Heath 2001 on the use of
epithet for Telemachus over the course of the *Odyssey*.

[36] 90, 186, 225, 258, 266.

uses πολύμητις (resourceful, 201).[37] In Book 17, there are six single-verse reply formulas for Odysseus: two have πολύτλας (280, 560) and four use πολύμητις. In the poem as a whole, there are 45 instances of τὸν δ' ἀπαμειβόμενος προσέφη πολύμητις Ὀδυσσεύς (then resourceful Odysseus spoke in turn and answered him) and just nine reply introductory formulas with the epithet πολύτλας. Both of these epithets are used only for Odysseus. Thus, the patterns governing the reply formulas in Book 16 differ substantially from those which apply in Book 17 and in the remainder of the poem as a whole.

The reunion of Odysseus and Telemachus in Book 16 begins with Odysseus and Eumaeus eating breakfast and the return of Telemachus from his voyage in search of news of his father. Odysseus asks Eumaeus who this young man is (8-10). However, Telemachus arrives at the hut before Odysseus finishes asking his question (οὔ πω πᾶν εἴρητο ἔπος [his whole word had not been spoken], 11). Although his speech is not so abbreviated as to contain any partial lines, Homeric speakers are not generally interrupted before they get to the end of what they want to say. Thus, at the very beginning of the reunion, contact between Odysseus and Telemachus disrupts the usual conventions of Homeric conversation.

Eumaeus recognizes Telemachus with joy and greets him affectionately. Eumaeus, at this point in the story, is essentially a father figure to Telemachus. Indeed, a simile compares Eumaeus' feelings at seeing him to those of a father greeting his son when he returns from a foreign land (17-20):

> ὡς δὲ π<u>ατὴρ</u> ὃν <u>παῖδα</u> φίλα φρονέων ἀγαπάζῃ
> ἐλθόντ' ἐξ ἀπίης γαίης δεκάτῳ ἐνιαυτῷ,
> μοῦνον τηλύγετον, τῷ ἔπ' ἄλγεα πολλὰ μογήσῃ,
> ὣς τότε Τηλέμαχον θεοειδέα . . .

> And as a <u>father</u>, with heart full of love, welcomes his only <u>son</u>,
> for whose sake he has undergone many hardships
> when he comes back in the tenth year from a distant
>   country,
> so now godlike Telemachos . . .

Odysseus, who is indeed an only child, has been absent not ten years but twenty. He is also the actual father of the child, παῖδα (son), referred to in line 17. The relationship between the situation in the narrative and this simile

---

[37] See the appendix of Pope 1960 (129-135) on the various epithets for Odysseus in the *Iliad*, *Doloneia*, and *Odyssey*.

indirectly draws attention to Odysseus' concealed identity; the emotion that the simile depicts reminds the audience of the strength of the emotions that Odysseus is hiding in order to maintain his concealment. The simile is in striking sympathy with the upcoming reunion of Odysseus and Telemachus, the central subject of Book 16 and indeed of much of the rest of the poem.[38] In Eumaeus' welcoming speech to Telemachus, which immediately follows the simile, he calls him γλυκερὸν φάος (sweet light, 23), a term of endearment used otherwise only by Penelope,[39] and φίλον τέκος (dear child, 25). Observing these emotions, we imagine, must increase the difficulty of Odysseus' concealment: the simile reminds the audience of Odysseus' self-restraint, while his presence as a bystander during this affectionate welcome heightens the difficulty of the concealment for Odysseus himself.

When Telemachus first speaks to Odysseus after his exchange of welcome and greeting with Eumaeus, he thinks the old beggar is a ξεῖνος (friend, guest: 44), having as yet no reason to think anything else. An unusual speech introduction, Τηλέμαχος δ' ἑτέρωθεν ἐρήτυε φώνησέν τε (but Telemachos from the other side checked him and said to him, 43), precedes his courteous greeting to the supposed stranger. His appropriate behavior as a host toward Odysseus contrasts with his awkward performances as a guest of Nestor and Menelaus in Books 3 and 4 of the poem. The description of Telemachus immediately after this speech as Ὀδυσσῆος φίλος υἱός (beloved son of Odysseus, 48), implicitly contrasts their polite and unemotional contact as ξεῖνοι (guest-friends) with the love that they bear for each other as father and son.

The father-son relationship, then, has a prominent and complex role from the very beginning of Odysseus and Telemachus' meeting. The simile before Eumaeus' greeting simultaneously brings forward the general idea of fathers and sons and refers indirectly to the web of connections among the characters present. This very effectively brings out the strength of the watching Odysseus' emotions, and accordingly, his strength in concealing them. Telemachus is the acknowledged surrogate son of Eumaeus and the (as yet) unacknowledged child of Odysseus, whose own position as a son as well as a father is invoked by the simile's description of a child who has been away from home for a long time. When Telemachus speaks to his father for the first time, the unusual introductory verse at 16.43 makes his words stand out. Yet the words themselves are nothing but the merest social politeness of inviting a

---

[38] Danek 1998:301 sensitively brings out the various undercurrents in this simile, and connects it with his more general idea that Eumaeus is consistently a parallel figure to Laertes in the *Odyssey*.

[39] Also as a greeting when she first meets her son after he returns from his journey, *Odyssey* 17.41.

guest to sit down. The use of a patronymic in the verses immediately following this speech reinforces the contrast between the momentousness of the first meeting between father and son and the banality of the words and actions of the meeting. Watchers of the action from outside the poem feel this contrast, as does Odysseus, but Telemachus is ignorant of it. His ignorance, in light of the strength of his desire for his father throughout the earlier books of the poem, lends pathos to the situation. Moreover, the gap between his ignorance and Odysseus' understanding and self-control that is depicted so effectively here plays a central role in unfolding of their meeting, as we are about to see.

In the ensuing conversation among the three characters, the name-epithet formulas for Odysseus emphasize the suffering that his equivocal position at this point causes him, while the name-epithet formulas for Telemachus are the same as they usually are elsewhere in the poem. At this level of diction, the conversation depicts Odysseus feeling his separation from Telemachus, but the ignorant Telemachus feeling the same way he would with any other guest. All of Telemachus' speeches are introduced by the reply formula τὸν δ' αὖ Τηλέμαχος πεπνυμένος ἀντίον ηὔδα (then the thoughtful Telemachos said to him in answer, 68 = 112 = 146). Odysseus, on the other hand, is πολύτλας δῖος Ὀδυσσεύς during this conversation (τὸν δ' αὖτε προσέειπε πολύτλας δῖος Ὀδυσσεύς [then long-suffering great Odysseus spoke to him], 90). In contrast, he is πολύμητις Ὀδυσσεύς (τὸν δ' ἀπαμειβόμενος προσέφη πολύμητις Ὀδυσσεύς [then resourceful Odysseus spoke in turn and answered him]) in the vast majority of his reply introductions in the rest of the Odyssey.[40] Indeed, reply formulas that emphasize Odysseus' suffering rather than his cleverness appear primarily in Book 16,[41] where his suffering rather than his resourcefulness take center stage. Here we find a formulaic but comparatively rare epithet occurring in both the Iliad and the Odyssey that focuses attention not on the crafty side of Odysseus' character, but on the suffering and self-denial he endures during the long process of making his way home to his family. This is one of a number of different techniques that appear during this conversation

---

[40] Machacek's very interesting and useful article points out that there are several speech introductory lines for Odysseus that are equivalent except for the epithet(s) applied to Odysseus (1994:324), but he does not explore in detail how such a set of alternatives might be used by the poet.

[41] τὸν δ' αὖτε προσέειπε πολύτλας δῖος Ὀ., 14.148; 16.90, 225, 258, 266; 17.560 and τὸν δ' ἠμείβετ' ἔπειτα πολύτλας δῖος Ὀ., 15.340, 16.186, 17.280 (then long-suffering Ὀ. spoke to him in answer). Examples outside the reunion of Telemachus and Odysseus in Book 16 appear in contexts closely related to Odysseus' return, as in 14.148, which introduces a speech in which Odysseus swears an oath to Eumaeus (concealing his identity) that "Odysseus" will come home, or 17.560, where he learns that Penelope wants to see him and replies that he will tell the truth to her.

to highlight the difficulty that Odysseus has in balancing his circumspection and his desire to be reunited with his family while speaking with Telemachus. At this point, Telemachus feels nothing unusual, which contributes indirectly to the emotions of Odysseus.

Once Eumaeus journeys to the city to relay the message that Telemachus has returned safely (154-155) and the coast is clear, father and son converse alone. Athena transforms Odysseus' appearance to a strong and hearty man and departs (155-177). The emotions of each come out much more strongly here than when Eumaeus is still with them. The astonished Telemachus casts his eyes reverently down at the sight of the transformed erstwhile beggar who reenters the hut. At the same time, the narrator calls him φίλος υἱός (beloved son, 178). In the speech immediately following, Telemachus not unreasonably concludes that his suddenly changed "guest" is in fact a god who should be propitiated (181-185). For Telemachus, in contrast to his father, the conflict which arouses the audience's sympathy does not take place within himself or between conflicting impulses of his own. Rather, the tension here arises between his partial understanding of the situation (and his perfectly sensible response to it as he understands it), shown through his behavior and his speech; and the real state of matters, underlined by the narrator's way of identifying him before his speech. Nevertheless, this conflict draws on the same basic notions of concealment versus reunion that underlies the internal conflicts that Odysseus feels.

At this point, we see that Telemachus is feeling the opposing pull of his desire to believe Odysseus and his skepticism, while Odysseus has put aside his desire to conceal his identity and whole-heartedly desires a reunion with his son. This puts him and Telemachus into a kind of tension as well. With one exception, the reply formulas for Odysseus in this conversation use the πολύτλας δῖος (long-suffering great) epithet, not the more regular πολύμητις (resourceful) one. The "long-suffering" epithet appears in the introduction to Odysseus' reply to Telemachus' first speech (186), in which Odysseus identifies himself as the young man's father (187-189). Odysseus tells his doubtful and wary son that he is not a god, but Telemachus' father (ἀλλὰ πατὴρ τεός εἰμι [but I am your father], 188). The expanded speech frame before Telemachus' reply to this assertion, at 190-193, calls further attention to Telemachus' dogged insistence that this mysterious changeling beggar is a god and not his long hoped-for father.

> τὸν δ' ἠμείβετ' ἔπειτα <u>πολύτλας δῖος Ὀδυσσεύς·</u>
> "οὔ τίς τοι θεός εἰμι· τί μ' ἀθανάτοισιν ἔΐσκεις;
> ἀλλὰ πατὴρ τεός εἰμι, τοῦ εἵνεκα σὺ στεναχίζων

πάσχεις ἄλγεα πολλά, βίας ὑποδέγμενος ἀνδρῶν."
ὣς ἄρα φωνήσας υἱὸν κύσε, κὰδ δὲ παρειῶν
δάκρυον ἧκε χαμᾶζε· πάρος δ' ἔχε νωλεμὲς αἰεί.
<u>Τηλέμαχος δ', οὐ γάρ πω ἐπείθετο ὃν πατέρ' εἶναι,</u>
<u>ἐξαῦτίς μιν ἔπεσσιν ἀμειβόμενος προσέειπεν·</u>

Then in turn <u>long-suffering great Odysseus</u> answered him:
"No, I am not a god. Why liken me to the immortals?
But I am your father, for whose sake you are always grieving
as you look for violence from others, and endure hardships."
    So he spoke, and kissed his son, and the tears running
down his cheeks splashed on the ground. Until now, he was
    always unyielding.
<u>But Telemachos, for he did not yet believe that this was</u>
<u>his father, spoke to him once again in answer, saying:</u>

                                    16.186-193

Odysseus, who at long last has put aside concealment in favor of making
a connection with Telemachus, is now stymied by the same circumspection
that has marked his own behavior in the past. The language and structure of
the conversation here dramatize the shifting gulf that exists for Telemachus as
the scene progresses: whereas at the beginning of his meeting with Odysseus,
his partial understanding contrasts with the real identity of his "guest,"
Telemachus now faces an internal conflict between the information he has
received and his own skepticism of it. This is similar to the opposing claims
of honesty and concealment that Odysseus has experienced before, but at this
point has put aside. Telemachus' hesitation creates a gulf between himself and
Odysseus.

    Indeed, Odysseus explicitly mentions the disjunction between
Telemachus' suspicion and the misery the youth has endured because of the
absent father who now stands before him in language which echoes that of the
simile at the beginning of Book 16 (ἄλγεα πόλλα [many hardships], 16.19 and
189). While Odysseus weeps and kisses his son, a reaction that characterizes
the great joy of another important reunion in the poem,[42] Telemachus remains
suspiciously aloof. Indeed, the syntax of line 192 stops the action briefly and
focuses on Telemachus' isolation: the adversative sense of δ' separates him

---

[42] Of Penelope reunited with Odysseus, δακρύσασα . . . κάρη δ' ἔκυσ' ἠδὲ προσηύδα (she burst
into tears . . . and kissed his head, saying), *Odyssey* 23.207-208. See Murnaghan 1987:22 on the
physical accompaniments to reunions in the *Odyssey*.

grammatically and emotionally from his father, who has been mentioned in the previous verse. The increased prominence of the narrator's voice in the rest of the verse makes a pause in the flow of the story that heightens the sense of the youth's reserve.

The use of γάρ (for) in this aside syntactically isolates the clause in verse 192 from the surrounding narrative, suggesting that this is the narrator's own explanatory comment on the situation rather than the thoughts of any of the characters in the story.[43] γάρ appears here as part of a formulaic particle cluster οὐ γάρ πω (for not yet), which appears ten times in the Iliad and 21 times in the Odyssey. In the Iliad, this cluster appears predominantly in passages of direct speech (8 of 10 occurrences) and almost always at the beginning of the verse (except Iliad 4.331, where οὐ falls at the beginning of the second foot). In the Odyssey, although this cluster appears more than twice as often as in the Iliad, only at 16.192 does it fall outside of direct speech. As in the Iliad, in the Odyssey this formula tends to be localized at the beginning of the verse (15 of 21 examples). When it falls elsewhere, in all cases but this one οὐ falls at the beginning of the third foot. Thus, although the cluster οὐ γάρ πω can regularly be found in Homeric epic, this particular example is a unique and glaring departure from patterns of localization and usage that occur elsewhere.

These unique aspects of the formula draw out the conflict Telemachus is feeling between openness and skepticism, and they dramatize in a very concrete way the gap between him and Odysseus. Moreover, these two verses are not enjambed with the preceding lines describing Odysseus' tender and emotional greeting of Telemachus, so that the usual one-line reply formula for Telemachus could have been used here instead of this couplet commenting on Telemachus' demeanor. Indeed, the common reply formula for Telemachus could have taken the place of the entire passage (16.190-193) without loss of clarity. Yet the narrator's aside describing the wary and suspicious son contrasted with the kisses and tears of the father in the previous verses, very effectively depicts the gap between father and son and the shifting tensions between circumspection and acceptance that each experiences over the course of their interaction. However tempted he might be to welcome this supposed Odysseus, Telemachus is not convinced at all by Odysseus' statement

---

[43] de Jong 1987a:62 discusses γάρ in connection with the primary narrator-focalizer's transmission of information to the primary recipient of the story. She is interested in γάρ as an explanation of a negative statement by the narrator ("X did not Y, γάρ . . . "), while here it takes the more unusual form of a negative explanation for a positive statement: Telemachus <u>did</u> answer γάρ he did <u>not</u> believe . . .

f his real identity. He now repeats in essentially the same language as before
his conviction that the beggar must be a god trying to cause him even more
misery (194-200).

Interestingly, the only instance of the epithet πολύμητις in the reunion
of Book 16 appears at 16.201, which introduces Odysseus' reply to this speech.
Yet again, Odysseus asserts the truth of his statement that he is Odysseus
(202-203). He tells his doubtful son that no other Odysseus than the one he
sees before him will be arriving on Ithaca (204-206). This speech contrasts
most strikingly with the array of untruths Odysseus has told about his iden-
ity throughout the poem, untruths that are uniformly believed.[44] In those
cases, the epithet is indeed descriptive. Here, in contrast, it calls attention
to Odysseus' complete and uncharacteristic honesty, and also to the irony of
his not being believed when he is in fact telling the truth and wants so
desperately to be believed. We can see, in fact, that the speech frames have at
least as important a role as the speeches themselves in depicting the conflicts
that each character experiences in this scene and the nature of the gap
between father and son.

Odysseus' explanation, however, that Athena is responsible for his dramatic
shifts in physical appearance (207-212) now persuades Telemachus that this
man is his father returned home. The emotion of the reunited pair now engulfs
them, and similarly overwhelms the usual structure of rapid interchange in one-
on-one conversations in the Homeric epics. A long and elaborate speech frame
consisting of several different components appears between Odysseus' speech
(the fourth turn of eleven) and Telemachus' reply (fifth turn, 16.213-221). This
speech frame very movingly describes the emotions of the two weeping men at
the moment when both have resolved their respective conflicts between skep-
tical distance and open acceptance in favor of the latter. First, we have a speech
conclusion, which as we have seen is unusual in a one-on-one conversation. Here,
moreover, the narrator takes several verses to describe the behavior of the father
and son, behavior which is the reverse of what appeared at 16.190-193. Odysseus
sits down, and Telemachus weeps as he embraces his father. In other words,
Telemachus physically acts out that he is no longer keeping a skeptical distance
from Odysseus.

> ὣς ἄρα φωνήσας κατ' ἄρ' ἕζετο, Τηλέμαχος δὲ
> <u>ἀμφιχυθεὶς πατέρ' ἐσθλὸν</u> ὀδύρετο, <u>δάκρυα λείβων</u>.
> <u>ἀμφοτέροισι δὲ τοῖσιν</u> ὑφ' ἵμερος ὦρτο <u>γόοιο·</u>

---

[44] Most recently to Eumaeus, *Odyssey* 14.149-408.

> So he spoke, and sat down again, but now Telemachos
> <u>folded his great father in his arms</u> and lamented,
> <u>shedding tears</u>, and desire for <u>mourning</u> rose in <u>both</u>
> <u>of them</u>;

16.213-215

16.213 contains three formulaic expressions that are repeated elsewhere but are combined in this way only here. ὡς ἄρα φωνήσας (so he spoke) is a common speech concluding formula;[45] κατ' ἄρ ἕζετο (and sat down again) appears 13 times in this position in the verse; the expression Τηλέμαχος δέ is found often.[46] However, in the other places where κατ' ἄρ' ἕζετο is combined with a verse-initial formula for "having spoken," we find #ἤτοι ὅ γ' ὡς εἰπὼν κατ' ἄρ' ἕζετο (he spoke thus, and sat down again).[47] In fact, κατ' ἄρ' ἕζετο is the only component of the full-verse formula ἤτοι ὅ γ' ὡς εἰπὼν κατ' ἄρ ἕζετο· τοῖσι δ' ἀνέστη (he spoke thus and sat down again, and among them stood up) that appears outside of the full-verse formula. Thus, although verse 213 is composed of formulaic elements that regularly appear in other speech conclusions, these elements are used in unusual ways here.

In our passage, the basic idea of "they desired to grieve" fills not one or even two but three verses. A single-verse speech concluding formula exists for this idea,[48] which is expanded to a couplet at *Iliad* 23.152-153. Our expanded version of this formulaic notion focuses first on Telemachus' physical acceptance of his father in 214 by embracing him (ἀμφιχυθεὶς πατέρ' ἐσθλόν) and weeping (δάκρυα λείβων), just as Odysseus had kissed his son and wept when he first told the resisting and skeptical Telemachus who he really was (190-191). 215 describes this emotion as γόος (mourning), drawing out the feelings of Odysseus as well as Telemachus by means of the unusual initial half-verse ἀμφοτέροισ δὲ τοῖσιν, which refers to them as a pair. In contrast, the formula ὡς φάτο, τῷ δ' ἄρα πατρὸς ὑφ' ἵμερον ὦρσε γόοιο (he spoke, and stirred in the other the longing to weep for his father)[49] would have directed attention to Telemachus rather than to Odysseus in the moment immediately after the speech. ὡς φάτο, τοῖσι δὲ

---

[45] 57 times in the *Iliad* and *Odyssey*, with either masculine or feminine participle.

[46] Only here is it verse-final, however, and of 29 occurrences, the majority (19 cases) have δ elided.

[47] See Chapter 5 on this formula and its use in formal assemblies.

[48] Listed in Appendix IV.

[49] *Iliad* 24.507, *Odyssey* 4.113. See Chapter 3 (141) on this verse in the conversation between Achilles and Priam in *Iliad* 24.

πᾶσιν ὑφ' ἵμερον ὦρσε γόοιο (he spoke, and started in all of them the desire for weeping)⁵⁰ would not connect the two as a *pair*, but rather as a less intimate and moving *group*. Moreover, the verses here that convey the general idea of "thus X spoke, and [someone] desired to grieve" contain additional information that increases the pathos of this moment still further. They lend special vividness to what Telemachus felt by showing how he acted on his feelings. These welcoming actions of acceptance and affection must be particularly gratifying to Odysseus after Telemachus initially greets the announcement that Odysseus is his father with suspicious aloofness (192-193).

Next, a simile further explores the emotions of the father and son with an image of parenthood taken from the animal world.

> κλαῖον δὲ λιγέως, ἀδινώτερον ἤ τ' οἰωνοί,
> φῆναι ἢ αἰγυπιοὶ γαμψώνυχες, οἷσί τε τέκνα
> ἀγρόται ἐξείλοντο πάρος πετεηνὰ γενέσθαι·
> ὣς ἄρα τοί γ' ἐλεεινὸν ὑπ' ὀφρύσι δάκρυον εἶβον.

> They cried shrill in a pulsing voice, even more than the
>   outcry
> of birds, ospreys or vultures with hooked claws, whose children
> were stolen away by the men of the fields, before their wings
>   grew
> strong; such was their pitiful cry and the tears their eyes wept.

16.216-219

The presence of the simile draws out this moment, the first reunion of Odysseus and a member of his family. The narrative, indeed, could proceed smoothly from verse 214 or 215 to verse 220, but the simile draws out and thereby emphasizes this crucial and moving scene. Although Telemachus and Odysseus are presumably overjoyed to be restored to each other, the language of the narrative and the subject of the simile show instead a rending sadness. At first glance, it seems strange that the narrator should illustrate what should be a happy occasion with a comparison of sadness and bereavement. Many scholars have explained this as some type of reversal of the context⁵¹ or as an expression of the peril and fear that Odysseus and Telemachus face.⁵²

---

⁵⁰ *Iliad* 23.108, *Odyssey* 4.183; cf. *Iliad* 23.152-153.
⁵¹ E.g. Podlecki 1971:85; Foley 1978:7-8.
⁵² Moulton 1977:133-134 relates the simile to the danger the two still must encounter, Minchin 2001:147-148 to Odysseus' fear that he would never be reunited with his son.

I believe that the simile illustrates an aspect of the situation that the narrative itself does not directly explore: the sadness and bereavement of the two because of the time together that has been lost to them. The birds of the simile have had their chicks, τέκνα . . . πάρος πετεηνά (children before their wings grew, 217-218), stolen by hunters. The detail of winglessness emphasizes both the youth of the chicks and their inability to defend themselves. Despite their own power as hunters—φῆναι ἢ αἰγυπιοὶ γαμψώνυχες (ospreys or vultures with hooked claws, 217) are both fierce birds of prey—the parents are unable to protect their offspring from harm. Just as the mighty parent birds are unable to keep their children safe, so the warrior and hero Odysseus has not fended off the incursions of the suitors against his still immature son Telemachus. The bereft birds, too, suggest that for Odysseus and Telemachus, the Trojan War and Odysseus' long wanderings have irrevocably stolen the first stage of their father-son relationship. While we have seen several examples of speech frames that supply details that are otherwise not explicit about the emotional state of one or both speakers in a conversation, this simile goes far beyond the brief comments that appear in other conversations in terms of its length, its vividness, and the great deal of information that it implies.

Unlike other reunions between Odysseus and his household, the meeting with Telemachus marks the establishment of a relationship that did not previously exist, not the resumption of an interrupted one. They accept each other not by exchanging and recognizing σήματα (signs), as in other scenes of recognition between Odysseus and his household, but because Odysseus repeatedly states his identity and essentially forces Telemachus to accept him. Between Odysseus and Telemachus, indeed, there *are* no σήματα because as yet there has been no relationship between them. Telemachus has had to grow up without a father. While the father has now returned, they can never recover the loss of Telemachus' boyhood, which is gone just as surely as the stolen chicks of the simile. Thus, while the simile seems at first glance to contrast with the narrative, in fact it brings out the underlying sadness of the happy reunion. The gap between the two characters is closed, and the conflict that each has felt between openness and concealment is over, but at the moment when this is finally accomplished, the simile tells us that the damage done by their former separation cannot be entirely undone.

At length, the pair returns to the business at hand, but the form of the lines introducing Telemachus' first speech after the reunion scene gives a final glimpse of the great depth and strength of the emotions of Odysseus and Telemachus.

καί νύ κ' ὀδυρομένοισιν ἔδυ φάος ἠελίοιο,
εἰ μὴ Τηλέμαχος προσεφώνεεν ὃν πατέρ' αἶψα·

And now the light of the sun would have set on their crying,
had not Telemachos spoken a quick word to his father:

16.220-221

The usual one-verse reply formula is discarded in favor of a multi-verse intro-duction. Here a fairly straightforward aspect of the context partly explains why a reply formula is not used. After a speech conclusion and simile delay Telemachus' reply (in the text, if not necessarily to the same extent in the story), Telemachus can no longer be said to be replying directly to the previous speech. However, this is not the only explanation for the expansion. The contrary to fact condition here allows the audience to see how deep their grief was, since it would have gone on indefinitely but for Telemachus' remarks. Contrary to fact speech introductions are both rarer and more systematized in their connection to the narrative in the *Odyssey*, where the only two examples occur in reunion scenes involving Odysseus, than they are in the *Iliad*.[53] The expanded introduction at 16.220-221 extends the grief of Odysseus and Telemachus even further, both by devoting additional verses to describing it and through the image it uses to represent their emotion. Not only that, but it is Telemachus, not Odysseus, who effectively takes charge of the situation by asking his father about the details of his voyage.[54] This is the proper behavior of a host toward a guest, which Odysseus might be said to be after such a long absence. Furthermore, this verbal initiative on the part of the young man may be seen as a step along the path to adulthood, which his father's return and the subsequent restoration of his own proper position make possible.

This extremely elaborate and moving speech frame marks the high point of the episode when both characters have put aside their cautious skepti-cism and have been reunited. The shorter but still elaborate speech frame at

[53] Speeches that begin "and [such and such] would have happened, if X hadn't . . . ." are a variant of the usual speech introduction structure that appear from time to time in the Homeric epics, *Iliad* 11.311-312, 21.211-212, 23.154-155, 490-491, 540-542; 24.713-715; *Odyssey* 16.220-221, 21.226-227 (during Odysseus' reunion with Eumaeus). On if-not situations generally, see de Jong 1987a:68-81. Lang 1989 surveys conditions in Homer, making the extremely useful and important distinc-tion between affirmative and negative protases; Louden 1993 argues that what he calls "pivotal contrafactuals" may sometimes connect related episodes, among which he includes the reunions of Odysseus with Telemachus, Penelope, and his herders (193-194).

[54] Louden 1993:194 notes this as a consistent feature of the Odyssean reunions in which condi-tions are found: the person who ends the situation referred to in the condition takes charge of the situation generally.

190-193 builds a kind of crescendo leading to this moment. After this climactic moment, which appears approximately one-third of the way through the conversation, there is a corresponding decrescendo. The conflict that Odysseus and Telemachus have experienced between concealment and openness is now over, and accordingly, there are no elaborate speech frames in this part of the conversation. Telemachus and his father now talk at some length about Odysseus' experiences and the problem of the suitors (seven more turns, each preceded by a single verse reply formula). The conversation ends with a long speech (16.267-307) in which Odysseus gives Telemachus a series of instructions. At the end of his speech, Odysseus tells the youth to keep his true identity secret from everyone in the palace.

> εἰ ἐτεόν γ' ἐμός ἐσσι καὶ αἵματος ἡμετέροιο,[55]
> μή τις ἔπειτ' Ὀδυσῆος ἀκουσάτω ἔνδον ἐόντος,
> μήτ' οὖν Λαέρτης ἴστω τό γε μήτε συβώτης
> μήτε τις οἰκήων μήτ' αὐτὴ Πηνελόπεια,
> ἀλλ' οἶοι σύ τ' ἐγώ τε γυναικῶν γνώομεν ἰθύν . . .

> If truly you are my own son, and born of our blood,
> then let nobody hear that Odysseus is in the palace;
> let not Laertes hear of it, neither let the swineherd;
> let no one in the household know, not even Penelope
> herself; you and I alone will judge the faith of the women . . .

> 16.300-304

Here Odysseus explicitly connects the capacity to conceal important information with kinship to him. Moreover, this statement brings up in a new context the ongoing tension between concealment and openness that characterizes Odysseus' actions throughout the second half of the poem.

The language of the verse introducing Telemachus' reply to this speech seems to affirm that Telemachus will be able to perform the task he is given: τὸν δ' ἀπαμειβόμενος προσεφώνεε <u>φαίδιμος υἱός</u> (then in answer again his <u>glorious son</u> said to him, 16.308). By omitting Telemachus' name and instead referring to him in terms of his relationship to Odysseus, the verse suggests that, as the youth is indeed the son of his father, he will be able to do what

---

[55] An alternate reading of this line is found in three MSS and read by Plutarch at *vita Homeri* ii.149 ἐμοὶ δέ σ' ἐγείνετο μήτηρ (your mother bore you to me). In fact, this variant makes basically the same point about family resemblance being shown through concealment as does the reading given here, but via the mother more than the father.

s asked of him. This particular verse appears nowhere else in the poem,[56] although Telemachus is often described as the "dear son of Odysseus" outside of speech frames.[57] It seems significant that this line appears only here, as a signal to the audience that Telemachus will succeed both in helping Odysseus restore order to the palace and, more generally, in reestablishing himself in the position due him as Odysseus' son (φαίδιμος υἱός). Likewise, Telemachus accepts Odysseus' charge in his reply (309-310). Here the narrator and the characters depict the conversation in similar terms: Odysseus and Telemachus are focused not on concealment aimed by one at the other, as in the earlier portion of their conversation, but on a deception in which they both participate that is aimed at others (the household). Earlier in the conversation, in contrast, we saw that the narrator and the characters often illustrate different, complementary aspects of the conversation when it contains a conflict that in some sense pits the two characters against each other.

The scene now changes for a while to the suitors, but Telemachus and Odysseus reappear at the end of Book 16 before night falls and the poem moves on from the reunion between father and son (16.452-481). Here Telemachus begins to practice the concealment that Odysseus has enjoined on him and for which Odysseus himself is justly famous.[58] When Telemachus asks what the suitors are now doing about their ambush (461-463), Eumaeus tells him about a ship he saw in the harbor that he believes was carrying them (465-475). At this point the conversation ends, and the three men retire for the night. Before the scene closes, however, the narrator offers a brief final glimpse of the three characters.

> ὣς φάτο, μείδησεν δ' ἱερὴ ἲς Τηλεμάχοιο
> ἐς πατέρ' ὀφθαλμοῖσιν ἰδών, ἀλέεινε δ' ὑφορβόν.

> So he spoke, and Telemachos, the hallowed prince, smiled
> as he caught his father's eye, but avoided the eyes of the
> swineherd.

> 16.476-477

---

[56] But compare 24.243, of Odysseus speaking to Laertes: τὸν δὲ παριστάμενος προσεφώνεε φαίδιμος υἱός (and now his glorious son stood near, and spoke to him, saying). Edwards 1969 notes that in these passages φαίδιμος υἱός "is used to stress, very effectively, the father-son relationship of the two parties" (85).

[57] A full-verse formula in the nominative or accusative, Τηλέμαχος/ον φίλος/ον υἱὸς/ον Ὀδυσσῆος θείοιο (Telemachos, beloved son of godlike Odysseus), is found at Odyssey 3.398, 15.554, 17.3, 20.283, and 21.432.

[58] In that Odysseus is himself famous for his ability to dissemble and conceal, Telemachus' own power of concealment may be considered not just a test of loyalty but a mark of family resemblance (Lateiner 1995:153).

Telemachus responds to Eumaeus' remarks about the suitors' ambush and the situation in the town in a mature, even Odyssean manner. By smiling in response to speech, Telemachus shows a filial resemblance to Odysseus who often smiles at someone's statement before answering it to show his understanding, appreciation or control of a situation.[59] Here, at the end of Book 16, Telemachus goes his father one better by *not* answering someone in language that generally appears elsewhere as part of a formulaic speech frame before a reply. This unexpected use of language strongly reminiscent of reply formulas emphasizes Telemachus' self-control in keeping silent, an unusual ability that Odysseus also has. Indeed, this capacity distinguishes Odysseus from virtually every other Homeric hero.[60]

Thus, this apparently simple speech conclusion demonstrates Telemachus' newly emerging adulthood in several ways. His smile suggests control of, or at least comfort with, the general situation as well as a family resemblance to his father. He shows self-control by remaining silent instead of speaking when he knows, as Eumaeus does not, that the wretched beggar crouched in his hut is in fact Odysseus. Finally, the reappearance of an epithet used only for Telemachus that has appeared just once before in the poem,[6] ἱερὴ ἲς Τηλεμάχοιο (Telemachos the hallowed prince), confers some of the κλέος (reputation) of an adult Homeric hero on the youth.[62] In other words, the shift from a shared to an individualized epithet for Telemachus parallels the development of his character in the story from an uncertain boy to a young man.[63]

And how does Telemachus acquit himself for the remainder of the poem? As the modern audience, and most likely the ancient audience as well, is fully aware, the reunited father and son successfully remove the suitors from the palace, Penelope eventually accepts Odysseus' assertion that he is her long lost husband, and order is restored. Athena appears at the poem's conclusion

---

[59] See Levine 1984 on Odysseus' smiles.

[60] Murnaghan 1987:4.

[61] 2.409, where he tells his companions of his intention to leave in quest of information about his father without telling his mother.

[62] Hainsworth 1968:10, "within the context of the poet's technique it is a simple matter to assume that a hero of the stature of Achilles or Odysseus is *sui generis*, and so merits his own honorific [epithet]."

[63] Another difference between the two expressions is where the name "Telemachus" falls in the verse. Kahane 1994 asserts that names which fall in the middle of the verse deny the character in question "the nominative markers of a 'hero'" (135) while major characters' name-epithet tend to fall at the end of the verse. The periphrasis may be seen, according to this line of reasoning, as a way of increasing Telemachus' heroic stature by moving the location of his name within a speech introductory verse.

o force the characters into amicable coexistence, but the audience is never-heless left wondering about how the feelings of uncertainty and hostility hat must still remain among the inhabitants of Ithaca will be resolved. This eeling of being in progress even at the conclusion of the poem is as true of Telemachus' emerging adulthood as it is of any other story line in the tale.

The return of Odysseus does not instantly make Telemachus a self-sufficient, ndependent adult: for the most part it is still Odysseus who makes the plans ınd arranges events to his own satisfaction. Yet the young man does show real :hanges as a result of his own travels and the return of Odysseus, beginning with his self-control and self-reliance at the end of the reunion of Book 16. "or the remainder of the poem, he consistently dissembles to the suitors and o the members of his own family in order to conceal the fact of Odysseus' eturn, a degree of self-command that is hard to imagine in connection with he awkward, uncertain youth of the early part of the poem. For Telemachus, unlike for Odysseus, the simple fact of his ability to conceal things from others vho would be interested in the concealed information merits special notice rom the narrator (in the form of the epithets that describe him when he speaks misleadingly). There is no sense in these scenes that Telemachus feels ıny internal conflict from a desire to reveal his privileged information. The 10teworthy feature of his deceptions is not any conflict they entail for him, ıut his newly developed ability to practice them at all.

The epithets that modify Telemachus parallel this development in his :haracter. In the first two thirds of the poem, he is described in reply introduc-.ions predominantly by relatively colorless adjectives used of various Homeric :haracters.[64] In the last third, in contrast, group reply formulas containing the ınique expression ἱερὴ ἲς Τηλεμάχοιο (hallowed prince Telemachos) appear :onsistently (if not uniformly).[65] Similarly, periphrases calling him φίλος ›ιὸς Ὀδυσσῆος θείοιο (dear son of godlike Odysseus) or some variant thereof ıppear much more frequently in the last third of the poem than they did in he first two thirds of the poem.[66] Thus, the language for Telemachus changes n the same way as the character himself does: it recognizes, or at any rate ›arallels, his reunion with his father and his subsequent increase in maturity.

But, it may be objected, τοῖσι δὲ καὶ (or τοῖς αὖτις) μετέειφ' ἱερὴ ἲς Τηλεμάχοιο the hallowed prince Telemachos now spoke out among them) is a group reply

---

[64] A characterization with which Heath 2001 disagrees.
[65] 18.60, 18.405, 21.101, 21.130, 22.354-355 (combining a speech concluding verse that contains our formula for Telemachus with a context-specific speech introduction).
[66] 17.3, 18.214, 20.283, 21.432, 22.350, 24.505.

formula. τὸν δ' αὖ Τηλέμαχος πεπνυμένος ἀντίον ηὔδα (then the thoughtful Telemachos spoke to him in answer), on the other hand, is a reply formula that generally appears in one-on-one conversations. Certainly such contextual factors do have some effect on which of the two verses appears. And yet, the line between addressing one character and addressing more than one is not always sharply drawn: a character may address one person out of a group as synecdoche for the whole group. For example, at *Odyssey* 2.208, we have τὸν δ' αὖ Τηλέμαχος πεπνυμένος ἀντίον ηὔδα with a singular accusative pronoun, but this introduces a speech whose first line (2.209) is "Εὐρύμαχ' ἠδὲ καὶ ἄλλοι, ὅσοι μνηστῆρες ἀγαυοί (Eurymachos and all you others who are haughty suitors)." The remainder of the speech uses plural forms of address (ὑμέας, 210; δότε, 212). Conversely, the formulaic half-verse τοῖσι δὲ μύθων ἦρχε (s/he began the talk among them) appears more than once in contexts where the plural pronoun is not applicable.[67]

Furthermore, Telemachus does address groups of people in the early part of the poem, and these remarks are introduced without recourse to the expression ἱερὴ ἲς Τηλεμάχοιο.[68] This suggests that, while context does limit the use of the group reply formula τοῖσι δὲ καὶ/τοῖς αὖτις μετέειφ' ἱερὴ ἲς Τηλεμάχοιο, the story is told without this verse in the first part of the poem and could have continued to move forward without it throughout. Conversely, ἱερὴ ἲς Τηλεμάχοιο could have appeared indiscriminately throughout the poem, which would preclude the effect I have described above. Indeed, it is significant that ἱερὴ ἲς Τηλεμάχοιο appears in the first 15 books of the poem only when Telemachus tells his comrades that they are going on an expedition to look for news of Odysseus and denies having heard any news of his father (*Odyssey* 2.409). This is an important moment in the youth's development, when for the first time he takes the initiative, eluding both the suitors and his mother in pursuit of his own aims.

All of the speeches introduced by τοῖσι δὲ καὶ/τοῖς δ' αὖτις μετέειφ' ἱερὴ ἲς Τηλεμάχοιο (now the hallowed prince Telemachos spoke his word to them) show Telemachus making deceptive speeches either to the suitors or for their benefit.[69] At 18.60, although this group reply formula appears, Telemachus speaks to Odysseus himself in the body of his speech. He pretends

---

[67] See Introduction, 38–39.

[68] τοῖσι δὲ Τηλέμαχος πεπνυμένος ἄρχετο μύθων (the thoughtful Telemachos began speaking among them) appears at *Odyssey* 1.367 (with an alternate reading of ἀντίον ηὔδα, which is not used elsewhere of a speech not immediately preceded by another speech) and 15.502. This verse does not occur after Book 16.

[69] The epithets for Hera in *Iliad* 14 function in a similar way; see Chapter 3. Lateiner 1995:154 makes the suggestion that the newly mature Telemachus has assumed his adolescent-self as a disguise: "paradoxically, Telemachus' assuming the disguise of an adolescent proves his manhood. No adolescent would or could perform that fraud."

not to know the true identity of the beggar, calling him ξεῖν' (stranger, 61). He tells the "beggar" to fight Iros if he wants to, reasserts his own position as the host, and refers to Antinous and Eurymachus in possibly ironic terms (Ἀντίνοός τε καὶ Εὐρύμαχος, πεπνυμένω ἄμφω [Antinoös and Eurymachos, both men of prudence], 65).[70] At 18.405, this formula introduces a speech in which Telemachus tells the suitors that some god must be inciting them to their current behavior and suggests that they go home, while denying that he will force them to leave (406-409). Although this seems a harmless and ordinary remark on its face, it clearly had a different significance to the suitors, who are struck dumb at Telemachus' words:[71]

ὣς ἔφαθ', οἱ δ' ἄρα πάντες ὀδὰξ ἐν χείλεσι φύντες
Τηλέμαχον θαύμαζον, ὃ θαρσαλέως ἀγόρευε.

So he spoke, and all of them bit their lips in amazement
at Telemachos, and the daring way he had spoken to them.

18.410-411

The other two speeches preceded by τοῖσι δὲ καὶ/τοῖς αὖτις μετέειφ' ἱερὴ ἲς Τηλεμάχοιο both occur during the contest of the bow, and show Telemachus actively pretending to be either weaker or stupider than he really is. 21.101 introduces the speech in which he announces his intention to try to string the great bow of Odysseus (102-117). In the course of the speech, he twice refers to himself with the adjective ἄφρων (witless, 102 and 105), when in fact by this point in the story he is nothing of the kind. His attempt to string the bow, so nearly successful but for the intervention of Odysseus himself, is followed by extravagant lamentations about his own youth and inability.

καί νύ κε δή ῥ' ἐτάνυσσε βίῃ τὸ τέταρτον ἀνέλκων,
ἀλλ' Ὀδυσεὺς ἀνένευε καὶ ἔσχεθεν ἱέμενόν περ.
τοῖς δ' αὖτις μετέειφ' ἱερὴ ἲς Τηλεμάχοιο·
"ὢ πόποι, ἦ καὶ ἔπειτα κακός τ' ἔσομαι καὶ ἄκικυς,
ἠὲ νεώτερός εἰμι . . . "

---

[70] Edwards 1966:165 notes that this is the only time a suitor is called πεπνυμένος, and he suggests that Telemachus uses the word on purpose here ("[πεπνυμένος] is never attributed to any of the suitors . . . except by the crafty lips of the young man himself"). While I find this suggestion provocative, I also find it problematic, since it seems to me to imply that the characters are using the narrator's vocabulary in the same way that the narrator does.

[71] The same couplet appears at 1.381-382 (omitted by some manuscripts) and 20.268-269. Olson 1995:75 suggests that the suitors are surprised in Odyssey 1 (381-382), when this couplet first appears, because until this point, Telemachus and the suitors have had good relations. It is not clear according to this line of reasoning why the suitors are still surprised in Book 18.

> And now, pulling the bow for the fourth time, he would have
>   strung it,
> but Odysseus stopped him, though he was eager, making
>   a signal
> with his head. The hallowed prince, Telemachos, said to them:
> "Shame on me. I must then be a coward and a weakling,
> or else I am still young . . . "

21.128-132

This pretense distracts the suitors from noticing that in fact Telemachus almost strung the bow, and the contest proceeds without the suitors seeming to realize Telemachus' feat. Moreover, except for Odysseus himself, only Telemachus speaks more than once while attempting to string the bow. This gives Telemachus prominence in the contest of the bow, implicitly showing that of the young men present, he is the most nearly able to match his father's strength and skill. Generally speaking, τοῖς αὖτις μετέειφ' ἱερὴ ἲς Τηλεμάχοιο is found in the section of the poem in which Telemachus is capable of concealment and adult behavior. The specific contexts in which it appears all show Telemachus either dissembling for the suitors or frightening them with bold language, neither of which he was able to do persuasively in the early part of the poem.

The Analyst idea that the Telemachy (the story of Telemachus' journey in Books 1-4) is a later addition or an inexpert grafting of a different story onto the story of Odysseus' homecoming has now been generally abandoned. Recent scholars of various persuasions have accepted this episode as an integral part of the story that the *Odyssey* tells, albeit one that had alternative versions.[72] Both the prominence in the construction of the poem of the traditional story line involving Telemachus and the reunion that takes place between him and Odysseus demonstrate a consistent approach to the tools of Homeric storytelling: a skillful and effective use of traditional materials in order to tell the story of Odysseus' homecoming in a particular way. This Odysseus derives much of his meaning and importance for the audience from his effect on those left behind, including Telemachus. The story line involving Telemachus has unusual prominence, perhaps more than normally appeared in a story about a husband returning to a wife besieged by suitors and about

---

[72] See Reece 1994 for an interesting speculation about versions in which Telemachus goes to Crete, meets Odysseus there, and returns with him to Ithaca. At the end of his paper (170-171), he offers a concise and well-observed appreciation of the role of the Telemachy in our *Odyssey*.

to remarry,[73] thus setting up an expectation in the audience for a developed scene of reunion between Telemachus and Odysseus. When this scene does take place, it develops the type of "one-on-one conversation" at unusual length, relying on traditional types of elaboration at key points in order to bring out the strength of the conflicting feelings each feels about wanting, on the one hand, to maintain a cautious distance while also desiring closeness and reunion. The most elaborate description of their emotions occurs when this tension is finally resolved and their separation has ended in mutual acceptance and recognition.[74]

Laertes and Odysseus: Book 24

Here this chapter stops following the sequence of reunions as they appear in the *Odyssey*, postponing the drawn out series of encounters between Odysseus and Penelope to the next chapter. Instead, I will now skip to the end of the poem and consider the reunion of Odysseus with his old father, Laertes. Analyses of this reunion have long been plagued by questions about the status of the end of the poem. A famous scholion of Aristophanes and Aristarchus says that the πέρας or τέλος of the *Odyssey* occurs at 23.296, and generations of scholars have puzzled and argued over what this might mean.[75] Some have asserted, based on this scholion, that τέλος means the end of the poem, and that the part of the poem following this verse is a later interpolation. Others have felt that the word refers to the "goal" or "aim" of the story rather than the literal end of the poem, and have defended the unity of the last part of the *Odyssey* as it has been transmitted to us. Within this general controversy concerning the entire section of the poem within which the reunion between Odysseus and Laertes takes place, the reunion in particular has come in for its own share of criticism and debate.

This reunion, like others between Odysseus and his family members, takes the form of a one-on-one conversation in which the usual patterns of this type are manipulated to dramatize the conflict Odysseus feels between

---

[73] Reece 1994:161.

[74] Danek 1998:308 discusses the specific construction of this reunion and its relation both to the underlying themes of our *Odyssey* and to alternative versions of the Telemachus aspects of the story.

[75] Rather than attempt myself to recapitulate this "indigestible mass of material" (Heubeck in Russo et al. 1992:342), interested readers are referred to Heubeck's discussion of the scholion, the "τέλος" of the *Odyssey*, and the immense bibliography that has grown up around the question (Russo et al. 1992:342-345). He espouses the unitarian position, which is very ably opposed by West 1989.

revealing himself at once to his father and telling him some circumspect untruths instead. However, the kinds of manipulations we find here are quite different from those of other reunions in the poem. It is a less lengthy conversation than those that take place between Odysseus and either Telemachus or Penelope; it does not contain any extended similes to draw out and bring to life the moment of reunion; it barely contains a test of recognition. Moreover, Odysseus' behavior toward his elderly father, in testing him at all, has been widely criticized as cruel and pointless after the suitors have already been killed and Odysseus' position in his household has become much more secure.[76] The unusual aspects of this reunion could lend support to the notion that the Laertes scene is not part of the same fabric as the rest of the *Odyssey*.

The observations I will make about this reunion largely parallel the conclusions of West 1989, namely that the end of the *Odyssey* was added to the main body of our *Odyssey* at a later time. I would like to emphasize that although I find West's comments very plausible, and my own observations *parallel* her conclusions about the later addition of the end of the *Odyssey*, I myself am not convinced that this is what happened.[77] Alternatively, since the basic pattern that is used to create these effects is the same one-on-one conversation type that we have seen repeatedly in reunion scenes, one could claim that Odysseus' reunion with his father in fact does resemble his reunions with other family members, thereby strengthening the case against the idea that the end of the *Odyssey* and Book 24 in particular should be considered differently from the rest of the poem.

The scene gets under way when Odysseus brings Telemachus and servants with him to his father's dwelling. Once they arrive, he tells the other members of his party to prepare a meal while he tests his father to see whether he will know Odysseus or not (24.214–218). When Odysseus first sees his father, wretchedly dressed and toiling in his orchard, he weeps and debates whether to embrace him immediately or make his trial of the old man (232–238).[78] Here,

---

[76] Danek 1998:488-492 provides a useful overview of these various problems and of possible alternative story versions pertaining to the reunion of Odysseus and Laertes.

[77] To me this is one of the questions about the Homeric epics that remain unanswerable because of our ignorance about the composition and transmission of the poems in the period before the Hellenistic editors. These are matters to which I will return in the Conclusion.

[78] See the note of Heubeck *ad* 24.235-240 (in Russo et al. 1992) on the unusual construction of this passage in comparison to other cases where someone debates among various possible alternatives. He condemns the passage, but I think it is consistent with the lack of resolve that Odysseus demonstrates throughout the episode, which contrasts so strongly and movingly with his firm resolve in similar situations earlier in the poem.

n fact, the narrator explicitly says that Odysseus feels torn between open-
ness and concealment. In previous reunions, as we have seen, the narrator
describes the emotions of one or both speakers which, taken in conjunction
with what the character(s) actually say, implicitly depicts this tension. The
description here puts Odysseus' dilemma squarely before the audience.

> τὸν δ' ὡς οὖν ἐνόησε πολύτλας δῖος Ὀδυσσεὺς
> γήραϊ τειρόμενον, μέγα δὲ φρεσὶ πένθος ἔχοντα,
> στὰς ἄρ' ὑπὸ βλωθρὴν ὄγχνην <u>κατὰ δάκρυον εἶβε</u>.
> μερμήριξε δ' ἔπειτα κατὰ φρένα καὶ κατὰ θυμὸν
> <u>κύσσαι καὶ περιφῦναι ἑὸν πατέρ'</u> ἠδὲ ἕκαστα
> εἰπεῖν, ὡς ἔλθοι καὶ ἵκοιτ' ἐς πατρίδα γαῖαν,
> ἦ πρῶτ' ἐξερέοιτο ἕκαστά τε πειρήσαιτο.

Now when much-enduring great Odysseus observed him,
with great misery in his heart, and oppressed by old age,
he stood underneath a towering pear tree and <u>shed tears</u> for him,
and deliberated then in his heart and his spirit
whether to <u>embrace his father and kiss him</u> and tell him
everything, how he was come again to his own dear country,
or question him first about everything, and make trial of him.

Only here does Odysseus hesitate at all in his dealings with a family member or
friend whom he is meeting for the first time. In every other case, most notably
with Penelope (on which see the next chapter), Odysseus sticks inexorably to
his plan to reveal himself only after testing and reassuring himself about the
loyalty of the person whom he is meeting again. Kisses, tears, and embraces all
characterize the moment when reunion actually occurs in the other important
reunions in the *Odyssey*,[79] but Odysseus either does or feels the need to do
these things before he has even spoken to his father. The greater strength and
prominence of Odysseus' conflicted emotions here puts his relationship with his
father, and hence his reunion with him, on a different and in some sense higher
footing than his meetings with other loved ones, even with Penelope.[80]

The conversation between Odysseus and Laertes has eight turns in all,
several of which have multi-verse speech frames. In addition, the climax of

---

[79] Murnaghan 1987:22.
[80] Similarities between this scene and the meeting with Penelope include: testing not only by but
  of Odysseus; the grief of the other person upon hearing Odysseus' description of a false "sign";
  Odysseus provides a true sign of his identity after he has told his relation the truth about who
  he is.

the conversation halfway through is marked not by an elaboration like the one we saw in the reunion with Telemachus, but by a unique disruption in the turn structure of this one-on-one conversation. Odysseus—at least initially—decides that testing his father is the best course and addresses him accordingly (244-279). The grief-stricken father laments his lost son and asks the supposed stranger who he is (281-301). Odysseus replies with another of his false identities and asserts that "Odysseus" had visited him five years before (303-314).[81] Laertes now bursts into tears upon hearing what he imagines to be a true report of his son. A formulaic speech conclusion begins the passage that describes the grief of the father upon hearing this news of his son, grief that has a striking effect upon the son as he watches it.

> ὣς φάτο, τὸν δ' ἄχεος νεφέλη ἐκάλυψε μέλαινα·
> ἀμφοτέρῃσι δὲ χερσὶν ἑλὼν κόνιν αἰθαλόεσσαν
> χεύατο κὰκ κεφαλῆς πολιῆς, ἁδινὰ στεναχίζων.
> τοῦ δ' ὠρίνετο θυμός, ἀνὰ ῥῖνας δέ οἱ ἤδη
> δριμὺ μένος προὔτυψε φίλον πατέρ' εἰσορόωντι.
> κύσσε δέ μιν περιφὺς ἐπιάλμενος ἠδὲ προσηύδα·
> "κεῖνος μέν τοι ὅδ' αὐτὸς ἐγώ, πάτερ, ὃν σὺ μεταλλᾷς,
> ἤλυθον εἰκοστῷ ἔτεϊ ἐς πατρίδα γαῖαν.
> ἀλλ' ἴσχευ κλαυθμοῖο γόοιό τε δακρυόεντος."

> He spoke, and the black cloud of sorrow closed on Laertes.
> In both hands he caught up the grimy dust and poured it
> over his face and grizzled head, groaning incessantly.
> The spirit rose up in Odysseus, and now in his nostrils
> there was a shock of bitter force as he looked on his father.
> He sprang to him and embraced and kissed him and then
>   said to him:
> "Father, I am he, the man whom you ask about. I am
> here, come back in the twentieth year to the land of
>   my father.
> But stay now from your weeping, shedding of tears,
>   and outcry."

24.315-323

The formulaic verse at 315, appearing three times in the Homeric poems, also describes the grief-stricken Achilles after Antilochus comes to him at the

[81] Introduced by a regular reply formula containing the epithet πολύμητις (resourceful), 302.

beginning of *Iliad* 18 to tell him of the death of Patroclus. Similarly, Laertes performs the actions of a newly bereaved person when he puts dirt on himself and groans aloud.[82] It is unclear exactly why he acts like a bereaved person here: is he showing his sorrow that Odysseus is not, in fact, here to welcome this stranger who was hoping to see his guest-friend again (314-315)? Expressing his belief that Odysseus is dead, in spite of this report that he was alive relatively recently? Neither the immediate context nor comparison with the behavior of other characters elsewhere permits a firm conclusion on this point. Whatever the specific reason for Laertes' grief about Odysseus may be, the use of the language of mourning to describe it sets his grief apart from that of other members of Odysseus' family. Neither Penelope nor Telemachus, however much they were grieved by Odysseus' absence, ever behaved like a person in mourning on his account.

In fact, this passage gives equal prominence to the response of *Odysseus* to his father's grief as to the father's response to what Odysseus has said. This is quite remarkable: not only are extended speech frames of any sort unusual in one-on-one conversation, but a speech frame that describes the effect of the listener's emotion on the speaker who has just finished speaking is anomalous. This is also unlike Odysseus' behavior on other occasions when he is confronted with a grieving relation. Odysseus does, of course, respond to the grief of other people many times during the poem, but he generally does this either in the breach (as in his first meeting with Penelope in Book 19) or else after he has already declared himself to be Odysseus (which happens with both Telemachus and Penelope). Elsewhere, Odysseus can manage the conflict between his desire for openness and his impulse to conceal himself, but here, it appears, he cannot.

Moreover, Odysseus responds to his father's displays of grief by abandoning not only his plan to test Laertes, but even the alternating turn structure of the conversation. Laertes weeps and disfigures himself here in response to Odysseus' reference to hosting "Odysseus" in his false persona, and Odysseus also makes the speech after this one (that is, he takes both the third and the fourth turn in the sequence of eight). There are only seventeen successive speeches in the entire *Odyssey*, and the other sixteen are made either to or in a group. This is the only one that occurs in a one-on-one conversation. Only in his father is Odysseus unable to face the spectacle of the grief and bereavement

---

[82] Indeed, the language that describes his groaning in verse 317 closely resembles that which is used in the formulaic speech frames for formal laments, on which see Chapter 6.

of a relative who wrongly believes him to be lost. Only here does he abandon a previously designed plan to test and to lie because he is so deeply affected by the emotions of the person he sees weeping for him. The disruption of the turn structure itself is a fitting way to show that Odysseus cannot control the tension he feels between honesty and circumspection. Rather than simply describing this overwhelming emotion, the narrator depicts it overwhelming a typical pattern of one-on-one conversation that is observed everywhere in the *Odyssey* except for here.

Indeed, when he speaks, he does not say "I am Odysseus" or even "I am your son," as he says "I am your father" to Telemachus in Book 16. Instead, he simply says κεῖνος μέν τοι ὅδ᾽ αὐτὸς ἐγώ, πάτερ, ὃν σὺ μεταλλᾷς (Father, I am he, the man whom you ask about, 321) asserting his own identity through the actions of his father. Although the structural anomaly in this conversation differs markedly from the long emphatic passages of simile and description that occur in other reunions in the poem, like those elaborations, it does rely on the typical patterns of one-on-one conversation to create its effect. In its own way, it shows a starker and more basic emotional upheaval for Odysseus than the striking similes that audiences have loved since antiquity in the reunion scenes with Telemachus and Penelope.

Now that Odysseus has broken down under the weight of his father's grief and given up his testing plan, the tables are turned on him and Laertes tests him instead.[83] Just as Penelope did in Book 23, Laertes responds to Odysseus' statement of his identity by asking him for a σῆμα, a sign to prove his identity (328-329). In his reply, Odysseus provides not just one but two such tokens: he points to his scar (331-335), which has already revealed him inadvertently to Eurycleia, and he describes the trees in the orchard that the two used to walk among together when Odysseus was a little boy (336-344). Hearing these "signs," and recognizing them, Laertes is again overcome with emotion.[84]

> ὣς φάτο, τοῦ δ᾽ αὐτοῦ λύτο γούνατα καὶ φίλον ἦτορ,
> σήματ᾽ ἀναγνόντος, τά οἱ ἔμπεδα πέφραδ᾽ Ὀδυσσεύς·
> ἀμφὶ δὲ παιδὶ φίλῳ βάλε πήχεε· τὸν δὲ ποτὶ οἷ
> εἷλεν ἀποψύχοντα πολύτλας δῖος Ὀδυσσεύς.

---

[83] As we will see in the next chapter, Penelope too tests Odysseus, but in Book 19, Odysseus is able to bear the spectacle of his grieving wife as he is not able to bear that of his weeping father here.

[84] The formulaic language that occurs here also appears earlier in the *Odyssey* when Penelope hears the Odysseus describing their bed to her (24.345-346 ~23.205-206).

αὐτὰρ ἐπεί ῥ' ἔμπνυτο καὶ ἐς φρένα θυμὸς ἀγέρθη,
ἐξαῦτις μύθοισιν ἀμειβόμενος προσέειπε·

> He spoke, and Laertes' knees and the heart within him went
> slack,
> as he recognized the clear proofs that Odysseus had given.
> He threw his arms around his dear son, and much-enduring
> great Odysseus held him close, for his spirit was fainting.
> But when he had got his breath back again, and the spirit
> gathered
> into his heart, once more he said to him, answering:

24.345-350

Laertes physically demonstrates rather than saying in words that he accepts Odysseus as his son; moreover, in his speech (351-355), he hopes that the suitors will get their just desserts but fears that they will attack (presumably because they have heard that Odysseus has returned, although Laertes does not specify the reason for their hypothetical hostilities). This assumes that Odysseus is going to avenge the suitors and that he has the standing as the head of the household to do so.

The structure of this particular passage resembles the structure of two closely related passages that appear in the reunion of Penelope and Odysseus.[85] However, the two reunions take different courses. Whereas Penelope is only able to succeed in her attempts to test Odysseus after a prolonged period of being tested herself, and after failing initially to test him, Laertes breaks Odysseus' resolve to test him and almost immediately takes over the role of tester. The somewhat elaborate speech frame here provides a second emotional peak in the reunion scene at the by-now expected point when both characters have put aside any impulse toward concealment and have identified and recognized each other. This high point, unlike the unique successive speeches by Odysseus earlier in the scene, resembles the techniques of elaboration that we find in other reunion scenes in the poem in both its structure and what the structure depicts. Unlike the reunions with Telemachus or with Penelope, however, which both contain multiple elaborations that build up to one climactic moment in the episode, the two different high points of emotion in the reunion with Laertes operate rather

---

[85] 19.249-252, when Penelope "recognizes" the description of "Odysseus'" clothes by the disguised beggar, and 23.205-208, after Odysseus describes their bed (23.205-206 ~ 24.345-346). Danek 1998:490 suggests, in fact, that there may have been versions of the Laertes aspect of the story in which the recognition was split into two sections similar to the construction of the Penelope-Odysseus reunion.

differently from one another from an aesthetic standpoint. As a result, they do not tend to reinforce one another to create one unified crescendo effect. Instead, the scene contains two intertwined tensions or developments: a unique one, in which Odysseus is overmastered against his will by his desire for frankness; and another more usual one in which the frankness Odysseus finds himself practicing gradually results in the mutual recognition of two characters.

The unusual strategies that are employed in this episode to create aesthetic and emotional effects parallel the discussion about the place of Book 24 in the *Odyssey*. That is to say, these strategies are markedly different from those that are used in similar scenes earlier in the poem, but they are certainly recognizable as belonging to the same basic aesthetic as these other parts of the *Odyssey*. Depending on the bent of the interpreter, this analysis could support different hypotheses. It could prove either that this part of the poem is sufficiently different from what precedes it that we must posit a different (probably later) origin, as West suggests. Alternatively, it could be argued that the similarities between the construction of Odysseus' reunion with Laertes and his reunions with Penelope and Telemachus are substantial enough to support the unity of Book 24 with the rest of the poem. Similarly, we may see the references to Laertes before Book 24 either as contrived[86] or as leading up to Laertes' role later in the poem. Rather unsatisfactorily, I do not have a firm position on this point. I think there are some issues on which our knowledge is simply inadequate to allow us to draw firm conclusions—as opposed to plausible hypotheses—and the status of *Odyssey* 24 is one of them.

Conclusions

This chapter has argued that a consistent aesthetic outlook and approach to traditional materials operates in the various conversations in the second half of the *Odyssey* that mark important points in Odysseus' homecoming. In each of these scenes, the narrator highlights a tension that Odysseus feels between revealing himself at once to the person with whom he speaks in order to re-establish a relationship with that person, and concealing his identity. Typical conversation patterns depict this conflict: the narrator manipulates or draws out the usual structures of one-on-one conversation without substantially changing them. When Odysseus meets Athena, his first conversation on Ithaca, and when he is reunited with his son, wife (as we will see shortly), and father,

---

[86] West 1989:117.

a one-on-one conversation occurs that is unusually long and that contains elaborations of various kinds in between the individual speeches where we would normally expect single-verse reply formulas. These elaborations are one of the main sources of emotion and pathos in these various scenes.

This emotion focuses in almost every case on the sadness, tension, and pain that Odysseus experiences as he reunites with his home and family because of the conflicting pressures of emotional closeness and strategic concealment. Often this tension emerges through a contrast between a speech frame describing strong emotions and a speech that does not betray any particular feeling. In no case does an elaborate conversation like this appear outside of a reunion context. Concealment on its own, as in the scenes between Odysseus and Eumaeus in Books 14 and 15, does not give rise to the same conflicts or the same narrative effects. This pattern distinguishes the *Odyssey* from the *Iliad*, in which this kind of elaboration of one-on-one conversation focuses not on the emotions of reunion, but—for the most part—on the feelings of hostility, power, and triumph that arise between enemies on the battlefield.[87] The reunion between Penelope and Odysseus, the topic of the next chapter, displays the same aesthetic tendencies, but over a longer stretch of the poem than any of Odysseus' other reunions.

---

[87] For one-on-one conversations in the *Iliad* see Chapters 3 and 4.

2

ONE-ON-ONE CONVERSATIONS
(ODYSSEUS AND PENELOPE)

THE STORY OF PENELOPE AND ODYSSEUS and their drawn-out reunion over the course of the last third of the *Odyssey* is one of the most extensively studied portions of the Homeric epics.[1] The gradual rapprochement between Penelope and Odysseus, stretching over several books of the *Odyssey* contains two major movements or sections, one in Book 19 and one in Book 23. Penelope and Odysseus first meet face to face in a long conversation that essentially takes up all of Book 19. This conversation falls into two parts, separated by the incident of Eurycleia and her recognition of Odysseus' scar. At the end of the second section of this conversation, Penelope decides to hold the bow contest. Odysseus now goes among the suitors, wins the bow contest and slaughters the suitors. The Penelope-Odysseus reunion returns to center stage at the beginning of Book 23, when Eurycleia rushes up to her mistress quarters to tell her that the suitors are dead and the anonymous beggar who killed them is Odysseus. This information brings Penelope down to talk to the stranger for herself, and in another long conversation, Penelope tests the stranger and satisfies herself that he is indeed her husband.[2] This climactic conversation, for many the highlight of the entire poem, contains the single most elaborate speech frame in the Homeric epics.

---

[1] Russo (in Russo et al. 1992:4-14) provides an excellent overview of the main issues for modern scholarship concerning the narrative construction of the reunion. de Jong 2001:458-460 surveys some of the same issues but in a more limited manner. Argument has centered on the length of the reunion (on which see Emlyn-Jones 1984), which some have seen as excessive and lacking in motivation; whether Penelope does, in fact, recognize Odysseus before Book 23; and what her motivation is for setting the bow contest.

[2] Emlyn-Jones 1984 argues that there is a "reunion" type in the *Odyssey* that is not complete until Book 23, thereby disagreeing with critics who have suggested either 1) that the narrator's technique in fashioning Penelope lacks finesse or traditionality or 2) that Penelope recognizes Odysseus before Book 23.

The reunion of Penelope and Odysseus—unlike those we have studied in Chapter 1—contains not just one conversation, but many conversations, each of which uses speech frames and interruptions in the conversation to dramatize at unparalleled length the tension between openness and circumspection that to some degree drives all of Odysseus' reunions on Ithaca. The conflict has much greater prominence and poignancy here than in any other reunion not only because of the unique level of detail in individual conversations, but because several conversations stretching over the last third of the poem feature this tension. In particular, this series of conversations shows the intertwining feelings of the husband, steeling himself to remain unmoved in the face of his wife's grief until he has determined that the time has come to do so; and the wife, who over the course of her conversations with the strange beggar masters her grief to successfully test Odysseus without his knowing it, a feat that she alone among the characters in the *Odyssey* is able to achieve. In other words, this reunion is constructed in the same way as other elaborate conversations we have seen in Chapter 1 (and will see in Chapter 3 and 4), only much more so.

Penelope and Odysseus, Prelude: Book 18

Although the reunion of Penelope and Odysseus is a recurring motif throughout the *Odyssey*, actual contact between the two first gets underway in Book 17, when Penelope invites the beggar to speak with her via a message to Eumaeus (17.505-511). When Athena arouses in Penelope the idea of showing herself to the suitors (18.158-163),[3] Odysseus is present in the hall to observe her interactions with the young men who want to supplant him. This scene between Penelope and the suitors forms an effective prelude or backdrop to the meeting between her and her disguised husband in Book 19. In the first pair of speeches in the conversation between Penelope and the suitors, each of the speakers shows his or her nature as a speaker and as an adversary in the ongoing battle between them about the legitimacy of the suitors' behavior and Penelope's refusal to marry any of them. Eurymachus straightforwardly compliments Penelope on her beauty (245-249), while Penelope in her reply does a masterful job of saying one thing that effectively and indirectly communicates something different

---

[3] Byre 1988:162-163 argues persuasively that the idea that Penelope should show herself to the suitors belongs to Athena, not Penelope. He suggests that her laugh before she tells Eurynome of her intention to go among them (*Odyssey* 18.158-163) results from the fact that she is doing something she doesn't understand or even desire to do.

to the suitors. She recalls at length what Odysseus said to her when he left for the Trojan War (253-270) and she berates the suitors for their rude behavior in using up the goods of her household instead of wooing her with gifts as would normally be expected of a suitor (272-280).

From a pragmatic point of view, Penelope is an extremely effective speaker here. The intention behind Eurymachus' speech is to legitimize the suitors' pursuit of her: any Greek who saw her would want to court her because of her beauty, and therefore, the suitors are only doing what anyone might do under the same circumstances. Penelope counters this basic point in two different ways: by discussing her husband at such length, she indirectly reminds the suitors that as a married woman, she is not a suitable bride for any of them; and by speaking about the proper behavior of suitors, she successfully induces the suitors to bring her presents. Not surprisingly, the suitors focus on the second part of her speech, with its implicit suggestion that she might accept the goods and marry one of them, and ignore the first part, even though the first part of the speech is more prominent because of both its length and the order of the different parts of the speech. Antinous, who responds to her speech, promises gifts from the suitors (285-89), but makes no reference to Odysseus.

Between Penelope's speech and the reply to it, an extended passage in the form of a speech conclusion describes the response elicited by Penelope's words (281-283).

> " . . . μνηστήρων οὐχ ἥδε δίκη τὸ πάροιθε τέτυκτο,
> οἵ τ' ἀγαθήν τε γυναῖκα καὶ ἀφνειοῖο θύγατρα
> μνηστεύειν ἐθέλωσι καὶ ἀλλήλοις ἐρίσωσιν·
> αὐτοὶ τοί γ' ἀπάγουσι βόας καὶ ἴφια μῆλα,
> κούρης δαῖτα φίλοισι, καὶ ἀγλαὰ δῶρα διδοῦσιν.
> ἀλλ' οὐκ ἀλλότριον βίοτον νήποινον ἔδουσιν."
> ὣς φάτο [sc. Penelope], <u>γήθησεν δὲ πολύτλας δῖος</u>
>   <u>Ὀδυσσεύς,</u>
> οὕνεκα τῶν μὲν δῶρα παρέλκετο, θέλγε δὲ θυμὸν
> μειλιχίοις ἐπέεσσι, νόος δέ οἱ ἄλλα μενοίνα.
>   <u>τὴν δ' αὖτ' Ἀντίνοος προσέφη, Εὐπείθεος υἱός·</u>
> "κούρη Ἰκαρίοιο, περίφρων Πηνελόπεια . . . "

" . . . The behavior of these suitors is not as it was in times past
when suitors desired to pay their court to a noble woman
and daughter of a rich man, and rival each other. Such men
themselves bring in their own cattle and fat sheep, to feast

the family of the bride, and offer glorious presents.
They do not eat up another's livelihood, without payment."
    She spoke, and <u>much-enduring great Odysseus was happy</u>
because she beguiled gifts out of them, and enchanted their
    spirits
with blandishing words, while her own mind had other
    intentions.
    <u>Then Antinoös the son of Eupeithes answered</u>:
"Daughter of Ikarios, circumspect Penelope . . . "

18.275-285

Contrary to the usual pattern for speech conclusions between one speech and another in an ongoing conversation—which in itself is already unusual—this passage does not describe the reaction of anyone directly involved in the ongoing exchange. Instead, it briefly diverts the attention of the audience to a silent bystander. Moreover, this description falls between one speech and the single-verse reply formula preceding the next one in the conversation, making it unnecessary to the narrative structure of the scene. From the standpoint of narrative structure and clarity, the reply formula for Antinous at verse 284 could directly follow verse 280. Instead, we get a brief glimpse of a silently appreciative Odysseus, in disguise as a beggar, observing from the sidelines his wife's sparring with the suitors.[4]

Even before the two meet face to face, they show an unstated—and unknown, in Penelope's case—fellowship in their ideas about overcoming the suitors. Without directly connecting the two characters, the narrator vividly conveys their basic similarity and suitability for each other in an area that the poem delves into in detail: each is capable of falsely representing him- or herself in the interest of some larger goal. Penelope manipulates the suitors to bring her presents, even though the bulk of her speech suggests that she has no interest in marrying any of them; Odysseus enjoys the spectacle of his wife's cleverness and does not feel impelled to reveal his identity when confronted face to face with other men trying to marry her. This increases the

---

[4] Hölscher 1972, the most persuasive and influential treatment of this passage, argues that the much-debated phrase νόος δέ οἱ ἄλλα μενοίνα (while her own mind had other intentions) distinguishes between what Penelope says and "the feelings in her heart" rather than between her words and some secret plan (136). Odysseus, he goes on to say, is not worried about Penelope's fidelity here or elsewhere because her speech clearly shows this distinction between what she says to the suitors and how she feels.

involvement of the audience in their ultimate reunion and the sense of fitness that surrounds it. Furthermore, Odysseus' silent and acute appreciation for Penelope falls amid the two speeches by his wife's two most prominent suitors, throwing their lack of understanding of her motives or the situation into relief.

Two Competing Vocatives for Penelope

Penelope is addressed with a full-verse vocative by both Eurymachus (18.245) and Antinous (18.285). Both here and elsewhere, these young men address Penelope as κούρη Ἰκαρίοιο, περίφρον Πηνελόπεια (daughter of Ikarios, circumspect Penelope).[5] These men define Penelope's identity in terms of her father Icarius. Furthermore, she is referred to as a κούρη (daughter, young woman). Here the word should be taken with her father's name to mean "daughter of Icarius," but its connotation of youth is also present. This way of describing Penelope implicitly ignores her relation to Odysseus and to Telemachus, as well as the long years of fending for herself since Odysseus went to war. Such language, in fact, illustrates the suitors' ongoing attempt to define Penelope's identity in a way that makes her a suitable target of their attentions.[6] Penelope uses speech to successfully manipulate the suitors, insofar as she gets them to bring her gifts without directly ordering them to do so. In contrast, they attempt without success to manipulate her identity through their addresses to her so as to make her an appropriate bride for one of them.[7]

In contrast, Odysseus uses a full-verse vocative to address his wife that differs from the one that the suitors use: ὦ γύναι αἰδοίη Λαερτιάδεω

---

[5] Eurymachus, *Odyssey* 16.435, 18.245, 21.321; Antinous, *Odyssey* 18.285.

[6] Kahane 1994 briefly refers to this verse (98) in his chapter on the "heroic" properties of verse-final proper names in the vocative case. He sees the verse as a way of connecting Penelope and Odysseus: "the diction creates a very desirable reference and hence analogy. After all, Penelope is not just Odysseus' formal spouse, she is also his counterpart in cunning, self-control, and perseverance." Because Kahane focuses exclusively on vocatives where a nominative proper name appears at the end of the verse, he does not mention the other full-verse vocative for Penelope, which in my opinion makes a much closer connection between her and her husband (see below).

[7] Conversation analysis has shown that speakers identify things they talk about in particular ways that depend on the interaction between the speaker, the thing they are talking about, and the context (Silverman 1998:14-17): "having multiple terms for one 'object' represents not just more 'interest' in that object but an attempt to enforce authority . . . In that sense, the categories we use in our descriptions are instruments of social control, and contested categories are one way that one does 'rebellion'" (16-17).

Ὀδυσῆος (O respected wife of Odysseus, son of Laertes), 19.165. Throughout the conversation between him and Penelope in Book 19, Odysseus begins several speeches to her with this full-verse vocative.[8] These words present her in an entirely different light from the language used by the suitors when they address Penelope with a full-verse vocative. The suitors, naturally, are not anxious to dwell on the fact that Penelope is already married. Odysseus, in contrast, calls Penelope a γυνή, or a sexually mature woman; the word may also mean, among other things, the mistress of a house[9] and a wife.[10] Alone, it may be used in the vocative as a form of respectful address.[11] While a κούρη (young maiden) would be unlikely to have a husband, much less an adult son, a γυνή certainly could be married and have a family of her own. The modifying adjective αἰδοίη (respected) calls attention to the honor a married woman should get, and subtly jibes at the suitors for their improper behavior. Finally, this verse refers to Odysseus using both his name and his patronymic. This reminds the listeners, who include the suitors since this conversation takes place in the crowded hall of the palace, of the existence of Penelope's husband and of that husband's important place in the social structure of Ithaca.[12] In a larger sense, it pits Odysseus' notion of the proper role for Penelope against that of the suitors.

The verse that the suitors use to address Penelope is numerically more frequent than this expression of Odysseus', largely because κούρη Ἰκαρίοιο, περίφρον Πηνελόπεια (daughter of Ikarios, circumspect Penelope) can be used in several cases besides the vocative without changing the metrical shape of

---

[8] Odyssey 19.165, 262, 336, 583; the appearance of this verse at 17.152 will be discussed below.

[9] Cunliffe def. 2. I use Cunliffe rather than LSJ in this and the following notes because LSJ mixes Homeric and post-Homeric usage, whereas Cunliffe is confined to Homer.

[10] Cunliffe def. 4b.

[11] E.g. by Odysseus to Penelope at Odyssey 19.107, or (in quite different circumstances) by Antenor to Helen during the Teichoscopia (Iliad 3.204); Cunliffe def. 5. In fact, with the exception of Antenor's address to Helen and Odysseus' first approach to Nausicaa at Odyssey 6.149-185, γυνή in the vocative case is used only by a husband addressing his wife (6.168-169, where he is comparing Nausicaa to a goddess: ὡς σέ, γύναι, ἄγαμαί τε τέθηπά τε δείδιά τ' αἰνῶς/γούνων ἅψασθαι . . . [so now, lady, I admire you and wonder and am terribly / afraid to clasp you by the knees]).

[12] Discussing this verse from a different point of view, Austin 1975:48 makes the very interesting point that although most characters do not use the kind of name-epithet formulas that appear with such regularity in the narrative sections of the Homeric epics, Odysseus does use them: "only Odysseus shows any inclination to follow in the poet's path; in his case all but one of his name-epithet formulas occur not when he is speaking about Odysseus, but when he is addressing Penelope as the wife of Odysseus, son of Laertes."

the noun κούρη. In addition to its four occurrences in the vocative,[13] κούρη Ἰκαρίοιο, περίφρον Πηνελόπεια is used in the nominative case four times[14] and in the dative three times,[15] once by Odysseus himself. Odysseus' character does use this formula in the dative case, where it is the only expression available, but he avoids it for Penelope in the vocative case. ὦ γύναι αἰδοίη Λαερτιάδεω Ὀδυσῆος (O respected wife of Odysseus, son of Laertes), although slightly more common in the vocative case than κούρη Ἰκαρίοιο, περίφρον Πηνελόπεια, can only be used as a vocative because of the initial metrically distinct ὦ γύναι.[16]

The issue of focalization is a very interesting one here: is it the character of Odysseus who purposefully avoids the vocative used by the suitors or does the narrator make him do so without his awareness?[17] Is this a piece of characterization or an aspect of poetic craft? It would be entirely in character for Odysseus to use language in this way, and conversation analysis demonstrates that this kind of intentional categorization is a regular feature of the way people talk. However, there are no obvious signals from the narrator that Odysseus is consciously setting out to identify either himself or Penelope with this language. Whichever is the case, Penelope may well recognize the difference between the suitors' mode of address and that of the beggar, and attach importance to this. For reasons that I will explain in detail later on, I do not believe that Penelope recognizes Odysseus until Book 23, but I do think that clues like this in Odysseus' way of talking attract her attention and unsettle her.

One might be tempted to argue that, since all of the instances of calling Penelope "wife of Odysseus" appear quite close together, the pattern in which they appear is due to clustering rather than to their particular appropriateness to this context.[18] However, there is one additional instance of ὦ γύναι αἰδοίη Λαερτιάδεω Ὀδυσῆος (O respected wife of Odysseus, son of Laertes) which makes this explanation unlikely. Theoclymenus the seer, whom Telemachus brings back to Ithaca with him from his travels to Pylos and Sparta, addresses

---

[13] *Odyssey* 16.435, 18.245, 18.285, 21.321.

[14] *Odyssey* 1.329, 11.446, 19.375, and 20.388.

[15] *Odyssey* 17.562 (by Odysseus, when he asks Eumaeus to tell Penelope that he will speak with her later on), 18.159, 21.2.

[16] This verse appears five times: 17.152; 19.165, 262, 336, 583.

[17] See de Jong 1987a:31-40 for an overview of narratological terminology, including "focalization," in the context of Homeric studies. The glossary in de Jong 2001:xi-xix covers similar territory, but in a less full and accessible form.

[18] On clustering, see Janko 1981.

'enelope in this way also.[19] Theoclymenus meets Penelope when he accompa-
ies Telemachus to the palace after their travels in Book 17 of the poem. After
'elemachus has told his mother about his trip, including what he learned
rom Menelaus about the whereabouts of Odysseus (17.140-49), Theoclymenus
olemnly asserts that what Telemachus has said is true.

> "ὦ γύναι αἰδοίη Λαερτιάδεω Ὀδυσῆος,
> ἦ τοι ὅ γ' οὐ σάφα οἶδεν, ἐμεῖο δὲ σύνθεο μῦθον·
> ἀτρεκέως γάρ τοι μαντεύσομαι οὐδ' ἐπικεύσω.
> ἴστω νῦν Ζεὺς πρῶτα θεῶν ξενίη τε τράπεζα
> ἱστίη τ' Ὀδυσῆος ἀμύμονος, ἣν ἀφικάνω,
> ὡς ἦ τοι Ὀδυσεὺς ἤδη ἐν πατρίδι γαίῃ,
> ἥμενος ἢ ἕρπων, τάδε πευθόμενος κακὰ ἔργα
> ἔστιν, ἀτὰρ μνηστῆρσι κακὸν πάντεσσι φυτεύει·
> οἷον ἐγὼν οἰωνὸν ἐϋσσέλμου ἐπὶ νηὸς
> ἥμενος ἐφρασάμην καὶ Τηλεμάχῳ ἐγεγώνευν."

"O respected wife of Odysseus, son of Laertes,
attend my word, because he does not understand clearly,
but I shall prophesy truly to you, and hold back nothing.
Zeus be my witness, first of the gods, and the table of friendship,
and the hearth of blameless Odysseus, to which I come as
    a suppliant,
that Odysseus is already here in the land of his fathers,
sitting still or advancing, learning of all these evil
actions, and devising evils for all of the suitors.
Such was the bird sign I interpreted, and I told it
to Telemachos, as I sat aboard the strong-benched vessel."

17.152-161

Theoclymenus not only confirms Telemachus' information, he adds that
)dysseus is at that moment on the island itself. Furthermore, he uses language
issociated with prophecy and oath-taking to declare the truth of what he says.
\t the start of these strongly worded assertions that Odysseus is nearing the
:nd of his long journey homeward, Theoclymenus addresses Penelope as the
vife of the returning hero (17.152) rather than as the daughter of her father in
he manner of the suitors.

---

[19] Reece 1994, in fact, argues that Theoclymenus is a doublet for Odysseus, performing functions
that would have belonged to Odysseus himself in alternative versions of the story.

In fact, these two different full-verse vocatives reflect one of the impor tant themes of the story: whether Penelope will return to her father's hous and marry one of the suitors or Odysseus will come home and reestablish he footing and his own in the social structure of Ithaca. Not only do these tw verses present different views of Penelope herself. By using one or the other individuals in the poem implicitly characterize themselves and their attitud toward the impasse about Penelope's status. These two different regularl occurring full-verse vocatives dramatize an important conflict of the poem whether she is to remain the wife of Odysseus or give him up for dead, resum her identity as the daughter of her father rather than the wife of her husband and marry again. This central conflict is depicted partly through regularl occurring formulas and structures that characterize conversation, structure which follow principles of conversation analysis.

Penelope and Odysseus (i): Book 19

This brief meeting in Book 18 between Penelope and her suitors in the presenc of Odysseus gives a vivid glimpse of all the characters involved behaving i a typical manner, providing a base line or backdrop for the reunion as i begins to unfold. Moreover, this scene lengthens the overall reunion betweer Odysseus and Penelope by giving them their first sight of each other befor they meet face to face. Book 19 consists almost entirely of a long conversatior between Penelope and Odysseus. This conversation opens with the vers ἔνθα καθέζετ' ἔπειτα πολύτλας δῖος Ὀδυσσεύς (on this, much enduring grea Odysseus was seated, 19.102). In the reply introductions for Odysseus onc the conversation gets under way, however, his remarks to Penelope alway start off with the reply formula most common elsewhere in the poem, τὴ δ' ἀπαμειβόμενος προσέφη πολύμητις Ὀδυσσεύς (then resourceful Odysseu spoke in turn and answered her).[20] This reply formula also introduces tw of three of his speeches to Eurycleia while she bathes his feet.[21] Thus, th consistent use of the epithet πολύτλας in reply formulas does set off Odysseus reunion with his son from other extended conversations he has, includin exchanges in similar circumstances with his wife and his old nurse.[22]

---

[20] *Odyssey* 19.106, 164, 220, 261, 335, 554, 582.

[21] 382, 499. The exception, 19.479-481, is an expanded introduction containing a variety c context-specific information, which means that the usual single-verse reply formula is no semantically equivalent.

[22] Of course, Odysseus conceals his identity throughout his first conversation with Penelop while he reveals it to Telemachus in the course of Book 16.

Odysseus' first conversation with his wife is distinguished not only by the elaborate speech frames it contains at several key points, but also by its great length. In different ways, both the length and the quantity of elaborate speech frames draw out the tension Odysseus feels between openness with Penelope and circumspection towards her. It also depicts the emotions of Penelope, who feels a corresponding tension that is openly displayed to both Odysseus and the audience between believing what the stranger tells her about her absent husband and remaining skeptical. The similarity and yet the difference between the responses of husband and wife as they confront these tensions give this conversation its tone and its impact. The first section of the conversation is composed of eleven turns between the two of them, with an additional two turns involving Eurycleia (103-388), followed after Eurycleia bathes Odysseus' feet by an additional five turns between Odysseus and Penelope (508-601).

The conversation between Penelope and Odysseus opens with the usual formalities between host and guest, which comprise the first three turns of the conversation. In his second speech (the fourth turn), Odysseus finally identifies himself to Penelope, or pretends to. Like the other three speeches in the conversation up to now, this is introduced by the most common reply formula for his character.[23] This formulaic introduction contrasts with the striking content of the speech itself, and with its effect on both husband and wife. For the first time, Odysseus addresses Penelope using the full-verse vocative that identifies her as "wife of Odysseus" (165). Then, although he claims to be answering Penelope's question about who he is (166-171), he falsely represents himself as a Cretan who met Odysseus[24] and offered him hospitality for several days when Odysseus' ship had been blown off course (185-202).

While the four speeches of Penelope and Odysseus up to this point have all been introduced by common reply formulas, a highly developed and extremely effective multi-verse speech frame spans the interval between Odysseus' speech here and Penelope's reply (203-214). This elaborate passage could be replaced by the single verse τὸν δ' ἠμείβετ' ἔπειτα περίφρων Πηνελόπεια (circumspect

---

[23] Speech introductory verses to this point for Penelope: τοῖσι δὲ μύθων ἄρχε περίφρων Πηνελόπεια (their discourse was begun by circumspect Penelope, 103); τὸν δ' ἠμείβετ' ἔπειτα περίφρων Πηνελόπεια (circumspect Penelope said to him in answer, 123). For Odysseus: τὴν δ' ἀπαμειβόμενος προσέφη πολύμητις Ὀδυσσεύς (then resourceful Odysseus spoke in turn and answered her, 106 and 164).

[24] This name is emphatically placed in the verse. "Odysseus" is the first word in its clause after the conjunction ἔνθα (ἔνθ' <u>Ὀδυσῆα</u> ἐγὼν ἰδόμην καὶ ξείνια δῶκα [it was there I knew <u>Odysseus</u> and entertained him], 185). Note the hiatus entailed by the emphatic initial position of Odysseus' name and its juxtaposition with the pronoun ἐγών; on this hiatus in Homer see Russo *ad loc.* in Russo et al. 1992.

Penelope said to him in answer), which introduces all but two of her speeches to Odysseus in Book 19, without loss of narrative clarity. However, our passage is one of the most striking and effective in the *Odyssey*, and its presence here elevates the typical motif of "returning husband in disguise tests loyalty of wife"[25] to a deeply moving encounter. In this passage, a pair of separate similes describes Penelope's emotion at hearing news of her long-absent husband and that husband's (lack of) reaction to her tears.[26]

> ἴσκε ψεύδεα πολλὰ λέγων ἐτύμοισιν ὁμοῖα·
> τῆς δ' ἄρ' ἀκουούσης ῥέε δάκρυα, τήκετο δὲ χρώς.
> ὡς δὲ χιὼν κατατήκετ' ἐν ἀκροπόλοισιν ὄρεσσιν,
> ἥν δ' Εὖρος κατέτηξεν, ἐπὴν Ζέφυρος καταχεύῃ·
> τηκομένης δ' ἄρα τῆς ποταμοὶ πλήθουσι ῥέοντες·
> ὣς τῆς τήκετο καλὰ παρήϊα δάκρυ χεούσης,
> κλαιούσης ἑὸν ἄνδρα παρήμενον.
>   αὐτὰρ Ὀδυσσεὺς
> θυμῷ μὲν γοόωσαν ἑὴν ἐλέαιρε γυναῖκα,
> ὀφθαλμοὶ δ' ὡς εἰ κέρα ἕστασαν ἠὲ σίδηρος
> ἀτρέμας ἐν βλεφάροισι· δόλῳ δ' ὅ γε δάκρυα κεῦθεν.
> ἡ δ' ἐπεὶ οὖν τάρφθη πολυδακρύτοιο γόοιο,
> ἐξαῦτίς μιν ἔπεσσιν ἀμειβομένη προσέειπε·
> "νῦν μὲν δή σευ, ξεῖνε, ὀΐω πειρήσεσθαι . . ."

He knew how to say many false things that were like true
    sayings.
As she listened her tears ran and her body was melted,
as the snow melts along the high places of the mountains
when the West Wind has piled it there, but the South Wind
    melts it,
and as it melts the rivers run full flood. It was even
so that her beautiful cheeks were streaming tears,
    as Penelope
wept for her man, who was sitting there by her side.

---

[25] On the themes in this part of the *Odyssey*, see e.g. Lord 1960:170-177. Foley 1999:125 has recently argued persuasively that doubtfulness about the wife's fidelity is a normal motif in this story type in South Slavic epic.

[26] This analysis overlaps to some extent with that of Russo in Russo et al. 1992:87-88. His appreciation of the Penelope simile is particularly good. Podlecki 1971:87-88 mentions this simile in the larger context of noting the "unusually large number of similes" in Book 19.

> But Odysseus
> in his heart had pity for his wife as she mourned him,
> but his eyes stayed, as if they were made of horn or iron,
> steady under his lids. He hid his tears and deceived her.
> But when she had taken her fill of tearful lamentation,
> then she answered him once again and spoke and addressed him:
> "Now, my friend, I think I will give you a test . . . "

19.203-215

While Penelope yields easily to the emotion she feels at the prospect of information about Odysseus, Odysseus—apparently without difficulty—masters the possible impulse to openness that his pity for Penelope might cause. His pity shows that he does feel some tug in the direction of openness with Penelope, but his calm behavior continues the deception that his words have begun. Both characters feel a desire for true information about Odysseus, but they respond in very different ways to that desire. Our passage depicts that difference, and makes it one of the things the conversation as a whole is about.

The first verse after the speech contains no direct references to the preceding speech, which is unusual at the start of a multi-verse passage following direct speech.[27] This verse is connected very loosely, both syntactically and semantically, to the preceding speech and to the following description of Penelope's reaction to what Odysseus has said. In fact, it does not provide any essential information about the situation or the reactions of the characters. However, its presence here emphasizes Odysseus' capacity to tell believable untruths at a moment when he has just done so under particularly challenging circumstances. In addition, it throws into relief the following verses describing Penelope's natural and spontaneous reaction to what she believes to be the truth.

This passage describes the emotions of both Penelope and Odysseus using comparisons. Penelope's chill loneliness melts in a flood of tears like winter snows on the mountains when spring winds blow (205-208); in contrast, Odysseus maintains his deception and his composure with rock-like steadiness even in the face of his wife's grief (211-212).[28] The two

---

[27] The resemblance between this verse and Hesiod *Theogony* 27 has been frequently commented upon. See e.g. West 1997 *ad Theogony* 27.

[28] Erbse 1972:93 writes of this simile for Odysseus' feelings, "Das ist das Meisterstück des Maskierten. Man spürt, welche Kraft der Selbstbeherrschung es erfordert" (This is the masterpiece of the disguise. One feels what power of self-mastery it requires).

comparisons are separate: the disjunctive conjunction αὐτάρ (but, 209) begins the description of Odysseus' immovability, marking a strong syntactical boundary between the two. In addition, the wife and the husband have very different emotions that are described with two distinct images. These two comparisons, in a sense, emphasize the division that exists at this point between the lonely, sorrowing queen and her disguised husband, who is sad also but conceals his grief. This gulf, however, contrasts movingly with the physical nearness of the two: Penelope weeps for ἑὸν ἄνδρα παρήμενον (her man, who was <u>sitting there by her side</u>, 209).[29] The similes describing their different emotions also sit side by side, as it were, echoing the narrative in describing two characters who are both alone and together in their sadness. Finally, after the very different reactions of the two are described, a couplet focusing on Penelope introduces her next speech (213-214). 213 is a full-verse formula that appears three time before speeches by Penelope, each time after she has had some kind of reminder of her absent husband, but the verse is only used after Odysseus himself has actually arrived in the palace.[30]

In the speech introduced by this affecting passage, which is the fifth turn in the conversation, Penelope tests the veracity of the stranger (ὀΐω πειρήσεσθαι [I think I will give you a test], 215) by asking him to describe "Odysseus'" clothing. Just as Penelope openly displays her grief, here she clearly identifies her question as a test. Of course Odysseus is able to pass (221-248). Once again, Penelope is overcome with emotion (249-252), described in a passage that could be replaced by a single-verse reply formula with no loss of narrative clarity. This passage forms an instructive pair with 19.203-214 above. The language in the two passages displays a number of similarities, but 19.249-252 includes no similes and no description of Odysseus' feelings.

> ὣς φάτο, τῇ δ' ἔτι μᾶλλον ὑφ' ἵμερον ὦρσε γόοιο,
> σήματ' ἀναγνούσῃ τά οἱ ἔμπεδα πέφραδ' Ὀδυσσεύς.
> ἡ δ' ἐπεὶ οὖν τάρφθη πολυδακρύτοιο γόοιο,
> καὶ τότε μιν μύθοισιν ἀμειβομένη προσέειπε·

---

[29] Different commentators locate the pathos and irony of this vignette in different places. Russo in Russo et al. 1992 *ad* 209 notes the participle παρήμενον and its effective positioning after the third-foot caesura, while de Jong 2001:470 mentions both this participle and the possessive pronouns ἑόν (209) and ἑήν (210).

[30] In addition to our passage, the verse appears later in Book 19 (see below on 19.251) and when Penelope brings out Odysseus' bow for the trial of the suitors (21.57).

He spoke, and still more aroused in her the passion for
    weeping,
as she recognized the certain proofs Odysseus had given.
But when she had taken her pleasure of tearful lamentation,
then once again she spoke to him and gave him an answer:

Verse 251 is very similar to verse 213. In the earlier passage, two comparisons precede 19.213; syntactically and structurally speaking, verse 251 could also have followed a simile or similes. The similes greatly expand the moment at which Penelope first hears news of Odysseus from her husband himself, giving that event prominence and heightened poignancy. The second simile (211-12), in particular, draws Odysseus into the first scene, which increases its impact by including both husband and wife and also by portraying their very different reactions to the same event. The focus in 249-252, on the other hand, is only on Penelope.

Penelope's emotion here comes from "recognizing signs" (σήματ' ἀναγνούσῃ). This verse, which appears in two other reunion scenes in the poem,[31] has a somewhat ironic effect here since the signs that Penelope believes she recognizes do not represent what she thinks they do. This is the last time that a passage between two speeches in this conversation betrays any unusual emotion from Penelope. Speech introductions for her in the remainder of Book 19 are all single verse reply formulas, as were those in the first part of her conversation with Odysseus. Put another way, a key role of this conversation is to dramatize the gap between Penelope's craving for information about Odysseus and her emotional response to receiving such information; and Odysseus' self-control in providing false information without giving in to whatever desire he might feel to tell Penelope the truth in response to the questions she asks him. Once she has mastered herself enough to be circumspect about what the stranger tells her, the emotional drama of the conversation largely dissipates.

In the second half of this part of the conversation, comprising five of the eleven turns, Penelope continues to disbelieve the stranger's assertion that "Odysseus" will soon come home, and Odysseus reiterates his claims in the face of her doubt. Whenever he speaks, he uses the "wife of Odysseus" vocative (262, eighth turn; and 336, tenth turn). Toward the end, the conversation

---

[31] 19.250=23.206, on which see below; 24.346 is nearly identical but with a male instead of a female as the subject of the participle. Emlyn-Jones 1984:8 suggests the narrator creates irony here by frustrating the audience's expectation that displaying signs in this way is associated with recognition.

turns to the necessity of bathing Odysseus' feet. In Penelope's last speech she offers him the services of Eurycleia, remarking at the end of her speech that perhaps Odysseus' feet resemble those of the stranger now before her (358-360). This has been interpreted by some scholars as a sign that Penelope sub- or unconsciously recognizes Odysseus.[32] I prefer the idea that the sudden evocation of the long-absent Odysseus through this conversation has aroused particularly vivid memories of and longing for him in his wife. She is therefore naturally inclined to think of him in connection with the stranger who has brought her news of him. In addition, she may have noticed at some level that the stranger addresses her as her own husband might have done, and not as the suitors do, strengthening any affinity she is inclined to see between the stranger and her husband. If she does recognize Odysseus, on the other hand, both the earlier focus on the strength of her desire for news of him and the eagerness of Odysseus to prevent Eurycleia from revealing his identity to her make no sense. Moreover, the quantity and quality of emphatic technique that draw the audience's attention to this reunion as it progresses through the last third of the poem fall to the ground if we are meant to imagine that Penelope actually recognizes Odysseus all the time.

Penelope essentially disappears from the story while Eurycleia bathes Odysseus and the story of his scar is told. The second section of her conversation with Odysseus is much briefer than the first section, at five turns; similarly, it has a lower emotional tone, although it contains some notable images and ideas.[33] The most important item in this second phase of the conversation is Penelope's decision to set the contest of the bow (571-581). This part of the conversation contains one group reply formula and four single-verse reply introductions, without any elaboration of the kind that appears after some of the speeches in the first and longer part of the conversation. Odysseus also has one "wife of Odysseus" full-verse vocative for Penelope (583). Although there is only one, this vocative, like the three in the first part of the conversation, occurs in a significant context. It begins Odysseus' last speech to Penelope, in which he tells her to hold the contest without delay, for Odysseus will return

---

[32] In Felson-Rubin's 1994 discussion, she rightly emphasizes that those who would argue for an early recognition will have great difficulty in explaining Odysseus' eagerness that Eurycleia not reveal his identity at this point (59). The almost lyrical treatment in Austin 1975 of the leisurely progression of the reunion (223-233) argues strongly for a late recognition: "it is a mistake to concentrate on that second when recognition is crystallized rather than on the formation of that crystal" (224).

[33] E.g. Penelope's comparison of herself to the daughter of Pandareus, 19.518-524, and her dream of the geese with the gates of horn and ivory (560-569).

efore any of the suitors can string the bow (583-587). Penelope, now quite
er own mistress, does not directly answer his request, but instead announces
nat she is going to bed and offers the stranger a bed in the palace as well
589-599). She leaves the room, and both the conversation and this book of
he poem end.

It is important to notice that the first part of the conversation, by far the
onger and more elaborate in presentation, focuses on the ironies and tensions
hat surround Odysseus' identity and on Penelope's emotions upon hearing
ews of her long-absent husband. The part of the conversation that contains
enelope's decision to hold the bow contest, on the other hand, is much
horter and it receives essentially no unusual attention or elaboration. This
trongly suggests that at this point in the story, the narrator is not particularly
iterested in Penelope's decision to hold the bow contest, her motivation in
oing so, the effect of her statement to this effect on Odysseus, etc. These are
ome of the very matters have attracted the most scholarly attention: many
eaders have felt dissatisfied with Penelope's behavior[34] and have accordingly
ocused their attention on what motivates her to behave as she does, particu-
arly in relation to setting the bow contest at this particular moment.[35] If we
llow the narrator to guide us, and we focus our attention on those aspects of
he scene that are the longest and most elaborate, it becomes clear that the
hrust of this episode is the ironic and moving gulf between the sorrowing
enelope, ignorant of the stranger's identity and mourning her husband's
upposed absence, and the ease and skill with which Odysseus conceals his
dentity from her.

enelope and Eurycleia: Book 23

ow the story focuses for a while on other aspects of Odysseus' situation,
nd Penelope and Odysseus interact with one another only occasionally in
ooks 20-22. For the most part, where both are present, one is speaking to
he suitors and the other is listening. Once the suitors have been killed in
ook 22, Odysseus sends Eurycleia to Penelope to tell her what has been
appening, setting in train the fulfillment of the recognition and reunion
f the two. The conversation between Eurycleia and Penelope, although not

---

[34] A rare voice that approves of Penelope's behavior not merely as a plot device that furthers the
story, but also as positively admirable from a moral and ethical standpoint, is Foley 1995.
[35] For further discussion of these scholarly problems, see the end of this chapter (Penelope and
Neoanalysis).

as intensely gripping for the audience as the various conversations betwee Odysseus and Penelope, displays both unusual length (eight turns) and a elaborate speech frame at the point in the conversation when Penelop reacts to a report that Odysseus is present in the palace. This exchang also contributes to the audience's anticipation of the actual reunion an recognition of Odysseus and Penelope by talking about it but at the sam time postponing its occurrence. Hence, this conversation contributes to th overall program of elaboration and elongation that so strongly marks th reunion of Odysseus and Penelope.

At the beginning of Book 23, Eurycleia goes to the women's quarter to tell her mistress that Odysseus has returned and has killed the suitors (5 9). Although the nurse is laughing, Penelope shows no emotion in respons to this report. She immediately answers Eurycleia with skepticism and eve abuses the old nurse for telling lies (11-24). After a second repetition, howeve Penelope reacts strongly to the nurse's report.

> ὣς ἔφαθ', ἡ δ' ἐχάρη καὶ ἀπὸ λέκτροιο θοροῦσα
> γρηῒ περιπλέχθη, βλεφάρων δ' ἀπὸ δάκρυον ἧκε,
> καί μιν φωνήσασ' ἔπεα πτερόεντα προσηύδα·

> So she spoke, and Penelope in her joy sprang up
> from the bed, and embraced the old woman, her eyes
> streaming
> tears, and she spoke to her and addressed her in winged
> words:

23.32-34

This speech frame is the only one in this conversation between Penelop and Eurycleia that is not the usual formulaic single verse reply introductio for Penelope.[36] Furthermore, it has a very high density of words that describ Penelope's emotions. Even beyond the three underlined words, which indis putably refer to her feelings, ἀπὸ λέκτροιο θοροῦσα (sprang up from the bed in 32 indirectly suggests the depth of her sensations before she asks the nurs to tell her more. This description of Penelope's joyful reaction suggests tha she believes the nurse, or that she wants to believe her, but her words in th speech itself are less wholehearted than her actions.

---

[36] With alternation between the initial half-verses τὴν δ' ἠμείβετ' ἔπειτα (80) and τὴν δ' αὖτ προσέειπε (10, 58). Both are translated "said in answer" by Lattimore.

εἰ δ' ἄγε δή μοι, μαῖα φίλη, νημερτὲς ἐνίσπες,
εἰ ἐτεὸν δὴ οἶκον ἱκάνεται, ὡς ἀγορεύεις,
ὅππως δὴ μνηστῆρσιν ἀναιδέσι χεῖρας ἐφῆκε
μοῦνος ἐών, οἱ δ' αἰὲν ἀολλέες ἔνδον ἔμιμνον.

Come, dear nurse, and give me a true account of the matter,
whether he really has come back to his house, as you tell me,
to lay his hands on the shameless suitors, though he was only
one, and they were always lying in wait, in a body.

23.35-38

Although the description of Penelope immediately before this speech strongly suggests that she is full of joyful emotion, there is no word in the speech that conveys any emotion whatever.[37] Penelope merely asks how the stranger, whom she does not name or call by any title, was able to defeat the suitors when they outnumbered him. This is an entirely reasonable question under the circumstances and one that might have been asked by any observer, regardless of their personal involvement in the situation.

In fact, the description of Penelope's joyful behavior in contrast to the dispassionate, even skeptical answer she gives resembles closely what we saw in Book 13 for Odysseus when he first learns from Athena that he is on Ithaca.[38] Odysseus feels an *inward* joy that has neither an outward, non-verbal manifestation nor any role in the answering speech he makes to Athena; Penelope, while briefly displaying her emotions in her behavior toward Eurycleia, masters herself almost immediately and gives no indication of her feelings in the answer she gives to the nurse. If the same reply formula appeared at verse 32 as precedes all of Penelope's other speeches to Eurycleia, there would be no sign of the strength and suddenness of her feelings when she hears that Odysseus is believed by the rest of his family to be within the palace. As it stands, this speech frame gives a brief glimpse of the strength of the feelings that Penelope subdues in order to approach the news of Odysseus' return with what she deems the necessary caution.[39] It also likens her to her husband

---

[37] With the dubious exception of hesitation, which is implied by her repeated use of εἰ-clauses in combination with adjectives meaning "true" (νημερτές, 35; ἐτεόν, 36) in the first part of the speech.

[38] See Chapter 1, 55-58.

[39] Danek 1998:442 suggests that Penelope's refusal to believe the various reasons that Eurycleia gives her to accept that the beggar is Odysseus stems from her desire for some kind of emotional or psychological recognition of him ("einem inneren Anagnorismos"), which would be consistent with the poem's consistent focus on Penelope's emotions at moments when her husband and his homecoming are mentioned.

through her ability to govern the tension she feels between a desire to believe what she hears and the need to be circumspect until the information can be verified. Moreover, this passage provides further evidence that the narrator wants the audience to notice Penelope's emotions at moments when she is strongly moved by receiving news of her husband. This consistent strategy seems pointless if the narrator also means us to understand that Penelope actually has recognized Odysseus already.

Penelope and Odysseus (ii): Book 23

Penelope and the audience are prepared for a meeting between the two spouses now that Penelope has learned of Odysseus' identity. The audience's impatience for this meeting has been sharpened by the long interval since their first meeting in Book 19 and more immediately by Penelope's conversation with Eurycleia in which she learns who Odysseus is.[40] But the narrator postpones the business of reunion even further, creating additional suspense not only for the audience but also for the characters themselves. When Penelope descends to the hall after this conversation and does not immediately throw herself into Odysseus' arms, the incensed Telemachus berates her for her lack of feeling (97-103). Penelope excuses herself by saying that she is astounded by the news, and tells him that if the beggar is really Odysseus, they will recognize one another.

> " . . . γνωσόμεθ' ἀλλήλων καὶ λώϊον· ἔστι γὰρ ἡμῖν
> <u>σήμαθ'</u>, ἃ δὴ καὶ νῶϊ κεκρυμμένα ἴδμεν ἀπ' ἄλλων."
>   ὣς φάτο, <u>μείδησεν</u> δὲ πολύτλας δῖος Ὀδυσσεύς,
> αἶψα δὲ Τηλέμαχον ἔπεα πτερόεντα προσηύδα·

> " . . . [we shall find other ways,] and better,
> to recognize each other, for we have <u>signs</u> that we know of
> between the two of us only, but they are secret from others."
>   So she spoke, and much-enduring noble Odysseus
> <u>smiled</u>, and presently spoke in winged words to Telemachus:

23.109-112

A single verse is available that would accomplish the change in conversation participants, from Penelope addressing Telemachus to Odysseus addressing

---

[40] This view of the reunion as a unity has implications for our ideas about the composition and transmission of the poems. These will be discussed in the Conclusion.

Telemachus: e.g., δὴ τότε Τηλέμαχον προσέφη πολύμητις ᾿Οδυσσεύς (then resourceful Odysseus said to Telemachus[41]), *Odyssey* 22.390. However, the description of Odysseus' lively appreciation of his wife's caution significantly increases the impact of the scene: the audience sees her behavior both through Telemachus' uncomprehending eyes and through Odysseus' older and wiser ones, emphasizing in an extraordinarily effective way the similar capacity of these two people to put self-control and disguise ahead of a desire for frankness. Indeed, this vignette resembles somewhat the description of the silently admiring Odysseus as he watches Penelope's sparring with the suitors in Book 18 (281-283).[42] These interactions between husband and wife show us that they share, among other qualities, an appreciation of their spouse's ability to master an impulse for openness when it conflicts with a more important need for concealment or misdirection.

In fact, Telemachus acts as a sort of conversational buffer between the husband and wife during this three-way conversation. Telemachus is involved in every turn, either as speaker or addressee; his parents directly address only him and not one another.[43] The conversation falls into two halves, essentially: Telemachus addresses Penelope, and she replies; then Odysseus responds to what Telemachus said, and there are two more turns between Telemachus and Odysseus. Nevertheless, Odysseus and Penelope speak to each other, in the sense that although they address Telemachus at the literal level (with vocatives, for example), the substance of what they say is directed at each other more than at him.[44] This provides a prelude to the one-on-one conversation between Odysseus and Penelope, in which the audience sees them together when Penelope finally knows—or at least, has been told by reliable sources—that the stranger is her husband. However, the satisfaction of seeing the husband and wife alone together, with no third person to smooth things over between them, is still to come.

Before this conversation takes place, Odysseus orders that the household should pretend that a wedding is in progress, and he is bathed by Eurycleia

---

[41] Slightly adapted from Lattimore.

[42] See above, 94-96.

[43] This dynamic is noted by Schadewaldt 1966:15-17 as he examines the to-and-fro between the two throughout the part of Book 23 leading up to their mutual recognition and reunion.

[44] This distinction in a conversation involving more than two participants between the person who is addressed and the person from whom some kind of response is expected is noted by Goffman 1981:9-10. This passage exploits that distinction in a particularly subtle and interesting way, in that the person directly addressed is *not* the person from whom a response is expected or to whom the speech is mainly directed.

(130-164).[45] The conversation between Penelope and Odysseus that eventually results in mutual recognition and reunion consists of eight alternating turns between the two of them (166-287). It contains three successive multi-verse speech frames (181-182; 205-208; 231-247), which is unique in the Homeric epics: all the other elaborate one-on-one conversations that have been discussed in Chapters 1-3 contain one or at most two elaborate speech frames in a row. Here, each of three succeeding speech frames is longer than the last, drawing out the episode more and more as its climax approaches. Moreover, the first two expanded speech frames focus on the emotional responses of Odysseus and Penelope respectively to what is said to them. In the third expanded passage, the famous simile at 23.233-239 describes the emotions of both spouses at once after Penelope has stated that she accepts the man before her as her husband (209-230).

The speech frames, in fact, parallel the progress of the episode. They focus our attention on each character alternately, and finally on both together at the point when they have recognized and accepted each other. This dramatizes the last moments of the enduring tension between frankness and concealment that both husband and wife have spent so much time and energy to control so that they can reach the moment when each feels able to be candid and let go of skepticism and concealments. Each of these expansions can be appreciated by itself, but as a group, they work together to contribute to the simultaneous slowing and crescendo effects which so effectively dramatize the end of the conflict between concealment and openness. Not only is the crescendo effect in this conversation more elaborate than in other conversations we have seen, but earlier conversations lead up to it in an elongated, extended crescendo effect that spans the last third of the poem. This crescendo itself emphasizes the strength that each has to have to manage this tension by emphasizing how long and how much the tension has affected them both.

After Odysseus' bath, the process of testing that to some degree characterizes all the interactions between Penelope and Odysseus resumes. Odysseus, beautified by Athena as well as bathed by Eurycleia, sits down with Penelope (159-165). She, unlike Telemachus in Book 16, makes no response at all to the newly transformed man who has appeared before her. Here, for the first time in Book 23, Odysseus directly addresses Penelope, and like Telemachus did earlier, he criticizes her for remaining aloof from him when no other wife would do so (166-172). Apparently her Odyssean capacity for distrust is

---

[45] Those who see interpolation here have generally placed it at 117-172 (e.g. Page 1955:114-115 asserting that this is an interpolation designed to prepare for the final scene in Book 24). Lesky 1968:807-808 and Erbse 1972:57-72 have been among the most enthusiastic and influential defenders of the passage.

amusing and praiseworthy when he is in disguise (and so is also practicing a kind of concealment), but annoying when he has resumed his usual appearance and is expecting her as well as himself to lay aside her skepticism. At the end of his speech, he asks for a bed to be laid for him.

Odysseus, as well as the audience, wants Penelope to be ready to accept him at the same time as he is ready to be accepted, but at no time does she show as clearly as she does here that she is a match for him in her capacity to master an impulse to be open in order to conceal or misrepresent herself. She replies (174-180) by directing Eurycleia to make up a bed for Odysseus outside his bedroom (178). The introduction to this remark is the normal reply formula for Penelope (173); only *after* the speech does the narrator explicitly state that her speech was a test.

> "ἀλλ' ἄγε οἱ στόρεσον πυκινὸν λέχος, Εὐρύκλεια,
> ἐκτὸς ἐϋσταθέος θαλάμου, τόν ῥ' αὐτὸς ἐποίει·
> ἔνθα οἱ ἐκθεῖσαι πυκινὸν λέχος ἐμβάλετ' εὐνήν,
> κώεα καὶ χλαίνας καὶ ῥήγεα σιγαλόεντα."
> ὣς ἄρ' ἔφη πόσιος <u>πειρωμένη</u>· αὐτὰρ Ὀδυσσεὺς
> ὀχθήσας ἄλοχον προσεφώνεε κέδνα ἰδυῖαν.
> "ὦ γύναι, ἦ μάλα τοῦτο ἔπος θυμαλγὲς ἔειπες."

"Come then, Eurykleia, and make up a firm bed for him
outside the well-fashioned bedchamber: that very bed that
    he himself
built. Put the firm bed here outside for him, and cover it
over with fleeces and blankets, and with shining coverlets."
    So she spoke to her husband, <u>trying him out,</u> but Odysseus
spoke in anger to his virtuous-minded lady:
"What you have said, dear lady, has hurt my heart deeply."

23.177-83

The way the passage is constructed means that the impact of the speech falls belatedly on both the audience and Odysseus. The audience shares Odysseus' surprise rather than being prepared for Penelope's duplicity with a speech introduction that characterizes the speech as a test.[46] Between these

---

[46] Danek 1998:449 argues that this motif of the bed as a test is a new invention in our *Odyssey*, mainly because the passage provides all the information that the audience needs to understand it. If true, this would mean that the audience is indeed just as surprised and confused as Odysseus is, albeit for different reasons. For a speech by Penelope that she describes as a test at the beginning, cf. *Odyssey* 19.215-219. Note that this identified test fails to penetrate Odysseus' disguise, whereas her second, unidentified test succeeds.

two speeches, the verse *τὴν δὲ μέγ᾽ ὀχθήσας προσέφη πολύμητις ᾿Οδυσσεύ[s] (resourceful Odysseus, greatly angered, addressed her)[47] would show tha[t] Odysseus was angry at what Penelope had said, but would omit the crucia[l] information that she intended her speech as a test. It may also be the case tha[t] the epithet πολύμητις (resourceful), which would appear in a formula like th[e] hypothetical "angry Odysseus replied" verse suggested above, would be ou[t] of place in a context where Odysseus is being successfully tested by the μῆτι[ς] of someone else. In sum, this couplet (181-182) describes the intentions c[f] Penelope, the emotion of Odysseus, and the relationship that exists betwee[n] them as this relationship is being re-established. The combination of thes[e] features effectively portrays Penelope's skill in testing Odysseus at a momer[t] when he thinks that his testing and concealment days are over, and hi[s] discomfiture at what she has done.

In the third turn of eight in their conversation, the angry Odysseus nov[v] proves his identity to Penelope by describing at length the process by which h[e] built their bed. This story is structured with ring composition that repeats th[e] central story: compare verse 184, τίς δέ μοι ἄλλοσε θῆκε λέχος (what man ha[s] put my bed in another place?) with verses 203-204 λέχος, ἠέ τις ἤδη / ἀνδρῶ[ν] ἄλλοσε θῆκε (whether some man has moved [my] bed elsewhere). At the en[d] of his story, Odysseus says, οὕτω τοι τόδε σῆμα πιφαύσκομαι (I tell you this as [a] sign,[48] 202). This phrasing makes it unclear whether he means that the story c[f] the bed is the σῆμα, and in fact makes such a distinction irrelevant and unnec[-] essary.[49] Instead of a reply formula for Penelope's next speech, several verse[s] fall between Odysseus' σῆμα and Penelope's response to it.

> ὣς φάτο, τῆς δ᾽ αὐτοῦ λύτο γούνατα καὶ φίλον ἦτορ,
> σήματ᾽ ἀναγνούσῃ τά οἱ ἔμπεδα πέφραδ᾽ ᾿Οδυσσεύς·
> δακρύσασα δ᾽ ἔπειτ᾽ ἰθὺς δράμεν, ἀμφὶ δὲ χεῖρας
> δειρῇ βάλλ᾽ ᾿Οδυσῆϊ, κάρη δ᾽ ἔκυσ᾽ ἠδὲ προσηύδα·
> "μή μοι, ᾿Οδυσσεῦ, σκύζευ . . . "

---

[47] Although there is nothing apparently wrong with this verse, in fact the formula μέγ᾽ ὀχθήσα[ς] (greatly angered) is much more common in the *Iliad*, where it appears ten times (of which nir[e] occur with either gods or Achilles), than in the *Odyssey*, where it is found only three times (4.3[0] and 4.332, both Menelaus, and 15.325 [Eumaeus]). See Scully 1984 on this expression in relatio[n] to Achilles in particular.

[48] This is my translation; Lattimore renders "there is its character, as I tell you."

[49] Felson-Rubin 1994:38 suggests that the narrative is the σῆμα.

So he spoke, and her knees and the heart within her went
 slack
as she recognized the clear proofs that Odysseus had given;
but then she burst into tears and ran straight to him,
 throwing
her arms around the neck of Odysseus, and kissed his head,
 saying:
"Do not be angry with me, Odysseus . . . "

23.205-209

he entire speech frame (205-208) between the third and fourth speech in
ie conversation is equivalent to τὸν δ' ἠμείβετ' ἔπειτα περίφρων Πηνελόπεια
:ircumspect Penelope said to him in answer) from the standpoint of narrative
larity, but the telling of the story would suffer significantly without this
icture of the previously cautious and hesitant Penelope giving way to her joy
'ith tears and kisses of welcome. Her happy reaction here corresponds to the
nger of Odysseus after her speech about the bed. In her reply to the angry
dysseus (209-230), Penelope declares that she does recognize and accept
im. However, she focuses primarily on her fears about what would have
appened if she had let her guard down prematurely, not on her happiness
1at Odysseus has come home at last. She names him only once in the passage
!09) and does not call him by any affectionate epithet or title. The speech
self, in other words, is not particularly overjoyed. So, the speech frame
efore Penelope's speech describing her happy tears and embraces (205-
)8) is the primary vehicle for conveying her emotions at this point in the
pisode. Although kisses, tears, and embraces also characterized Odysseus'
:union with Telemachus (16.191-192 and 214),[50] this passage describes
enelope's emotions and behavior at more length than in the earlier and less
ignificant reunion. The motif of "loosening of knees" is associated elsewhere
'ith erotic—or at least an emotional—response.[51] This response is fittingly
voked in the circumspect and thoughtful Penelope not by Odysseus' newly

---

[50] See Murnaghan 1987:22 on the physical actions that accompany reunions in the *Odyssey*.

[51] Felson-Rubin 1994:62-63 argues for a specifically erotic connotation. Segal's remarks on the same expression (1971:45) offer a wider variety of possible meanings for it. He characterize its predominant significance in the *Odyssey* as "emotional or psychological" in contrast to the *Iliad*, where it often describes "simple physical reactions," as of warriors on the battlefield. Sometimes we find both senses at once, as when Lycaon accepts his defeat at the hands of the berserk Achilles in *Iliad* 21 (on which see Chapter 4, 174-175).

fine appearance, which at the start of this conversation aroused no apparen response from her (156-165), but by the recognition of σήματα (206).[52]

Even though husband and wife have both accepted Odysseus' identity, th idea of skepticism as an appropriate and necessary response to the uncertair ties of life remains prominent. When Penelope tells Odysseus that she made u her story about their bed being moved in order to test him (209-224), she pu forward their mental affinity as the reason he should forgive her deceptio τά περ ἄλλα μάλιστα / ἀνθρώπων πέπνυσο (beyond other men / you have th most understanding, 209-210). Indeed, the word πέπνυσο may also link him t their son Telemachus through his epithet πεπνυμένος. Penelope elaborates o deceptions that unwary people have fallen prey to, further justifying her war response to Odysseus, and she concludes by verbally accepting the σῆμα he ha given in his previous speech (225-230). Here Penelope's behavior and her wor finally act in concert to affirm the true identity of Odysseus as her husband. I this way, we can clearly see that she has accepted him in both word and deed.

A particularly striking—and long—passage occurs at the midpoint of th conversation, incorporating many elaborate details to form a dramaticall effective whole. This is the most highly developed passage in the Homer epics that is the functional equivalent to a single verse reply formula. Indee this moment of mutual recognition and acceptance between a husband an wife who have waited and striven so long to be reunited is, for many, th climax of the poem. For ease of reference in the quotation below, I have sep rated the passage into the different sections that I will be discussing.

> ὣς φάτο, τῷ δ' ἔτι μᾶλλον ὑφ' ἵμερον ὦρσε γόοιο·
> κλαῖε δ' ἔχων ἄλοχον θυμαρέα, κεδνὰ ἰδυῖαν.
>
> ὡς δ' ὅτ' ἂν ἀσπάσιος γῆ νηχομένοισι φανήῃ,
> ὧν τε Ποσειδάων εὐεργέα νῆ' ἐνὶ πόντῳ
> 235 ῥαίσῃ, ἐπειγομένην ἀνέμῳ καὶ κύματι πηγῷ·
> παῦροι δ' ἐξέφυγον πολιῆς ἁλὸς ἤπειρόνδε
> νηχόμενοι, πολλὴ δὲ περὶ χροῖ τέτροφεν ἅλμη,
> ἀσπάσιοι δ' ἐπέβαν γαίης, κακότητα φυγόντες·
> ὣς ἄρα τῇ ἀσπαστὸς ἔην πόσις εἰσοροώσῃ,
> 240 δειρῆς δ' οὔ πω πάμπαν ἀφίετο πήχεε λευκώ.

[52] Contrast the contexts for verse 206 here and for the same verse at 19.250. Here, Penelope se up a test of which Odysseus is unaware, as a result of which she gets information that he giv without knowing what her real intention was. In Book 19, on the other hand, she explicit identifies her request for information as a test and is given false information that misleads h about the true identity of Odysseus.

116

καί νύ κ᾽ ὀδυρομένοισι φάνη ῥοδοδάκτυλος Ἠώς,
εἰ μὴ ἄρ᾽ ἄλλ᾽ ἐνόησε θεὰ γλαυκῶπις Ἀθήνη.
νύκτα μὲν ἐν περάτῃ δολιχὴν σχέθεν, Ἠῶ δ᾽ αὖτε
ῥύσατ᾽ ἐπ᾽ Ὠκεανῷ χρυσόθρονον, οὐδ᾽ ἔα ἵππους
245 ζεύγνυσθ᾽ ὠκύποδας, φάος ἀνθρώποισι φέροντας,
Λάμπον καὶ Φαέθονθ᾽, οἵ τ᾽ Ἠῶ πῶλοι ἄγουσι.

καὶ τότ᾽ ἄρ᾽ ἦν ἄλοχον προσέφη πολύμητις Ὀδυσσεύς·
"ὦ γύναι . . ."

> She spoke, and still more roused in him the passion for
> weeping.

He wept as he held his lovely wife, whose thoughts were virtuous.

And as when the land appears welcome to men who are
swimming,
after Poseidon has smashed their strong-built ships on the open
water, pounding it with the weight of wind and the heavy
seas, and only a few escape the gray water landward
by swimming, with a thick scurf of salt coated upon them,
and gladly they set foot on the shore, escaping the evil;
so welcome was her husband to her as she looked upon him,
and she could not let him go from the embrace of her
white arms.

Now Dawn of the rosy fingers would have dawned on their
weeping,
had not the gray-eyed goddess Athena planned it otherwise.
She held the long night back at the outward edge, she
detained
Dawn of the golden throne by the Ocean, and would not let her
harness her fast-footed horses who bring the daylight to people:
Lampos and Phaethon, the Dawn's horses, who carry her.

Then resourceful Odysseus spoke to his wife, saying,
"Dear wife . . ."

23.231-248

This passage has a structure similar to the reunion of Odysseus and
Telemachus in Book 16 (213-221), but most of the components are extended
to even greater length and complexity than in that episode, as befits this more
significant reunion.

As we have seen, there are various forms of the dative that complet
the formulaic speech conclusion ὣς φάτο [dative phrase, indirect object] ὑφ
ἵμερον ὦρσε γόοιο (so he spoke, and in [dative] <u>stirred</u> a passion for grieving)
The particular verse ending in the formulaic half-verse ὑφ' ἵμερον ὦρσε γόοιο
(roused the passion for weeping) that is found at 231 is limited to two linke
scenes in the *Odyssey*. In each of these, Odysseus and then Penelope arous
grief in each other towards the end of an episode in which emotion has bee
steadily building in intensity.[53] In both passages, an additional verse directl
follows the ὑφ' ἵμερον ὦρσε γόοιο speech conclusion to describe how, or wh
grief is expressed. In Book 19, the other place where we find ὣς φάτο, τῷ δ' ἔτ
μᾶλλον ὑφ' ἵμερον ὦρσε γόοιο (s/he spoke, and still more roused in him/he
the passion for weeping), the next verse describes Penelope's response whe
she has just heard an accurate description of Odysseus' clothes. Odysseus, th
person grieving in this second passage, has just heard Penelope accept him a
her long-lost husband.

> ὣς φάτο, τῇ δ' ἔτι μᾶλλον ὑφ' ἵμερον ὦρσε γόοιο,
> σήματ' ἀναγνούσῃ τά οἱ ἔμπεδα πέφραδ' Ὀδυσσεύς.

> He spoke, and still more aroused in her the passion for
>   weeping,
> as she recognized the certain proofs Odysseus had given.

> 19.249-50

> ὣς φάτο, τῷ δ' ἔτι μᾶλλον ὑφ' ἵμερον ὦρσε γόοιο·
> κλαῖε δ' ἔχων ἄλοχον θυμαρέα, κεδνὰ ἰδυῖαν.

> She spoke, and still more roused in him the passion for
>   weeping.
> He wept as he held his lovely wife, whose thoughts were
>   virtuous.

> 23.231-32

With this repeated full-verse expression that means "desired to grieve," th
two instances of the expression are confined to one poem and to episode
with strong thematic connections.[54] The reunion of Penelope and Odysseus i
distinguished in the Homeric corpus for the way in which it builds consistentl

---

[53] See Appendix IV for the various speech concluding verses that include this half-vers
formula.

[54] One thinks here of the two linked passages in the *Iliad* that contain the ancient formula λιποῦς
ἀνδρότητα καὶ ἥβην (see Chapter 4, 182 and 188).

ver a long period. This "grieved even more" verse that appears at two key points during the reunion is consistent with the ongoing, almost laborious ay these two characters make their way back to each other.

From the syntactical standpoint, verse 231 with its dative masculine ronoun τῷ (him) seems to focus only on Odysseus. Although Penelope is yntactically the object of a participle modifying Odysseus (ἔχων [holding], 32), her praiseworthy wifely attributes actually take up most of the space a this verse (ἄλοχον θυμαρέα, κεδνὰ ἰδυῖαν [lovely wife, whose thoughts 'ere virtuous]). The syntax and structure of this couplet, which focuses on dysseus' response to what he has just heard, naturally creates the assump- on that he is the subject of the long and celebrated simile of shipwrecked iilors that follows (233-238). The subject matter of the simile, the joy of iilors at finally returning to land after being shipwrecked by Poseidon, rein- orces this idea.

> ὡς δ᾽ ὅτ᾽ ἂν ἀσπάσιος γῆ νηχομένοισι φανήῃ,
> ὧν τε Ποσειδάων εὐεργέα νῆ᾽ ἐνὶ πόντῳ
> ῥαίσῃ, ἐπειγομένην ἀνέμῳ καὶ κύματι πηγῷ·
> παῦροι δ᾽ ἐξέφυγον πολιῆς ἁλὸς ἤπειρόνδε
> νηχόμενοι, πολλὴ δὲ περὶ χροῒ τέτροφεν ἅλμη,
> ἀσπάσιοι δ᾽ ἐπέβαν γαίης, κακότητα φυγόντες·
> ὣς ἄρα τῇ ἀσπαστὸς ἔην πόσις εἰσοροώσῃ,
> δειρῆς δ᾽ οὔ πω πάμπαν ἀφίετο πήχεε λευκώ.

And as when the land appears welcome to men who are
      swimming,
after Poseidon has smashed their strong-built ships on the open
water, pounding it with the weight of wind and the heavy
seas, and only a few escape the gray water landward
by swimming, with a thick scurf of salt coated upon them,
and gladly they set foot on the shore, escaping the evil;
so welcome was her husband to her as she looked upon him,
and she could not let him go from the embrace of her white arms.

23.233-40

This simile has an unusually involved relationship to its context, in terms f both its syntax and its subject matter. Although the verses immediately receding it create the expectation that Odysseus is the person whose feelings re illustrated by this simile, at the end of the simile, we discover from the eminine pronoun τῇ (to her, 239) that the (syntactical) point of reference in

119

the narrative is not Odysseus at all, but Penelope.[55] Such a sudden and unex‐
pected shift of viewpoint between the beginning and the end of a simile
unparalleled in the Homeric poems. While many similes have aroused debate
on what the point of reference is in the narrative, there are no other similes
that so explicitly have *two* points of reference, particularly two as intertwined
as these are.[56] This surprising development focuses exceptional attention on
the simile and its contexts; it tightly connects the husband and wife by making
both of them points of comparison to the simile. The simile and its relation‐
ship to its context, in fact, mirror the final reunion of Odysseus and Penelope
by joining the two together as referents of the same simile in a strikingly
appropriate and unusual construction.[57] In the previous two expanded speech
frames in the reunion scene, in contrast, the reaction of *one* partner at a time
has been described. This unusual and effective portrayal of the emotions of
both simultaneously emphasizes the actual moment of reunion, making it
special and different both from identifications of Odysseus and Penelope else‐
where in the poem and from other reunions in the poem.[58]

The subject matter of the simile makes this identification even more
moving. The many parallels between the situation of the sailors of the simile
and that of Odysseus are obvious. At the Phaeacian court, Odysseus begins
his tale of his own wanderings with Poseidon's anger at the blinding of
Polyphemus (cf. 23.234); the detail πολλὴ δὲ περὶ χροΐ τέτροφεν ἅλμη (with
a thick scurf of salt coated on them, 237) recalls the dirty and disheveled
Odysseus arriving on Scheria at the end of Book 5; unlike the sailors of the
simile, however, Odysseus is the only one of his companions to reach home
safely. This extensive similarity between Odysseus and the subject of the
simile, taken with the couplet preceding the simile, maximizes the surprise
when the simile concludes with a reference to Penelope instead.

[55] There are no textual variants for 23.239 surrounding this change of subject.

[56] Heubeck (in Russo et al. 1992) *ad* 233-239 cites several similes from the *Odyssey* that he suggests
have "similar shifts of emphasis" (5.394-399, 10.415-421, and 16.17-21, on which last see
Chapter 1). To my mind, although all of these have subtle and complex relationships to their
contexts, none comes close to creating the kind of surprise reversal of the point of comparison
that our passage so masterfully achieves. In Book 16, for example, there are many ways in
which the simile of the returning son is more appropriate to Odysseus than to Eumaeus, but
it is clear both before and after the comparison that the simile is describing Eumaeus and not
Odysseus.

[57] Compare the two separate similes for Odysseus and Penelope in Book 19 discussed above.

[58] While Podlecki 1971:90 says that "most important of all, husband and wife are *once more*
identified in a strikingly intimate way" [emphasis added], I suggest that the extremely close
and unusually constructed identification between Odysseus and Penelope in this simile marks
their reunion as being different from previous identifications of husband and wife.

This conclusion forces a reconsideration of the simile itself: how is Penelope like these sailors? As discussed above, one immediate effect of the arrangement of the simile is to identify husband and wife, an effect that is independent of the actual subject of the simile. The explicit point of comparison is the joy felt by both the sailor and Penelope on attaining a long-awaited goal (23.239).[59] Yet the simile indirectly suggests that Penelope, just as much as Odysseus, has had sufferings and long toil in order to reach this happy result. Indeed, although their specific circumstances are different, the simile points out that their experiences are similar: both have continued to struggle for a particular aim (Odysseus' homecoming) in spite of the determined and ongoing opposition of powerful people (Poseidon and Circe in the case of Odysseus; the suitors for Penelope) against whom resistance often seemed futile or even dangerous. Their shared ability to persevere even against such odds unites them and makes Odysseus' homecoming possible.[60] This simile celebrates that shared ability at the moment when Odysseus and Penelope have finally achieved his homecoming.

Thus, this unusual relationship between simile and narrative reflects a complex web of conflicting feelings binding together husband and wife. Both are simultaneously the point of comparison to the same simile, which in one sense unites them at the point when their reunion is accomplished. At the same time, the simile and surrounding narrative point to underlying differences in their experiences: Odysseus, weeping, seems to be a man overwhelmed by grief, while Penelope is filled with joy. Similarly, although they are both compared to sailors wrecked by Poseidon, it is only Odysseus who has actually been shipwrecked. Penelope has had her own trials of perseverance and adversity in Ithaca, but her experiences and Odysseus during the twenty years of separation are distinct and will remain so.

A conditional construction follows the simile, but in contrast to the condition that appears in the reunion of Telemachus and his father (16.220-221) the expansion of a conditional speech introduction in our passage is further enlarged by several additional verses (243-246).[61] In fact, the actual speech introduction for the following speech does not appear until 247,

---

[59] The root ἀσπασ- (glad, welcome) also appears repeatedly in the simile that highlights Odysseus' desire to set sail for Ithaca at the beginning of the second half of the poem (13.31-35).

[60] Crotty reads the simile this way too: "Penelope's story—less colorful, more private, and immersed in the domesticity that was the Greek woman's lot—is nonetheless essentially the same as Odysseus' own: a journeying through countless griefs to attain the beloved" (1994:202).

[61] On conditions in Homeric poetry, see de Jong 1987a:68-80, Lang 1989 and Louden 1993.

with καὶ τότ' ἄρ' ἦν ἄλοχον προσέφη πολύμητις Ὀδυσσεύς (then resourceful Odysseus spoke to his wife, saying). This verse could directly follow verse 240. Alternatively, a shorter and more regular conditional speech introduction of the form *καί νύ κ' ὀδυρομένοισι φάνη ῥοδοδάκτυλος Ἠώς, / εἰ μὴ ἦν (or τὴν) ἄλοχον προσέφη πολύμητις Ὀδυσσεύς (now Dawn of the rosy fingers would have dawned on their weeping / if resourceful Odysseus had not spoken to his wife, saying) could have appeared. Instead, an elongated condition reverses the usual pattern of such conditions: time would have continued to go by and dawn would have appeared, not if X had not spoken (as would be more usual), but if Athena had not held off the dawn! Here the emotions of the scene are so intense that they actually do break down normal temporal restrictions. The passage at 243-246 describing how Athena held back the night (243), kept Dawn at bay at the edge of Ocean (244), and prevented her horses from being hitched up (245-246) draws out the episode just as Athena draws out the night in order to allow the reunion of Penelope and Odysseus to run its course.[62] When Telemachus and Odysseus are reunited, their grief is so strong that it *would* have gone on till nightfall but does not; Odysseus and Penelope's emotion, in contrast, actually does take precedence over the coming of day.

Considered as a whole, *Odyssey* 23.231-247 is the functional equivalent of the verse τὴν δ' ἀπαμειβόμενος προσέφη πολύμητις Ὀδυσσεύς (then resourceful Odysseus spoke in turn and answered her). Like other moments of reunion in the *Odyssey*, this one is drawn out by several different elements to create a moving and effective vignette that in the hands of a less able artist could simply have gone by with a single-verse reply formula. In this passage, a larger *number* of different elements—speech conclusion (231-232), simile (233-240), condition (241-246) and speech introduction (247)—are combined than in any similar passage elsewhere in the Homeric poems. Moreover, the simile and the condition in particular are especially long examples of phenomena that occur elsewhere as part of extended speech frames. All of these components, in fact, contain repeated patterns and language. This passage achieves its effects by means of length and the effective use of expressions known from other parts of the Homeric epics. A shorter and less evocative passage could have been created here in several ways: the narrator could have combined some but not all of these different

---

[62] This may also be a very indirect reference to Dawn as an erotic goddess, in light of the association between Dawn, eroticism, and horses posited by Boedeker 1974 (especially 74-75).

122

lements, or could have fashioned a shorter simile or condition in place of the especially long ones that we find in our passage. This unusually elaborate and dramatic vignette appears at the end of a particularly rich and vivid series of speech frames, a fitting end to the crescendo that in a sense has been building since Penelope first asked to see the mysterious storytelling beggar back in Book 17.

The conversation is only half over at this point. It continues for four more turns after this exciting moment for both the characters and the audience. All of the speeches—after the one by Odysseus that follows the unusually elaborate passage we have just been considering—are preceded by regular reply formulas. The overall dynamic of this conversation, in terms of both the speeches and the speech frames, is one of ever-increasing emotion and tension to which each succeeding speech frame makes an additional contribution. This emotion culminates at the halfway point of the conversation in a prolonged outburst of weeping for both Penelope and Odysseus. By describing this scene of grief and joy in such length and detail, the narrator makes it the heart of the conversation. Afterwards, the emotional tone of both the speeches and the speech frames drops markedly until the reunited pair goes to bed together, where they enjoy lovemaking and storytelling. Direct speech, however, does not return to the narrative until after they wake up the next morning, drawing a sort of narrative veil over the bed of Odysseus and Penelope.

Penelope and Neoanalysis

Neoanalytical criticism is associated almost entirely with the *Iliad* rather than the *Odyssey*.[63] To the extent that there is any neoanalytical work on the *Odyssey*, it has focused to a significant extent on whether Penelope's motivation makes any sense in her dealings with Odysseus and the bow contest.[64] This is largely because historically, neoanalysis has been engaged in rescuing the Homeric epics from the lamentable patchwork of incompetence that the Analysts considered them to be.[65] In the case of the *Iliad*, this provided neoanalysts

---

[63] Clark 1986:379 states that neoanalytic scholarship is restricted to the *Iliad*, which in my opinion is not true, but the fact that he makes this statement is illuminating. Kullmann's 1984 overview of neoanalysis does not mention the *Odyssey*. Katz 1991:13-15 notes the dearth of neoanalytic scholarship on the *Odyssey*.

[64] Katz 1991:77-113 provides a thorough discussion of the scholarship that deals with—as Katz says—"what does Penelope want?" in Books 18 and 19 (77).

[65] More so in the case of the *Odyssey* than of the *Iliad*, as Danek comments (1998:2n1).

with an interesting and useful set of questions to which they provided helpful answers. In the case of the *Odyssey*, however, neoanalysis has been much less well served by the questions that the Analysts bequeathed to it.

For example, it has been argued that the "vengeance" motif concerning the suitors and Odysseus should follow the "spouses' recognition/reconciliation," not precede it. More specifically, neoanalysts have frequently discussed whether certain passages connected with the reunion of Penelope and Odysseus are or are not interpolations.[66] The difficulties of these questions have sometimes been located by neoanalysts in the imperfect combination of two different previous versions of the Penelope story, although unlike the Analysts, most neoanalysts would not suggest that more than one composer was at work. In one of these story versions, Penelope recognizes her husband, and in the other version she does not recognize him.[67] Our *Odyssey*, in combining these two, fails to reconcile the diametrically opposed versions of the story and hence leaves its audience sometimes confused or dissatisfied on the question of Penelope's behavior.

However, these questions fundamentally differ from the questions that neoanalysis so ably explores in the *Iliad*. Neoanalytical criticism of the *Iliad* has shown us how the poem skillfully makes use of other traditional stories about the fall of Troy and the heroes who fought there in order to broaden the scope of the story that the poem tells. Partly by using various stories and motifs that belong more naturally to different parts of the Trojan War, the *Iliad* becomes a story of the entire war even though it tells only about a few weeks near the end of the fighting. Neoanalysis reconciles the unity of the *Iliad* with its broad chronological and thematic reach.

The *Odyssey* has a number of characteristics suggesting that we can use a similar method of inquiry to better understand it. For instance, both the *Iliad* and the *Odyssey* begin their story near the end of what might appear to be the tale.[68] Yet both extend their reach both chronologically and thematically beyond the specific events that fall within the time span of

---

[66] Particularly the scene of the bath in Book 23 that appears between the first conversation of Penelope, Telemachus, and Odysseus, and the one-on-one conversation between husband and wife (see Erbse 1972:55-72).

[67] Schadewaldt is a prominent and influential proponent of the idea that there are multiple authors at work our *Odyssey* (1966 passim), in spite of his unitarian views on the *Iliad*. Page 1955 is an important study in English with the same basic thesis.

[68] Hölscher 1972:388.

ne specific story they relate.[69] If we ask questions about how the *Odyssey* roadens its scope to become a story that in some way extends beyond dysseus himself, Penelope and her opaque motivations do not provide he answers we seek. The broadening of time and scope that occurs in the *dyssey*, which neoanalysis is well suited to help us understand, primarily ccurs in two ways: through tales of the homecomings of other Greek eroes, especially Agamemnon; and through references to events that efall Odysseus and his family either before the *Odyssey* begins or after ends.[70]

Neoanalysis can best contribute to our understanding of the *Odyssey* y exploring the different traditional stories that seem to lie behind the ales that Telemachus hears on his journeys and how they are used to hape the *Odyssey*.[71] Similarly, neoanalysis can help us to explore further he traditional antecedents for the stories of the shroud of Laertes, the rials of Odysseus after his return to Ithaca, etc. and how these "before" nd "after" aspects of the story of Odysseus and his family operate in the oem.[72] By focusing on Penelope's motivation, whose opacity seems to tem not from imperfect use of conflicting traditional materials but in fact rom an appropriate use of traditional story patterns,[73] neoanalysis has ailed to produce the kind of important insights about the *Odyssey* that it as given us about the *Iliad*. It has, however, performed a useful service n rehabilitating the *Odyssey* from the incompetent hash of poetasters hat the Analysts believed it to be. It is to be hoped that future neoanalyst cholars will follow the direction of Danek 1998 and Reece 1994, and use heir methods to answer questions of their own choosing about the *Odyssey* ather than simply redeeming it from the incompetence that the Analysts ttributed to it.

---

[69] As Jensen 1980, an oralist scholar, has rightly said, "they [the *Iliad* and *Odyssey*] are poems of the wrath of Achilles and the homecoming of Odysseus; at the same time they are poems of the *whole* war of Troy and *all* the homecomings of the heroes" (171, emphasis original).

[70] To some extent, this also applies to the journey of Telemachus, one part of the *Odyssey* that has been studied extensively by neoanalyst critics (see recently Reece 1994 for an excellent study of Telemachus' journeying that combines neoanalytical and oral perspectives).

[71] See the remarks of Kullmann 1991 on this point (447-448). Kullmann here briefly mentions useful work that has been done on the way that Agamemnon and his family provide a foil for Odysseus and his family, but other homecomings mentioned in the *Odyssey* have not received the attention they should.

[72] Danek 1998 is a welcome change from this general pattern: he explores in exhaustive and illuminating detail the alternative stories that can be deduced to lie behind every aspect of the *Odyssey*, without being prejudiced by the questions that Analysts happened to be asking about the poem.

[73] Emlyn-Jones 1984 and Foley 1999:142-157.

Conclusions

The reunion between Penelope and Odysseus develops to a unique pitch c
length, elaboration, and effectiveness the techniques of emphasis that we se
operating in the one-on-one conversations discussed in Chapters 1, 3, and ·
This reunion involves traditional characters and a traditional story pattern; it i
developed largely through the common type of one-on-one conversation; an
it uses a full range of emphatic techniques consistent with the oral aesthetic
described in the introduction. Conversations involving Penelope and Odysseu
are unusually long. They contain single-verse formulaic variations (th
vocative that Odysseus uses, as contrasted with the one that the suitors favo
as well as passages of elaboration that range from two verses to long passage
containing several components (simile, condition, etc.) at key points. As in th
other reunions in the *Odyssey*, the consistent theme of the many conversation
between Penelope and Odysseus is the tension that both of them feel betwee
being truthful and open with each other, and maintaining a skeptical distanc
in order to protect themselves. Elaborate speech frames consistently describ
strong emotions that Penelope and Odysseus feel but do not act on or spea
about, thereby dramatizing this conflict. Indeed, the placement and conter
of elaborations in the conversations between Penelope and Odysseus clearl
show that the core of their interactions, and what primarily interest
the narrator in this section of the poem, is the ongoing struggle betwee
openness and concealment. It is not Penelope's motives toward the suitors c
her intention in setting the bow contest, neither of which receive any unusu
elaboration.

3

ONE-ON-ONE CONVERSATIONS (ILIAD)

THE ODYSSEY, AS WE HAVE SEEN, USES CONVERSATION to dramatize the conflict between honesty and concealment that underlies Odysseus' various reunions on Ithaca and indeed, much of the social interaction in the poem as a whole. The *Iliad*, too, uses one-on-one conversations to depict significant themes and types of social interactions. However, both the areas toward which conversation in the *Iliad* directs our emphasis and the manner in which conversation is used to focus our attention differ noticeably from what we find in the *Odyssey*. Conversation in the *Iliad* is both less prevalent and less widely used than it is in the *Odyssey*. As we will see in this chapter, the *Iliad* has very few one-on-one conversations outside of battle contexts. In addition, the average length of a conversation in the *Iliad* is three speeches; in the *Odyssey* it is four speeches.[1] It appears that the basically cooperative nature of conversational exchange between two people in some sense is at odds with the competitive and hostile ethos that pervades the poem.

Indeed, hostility and competition consistently characterize one-on-one conversations: the two speakers in the few extended conversations in the *Iliad* are either spouses who are at odds (Zeus and Hera) or enemies who have temporarily laid aside their hostility (Achilles and Priam). Conversely, characters who appear to have a harmonious relationship to one another in fact do not engage in the exchange sequences that typify one-on-one conversation (Hector and Andromache). Thus, although conversation in the *Odyssey* is an exchange system that to some extent presupposes a relation of equality between the participants, in the *Iliad*, the presence of a conversation tends to

---

[1] This rough and ready figure was derived by finding the ratio of initial speeches to non-solo speeches (that is, to all speeches that are part of a conversation in some way). This ratio is 1:3.1 in the *Iliad* and 1:4.1 in the *Odyssey*.

emphasize some kind of conflict or hostility rather than similarity or parit
between the speakers. This chapter will focus on variations and elaboration
in the typical one-on-one conversational structure that occur in the *Iliad*.

Hector and Andromache: Book 6

Let us begin with a one-on-one conversation in the *Iliad* that does *not* follov
the normal alternating sequence of such conversations. In a famous scen
between Hector and Andromache in Book 6, Andromache and Hector mee
for the last time before Hector is killed by Achilles. Andromache asks he
husband not to leave the city and he refuses. In this sequence, which appear
to be a conversation, Andromache only makes the first speech in the serie
(6.407-439). She reminds Hector of her past history and all that he means t
her, and begs him to remain with her in the city rather than go out of th
walls to meet Achilles. Hector makes all the rest of the speeches in this scene
First he refuses Andromache's request (441-465), alluding to his concern fo
his reputation among the Trojans as well as his concern for her fate after hi
death and the fall of Troy. Then, after the famous incident in which the youn,
Astyanax draws back screaming in fear from Hector's helmet, Hector pray
to Zeus on behalf of his son (476-481); finally, he addresses Andromache onc
again, telling her not to feel so sorry about that which is fated (486-493). Th
scene ends when Andromache leaves Hector to return to her quarters.

Mackie has argued that Hector, unlike the Greek leaders, consistentl
refuses to engage in give-and-take with his men in the public context of th
assembly about how to conduct the war against the Greeks.[2] By looking at th
structure of his "conversation" with Andromache, we can see that the sam
lack of engagement appears here too. Hector is, in fact, "confined to a worl
of his own for much of this encounter."[3] Although critics have long admire
this episode for its vivid, moving character,[4] it is striking that in fact, th
husband and wife never *exchange* ideas or feelings. After Andromache ha
reproached Hector for leaving her, she next speaks to him when she lament

---

[2] E.g. Mackie 1996:27, 31-32. Odysseus follows a similar pattern in *Odyssey* 9-12.

[3] Ibid. 120.

[4] See e.g. Schadewaldt 1959:207-232 ("Hektor und Andromache", translated in Wright and Jone
1997) for a famous appreciation of this scene and its role in the *Iliad*. Schadewaldt refers t
the speeches in this meeting as "das Urbild eines 'Redekampfes'" (the prototype of a disput
217), but I think this overstates the amount of engagement between the two via speaking (a
opposed to gesture or other non-verbal means, on which Schadewaldt is extremely effective i
the later part of his piece).

over his corpse in the final book of the poem. In comparison to the extensively developed conversations between Odysseus and Penelope that chronicle and ultimately effect the reunion between the two, these spouses are not engaged in any kind of substantive exchange. Indeed, the *Iliad* does not offer us any picture of two spouses who converse in cooperative harmony with each other. This is one of the ways in which the overall sense of conflict in the poem emerges.

Hera and the Seduction of Zeus: Book 14

A different husband and wife portrait emerges from the trickery of Hera in Book 14. Here, too, we see two spouses who are failing to engage in the kind of cooperative exchange that conversation implies in the *Odyssey*, but these two spouses are actively at odds rather than simply failing to connect. Here, Hera duplicitously acquires a magical girdle of sexual allure from Aphrodite, which she uses to seduce Zeus into post-coital exhaustion and insensibility while Poseidon helps the Greeks on the battlefield. Hera is repeatedly characterized in her conversations with both Aphrodite and Zeus as "tricky," an unusual epithet for her that is restricted almost exclusively to this episode and to specific remarks in which Hera is actively misleading someone.[5] Similarly, the conversation overall dramatizes the conflict between the two divine spouses over the fate of Troy and the lengths to which Hera is willing to go in order to prevail over Zeus. Depicting conflict through conversation between spouses indirectly shows the audience how pervasive conflict is in the world of the *Iliad*.

The mostly commonly found single-verse reply formula for speeches by Hera is

τὸν δ' ἠμείβετ' ἔπειτα <u>βοῶπις πότνια Ἥρη</u>[6]

Then <u>the goddess the ox-eyed Hera</u> answered him

The existence of a metrical doublet for βοῶπις πότνια Ἥρη, namely θεὰ λευκώλενος Ἥρη (the goddess Hera of the white arms) has given rise to much

---

[5] This is similar to the epithets for Telemachus in the last third of the *Odyssey*, as we saw in Chapter 1.

[6] *Iliad* 1.551, 4.50, 14.263 (verb of speaking is δ' αὖτε προσέειπε; various MSS give several different readings), 16.439, 18.360, 20.309. It is striking, given the preponderance of τὸν δ' ἠμείβετ' ἔπειτα βοῶπις πότνια Ἥρη (then the goddess the ox-eyed Hera answered) in speech introductions, that there are manuscript variants for only one such verse. Conversely, several MSS give τὴν δ' ἠμείβετ' ἔπειτα βοῶπις πότνια Ἥρη instead of τὴν δ' ἠμείβετ' ἔπειτα θεὰ λευκώλενος Ἥρη at 15.92.

scholarly debate.[7] Both of these noun-epithet formulas are the same length metrically, and both begin with a single consonant, so they are metrically equivalent. Inquiries into the overall pattern of distribution of the two expressions have been inconclusive. However, in the context "single-verse reply formulas," we find that βοῶπις πότνια Ἥρη dominates almost exclusively over θεὰ λευκώλενος Ἥρη, which appears in a single-verse reply formula equivalent to τὸν δ' ἠμείβετ' ἔπειτα βοῶπις πότνια Ἥρη only once in the *Iliad*:

> τὴν δ' ἠμείβετ' ἔπειτα <u>θεὰ λευκώλενος Ἥρη</u>[8]

> In turn <u>the goddess Hera of the white arms</u> answered her

> 15.92

Where θεὰ λευκώλενος Ἥρη does appear in a speech introductory context, with the single exception of the verse just quoted, the speech introduction usually does not precede a reply. Moreover, introductions containing θεὰ λευκώλενος Ἥρη are usually two verses long and the verb of speaking generally does not appear in the same verse as the noun-epithet formula, for example:

> ἔνθ' ἵππους στήσασα <u>θεὰ λευκώλενος Ἥρη</u>
> Ζῆν' ὕπατον Κρονίδην ἐξείρετο καὶ <u>προσέειπε</u>

> There <u>the goddess of the white arms, Hera</u>, stopping her
>   horses,
>   <u>spoke</u> to Zeus, high son of Kronos, and asked him a question:

> *Iliad* 5.755-756[9]

This couplet precedes an initial speech, not a reply. Other couplets similar to this one also contain information beyond the idea "Hera answered him/her" in the same verse as the formula θεὰ λευκώλενος Ἥρη, e.g. ἵππους στήσασα (stopping her horses, 5.755) or τοὺς δὲ ἰδοῦσ' ἐλέησε (seeing them she took pity, 8.350). In addition, they often appear with initial speeches rather than

---

[7] E.g. Parry 1987:182; Beck 1986.

[8] According to Janko 1981:259, this unusual verse appears under the influence of the appearance of θεὰ λευκώλενος Ἥρη at 15.78. Another verse, τὸν δὲ <u>χολωσαμένη</u> προσέφη λευκώλενος Ἥρη (then <u>bitterly</u> Hera of the white arms answered him, saying; *Iliad* 24.55), uses the less common noun-epithet phrase in order to accommodate the participle χολωσαμένη. This verse is particularly interesting, moreover, because it allows us to reconstruct an acceptable single-verse reply formula that does *not* appear in the Homeric poems: *τὸν/τὴν δ' ἀπαμειβομένη προσέφη λευκώλενος Ἥρη (white-armed Hera, taking an answering turn, addressed him/her).

[9] See also *Iliad* 5.784-786, 8.350-351, 21.377-378, 21.418-419.

replies. So, in speech introductory contexts, the formula βοῶπις πότνια Ἥρη appears in single-verse reply formulas, while θεὰ λευκώλενος Ἥρη appears in multi-verse introductions.[10]

In *Iliad* 14, on the other hand, the epithets in single-verse reply formulas for Hera change to fit the narrative context. During Hera's deception, we find several instances of the unusual reply formula

τὴν/τὸν δὲ <u>δολοφρονέουσα</u> προσηύδα πότνια Ἥρη[11]

Then, <u>with false lying purpose</u> the lady Hera answered him/her

The underlined participle, which literally means "being tricky-minded," is manifestly appropriate to this episode. The point that this word makes is not that Hera is δολοφρονέουσα by nature,[12] but that she is so in this particular context. Not only that, but the speeches introduced by the δολοφρονέουσα verse have a common thread: they are all actively deceptive utterances. As we will see, when Hera tells the truth during this episode, the "tricky" verse does not appear. In speaking to Aphrodite, for instance, when Hera begins the conversation by telling the goddess that she wants to talk to her, basically straightforward language introduces her request.

βῆ ῥ' ἴμεν ἐκ θαλάμοιο, καλεσσαμένη δ' Ἀφροδίτην
τῶν ἄλλων ἀπάνευθε θεῶν πρὸς μῦθον ἔειπε·

She went out from the chamber, and called aside Aphrodite
to come away from the rest of the gods, and spoke a word
to her:

Iliad 14.188-189

Hera asks Aphrodite if she would entertain a request from her, even though they are on opposite sides in the Trojan War (190-192). After a formulaic

---

[10] Hainsworth 1978:45 suggests that θεὰ λευκώλενος Ἥρη "has gained considerable ground" versus βοῶπις πότνια Ἥρη because of "the obscurity, or the embarrassment, of the sense of βοῶπις" (45). It is important to note that while this is true in the aggregate, it is almost entirely untrue in the context of traditional reply formulas. This reinforces the idea that reply introductions are an old and traditional part of the poetic vocabulary of Homeric epic.

[11] *Iliad* 14.197, 14.300, 14.329; none of these verses have variants in the *apparatus criticus*. See also 19.106. Note that the verb προσηύδα (answered) is not found in its usual verse-final position.

[12] See Parry 1987:21 on particularized vs. generalizing epithets. This concept goes back to a scholion of Aristarchus on *Iliad* 8.555, where he says οὕτως οὐ τὴν <u>τότε</u> οὖσαν φαεινήν (sc. σελήνην), ἀλλὰ τὴν <u>καθόλου</u> φαεινήν [not that the moon is bright <u>at that time</u>, but because it is bright <u>in general</u>, emphasis mine].

reply introduction (τὴν δ' ἠμείβετ' ἔπειτα Διὸς θυγάτηρ Ἀφροδίτη [then the daughter of Zeus, Aphrodite, answered her], 193), Aphrodite invites Hera to tell her what she has in mind (194-196). Now Hera tells an untruth. The reply introduction τὴν δὲ <u>δολοφρονέουσα</u> προσηύδα πότνια Ἥρη (then, with <u>false lying purpose</u> the lady Hera answered her, 14.197) highlights her wily intentions. The most common reply formula, τὴν δ' ἠμείβετ' ἔπειτα βοῶπις πότνια Ἥρη (then the goddess the ox-eyed Hera answered her), would do just as well here, but this unusual expression draws the audience in to Hera's tricky plot and so heightens their enjoyment of it. She disingenuously asks Aphrodite for φιλότητα καὶ ἵμερον (loveliness and desirability, 198) in order—as she claims—to patch up a matrimonial dispute between Oceanus and Tethys (198-210). Aphrodite once again has a formulaic reply introduction (τὴν δ αὖτε προσέειπε φιλομμειδὴς Ἀφροδίτη [then in turn Aphrodite the laughing answered her], 211).[13] She agrees to help Hera, giving her a mysterious object of female attire from her bosom and promising her that it will allow her to accomplish her purposes (212-221).

Hera next visits Hypnus, to whom she does not tell any lies (232-293). Hera never misrepresents her intentions to Hypnus during this encounter, nor does the word δολοφρονέουσα (with tricky intention) appear in it. However the "tricky" formula reappears in the conversation between Hera and Zeus where her duplicity is at its most prominent. In this conversation, all of Hera's speeches are deceptive, and they are all introduced by the reply formula that describes her *as* deceptive. These deceptions include a false reason for her supposed journey (301-311) and a factitious reluctance to make love when Zeus propositions her (330-340). Zeus, in contrast, whose thoughts and intentions are all too clear, has his replies introduced by the most common reply formula for him (τὴν δ' ἀπαμειβόμενος προσέφη νεφεληγερέτα Ζεύς [then in turn Zeus who gathers the clouds answered her], 312 = 341).

In this scene, the unusual reply formula for Hera accurately reflects not only the general context of this episode (the seduction of Zeus) but the content of the particular speech in question. The sole occurrence of the verse τὸν/τὴν δὲ δολοφρονέουσα προσηύδα πότνια Ἥρη outside of this episode in Book 14 reinforces this idea: Agamemnon uses it when he is relating a different occasion on which Zeus was deceived at the hands of his wife (*Iliad* 19.106). Agamemnon tells this story in the assembly in Book 19 as a sort of

---

[13] For a discussion of the significance of these two metrically equivalent name-epithet formulas for Aphrodite, see Boedeker 1974:31-42.

xplanation or apology for his own misconduct toward Achilles. His basic
·oint is that if Zeus can be deceived, what hope is there for mere mortals? In
·he story Agamemnon tells (19.85-133), Hera induces Zeus to swear an oath
·hat the baby born on the day when Alcmene's labor with Zeus' son Hercules
·egan would be a great ruler over his fellow men. Zeus thinks this will mean
Iercules, naturally enough, but in fact Hera stays the labor of Alcmene and
·rings Eurystheus prematurely into the world.

> τὸν δὲ <u>δολοφρονέουσα</u> προσηύδα πότνια Ἥρη·
> "ψευστήσεις, οὐδ' αὖτε τέλος μύθῳ ἐπιθήσεις.
> εἰ δ' ἄγε μοι ὄμοσσον, Ὀλύμπιε, καρτερὸν ὅρκον,
> ἦ μὲν τὸν πάντεσσι περικτιόνεσσιν ἀνάξειν,
> ὅς κεν ἐπ' ἤματι τῷδε πέσῃ μετὰ ποσσὶ γυναικὸς
> τῶν ἀνδρῶν οἳ σῆς ἐξ αἵματός εἰσι γενέθλης."
> ὣς ἔφατο· Ζεὺς δ' οὔ τι <u>δολοφροσύνην</u> ἐνόησεν . . .

> Then <u>in guileful intention</u> the lady Hera said to him:
> "You will be a liar, not put fulfillment on what you have
>   spoken.
> Come, then, lord of Olympos, and swear before me a strong
>   oath
> that he shall be lord over all those dwelling about him
> who this day shall fall between the feet of a woman,
> that man who is born of the blood of your generation."
>   So Hera
> spoke. And Zeus was entirely unaware of her <u>falsehood</u> . . .

> *Iliad* 19.106-112

Iere, Agamemnon's concluding sentence emphasizes that Zeus did not
⊥nderstand her crafty intentions (112). His statement contains a noun
epeating the idea of the participle δολοφρονέουσα,[14] which highlights
·he trickiness of Hera's action. In addition, it reminds the audience that it
⊽as Zeus, the powerful head of the Olympic pantheon, whom Hera tricked,
⊥st as she did in Book 14. Indeed, all the speeches preceded by τὴν/τὸν δὲ
·ολοφρονέουσα προσηύδα πότνια Ἥρη (then in guileful intention the lady
Iera said to him/her) deal with tricking Zeus; in all but one, Hera speaks to

---

[14] Though not a ἅπαξ, δολοφροσύνη appears only in this passage; besides 19.112 above, we find
Ἥρη θῆλυς ἐοῦσα δολοφροσύνης ἀπάτησεν (Hera who is female deluded even Zeus) at the
beginning of Agamemnon's account of the story (19.97).

Zeus himself in terms manifestly at variance with her intentions.[15] Her trickery in both episodes, deludes the generally all-powerful Zeus and produces the desired result.[16]

In sum, this alternative formula for Hera not only emphasizes her tricky behavior at moments when she is, in fact, being tricky. In a larger sense, the conflict between these two spouses dramatizes larger issues for the story of the *Iliad*: the poem is characterized by a pervasive sense of hostility and competition not only on the battlefield (as we will see in the next chapter), but in kinds of interactions which in another world—such as the *Odyssey*—would be harmonoius. Spouses in the *Iliad*, unlike spouses in the *Odyssey*, are in important ways not on the same wavelength. This point comes home more dramatically and effectively because it is represented through conversation, a basic kind of cooperative social interaction.

In some ways the formulas that appear for Hera in this conversation resembles the context-specific participles that are found instead of ἀπαμειβόμενος (taking an answering turn) in the reply formula τὸν δ᾽ [participle, ◡◡—◡◡—] προσέφη [name/epithet, ◡◡—◡◡——], and we can imagine a scenario in which a poet, wishing to create a reply formula with a participle that was not shaped ◡◡—◡◡—, came up with the verse form τὸ δὲ [participle, ◡—◡◡—◡] προσηύδα [name/epithet, —◡◡——].[17] However, metrical problems with the particular participle δολοφρονέουσα seem to me insufficient to explain the use of this verse in comparison to other context-specific participles.

The word δολοφρονέουσα appears in patterns that more closely resemble those for meaningful epithets[18] than for meaningful participles. By way of comparison, the context-specific participles listed in Appendix II almost never modify the same character more than once in the same scene. Their function appears to be to emphasize the speaker's demeanor at a peak of some kind, not to bring out a consistent or ongoing aspect of the scene or the character. Of the seven participles in Appendix II that appear more than once, only ὑπόδρα ἰδών (looking darkly) appears more than once in the same episode to modify the same character. In both scenes where this is the case, the character in question has reached a fever pitch of battlefield rage, and so the repetition

---

[15] The exception is her request for assistance from Aphrodite, 14.198-210.

[16] The only other Homeric character described in this way is Odysseus (*Odyssey* 18.51, 21.274).

[17] There is one other verse with a similar structure at *Odyssey* 1.252: τὸν δ᾽ ἐπαλαστήσασα προσηύδα Παλλὰς Ἀθήνη (Pallas Athene answered him in great indignation).

[18] On which see in particular remarks about Odysseus and Telemachus in Chapter 1.

f a formula that normally conveys a peak of anger is appropriate (Achilles n *Iliad* 22 [260 and 344] and Odysseus in *Odyssey* 22 [34 and 60, which have different addressees]). Moreover, in neither of these scenes does the context-pecific participle occur in two successive turns for the same speaker during a ne-on-one conversation. If we want to find a distributional pattern like that which we have observed for δολοφρονέουσα, which appears repeatedly in a ingle conversation between two individuals to bring out a pertinent aspect of he speaker's character when she makes certain speeches, we must look to the distribution of epithets for Telemachus and for Odysseus in the *Odyssey*.

Priam and Achilles: Book 24

This chapter closes with part of the conclusion of the *Iliad*, namely the meeting between Priam and Achilles in Book 24, where one-on-one conversation nce again plays a significant role. The elaborations in this conversation are onstructed much like those we have seen in the important reunions in the *Odyssey*. As in the *Odyssey*, these elaborations and the conversation overall draw out a key aspect of the conversation that also has a significant role in the tory of the *Iliad* overall. However, the particular idea that this conversation emphasizes differs substantially from the issues of concealment that underlie he *Odyssey*. This conversation, after which we bid farewell to Achilles, depicts imultaneously the emotional spectacle of two implacable enemies meeting n the common ground of filial relations, and the depth of the underlying hatred between them, which is overcome only temporarily and incompletely by this fleeting moment of mutual understanding and emotional release. This hows the essential similarity of the conversational type and its aesthetic possibilities in the *Iliad* and the *Odyssey*, but the very different thematic nterests of the two poems.

Some critics of the poem have called its final book a later composition, ften by a supposed younger poet who also composed the *Odyssey* (or some ections of it).[19] Other readers, in contrast, have asserted that it must be an inte-gral part of the design of the poem as a whole, since it provides a resolution that s both effective and necessary to many of the main elements of the *Iliad*.[20] This

---

[19] E.g. Reinhardt 1961:64n11, where he discusses the similarities between Books 1 and Book 24 in the context of asserting a later poet for Book 24 than for Book 1; and 469-506, which provides a list of similarities between *Iliad* 24 and the *Odyssey* (divided into older and younger *Odyssey*).

[20] A position argued with passion and persuasiveness by Bowra 1930:105-106. Here he discusses a different possible ending in which Achilles dies and suggests why the ending found in the *Iliad* appears instead.

argument about the status of Book 24 of the poem has not affected anyone'
appreciation for the meeting between Priam and Achilles in the Greek camp
which for most readers is one of the high points of the poem. That being the
case, the aim of this analysis is to discuss the effects of this well-loved and thor
oughly studied scene as one example of the overall system of type scenes and
aesthetics that are the subject of this study. As Edwards says in his brief remark
on Book 24,

> It may be thought . . . that no commentary is required to explain its
> emotional impact. But the effect is produced by art, and the tech-
> niques of that art are not simple; and a careful study of the choices
> the poet has made, the allusions that lie in the background, and the
> appropriateness of the treatment of traditional motifs will probably,
> for most readers, further enrich their appreciation of this superb
> episode.[21]

Iliad 24 contains several conversations that have unusual features o
various kinds.[22] Priam and Hermes have a particularly long conversation
when Hermes meets Priam on his way to Achilles' camp (24.352-441). Thi
conversation lengthens the dangerous journey that Priam is making agains
the advice and entreaties of his family; by doing so, it focuses the audience'
attention on the aged Priam's simultaneous fear, grief, and determination
to brave whatever dangers are in store for him. It also provides a way to
stretch out the journey in the poem. Most journeys, in contrast, pass very
quickly in the narrative, with little attempt to represent the passage of story
time in the text.[23] Thus, the conversation here draws the audience in during
Priam's experiences on this frightening and important journey. The narrato
uses conversation between Priam and Hermes to present this journey from
Priam's point of view and to create sympathy for him before the encounte
with Achilles begins.

Once Priam arrives, however, the simile that precedes his supplication to
Achilles encompasses the perspectives of both Achilles and Priam. At the sam
time, it inverts key aspects of the scene in which it appears.[24] Often, Homeri
similes emphasize a particular theme of an important episode through a

---

[21] Edwards 1987:308.

[22] The series of laments for Hector that closes the book will be discussed in Chapter 6.

[23] See Rimmon-Kenan 1983, Chapter 4 on time in the text (the particular version of the story) vs
the story (the series of events that the text is relating).

[24] See Edwards 1980:6 on this scene as an elaboration of the supplication type.

comparison of what is happening in the story to an image which somehow inverts a central aspect of the scene. The last extended simile of the Iliad uses such a reversal to describe the amazement of Achilles when Priam suddenly appears in his camp to ransom the body of Hector:[25]

τοὺς δ' ἔλαθ' εἰσελθὼν Πρίαμος μέγας, ἄγχι δ' ἄρα στὰς
χερσὶν Ἀχιλλῆος λάβε γούνατα καὶ κύσε <u>χεῖρας</u>
<u>δεινὰς ἀνδροφόνους</u>, αἵ οἱ πολέας κτάνον υἷας.
ὡς δ' ὅτ' ἂν ἄνδρ' ἄτη πυκινὴ λάβῃ, ὅς τ' ἐνὶ πάτρῃ
φῶτα κατακτείνας ἄλλων ἐξίκετο δῆμον,
ἀνδρὸς ἐς ἀφνειοῦ, θάμβος δ' ἔχει εἰσορόωντας,
ὣς Ἀχιλεὺς θάμβησεν ἰδὼν Πρίαμον θεοειδέα·
θάμβησαν δὲ καὶ ἄλλοι, ἐς ἀλλήλους δὲ ἴδοντο.
τὸν καὶ <u>λισσόμενος</u> Πρίαμος πρὸς μῦθον ἔειπε·
"μνῆσαι πατρὸς σοῖο . . ."

Tall Priam
came in unseen by the other men and stood close beside him
and caught the knees of Achilleus in his arms, and kissed <u>the
hands</u>
<u>that were dangerous and manslaughtering</u> and had killed so
many
of his sons. As when dense disaster closes on one who has
murdered
a man in his own land, and he comes to the country of
others,
to a man of substance, and wonder seizes on those who
behold him,
so Achilleus wondered as he looked on Priam, a godlike
man, and the rest of them wondered also, and looked at each
other.
But now Priam spoke to him <u>in the words of a suppliant</u>:
"Remember your father . . . "

24.477–486

The simile (480–483) compares Achilles' surprise to that which people feel when someone stained by bloodguilt appears at their house. However,

---

[25] The reversal in this passage has struck many modern readers. Heiden's recent article on this simile (1998b) is a fine analysis of the complex web of associations it contains.

the subject of the verses immediately preceding the simile is not Achilles, but Priam (477), and his behavior as he supplicates Achilles by touching his knees and kissing his hands. These hands receive particular emphasis as both the first and the last word of verse 478. They are modified by an adjectival relative clause in adding enjambment[26] that emphasizes the terrible suffering Priam has endured because of the hands he is now kissing: χεῖρας / δεινὰς ἀνδροφόνους, αἵ οἱ πολέας κτάνον υἷας (hands / that were dangerous and manslaughtering and had killed so many of his sons, 478-479).[27] Verse 479 directs attention even more strongly to Achilles' hands. In addition, the syntactical construction here allows us to imagine an alternative version of the passage that omits verse 479 and its affecting details about just what these hands of Achilles have done that Priam is now kissing. Without this verse, Priam's arrival at Achilles' tent would be more expeditious but less poignant.

Both Priam and Achilles in their different ways resemble the man in the simile who has killed another man and flees his homeland to seek asylum elsewhere. However, the language at the beginning of the simile discourages an audience from identifying this man too closely with either Priam or Achilles. ὡς δ' ὅτ' ἂν ἄνδρ' ἄτη πυκινὴ λάβῃ (as when dense disaster closes on one, 480) has an abstraction rather than a person as the subject and the direct object is a generalized ἄνδρ' (man) rather than a more identifiable individual. This means that while the vignette in the simile has points of similarity with both characters, the language prevents too strong an identification with either. This simile, in fact, resembles those used in Odysseus' reunions with his son and his wife:[28] it both draws the two speakers together and indirectly emphasizes some kind of difference or gulf between them. The supplication described in the simile also points forward to the supplication that Priam is about to make to Achilles (486-506), drawing out the importance of the idea of suppliancy for the scene as a whole.

Both the prelude to Priam's speech and the passage immediately following it contain many different elaborations that highlight the themes

---

[26] Higbie 1990 is the definitive work on enjambment in Homer. See 29 for a definition of adding enjambment, a common method of linking a verse to the previous one in which the syntax of the two verses is independent.

[27] This motif of "slaughtering hands" is repeated in the following speech (ἀνδρὸς παιδοφόνοιο ποτὶ στόμα χεῖρ' ὀρέγεσθαι [put my lips to the hands of the man who has killed my children], 506).

[28] Odyssey 16.213-221 and 23.231-247, respectively.

of supplication, parenthood, grief, memory, and bereavement that underlie not only this scene but the entire *Iliad*. Before and while Priam speaks, it is he alone who feels these emotions; the success of his appeal to Achilles, depicted in the speech frame immediately following his speech, comes from its appeal to Achilles' similar feelings and memories about his own family. For a more concise but less affecting prelude to the speech, the speech introduction which immediately precedes Priam's supplicatory speech to Achilles could follow directly after verse 479, or even verse 478, omitting the simile altogether.

Moreover, the speech introduction itself rewards further scrutiny, insofar as it displays a noteworthy variation on common initial formula patterns. The pattern τὸν καὶ [name/modifier] πρὸς μῦθον ἔειπε (and [name, with modifier] addressed a speech to him) occurs five times in the Homeric epics for characters whose names have unusual metrical shapes. All the examples with the exception of this one have the form τὸν καὶ —ᴗᴗ— [name] <u>πρότερος</u> πρὸς μῦθον ἔειπε (and [speaker] <u>first</u> spoke a word to [him]).[29] Only here does the expression τὸν καὶ <u>λισσόμενος</u> (to him . . . as a <u>suppliant</u>) appear. This is particularly striking in light of the fact that Priam is the first to speak, and so the formulaic πρότερος modifier could have been used. Instead, we find a participial form of λίσσομαι (supplicate). This verb provides yet another reference to the idea of suppliancy in the scene, giving Priam's words a kind of ritual status they would lack without it.

In one of the most moving speeches in the *Iliad*, Priam begs Achilles to accept ransom for the dead Hector. His speech focuses on many of the same ideas as the surrounding speech frames, and in some cases even use the same language as the speech frames. The very first words, μνῆσαι πατρὸς σοῖο (remember your father, 486), set the tone of the speech as a whole: Priam appeals to Achilles based on his memory for and emotional attachment to his own father, a feeling through which Priam links himself to his enemy. This idea appears again toward the end of the speech, after Priam has depicted his own greater paternal misery in contrast to Peleus' and mentioned the goods with which he hopes to ransom Hector's body: αὐτόν τ' ἐλέησον / μνησάμενος σοῦ πατρός (take pity upon me / remembering your father, 503-504). The essential idea with which Priam tries to appeal to his enemy is Achilles' memory of and feeling for his father.

---

[29] *Iliad* 5.632 (Tlepolemus), 13.306 (Meriones); *Odyssey* 16.460 (Telemachus), 17.74 (Peraeus).

A lengthy passage between this speech and Achilles' reply rivets the attention of the audience on the cathartic and unifying grief of the two men (506–518). This passage, like Priam's speech, focuses on the ideas of memory, grief, and filial relationships which Priam has succeeded in evoking in his previously implacable enemy.

> ἀνδρὸς <u>παιδοφόνοιο</u> ποτὶ στόμα χεῖρ' ὀρέγεσθαι.
>   <u>ὢς φάτο, τῷ δ' ἄρα πατρὸς ὑφ' ἵμερον ὦρσε γόοιο·</u>
> ἀψάμενος δ' ἄρα χειρὸς ἀπώσατο ἦκα γέροντα.
> τὼ δὲ μνησαμένω ὃ μὲν Ἕκτορος ἀνδροφόνοιο
> κλαῖ' ἀδινὰ προπάροιθε ποδῶν Ἀχιλῆος ἐλυσθείς,
> αὐτὰρ Ἀχιλλεὺς κλαῖεν ἑὸν πατέρ', ἄλλοτε δ' αὖτε
> Πάτροκλον· τῶν δὲ στοναχὴ κατὰ δώματ' ὀρώρει.
> <u>αὐτὰρ ἐπεί</u> ῥα γόοιο τετάρπετο δῖος Ἀχιλλεύς,
> καί οἱ ἀπὸ πραπίδων ἦλθ' ἵμερος ἠδ' ἀπὸ γυίων,
> αὐτίκ' ἀπὸ θρόνου ὦρτο, γέροντα δὲ χειρὸς ἀνίστη
> οἰκτίρων πολιόν τε κάρη πολιόν τε γένειον,
> <u>καί μιν φωνήσας ἔπεα πτερόεντα προσηύδα·</u>
> "ἆ δείλ', ἦ δὴ πολλὰ κάκ' ἄνσχεο σὸν κατὰ θυμόν . . . "

" . . . I put my lips to the hands of the man who has <u>killed my children.</u>"
   <u>So he spoke, and stirred in the other a passion of grieving</u>
for his own father. He took the old man's hand and pushed
         him
gently away, and the two remembered, as Priam sat huddled
at the feet of Achilleus and wept close for manslaughtering
         Hektor
and Achilleus wept now for his own father, now again
for Patroklos. The sound of their mourning moved in the
         house. <u>Then</u>
<u>when</u> great Achilleus had taken full satisfaction in sorrow
and the passion for it had gone from his mind and body,
         thereafter
he rose from his chair, and took the old man by the hand,
         and set him
on his feet again, in pity for the grey head and the grey beard,
<u>and spoke to him and addressed him in winged words:</u>
         "Ah, unlucky,
surely you have had much evil to endure in your spirit . . . "

his passage, whose narrative function is simply to effect a transition from Priam's plea to Achilles' response, is structurally equivalent to the single formulaic verse τὸν δ᾽ ἀπαμειβόμενος προσέφη πόδας ὠκὺς Ἀχιλλεύς (then in answer again spoke Achilleus of the swift feet). That reply formula would admit various participles to describe the emotion of Achilles if that were the sole purpose of this extended passage of narration.[30] Instead, the passage uses a number of different elaborations to prolong this moment and draw out the grief that unites these two enemies. This grief, we are told once again, arises from the fact that Achilles is a son, Priam is a father, and both feel common emotions when remembering the father or son from whom they are separated. Some of the elaborations here are themselves longer or unusual versions of formulas that occur in different forms elsewhere in the Homeric epics, which increases the emphasis here even further.

The passage begins with a formulaic speech conclusion, something that rarely appears between two speeches in an ongoing one-on-one conversation (507). This particular formula has the basic structure ὣς φάτο, [dative object, sometimes also genitive of person for whom dative object is grieving] ὑφ᾽ ἵμερον ὦρσε γόοιο (thus he spoke, and aroused in [object(s)] a passion for grieving).[31] One object found with this formula is τοῖσι δὲ πᾶσιν (in all of them), which would fit the context here, but is not used.[32] The speech conclusion that we have in our passage, ὣς φάτο, τῷ δ᾽ ἄρα πατρὸς ὑφ᾽ ἵμερον ὦρσε γόοιο, appears once in the Odyssey.[33] In our passage, it highlights the grief of Achilles for his aged father far away in Phthia rather than focusing attention on the two men together, as the expression τοῖσι δὲ πᾶσιν would do. In other words, the narrator begins this elaboration by saying that Priam's speech, which began and ended with the exhortation "remember your father," has succeeded in its effort to unite him and Achilles by appealing to their common involvement in father-son relationships.

Following the speech conclusion, the grief of both men as they remember a son and father respectively is described in vivid detail. Verse

---

[30] Indeed, this verse (with the participial formula ὑπόδρα ἰδών [looking darkly]) introduces Achilles' next speech (24.559).

[31] Twice Iliad (23.108, 24.507), four times Odyssey (4.113, 4.183, 19.249, 23.231). Compare also the closely related expression at Od. 16.215, ἀμφοτέροισι δὲ τοῖσιν ὑφ᾽ ἵμερος ὦρτο γόοιο# (in both of them passion for grieving was stirred) and the speech concluding couplet at Iliad 23.152-153 that contains the half-verse ὑφ᾽ ἵμερον ὦρσε γόοιο# in 153.

[32] At Iliad 23.108 and Odyssey 4.183. An expansion of this full-verse concluding formula that includes context-specific detail occurs at Iliad 23.152-153.

[33] At Odyssey 4.113; see Reinhardt 1961:493-494 on different tones in these two passages.

141

508, which is in adding enjambment with 507, in a few words shows Achilles gently (ἦκα) taking the old man (γέροντα) by the hand. This image contrasts vividly with the last verse of the speech, in which Priam kisses the same hand and calls the man whose hand it is παιδοφόνοιο (child-killing, 506). This emphasizes the transformative effect of Priam's speech on Achilles, who instead of being a figure who causes violence and sorrow for Priam's family is now united with Priam in healing grief for family members dead or far away. The picture of the two mourning men in 509-512 has points in common with a simile, including the repetition in verses 509-512 of vocabulary found in the speech immediately preceding the description: γόοι (grieving, 507), μνησαμένω (remembering, 509), forms of κλαίειν (to weep either with or without ἁδινά (close, 510 and 511), and στοναχή (sound, 512). These form a connected group of words evoking the themes of memory and loss in a manner analogous to what would occur in a simile.[34] Like a simile these verses form a self-contained group that could be omitted to create a shorter and less effective version of the same passage. In addition, this set of vocabulary strongly evokes the language of formal lament for a loved one. We have already seen each man lament over the body of a beloved friend or child;[35] now we see them share this grief with one another, bridging the gulf between the two enemies. This description of the memory, grief and bereavement of both men together and not simply Priam alone marks the emotional peak of the scene.

After this, Achilles begins to calm down. At the same time, the description in the speech frames shows the perspective of Achilles alone rather than describing the feelings of both Achilles and Priam. 513 tells us that Achilles had his fill of weeping, beginning with the transitional expression αὐτὰρ ἐπεί (then when), which often marks a shift from narrative to speech. This particular verse calls to mind a similar verse from the Odyssey, ἡ δ' ἐπεὶ οὖν τάρφθη πολυδακρύτοιο γόοιο (but when she had taken her pleasure of tearful lamentation, 19.251), which directly precedes a speech introduction at Odyssey 19.252. In our passage, however, the "when grief was satisfied" verse effects a transition not to speech but to further details of Achilles' thoughts and feelings. This elongates the emotional decrescendo here

---

[34] In contrast, similarly constructed passages in the Odyssey (discussed in Chapters 1 and 2) regularly have similes following speech concluding verses ending with the half-verse ὑφ' ἵμερο ὦρσε γόοιο#.

[35] A detailed discussion of typical patterns for lament will appear in Chapter 6.

elping the audience to experience the gradual ebbing of terrible sorrow along with the characters. 24.514, in adding enjambment with the preceding verse, amplifies the end of Achilles' grief, casting it as a physical departure of ἵμερος (passion) from his body.

Pity for the old man follows Achilles' cathartic emotion for Peleus, pity which is repeatedly evoked by focusing on Priam *as* an old man and not as a king: γέροντα (old man, 515), πολιόν τε κάρη πολιόν τε γένειον (the grey head and the grey beard, 516). 516, in adding enjambment with the preceding verse, shows that Achilles raised Priam from his suppliant position out of pity for his age, strongly emphasized by the syntactic parallelism and anaphora of πολιόν τε κάρη πολιόν τε γένειον. This detail makes the scene vivid to an audience and gives Priam life as an old man rather than (e.g.) as the king of Troy. [36] The pity described at such evocative length in 513-516 may, in fact, be considered an extra-long version of the more usual single verse of emotional reaction with name/epithet that often precedes καί μιν φωνήσας ἔπεα πτερόεντα προσηύδα. It is, in fact, an extended version of a pattern of speech introductory language which is itself an extended version of single-verse speech introductions.

Let us now review the overall structure of this impressive passage. It contains a sequence of speech conclusion (507-508), passage amplifying the conclusion (509-512), and speech introduction (513-517). For each of these three components, a common formula that elsewhere occupies one verse conclusion, although generally found at the end of a conversation rather than in the middle), two verses (ἔπεα πτερόεντα reply introduction), or no verses at all (description of the grief of Achilles and of Priam), expands to include a wider, richer variety of detail than would be possible in a shorter space. Not only that, but a single verse of the form τὸν δ' ἀπαμειβόμενος προσέφη πόδας ὠκὺς Ἀχιλλεύς (then in answer again spoke Achilleus of the swift feet) would perform the basic narrative function of the whole passage ("conclude speech A, introduce speech B") equally well. A complex inter-related series of elaborations transforms this moment from an ordinary transition between speeches to a finely wrought vignette of two lonely and

---

[36] It is noteworthy that although Priam is the king of Troy, the most common noun-epithet for him refers not to his high position but to his old age: γέρων Πρίαμος θεοειδής (aged Priam the godlike). It is also noteworthy that although this expression appears seven times, and may therefore be considered "formulaic" from a purely numerical standpoint, it is found only in speech introductions in Book 24, where the idea of Priam's age is most prominent in and important to the story.

bereaved enemies who briefly find common ground in their shared grief
This conversation depicts Priam's achievement in successfully supplicating
Achilles (in contrast to the many unfortunate Trojan warriors whom Achilles
kills on the battlefield) and in creating an emotional appeal to him that
breaks through his grief and anger. At the same time, the enmity of the two
heroes and of their respective peoples is never forgotten. Even at the height
of their emotion, these two men remain enemies. Their moment of mutual
harmony and understanding derives some of its force from the constant
awareness that it is temporary, and that the hostilities that will destroy both
Achilles and Priam will resume all too soon.

Conclusions

Overall, the *Iliad* contains few one-on-one conversations that are particularly
elaborate, further emphasizing the meeting between Priam and Achilles. The
Odyssey, on the other hand, contains many elaborate conversations. These
conversations make use of the same kinds of techniques for elaboration that
we have observed in the *Iliad*: unusually long turn sequences; variations of
language within single-verse speech framing formulas, as in the deception that
Hera carries out in *Iliad* 14; and lengthy and complex elaborations, as in the
meeting between Priam and Achilles in *Iliad* 24. The two poems share the same
typical patterns for one-on-one conversations, and the poetic techniques they
use in order to draw out a conversation for aesthetic effect are also similar.
Through extended conversations, each poem emphasizes a fairly consistent
set of themes that relates to the poem's depiction of interpersonal relations.
The *Odyssey*, as we have seen, views personal relationships as complicated for
Odysseus and his family by the conflicting claims of concealment and honesty.
Relationships in the *Odyssey* are far from simple, but they are not essentially
hostile in spite of the tensions they may engender in the poem's characters.
When Odysseus deceives Penelope, he does so in aid of their common goal of
his return home.

The *Iliad*, on the other hand, depicts personal relationships as much more
fleeting and problematic. People who should have harmonious and coopera-
tive relationships do not, in fact, engage in conversational exchange, or else
they use conversation to win a conflict; the only people in the poem depicted
in an extended conversation that does not take place on the battlefield are
enemies who put aside their hatred for each other only long enough to allow
one of them to supplicate the other. The *Iliad* uses conversation, or the lack
of it, to show the isolation of its characters and the primacy of conflict in

human interaction. Indeed, the genres of conversation that the *Iliad* uses most extensively tend to involve a power differential between the speakers and/or groups rather than individuals as the defining participants in the conversation, or both. These genres are the subject of Part II.

PART II

SINGLE SPEECHES AND
GROUP CONVERSATIONS

4

SINGLE SPEECHES AND VARIATIONS ON THE BATTLEFIELD

THE FIRST THREE CHAPTERS FOCUSED ON THE EXTENDED ONE-ON-ONE CONVERSATIONS in the *Odyssey* and the *Iliad*. We have seen that the *Odyssey* makes much more extensive use of one-on-one conversation than the *Iliad* does, and indeed, the *Iliad* presents its view of human relations partly by the comparative lack of one-on-one conversation. Conversely, the *Iliad* depicts its characters engaged in a wide range of speech exchange systems other than one-on-one conversation. These systems, which include vaunts, challenges, assemblies, athletic games, and laments, either do not appear in the *Odyssey* or appear in a very limited way. The different kinds of speech exchange discussed in the following three chapters share some basic characteristics that link them to one another and distinguish them from one-on-one conversation. In all of these genres of speech, behavior as well as speech has an important role to play. On the battlefield, speech and physical attacks often have much in common with one another and to some degree are interchangeable, as we will see. In formal group contexts of various kinds, in order to perform a turn properly, a speaker must both do certain actions and make his remarks. In one-on-one conversations, in contrast, behavior appears only rarely as part of the conversation; it is not a typical or required part of the type; and when it does appear, it tends to be a physical enactment of an emotion rather than a separate feature of the conversation.

From a social standpoint, the genres of speech in which the *Iliad* is most interested highlight conflicts in power relations and group dynamics. These conflicts or tensions have central importance in different ways for the speeches that enemies make to each other on the battlefield; the competition of peers in athletic games; and the way that members of the same side figure out what to do during an assembly. The extensive one-on-one conversations in the *Odyssey*, on the other hand, highlight the relations of Odysseus with various individuals who are particularly important to him. The *Iliad* is a poem of war and conflict, and the speech genres in which it is most interested are those that directly relate to these topics. Lament, the subject of Chapter 6, is directly related to conflict insofar as the *Iliad* chooses to portray war partly through its effects on non-combatants.

Moreover, when one-on-one conversations do take place in the *Iliad*, they tend to appear in contexts that prominently feature hostility and conflict. Their purpose in these scenes is to dramatize various aspects of the conflict, whether the hostilities take place between enemies (as with Hector and Patroclus in Book 16) or between ostensible comrades (as between Achilles and Agamemnon in the assemblies in Books 1 and 19). Whereas conversation in the *Odyssey* dramatizes internal tensions and conflicts surrounding Odysseus' return to Ithaca, both one-on-one conversation and other forms of speech exchange highlight hostilities directed at others in the *Iliad*. In other words, conversation and speech exchange play a central role in each poem in portraying and emphasizing key themes; indeed, the particular speech exchange systems that appear in each poem and the way they are used are one of the most important factors in shaping the way the story is told.

Battlefield Speech Genres

This chapter focuses on battlefield speech in particular because the kinds of speeches that warriors most often make on the battlefield are predominantly single genres.[1] Single genres do appear in non-battle contexts, but single speech genres are the predominant mode of speech only on the battlefield. A fighting warrior gives instructions to his comrades, or exhorts them to fight their best; he challenges an enemy before attacking him or vaunts over him after killing him;[2] he prays for assistance to a god when afraid or in danger; occasionally he speaks aloud to himself, pondering what to do in a difficult situation. All of these genres of speech occur predominantly on the battlefield and predominantly as single speeches. Moreover, all of them feature an

---

[1] See Edwards 1987:92-94 for an overview of the genres of speech commonly found on the battlefield. I will be using his terminology of "challenge" for a speech before a physical attack and "vaunt" for a speech that celebrates a successful attack (93).

[2] Parks 1990:6-7 and Martin 1989:68-77 use the more general term "flyting" to refer to ad hominem verbal attacks (Parks) or contest genres of speech (Martin).

imbalance of power of some sort. Someone giving an exhortation is presumed to be a leader of the men whom he exhorts, not simply their peer, while enemies in battle are disputing over the basic fact of which one of them will remain alive. Prayer involves a god who has the power to grant a request and someone making such a request, but not any kind of extended interchange during the request itself. For single speech genres, unlike other types of speech exchange, a conversation is itself not only a lengthening but also an elaboration on the regular pattern for the speech sequence in question. The conversation need not display any other unusual features to be considered an elaboration if it takes place in a context where a single speech would be the more expected type of speech.

Most of these single genres of speech have formulaic conclusions that tend to follow them.[3] In other words, from the standpoint of the typical language of Homeric poetry, action rather than a reply is the expected response from the addressee(s) after the types of speech that most commonly appear on the Homeric battlefield. Following an exhortation, we frequently learn that ὣς εἰπὼν ὄτρυνε μένος καὶ θυμὸν ἑκάστου (so he spoke, and stirred the spirit and strength in each man, 11 times in the Homeric epics, all but one of which are found in the *Iliad*). In the case of a challenge, the challenger may proceed to throw his spear at his opponent: ἦ ῥα καὶ ἀμπεπαλὼν προΐει δολιχόσκιον ἔγχος (So he spoke, and balanced the spear far-shadowed, and threw it, 7 times in the *Iliad*). The formulaic conclusion for prayers, ὣς ἔφατ' εὐχόμενος, τοῦ δ' ἔκλυε [nominative name/epithet, subject] (so he spoke in prayer, and [subject] heard him), has been the subject of able and exhaustive attention by Muellner.[4] This chapter will examine both the regular patterns and the variations on these patterns, first for exhortations (speeches between comrades on the battlefield) and then for challenges and vaunts (speeches between enemies). These variations will sometimes consist of unusually long turn sequences that nevertheless follow the usual order, and sometimes of unusual turn sequences. The most unusual and elaborate battlefield scenes, as we will see, consist of both. These elaborate battlefield conversations appear specifically in connection with Agamemnon and Achilles to depict the way that the personality of each hero shapes his own experiences, the experiences of his comrades and enemies, and the *Iliad* as a whole.

---

[3] See the Introduction for the association of speech conclusions with the end of a speech sequence.

[4] Muellner 1976, particularly 18-30.

Exhortation

A king or hero urging his comrades on to ever-greater feats of bravery and slaughter against the enemy regularly appears in battle scenes in the *Iliad*. Most commonly, such exhortations do not receive a verbal reply from the men who have been addressed. Various things may happen after an exhortation. For instance, there may be another exhortation of some kind from someone on the same side (e.g. *Iliad* 5.471-492, Sarpedon rebukes Hector following Ares' exhortation to the Trojans). Sometimes the narrator goes on to describe the trail of carnage left by the newly exhorted troops (e.g. *Iliad* 16.268-274, in which Patroclus exhorts the Myrmidons, who then attack the Trojans en masse). Or, the person who gave the exhortation may display his own bravery, thereby further inciting his comrades by attacking the enemy (e.g. Agamemnon at *Iliad* 5.533, who kills a Trojan immediately after exhorting his men). If he himself is in trouble for some reason, he may leave the field of battle after urging his men not to give up the fight in his absence (as the wounded Agamemnon does at *Iliad* 11.280-283). Whatever the next event after a speech of exhortation turns out to be, it virtually never includes a verbal response from the troops who have been exhorted.

Let us now turn to a fairly typical example of a single exhortation, in which Hector rallies his men after the wounded Agamemnon is carried off the field (*Iliad* 11.284-291).

> Ἕκτωρ δ' ὡς ἐνόησ' Ἀγαμέμνονα νόσφι κιόντα
> <u>Τρωσί τε καὶ Λυκίοισιν ἐκέκλετο μακρὸν ἀΰσας·</u>
> "Τρῶες καὶ Λύκιοι καὶ Δάρδανοι ἀγχιμαχηταί
> <u>ἀνέρες ἔστε φίλοι, μνήσασθε δὲ θούριδος ἀλκῆς.</u>
> οἴχετ' ἀνὴρ ὥριστος, ἐμοὶ δὲ μέγ' εὖχος ἔδωκε
> Ζεὺς Κρονίδης· ἀλλ' ἰθὺς ἐλαύνετε μώνυχας ἵππους
> ἰφθίμων Δαναῶν, ἵν' ὑπέρτερον εὖχος ἄρησθε."
> <u>ὣς εἰπὼν ὄτρυνε μένος καὶ θυμὸν ἑκάστου.</u>

> When Hektor was aware of Agamemnon withdrawing
> <u>he called out in a great voice to the Trojans and Lykians:</u>
> "Trojans, Lykians, and Dardanians who fight at close quarters,
> <u>be men now, dear friends, remember your furious valour.</u>
> Their best man is gone, and Zeus, Kronos' son, has consented
> to my great glory; but steer your single-foot horses straight on
> at the powerful Danaans, so win you the higher glory."
> <u>So he spoke, and stirred the spirit and strength in each man.</u>

A context-specific formula that introduces exhortation or shouted instructions on the battlefield precedes Hector's speech (285). This introductory formula often appears with the full-verse formula in which Hector tells his men to "remember your furious valor" (287).[5] The content of the exhortation urges the men to be brave in order to win glory, which is typical for exhortations.[6] At the end of the speech, a concluding formula tells us that Hector succeeded in stirring up his men (291). After the exhortation, the narrator pauses to amplify this image of Hector with two expansions that do not advance the plot, but rather contribute to a dramatic and effective telling of the story: a simile likens Hector to a huntsman and his troops to hounds (292-295) and a second simile that follows immediately after the first compares Hector to a storm cloud (296-298). Then the narrator asks a rhetorical question about who the warriors were whom Hector killed (299-300).

Taken together, these various features—the exhortation to the Trojans based on memory, valor, and honor; the pair of similes; and the rhetorical question—create a vivid image of the powerful Hector at a moment when things are not going well for the Greeks. This sequence provides an example of the expansionist aesthetic of repetition and variation in which the single speech forms one element of a series of different elements rather than itself being expanded or adapted. Both the exhortation itself and the speech frames surrounding it are formulaic and follow the usual patterns for such speeches. The presence of a simile, or even a pair of similes, in a battle scene is also a common features of Homeric poetry.[7] Rhetorical questions are uncommon, but certainly not unprecedented.[8] This one simultaneously draws out the might of Hector and reminds the audience that his power, currently strong and terrible for the Greeks, is dependent on the favor of Zeus. In all probability the audience, familiar with the general outlines of the story, knows that this favor is soon to be withdrawn.

---

[5] [dative object] ἐκέκλετο μακρὸν ἀΰσας ([he] in a great voice cried out to [object]) appears eight times in the *Iliad*. In six of these instances, the speech so introduced contains the exhortation ἀνέρες ἔστε φίλοι, μνήσασθε δὲ θούριδος ἀλκῆς (be men now, dear friends, and remember your furious valor). Collins 1998:103-104 discusses the association of ἀλκή (valor) with memory in this formula. Mackie 1996:88 notes that this formula is "virtually confined" to speeches by Hector.

[6] For the use of memory as part of exhortation in connection with this formula, see Martin 1989:79-80.

[7] See Moulton 1977:18-27 on pairs of similes. He says that the second in a pair of successive similes like these generally "elaborate[s] or intensif[ies] the initial comparison" (19).

[8] See Hainsworth 1993 *ad* 11.299 for other passages in which this particular question formula appears.

Variation in Exhortation Patterns: The Epipolesis in Iliad 4

The exhortation speech itself may expand into a conversation in order to create emphasis. The Epipolesis,[9] the scene in *Iliad* 4 in which Agamemnon tours his forces and as he encounters each contingent either praises it for valor or reproaches it for substandard bravery, represents a different kind of expansion of the single genre of exhortation. In a sense, the Epipolesis provides an exhortation of unprecedented length and elaboration as a prelude to the fighting of the entire *Iliad*, which begins in earnest immediately after the Epipolesis ends. If we see the Epipolesis as an expansion of the typical "exhortation" pattern, it gives a larger context for this scene, both within the system of conversational types and within the battle narrative in the *Iliad*.

Other scholars have been interested in battle-related characteristics of the scene, considering it as a catalogue[10] or as an example of a compositional technique in which the poet begins with a general type and follows it with specific examples of the type.[11] For the most part, however, this scene has fallen between the stools of the more engrossing opening set pieces of the poem (the Catalogue of Ships, the scene in Book 3 of Helen on the walls of Troy) and the fighting proper that begins in Book 5. In fact, the Epipolesis itself helps to provide background for the opening of the poem, and makes a transition between the series of vignettes that introduce us to the characters and story of the *Iliad* and the sustained fighting that takes up much of the action. The various tribal heads that Agamemnon meets and harangues respond to his remarks in various ways, although as we have seen, in its most common form the exhortation does not receive a reply at all. These different responses illustrate the personalities of these individual leaders as well as the personality of Agamemnon himself. Furthermore, the dynamics of the various conversational exchanges between Agamemnon and his troops illuminate Agamemnon's relationships with the Greek forces under his command. Agamemnon has the status to exhort these men, but his remarks never have a clear relationship to the behavior of the fighter being exhorted. In one case, Agamemnon is forced to retract what he says. The overall picture that emerges from this is of a leader who does not know how to effectively use his position of power or to address his men in a manner that is suitable to their behavior and standing in the Greek community as a whole.

---

[9] Named from the verb ἐπεπωλεῖτο at 4.231, from ἐπιπωλέομαι "to go round, inspect, review."
[10] Fenik 1968:153.
[11] Krischer 1971:134.

Agamemnon's review of his troops essentially begins with two "topic sentences" that establish two broad categories for the exhortations he addresses later on to the various individuals whom he meets: Agamemnon urges on those men who are eager to fight, while he reproaches others who hang back from the fighting. [12] The arrangement of the five encounters in the Epipolesis follows this overall sketch: Agamemnon praises and encourages the first three leaders whom he meets (Idomeneus, the Ajaxes, and Nestor) and reproaches the last two (Odysseus and Diomedes). The conversation—or lack thereof—that takes place during each of these encounters is structured slightly differently, lending a pleasant variety to the composition of the episode as well as depth and individuality to the characterizations of the various figures involved in the Epipolesis. [13]

This initial set-up (232-250) tells the audience what to expect from Agamemnon as he tours the Greek forces, but does not give any indication of how the forces are going to respond when they are praised or reproached for their behavior. This focus on the person giving the exhortation is consistent with the usual pattern for battlefield exhortations that was outlined above: troops who have just been exhorted generally do not respond verbally to their leader's speech. However, Agamemnon's specific encounters with individual groups of warriors almost always include conversational exchange between him and the object of his exhortation. These responses represent the primary departure from common patterns of exhortation that we find in the Epipolesis. As such, they also represent one of its major points of interest. These exchanges show Agamemnon making contact with the important warriors among the Greeks, but they also show that he does not have a very comfortable relationship with any of these men.

Agamemnon first encounters Idomeneus, the commander of the Cretan contingent. Idomeneus receives a gracious and friendly address. Both the speech introductory language and the content of Agamemnon's remarks display his warm and respectful tone.

> τοὺς δὲ ἰδὼν γήθησεν ἄναξ ἀνδρῶν Ἀγαμέμνων,
> αὐτίκα δ' Ἰδομενῆα προσηύδα μειλιχίοισιν·
> "Ἰδομενεῦ, περὶ μέν σε τίω Δαναῶν ταχυπώλων
> ἠμὲν ἐνὶ πτολέμῳ ἠδ' ἀλλοίῳ ἐπὶ ἔργῳ
> ἠδ' ἐν δαίθ', ὅτε πέρ τε γερούσιον αἴθοπα οἶνον

---

[12] Krischer 1971:133-134 characterizes the first two speeches as compared to the five meetings with specific heroes as "Typus" (type) and "Einzelheiten" (particulars). He persuasively suggests that this is done in order that "sie von vornherein im Rahmen des Ganzen gesehen werden" (they be seen from the start in the setting of the whole).

[13] Kirk 1985:353-354 gives an overview of the organization and composition of the Epipolesis.

Ἀργείων οἳ ἄριστοι ἐνὶ κρητῆρι κέρωνται . . .
ἀλλ᾽ ὄρσευ πόλεμόνδ᾽, οἷος πάρος εὔχεαι εἶναι."

Agamemnon the lord of men was glad as he looked at them
and in words of graciousness spoke at once to Idomeneus:
"I honour you, Idomeneus, beyond the fast-mounted
Danaans whether in battle, or in any action whatever,
whether it be at the feast, when the great men of the Argives
blend in the mixing bowl the gleaming wine of the princes . . .
Rise up then to battle, be such as you claimed in time past."

Iliad 4.255-60 and 264

Idomeneus replies with a simple assent, at the level both of the formulaic
reply introduction that precedes his speech and what Idomeneus himself says
to Agamemnon.

τὸν δ᾽ αὖτ᾽ Ἰδομενεὺς Κρητῶν ἀγὸς ἀντίον ηὔδα·
"Ἀτρεΐδη, μάλα μέν τοι ἐγὼν ἐρίηρος ἑταῖρος
ἔσσομαι, ὡς τὸ πρῶτον ὑπέστην καὶ κατένευσα·
ἀλλ᾽ ἄλλους ὄτρυνε κάρη κομόωντας Ἀχαιούς,
ὄφρα τάχιστα μαχώμεθ᾽ . . . "

Then in turn Idomeneus lord of the Kretans answered him:
"Son of Atreus, I will in truth be a staunch companion
in arms, as first I promised you and bent my head to it.
Rouse up rather the rest of the flowing-haired Achaians
so that we may fight in all speed . . . "

4.265-69

Evidently, Idomeneus and Agamemnon agree on the merit of Idomeneus as a
fighter and a comrade, and that being the case, there is no point in Agamemnon
exhorting Idomeneus in the first place. This exchange shows that the two men
have a friendly and mutually respectful relationship, but it also indirectly
questions Agamemnon's judgment about where his encouragement is needed.

Agamemnon next reaches the Ajax contingent and their men, whose
activities are described with a simile of a goatherd watching the progress
of a dark cloud over the sea (275-80).[14] Although the goatherd in the simile
is dismayed by the bad weather he sees (279), Agamemnon is pleased by the

[14] Kirk 1985 *ad* 4.272-273 states that "Ajaxes" refers here to Telamonian Ajax and his brother
Teucer, not to Telamonian and Locrian Ajax. See Kullmann 1960:79-85 on the traditional
exploits, character, and antecedents of Telamonian Ajax.

sight of the Ajaxes busy with their armed men. The introductory couplet for his speech to them resembles that which introduced his speech to Idomeneus, but the content of this speech is unique in the Epipolesis.

κaὶ τοὺς μὲν γήθησεν ἰδὼν κρείων Ἀγαμέμνων,
καί σφεας φωνήσας ἔπεα πτερόεντα προσηύδα·
"Αἴαντ᾽, Ἀργείων ἡγήτορε χαλκοχιτώνων,
σφῶϊ μέν—οὐ γὰρ ἔοικ᾽ ὀτρυνέμεν—οὔ τι κελεύω . . . "

Strong Agamemnon was glad when he looked at them,
and he spoke aloud to them and addressed them in winged
    words:
"Aiantes, o leaders of the bronze-armoured Argives,
to you two I give no orders; it would not become me
to speed you . . . "

4.283-86

Nowhere else does Agamemnon greet a group of soldiers by telling them that he does *not* have orders for them. Moreover, after Agamemnon has announced that he is not giving the Ajax contingent orders, he leaves them there and immediately walks to the camp of Nestor. We hear nothing at all about how the Ajaxes responded to this speech, which suggests that this speech is not some kind of indirect or implicit suggestion. If it is intended as such, it fails in its intentions, insofar as the Ajaxes show no signs of being of aware of the fact.[15] Once again, it is not clear what if anything Agamemnon has actually accomplished with his address, increasing the sense that he lacks skill and acuity as a leader.

Nestor, who is famous for giving advice and is often seen doing so in Homeric epic, is first encountered by Agamemnon in the characteristic activity of exhorting his own troops (ὀτρύνοντα μάχεσθαι [urging (them) to battle], 294). The first speech in the encounter between Nestor and Agamemnon, indeed, is the exhortation that Nestor gives to his own men (303-309). Only after Nestor has had his say does Agamemnon speak (313-316); Nestor then has the last word in this exchange (318-325). Agamemnon's respect for the older man, and the fact that Nestor is shown exhorting his own men and

---

[15] Martin 1989:114 argues that the "limited praise" of Agamemnon in this speech does, in fact, urge on the Ajaxes while claiming not to give them any orders. It seems to me that the lack of information about how the Ajaxes respond—particularly in contrast to the focus on how other Greeks respond to Agamemnon during the Epipolesis—makes this a difficult conclusion to draw with certainty.

speaking more than Agamemnon does, both add depth and detail to the characterization of the aged and wise counselor of the Greek army. This exchange also makes an implicit contrast between the skillful speaker Nestor and the less adept Agamemnon, who once again achieves no clear result with his exhortation and in fact is overshadowed as a speaker by the man whom he is ostensibly trying to encourage. If we remember that the usual form of an exhortation entails no response at all from the person being exhorted, this imbalance of power and skill between Agamemnon and Nestor emerges even more clearly and is even more uncomplimentary to Agamemnon.

Agamemnon next encounters Odysseus and Menestheus. Here his speeches change from smiling encouragement to reproaches. The introductory formula for a reproach, however, is nearly the same as that for a complimentary speech, due to the identical metrical shape of νείκεσσεν (reproached) and γήθησεν (smiled).

> τοὺς δὲ ἰδὼν νείκεσσεν ἄναξ ἀνδρῶν Ἀγαμέμνων,
> καί σφεας φωνήσας ἔπεα πτερόεντα προσηύδα·
> "ὦ υἱὲ Πετεῶο διοτρεφέος βασιλῆος,
> καὶ σύ, κακοῖσι δόλοισι κεκασμένε κερδαλεόφρον,
> τίπτε καταπτώσσοντες ἀφέστατε, μίμνετε δ᾽ ἄλλους; ... "

> Seeing these the lord of men Agamemnon scolded them
>   and spoke aloud to them and addressed them in winged
>   words, saying:
> "Son of Peteos, the king supported of god; and you, too,
>   you with your mind forever on profit and your ways of
>   treachery,
>   why do you stand here skulking aside, and wait for the
>   others? ... "

4.336-40[16]

This speech, although addressed to both Menestheus and Odysseus, gives Menestheus a complimentary full-verse vocative (338) and Odysseus an abusive one (339). This strategy singles out Odysseus for particular

---

[16] Apthorp 1999 condemns both verse 337 (on the basis of its absence from several important papyri) and the very similar verse 4.369 (in spite of mounting evidence for the authenticity of 369, which he discusses and dismisses [19-20]). His grounds for doing so are the absence or questionability of the verses in several important early papyri, and the lack of necessity for an additional verb of speaking after νείκεσσεν (scolded) in verses 336 and 368. Whether the additional verse appears here or not is immaterial to the basic similarity between language introducing an exhortation based on praise and one based on blame.

condemnation while ostensibly addressing both heroes. Indeed, Agamemnon chooses his abusive language for Odysseus well: by calling Odysseus κακοῖσι δόλοισι κεκασμένε (which in a more literal translation than Lattimore's might be rendered "excelling in evil tricks"), he plays on a well-known characteristic of Odysseus that is contained in Odysseus' traditional epithet πολύμητις (translated by a gifted former student of mine as "multi-talented"). At this point, Agamemnon appears to have made a well-spoken address to the man he intends to reproach.

However, Agamemnon is unable to make his speech stick, so that this encounter too depicts him as an ineffectual giver of exhortations (and in a broader sense, therefore, as an ineffectual leader).[17] Odysseus does not take kindly to this reproach and replies angrily to Agamemnon's speech. His emotion appears, as in the other speeches in the Epipolesis, in both his remarks themselves and the formulaic introduction to his reply. The narrator introduces the speech as follows: τὸν δ' ἄρ' ὑπόδρα ἰδὼν προσέφη πολύμητις Ὀδυσσεύς (then looking at him darkly resourceful Odysseus spoke to him), 349. Odysseus tells Agamemnon bluntly that he is talking nonsense (350-355). Agamemnon immediately backs down rather than defending himself or his remarks.

> τὸν δ' <u>ἐπιμειδήσας</u> προσέφη κρείων Ἀγαμέμνων,
> ὣς γνῶ χωομένοιο· πάλιν δ' ὅ γε λάζετο μῦθον·
> "<u>διογενὲς Λαερτιάδη, πολυμήχαν' Ὀδυσσεῦ</u>,
> οὔτε σε νεικείω περιώσιον οὔτε κελεύω . . . "

> Powerful Agamemnon in turn answered him, <u>laughing</u>,
> seeing that he was angered and taking back the words
>   spoken:
> "<u>Son of Laertes and seed of Zeus, resourceful Odysseus</u>:
> I must not rebuke you beyond measure nor give orders . . . "[18]

4.356-59

Although Agamemnon began by berating Odysseus and Menestheus, he now smiles at them—the prelude to his praise of the other leaders he has encountered—and takes back his former negative remarks. Similarly, he uses the common full-verse vocative for Odysseus with which the Greeks usually address him (358).[19] This formulaic address refers to Odysseus' capacity for stratagems

---

[17] Martin 1989:59-65 discusses the power hierarchy that lies behind who gives successful commands in the *Iliad*.

[18] This verse is my translation; the rest of the quotation is Lattimore's.

[19] 7x *Iliad*, 15x *Odyssey*.

just as Agamemnon's abusive one does, but it does not make this capacity a matter for reproach. It combines Odysseus' cleverness with his illustrious lineage to create a typical honorific vocative.[20] Agamemnon told the Ajaxes that he would not give them orders in very similar language to that which he now uses to Odysseus in 359 (cf. οὔ τι κελεύω [I give no orders], 286). However, here the words have the ring of defeat, given the criticisms that Agamemnon has just made of Odysseus. So too does the phrase πάλιν δ' ὅ γε λάζετο μῦθον (taking back the words spoken) in 357. Agamemnon has tried to exhort Odysseus by rebuking him, and he has failed. Agamemnon's attempt to gain the upper hand over Odysseus by speaking harshly to him, Odysseus' resistance to the attempt, and Agamemnon's ready surrender when he sees that Odysseus is angry all contribute to the audience's understanding of the personalities of these two men. In this scene, Agamemnon does not follow through on his initial speech, and Odysseus resists the attempted rebuke by saying that Agamemnon is talking nonsense rather than by arguing against the rebuke in more specific terms. Once again, Agamemnon emerges from an encounter with one of the Greek leaders looking weak and ineffective in comparison to the man whom he is addressing. The specific context of exhortation strengthens this portrait, since this genre presupposes that the person giving the exhortation has the standing to give instructions to the person he addresses.[21]

Diomedes, the youngest warrior and the one with the least status of all those whom Agamemnon addresses in the Epipolesis, is the only leader whom Agamemnon can arguably be said to have successfully exhorted. Like Odysseus, he receives a rebuke; unlike Odysseus, Diomedes accepts the authority to make such a speech that Agamemnon's leadership gives him even though he does not endorse the specific content of the rebukes themselves.

> καὶ τὸν μὲν νείκεσσεν ἰδὼν κρείων Ἀγαμέμνων,
> καί μιν φωνήσας ἔπεα πτερόεντα προσηύδα·
> "ὤ μοι, Τυδέος υἱὲ δαΐφρονος ἱπποδάμοιο,
> τί πτώσσεις, τί δ' ὀπιπεύεις πολέμοιο γεφύρας;
> οὐ μὲν Τυδέϊ γ' ὧδε φίλον πτωσκαζέμεν ἦεν,
> ἀλλὰ πολὺ πρὸ φίλων ἑτάρων δηΐοισι μάχεσθαι . . . "

---

[20] Dickey 1996, although beginning chronologically with Herodotus, contains a number of extremely helpful insights on Homeric vocatives. She notes, e.g., the honorific function of the patronymic in Homeric poetry within a larger context of the association of vocatives with "formal, deferential, or courteous speech" (55). See Higbie 1995:190-91 on the importance of patronymic forms of address to a Homeric hero's good repute.

[21] Here I differ from Stanley 1993:71, who speaks positively of Agamemnon's "diplomacy" toward Odysseus.

<u>At sight of Diomedes the lord of men Agamemnon scolded him</u>
and spoke aloud to him and addressed him in winged words,
   saying:
"<u>Ah me, son of Tydeus, that daring breaker of horses,</u>
why are you skulking and spying out the outworks of battle?
Such was never Tydeus' way, to lurk in the background,
but to fight the enemy far ahead of his own companions . . . "

4.368-73

We can see once again that the tone of rebuke is set not only by the content of the speech itself, but also by the formulas and conventions that introduce the speech. Furthermore, the specific nature of rebuke is particularly appropriate to Diomedes: Agamemnon rebukes the young Diomedes for not being the man his father was, using both vocative address and a story from the past to drive his point home. It has been suggested that Diomedes accepts Agamemnon's criticisms because of his youth, which would make sense given Agamemnon's failure to give an effective exhortation to any of the older and more experienced fighters whom he has addressed thus far.[22]

Diomedes' usual full-verse vocative among the Greeks and their supporters is Τυδεΐδη Διόμεδες, ἐμῷ κεχαρισμένε θυμῷ (Son of Tydeus, you who delight my heart, Diomedes).[23] Agamemnon strikes a different and sharper note at the opening of his complaint that Diomedes is not the man his father was. In his address to Diomedes at 370, the only word in the verse which is in the vocative case (i.e. refers directly to Diomedes himself) is υἱέ (son). The focus of the verse is on Tydeus, who is described as δαΐφρονος ἱπποδάμοιο (daring breaker of horses). Furthermore, the introductory ὤ μοι creates an atmosphere of regret and grief.[24] Thus, this apparently ordinary full-verse vocative, while not overtly abusive, appears instead of the friendly Τυδεΐδη Διόμεδες, ἐμῷ κεχαρισμένε θυμῷ to show Agamemnon's disdain for Diomedes. Its language reinforces the idea of the story Agamemnon tells, namely that Diomedes is not a worthy son of his brave father. In addition, it subtly transforms the patronymic into a term of abuse rather than respect.

---

[22] Martin 1989:124, where he asserts Diomedes "is unsure of his language, but his lack of confidence is explicitly associated with his youth."

[23] 5.243 (Sthenelus), 5.826 (Athena), 10.234 (Agamemnon).

[24] This phrase, which functions as an interjection meaning something like "alas," always carries a note of sadness. Thetis' lament in *Iliad* 18, when she says ὤ μοι ἐγὼ δειλή, ὤ μοι δυσαριστοτόκεια (ah me, my sorrow, ah me, the bitterness in this best of childbearing, 18.54), is one of the most notable examples of this.

Similarly, both the length and the content of Agamemnon's speech (370-400, by far the longest of Agamemnon's speeches in the Epipolesis) delivers a particularly strong rebuke to Diomedes. Just as Agamemnon begins with a vocative identifying him as the inferior son of a brave and noble father, he tells a long story in his rebuke about a particular exploit of Tydeus (376-398). At the end of his story, he again abuses the son of Tydeus for failing to live up to the high standards of his father (399-400). The overall construction of the rebuke here resembles the one to Odysseus: an abusive or uncomplimentary vocative followed by a personal rebuke. Here, however, the target of the rebuke does not refuse to accept it. Diomedes, unlike Odysseus, does not respond angrily to this long and detailed criticism. In fact, he does not respond at all.

> ὣς φάτο, τὸν δ' οὔ τι προσέφη κρατερὸς Διομήδης,
> αἰδεσθεὶς βασιλῆος ἐνιπὴν αἰδοίοιο·
> τὸν δ' υἱὸς Καπανῆος ἀμείψατο κυδαλίμοιο·
> "Ἀτρεΐδη, μὴ ψεύδε' ἐπιστάμενος σάφα εἰπεῖν·
> ἡμεῖς τοι πατέρων μέγ' ἀμείνονες εὐχόμεθ' εἶναι . . . "

> So he spoke, and strong Diomedes gave no answer
> in awe before the majesty of the king's rebuking;
> but the son of Kapaneus the glorious answered him:
> "Son of Atreus, do not lie when you know the plain truth.
> We two claim we are better men by far than our fathers . . . "

4.401-405

Although Diomedes gives no answer to Agamemnon, he replies angrily to Sthenelus' challenge to what Agamemnon has said. His reply is worth quoting in full in spite of its length, because it brings forward with particular clarity the exhortation motif that runs through the entire Epipolesis. Diomedes appears to understand Agamemnon's project in the Epipolesis at least as fully and sympathize with it as entirely, as do the warriors whom Agamemnon has praised. Here Diomedes essentially summarizes the Epipolesis and cogently sums up the genre of exhortation.

> τὸν δ' ἄρ' ὑπόδρα ἰδὼν προσέφη κρατερὸς Διομήδης·
> "τέττα, σιωπῇ ἧσο, ἐμῷ δ' ἐπιπείθεο μύθῳ·
> οὐ γὰρ ἐγὼ νεμεσῶ Ἀγαμέμνονι, ποιμένι λαῶν,
> ὀτρύνοντι μάχεσθαι ἐϋκνήμιδας Ἀχαιούς·
> τούτῳ μὲν γὰρ κῦδος ἅμ' ἕψεται, εἴ κεν Ἀχαιοὶ
> Τρῶας δηώσωσιν ἕλωσί τε Ἴλιον ἱρήν,

τούτῳ δ' αὖ μέγα πένθος Ἀχαιῶν δῃωθέντων.
<u>ἀλλ' ἄγε δὴ καὶ νῶϊ μεδώμεθα θούριδος ἀλκῆς,"</u>
ἦ ῥα, καὶ ἐξ ὀχέων σὺν τεύχεσιν ἆλτο χαμᾶζε·
δεινὸν δ' ἔβραχε χαλκὸς ἐπὶ στήθεσσιν ἄνακτος
ὀρνυμένου· ὑπό κεν ταλασίφρονά περ δέος εἷλεν.

Then <u>looking at him darkly</u> strong Diomedes spoke to him
    [Sthenelus]:
"Friend, stay quiet rather and do as I tell you; I will
find no fault with Agamemnon, shepherd of the people,
<u>for stirring thus into battle</u> the strong-greaved Achaians;
this will be his glory to come, if ever the Achaians
cut down the men of Troy and capture sacred Ilion.
If the Achaians are slain, then his will be the great sorrow.
<u>Come, let you and me remember our fighting courage.</u>"
    He spoke and leapt in all his gear to the ground from
      the chariot,
and the bronze armour girt to the chest of the king clashed
      terribly
as he sprang. Fear would have gripped even a man stout-hearted.

4.411-21

Odysseus responds with an angry retort when Agamemnon casts base aspersions on his bravery. Diomedes, in contrast, becomes angry when Sthenelus argues with Agamemnon's base aspersions on himself. In Diomedes' view, Agamemnon has the right to exhort his own troops to battle however he thinks best. Diomedes' speech reminds the audience of the wider context in which these exhortations take place: the leader of the Greek troops has a particular responsibility for helping them to perform in battle as well as they possibly can, and the quality of their performance will reflect on him. In fact, although Diomedes berates Sthenelus for arguing with Agamemnon, he does so on the grounds Agamemnon has the right to speak to his men however he wants to, not because he agrees with what Agamemnon has said about him. Indeed, he does not mention the content of Agamemnon's speech at all. Because he approves of Agamemnon's general plan of action does not necessarily mean that he endorses the specific content of Agamemnon's criticisms of him personally.[25] So, even at the moment when Agamemnon gives his

---

[25] McGlew 1989:286 notes that Diomedes' actions here confirm Agamemnon's own statement (*Iliad* 2.73) that it is θέμις (right) for a king to test his troops.

most successful exhortation, the specific content of what he says receives no response. Rather, the youngest leader and the one with the least status among those whom Agamemnon has addressed accepts his right to give such a speech without endorsing the quality or the content of the speech itself. This is an incomplete success at best for Agamemnon.

At the end of this speech, the reference to Diomedes' armor (419-420) in a speech concluding formula that normally appears in battle contexts forcefully reminds the audience that we will soon have an opportunity to observe these men in battle. Diomedes himself, in fact, fights with outstanding courage and effectiveness in Book 5. Diomedes clearly understands and accepts that Agamemnon is exhorting his men for the upcoming fighting, that it is his privilege and his responsibility to do so, and that it is the concomitant responsibility of the troops to fight their best. By placing this especially long and detailed encounter last in the Epipolesis, the narrator leaves the audience thinking about these ideas, and reminds us that the fighting for which Agamemnon is exhorting his men is about to begin. Immediately after Diomedes' speech, a series of similes describing the Greeks, the Trojans, and the noise of battle introduces the beginning of fighting between the two sides.[26]

The sequence of exhortations that Agamemnon makes in the Epipolesis depicts Agamemnon's extremely limited effectiveness as a leader: when he praises his men, the praise seems gratuitous or irrelevant to the men who are praised, and when he attempts to use reproach to urge men on, he is not able to make his remarks stick except when his addressee is young and comparatively lacking in social status. Conversely, the men whom Agamemnon addresses are shown in typical pursuits: the Ajaxes, known more for their actions than their propensity for public speaker, are silently engaged in military maneuvers; Nestor's exhortations to his men overshadow the one that Agamemnon tries to give; Odysseus, a skilled and lively speaker, resists the rebuke aimed at him. Thus these encounters characterize not only Agamemnon, but his men. By framing these exchanges as exhortations, a genre of speech in which normally the speaker's words and the status that gives him the right to speak in such a fashion are accepted without comment by the addressee, the narrator emphasizes even more strongly Agamemnon's shortcomings as a speaker and a leader. Moreover, this elaborate portrait of the ineffectual Agamemnon and his main fighters appears effectively at this point in the poem, when the fighting in which these men will participate is about to begin.

---

[26] Compare the simile that follows Hector's exhortation to his troops in Book 11 that was used above as an example of the single genre of exhortation.

Challenge and Vaunt

Encounters between two enemies on the battlefield, unlike those between comrades, commonly consist of both speech and action combined: warriors threaten or attack one another both physically and verbally in alternation.[27] However, we do not see heroes shouting at one another *while* they throw their spears. Nor do we see extended exchanges of only speech, as we normally do in one-on-one conversations off the battlefield. Indeed, only in battlefield scenes[28] do we find speech concluding formulas that end an exchange between two speakers by describing the action of one of them.[29] Outside of battle contexts, in contrast, the only kind of physical action regularly found in speech concluding formulas is the much more general verse "having spoken thus, [X] went away" (e.g. the formula ὣς ἄρα φωνήσας ἀπέβη [nominative name/epithet, subject]). This unusual type of formulaic speech concluding language further shows that both action and speech commonly occur in the turns taken by two enemies who meet on the battlefield, in contrast to the speech-only exchanges that are the rule in one-on-one conversations outside of battle contexts. Conversely, speech-only exchanges are very rare in battle scenes. When one does occur, it generally depicts the death of a major hero whose death has important implications for both the plot and the overall themes of the poem.

The usual approach to speech in battle contexts has been either to view it in isolation from other kinds of speech,[30] or without comparing battle scenes that contain speech to battle scenes without speech.[31] In fact, speech on the battlefield derives its significance against the backdrop of both the battle context in which it occurs, which may or may not typically feature speech, and non-combat speech patterns. Particularly striking battle scenes may use speech in unusual ways either by containing more speech than a typical battle scene but

---

[27] Goffman 1981:142 has a helpful formulation of situations in which speech and action appear together in a context that is not primarily speech-driven: "the words spoken, whether by one participant or two, are an integral part of a mutually coordinated physical undertaking, not a talk."

[28] And related conversational genres: see Chapter 6 on athletic games.

[29] Such as ἦ ῥα καὶ ἀμπεπαλὼν προΐει δολιχόσκιον ἔγχος (so he spoke, and balanced the spear far-shadowed, and threw it). All of the most common speech concluding formulas describe emotional rather than physical response.

[30] E.g. Parks 1990, who implies (erroneously, in my view) that the competitive mode of the battlefield is the norm across many forms of human interaction (see e.g. 73-74); Fenik 1968, particularly 20-21 and 161-163.

[31] Krischer 1971, although extremely useful on the subject of similes in the typical *aristeia* pattern, does not include speeches in his typology of the *aristeia* (24). Martin 1989: 59-77 discusses various speech genres that commonly occur in battle contexts.

following the basic battlefield speech convention that avoids extended speech exchanges, or by containing conversations that are quite normal off the battle-field but rare in combat scenes. Before turning to these unusual cases, it will be useful to survey the typical sequences of speech and action in battle scenes.

Speech Exchange Followed by Attack Exchange

Speech and action combine in various sequences in battlefield encounters between two enemies. Sometimes attacks fall into two segments, an exchange of hostile speeches followed by an exchange of hostile actions. The meeting between Tlepolemus and Sarpedon in *Iliad* 5 takes this form. The common descent of the two warriors from Zeus provides an opportunity to contrast their genealogical relationship (which might be imagined to result in friendly relations) with their hostility toward one another on the battlefield, as we see in this formulaic introduction to Tlepolemus' first speech:

> οἳ δ' ὅτε δὴ σχεδὸν ἦσαν ἐπ' ἀλλήλοισιν ἰόντες
> υἱός θ' υἱωνός τε Διὸς νεφεληγερέταο,
> τὸν καὶ Τληπόλεμος πρότερος πρὸς μῦθον ἔειπε·

> Now as these in their advance had come close together,
> the own son, and the son's son of Zeus cloud-gathering,
> it was Tlepolemos of the two who spoke the first word:

> 5.630-32

Verses 630 and 632 are both formulaic and regularly occur one after the other to introduce the first speech after two enemies meet on the battlefield.[32] Here, the additional verse between the two formulaic verses reminds the audience that these particular enemies were actually cousins. This adds an extra resonance to their hostility to one another, given that relations might be expected to be friendly rather than hostile towards each other. In addition, it picks up on the "genealogy as abuse" aspect of battlefield speech,[33] which figures prominently in the pre-attack challenges that Tlepolemus (633-646) and Sarpedon (648-654) launch at one another. These speeches represent a pair of verbal attacks: each fighter tries to assert that his own ancestry is the more noble (partly by discrediting the

---

[32] E.g. *Iliad* 6.121-122, which begins the encounter between Glaucus and Diomedes. The verse οἳ δ' ὅτε δὴ σχεδὸν ἦσαν ἐπ' ἀλλήλοισιν ἰόντες illustrates the similarity of speech and action as battlefield attack strategies: although this verse frequently precedes a speech introduction and a verbal challenge, it may also precede a physical attack (as at *Iliad* 5.14, which is followed immediately by a spear cast).

[33] Parks 1990:108-109 discusses this under the more general heading of "retrojection," or reference to the past, as a means of attacking one's enemy in a flyting speech.

genealogy of his opponent) and that that he will prevail in the encounter. Then each hero makes a physical attack. At the same time, they throw their spears at one another, as a result of which Tlepolemus is killed and Sarpedon badly wounded (655-662). In a sequence like this one, we almost never find more than one speech for each warrior.[34] In this version of battlefield speech types, each warrior takes one challenge turn, and then each warrior takes a physical attack turn.

Speech + Action in One Turn

In fights between two enemies that include more than two speeches, the structure of an individual turn is different. In these cases, each warrior has a sort of extended attack "turn" that includes both speech and action. The fatal encounter between Pandarus and Diomedes in *Iliad* 5 (276-296) is a typical example of such a sequence. We can see in this scene that each character takes one "turn" composed of both speech and action: Pandarus, going first (there is an initial speech introductory formula at 276), speaks, then attacks, then speaks again (277-285). Diomedes "replies" first with a speech (introduced with a reply formula, 286) and then with a physical attack, which kills his opponent (287-296). The content of the speeches in this scene underscores the unique relationship between speech and action in one-on-one encounters on the battlefield: when Diomedes replies to Pandarus (287-289), he doesn't say "your boasts were groundless, but mine won't be," as we would expect if his challenge were a response to what Pandarus *said*. Instead, he derides Pandarus for missing him and promises to hit either Pandarus or his companion. Clearly, this speech responds to what Pandarus has done, not—or at least not primarily—to what Pandarus has said. This notion of speech as a kind of attack is the key difference between speech exchanges between two enemies on the battlefield and one-on-one conversations that occur in other contexts. A meeting of enemies on the battlefield can represent a responsive sequence. However, because it regularly includes both action and speech as part of a given turn, it is not the same as a one-on-one conversation where speech is generally the sole medium of exchange between the two characters.[35]

---

[34] For sequences of speech exchange/attack exchange where more than two speeches are given, see below.

[35] Hymes (in Gumperz and Hymes 1972:56) distinguishes situations like this, in which speech is one aspect of an essentially non-speech activity, from "speech events": "they are not in themselves governed by such rules [of speaking], or one set of such rules throughout. A hunt, e.g., may comprise both verbal and nonverbal events, and the verbal events may be of more than one type." He states that these situations cannot be described by the identical set of rules that characterize speech events, which are governed entirely by rules of speaking.

Within a particular speech-action "turn" of one participant in an encounter between two enemies, the sequence of speech and action may vary. This becomes clear if we compare the meeting between Pandarus and Diomedes with a similar encounter between Odysseus and Socus in *Iliad* 11. A schematic illustration of the two turns in this encounter as compared to the meeting of Pandarus and Diomedes looks like this:

Pandarus and Diomedes	Odysseus and Socus
Turn 1 (Pandarus)	Turn 1 (Socus)
threatening speech (5.277–279)	threatening speech (11.430–433)
throws his spear, hits enemy (280–282)	tries to pierce enemy's shield (434–438)
vaunt over apparently beaten foe (283–285)	
Turn 2 (Diomedes)	Turn 2 (Odysseus)
speech in reply (268–289)	threatening speech (441–445)
spear cast kills enemy (290–296)	fatal spear cast at retreating enemy (446–449)
	vaunt over dead enemy (450–455)

In each case, the two participants take one turn apiece composed of speech and then action. However, a particular turn may include more than one speech. Length of turn (i.e. how many segments the turn has) does not seem to be associated with whether the speaker is the winner or the loser in an encounter.

Variations in Challenge and Vaunt Pattern

Variations on this typical pattern of one turn each for two adversaries on the battlefield generally take two forms. Sometimes two characters or two groups of characters may attack each other in a sequence of more than two turns, but following the usual patterns just described. These scenes vary in length from the common pattern described above, but not in structure, in that speech does alternate with action in the attacks that each side makes. However, there are more than two turns in such lengthened encounters, either because several different characters each take one turn, or because one or both enemies get more than one turn in an encounter between two warriors. In such scenes, typical battlefield

peech conventions do not undergo any essential change. Alternatively, two
nemies may exchange speeches as though they were having a non-battlefield
onversation, without any action taking place between the speeches. In contrast
o the lengthened but essentially typical structures just mentioned, these
onversations transcend the typical patterns of battlefield interactions. Normally,
hese interactions are not talk-based, but rather include talk as one of several
ctivities. This in itself, besides the content of the conversation, creates emphasis
n the scene in which it appears. This strategy appears in some of the most
ramatic and significant death scenes in the *Iliad* in order to highlight the linkages
etween these different deaths, the depth of hostility between the Greek and
rojan heroes, and the costs these hostilities have for Greeks and Trojans alike.

More Than Two "Speech + Action" Turns: Iliad 14   Let us begin with attack-
um-speech exchanges that contain more than two turns. In *Iliad* 14 (453-507), a
nique sequence of vaunts and attacks occurs between several Greek and Trojan
arriors. This series takes place at the end of Poseidon's unauthorized activities on
he battlefield in aid of the Greeks. While Zeus and Hera sleep after Hera seduces
eus, Poseidon takes advantage of Zeus' inattention to what is going forward on
he battlefield to help the Greeks. After this scene, however, Book 15 opens when
eus wakes up, becomes furious, and prevents the other gods from interfering any
urther in the fighting at Troy. Following this divine discussion, the Greeks fall into
ruly desperate straits and Patroclus, in an effort to help them, sets forth to meet
is doom. The unusual series of back-and-forth attacks between the Greeks and
he Trojans at the end of Book 14 provides a sort of capstone to the Greeks' limited
uccess before Zeus intervenes, marking off the end of this section of the tale.[36]

Polydamas begins this sequence. Having killed the Greek Prothoenor
449-452), Polydamas vaunts over him (453-457). The Greeks are grieved by
earing Polydamas' mocking speech, in which he tells Prothoenor to lean on
he spear with which he has been killed on his way to Hades. Of the Greeks,
jax is the most indignant because Prothoenor had been standing by him
hen he was killed (459-460). A formulaic couplet that is used only in *Iliad*
3 and 14 describes the emotion of the Greeks and identifies the individual
arrior who was the most grieved by the vaunt they have just heard:

ὣς ἔφατ', Ἀργείοισι δ' ἄχος γένετ' εὐξαμένοιο·
Αἴαντι δὲ μάλιστα δαΐφρονι θυμὸν ὄρινε

[36] Although a back and forth series attacks, by itself, is quite usual (Fenik 1968:10 and 57), the
appearance of vaunts with each of the series of attacks is not.

> He spoke, and sorrow came over the Argives at his vaunting
> and beyond others he stirred the anger in wise Telamonian
> Aias . . .

14.458-459[37]

Ajax now throws his spear at Polydamas. He misses Polydamas and kills Archelochus instead (461-468). Then he vaunts over the dead Archelochus (469-474). The Trojans, like the Greeks before them, are grieved by his vaunt (ἦ ῥ' εὖ γιγνώσκων, Τρῶας δ' ἄχος ἔλλαβε θυμόν [he spoke, knowing well what he said, and sorrow fastened on the Trojans], 475).

This is the first of two pairs of Trojan-Greek attack-vaunt turns. In an exchange of vaunts between two individual warriors, which is the normal pattern, this would be the end of the encounter and the narrative would move on to a different aspect of the fighting. In this scene, however, a second pair of turns follows the first one. The sequence proceeds as follows: Polydamas kills Prothoenor and vaunts over him (turn 1); Ajax kills Archelochus in mistake for Polydamas and vaunts (turn 2); Acamas kills Promachus and vaunts over him (turn 3); Peneleus tries to attack Acamas, kills Ilioneus instead, and vaunts over him (turn 4). End of sequence marked by address to the Muses (508). This clash between the Greeks and the Trojans, which marks the high point of the Greeks' success in battle before their fortunes take a dramatic turn for the worse, consists of four turns of attack cum-vaunt instead of the usual pair of turns that we find in meetings between enemies. At the end of this unusual series, the address to the Muses further calls the attention of the audience to the Greeks' success.

> ἔσπετε νῦν μοι, Μοῦσαι Ὀλύμπια δώματ' ἔχουσαι,
> ὅς τις δὴ πρῶτος βροτόεντ' ἀνδράγρι' Ἀχαιῶν
> ἤρατ', ἐπεί ῥ' ἔκλινε μάχην κλυτὸς ἐννοσίγαιος.

> Tell me now, you Muses who have your homes on Olympos,
> who was the first of the Achaians to win the bloody
>   despoilment
> of men, when the glorious shaker of the earth bent the way
>   of the battle?

14.508-510

---

[37] Also 13.417-418 and 14.486-487. The couplet in Book 13 occurs after the second of a series of three challenges or vaunts, all of which involve Idomeneus in some way. However, that series differs from this one in that other events besides attack-vaunt turns occur in it. A number of heroes who do not speak make attacks and otherwise participate in the fighting, in which Idomeneus has a particularly prominent role.

his address, like the unusual series of vaunts it follows, emphasizes the point at which the Greeks as a group (as opposed to Achilles as an individual later on in the poem) achieve their greatest success on the battlefield during the course of the *Iliad*. However, it also reminds the audience that their current success is dependent on the help of Poseidon, and this help is about to be withdrawn.

More Than Two "Speech + Action" Turns: Iliad 21 The extended battlefield exchanges between individuals, as opposed to the group scene I have just been discussing, all relate to the central plot line of the last third of the *Iliad*: the death of Patroclus and i) its effect on Achilles from an emotional standpoint as well as ii) its connection with both the death of Hector in Book 22 and the death of Achilles after the events of the *Iliad*. Some of these individual meetings, which will be the focus of this section, take place between Achilles and the Trojans whom he kills in Book 21 during his *aristeia*. These encounters follow typical patterns for battlefield exchanges, but at greater length, often in such a way as to dramatize the extraordinary nature of Achilles' rage and alienation from the most basic norms of behavior on the battlefield. Others depart from the usual battlefield speech type and contain conversations. The presence of conversation, as we will see at the end of this chapter, is one of the many unusual features that link the deaths of Patroclus in Book 16 and Hector in Book 22.

Achilles re-enters the fighting after Patroclus dies in Book 16 and he is reconciled with his comrades in Book 19. He fights in Books 20 and 21 with a single-minded inexorability that appears nowhere else in the poem. These two books are closely linked, bound by an overall structure that creates parallels between the two Trojans whom Achilles attacks in Book 20, but who are rescued, and the two whom he meets and kills in Book 21.[38] Within Book 21, in turn, the encounter between Achilles and Lycaon at the beginning of *Iliad* 21 has several important similarities with Achilles' meeting with Asteropaeus shortly afterwards. As a result of Achilles' behavior toward these two Trojans, and several more which are mentioned pell-mell immediately after Asteropaeus' death, Achilles so angers the Scamander river that he is drawn into a fight with the river and so with the gods themselves. This berserk behavior, as it has recently been called,[39] depicts Achilles as utterly beyond the reach of normal human

---

[38] Whitman 1958:272-273.

[39] Shay 1994:77-99 argues that Achilles is berserk in his *aristeia* in Books 19-22 of the poem, asserting that "no restraint of any kind limits Achilles during his berserk state" (88).

emotions leading into his climactic meeting with Hector in Book 22, in which he displays many of the same feelings and actions toward Hector himself.

Many readers, including this one, have found great pathos in the encounter between Lycaon and Achilles. Lycaon, with his hopeful but doomed plea for mercy, is a universally sympathetic figure. Achilles, on the other hand, has disgusted some interpreters with what they see as the depravity of his behavior toward the suppliant Lycaon and later, toward Hector.[40] Others have defended his actions as not only excusable but required given one's obligation to avenge one's comrades and dishonor those who have harmed them.[41] When we look at Achilles' words and behavior in Book 21 in light of the typical patterns of battlefield speech genres in other scenes, we can see that the narrator is playing against these in order to place Achilles outside the norms of human behavior. At this point in the story, Achilles is not thinking about how others will regard his behavior. He often is not thinking very much even about himself. This sense of detachment exists alongside Achilles' battle frenzy. Frenzy (or berserk) is much more arresting to the audience than detachment, and it arouses strong negative reactions in some interpreters that may prevent them from giving Achilles' detachment the attention it deserves. However, as we will see, this sense that Achilles is somehow unable to connect to what is happening is one of the major forces driving the scene. Lycaon's pathetic appeal gets its force not simply from its lack of success, but also from its failure even to make an impression on Achilles.[42]

The meeting between the Trojan youth Lycaon and Achilles departs from typical patterns for battlefield encounters between enemies in several ways. Basically, this is an example of the "speech + action" turn type. However, Achilles has two turns, although one of them is extremely short and lacks a speech component. In addition, the action component of Lycaon's turn is not an attack. Lycaon is one of the last of the unfortunate Trojan youths whom Achilles meets in his bloodthirsty rampage in Books 20-21 after he returns to the battlefield following the death of Patroclus. The moment when Achilles first sees Lycaon occasions a narrative flashback: it describes a previous encounter between the two, when Achilles had sold Lycaon into slavery, and refers to the misfortune of the young man in falling into Achilles' hands so soon after returning home from this period of slavery (34-52). Indeed, Achilles is so surprised at the appearance of Lycaon before him that he exclaims to himself in amazement (53-63)

---

[40] E.g. Bowra 1930:20-21.

[41] Bassett 1938:203-204.

[42] Here we can profitably contrast Adrestus' supplication of Menelaus in Book 6 (45-65), which moving because of how close it comes to succeeding.

This extensive prelude to the actual meeting between the two fighters greatly increases the prominence of the episode and focuses the attention of the audience more closely on the meeting when it does occur.

As Achilles waits, Lycaon advances toward him eager to supplicate him; at the same time, Achilles tries to kill Lycaon with his spear, but his spear passes over the kneeling Lycaon (64-70), who thus has an opportunity to supplicate Achilles. This spear cast is the first turn in the encounter. Lycaon now takes a turn consisting of both action and speech, as is common in an encounter between enemies, but his behavior is that of a suppliant rather than of an attacker.[43] Unlike a fighter, who generally speaks first and attacks afterwards in a "speech + action" turn, he does the physical part of his turn first (pose of supplication, 68-72) and then makes his speech (74-96). What he says in his plea gains in impact for the audience because we have already heard the outlines of Lycaon's story in the flashback that begins the encounter between him and Achilles. Now, hearing the same facts in more detail, in the voice of the man who is living them, the audience feels personally involved in Lycaon's plight. Lycaon refers to the ransom that Achilles got for him the last time they met (74-80), describes his family (84-91), and finally suggests hopefully that Achilles need not kill him because he was born from a different mother than Hector (94-96).

Lycaon makes this plea for mercy,[44] but he acknowledges that his supplication is likely to be fruitless (92-93). Indeed, Achilles hears Lycaon's speech completely unmoved. The couplet that marks the transition between Lycaon's speech and Achilles' reply, very unusually, contains no verb of speaking to introduce the next speech. Like the plea itself, and indeed the construction of the episode to this point, this transitional couplet focuses the attention and sympathy of the audience on Lycaon.

> ὣς ἄρα μιν Πριάμοιο προσηύδα φαίδιμος υἱὸς
> λισσόμενος ἐπέεσσιν, ἀμείλικτον δ' ὄπ' ἄκουσε

> So the glorious son of Priam addressed him, speaking
> in supplication, but heard in turn the voice [i.e. of Achilles]
>   without pity:

21.97-98

---

[43] Parks 1990:59 considers this "the most dramatic episode of supplication." He asserts in connection with this scene that supplication is a kind of flyting. However (as Edwards 1987:91 notes), there is no successful supplication on the battlefield in the *Iliad*, which seems to me incompatible with the notion of supplication as flyting.

[44] Edwards 1980:5 lists the typical elements of a speech of supplication as "a vocative, a specific request, and an offer."

The verb προσηύδα appears in a speech *conclusion* rather than an introduction only here. Moreover, it is extremely unusual to find the listener rather than the speaker as the subject of a speech introductory expression.[45] So, several factors in the construction of the episode up to this point highlight the experiences of Lycaon and draw the audience in to these experiences: the flashback to his previous meeting with Achilles; Lycaon's own repetition of these events in his supplication to Achilles; and the transition to Achilles' reply, which casts his speech entirely in terms of its effect on the listening Lycaon. Conversely, it creates the idea that Achilles is not participating in the exchange, contributing to our sense of his detachment.

This unusual couplet, which extends Lycaon's turn right up to the first words of Achilles' turn, is the last reference to Lycaon as the central actor. Now Achilles takes his turn, and the Lycaon with whom the audience has been invited to sympathize becomes just one of a possibly endless series of victims of the bereaved and relentless Achilles. Achilles' turn has several parts. First he speaks to his enemy, but not to threaten Lycaon with his own bravery or employ any of the other motifs we have become accustomed to seeing in pre attack challenges. Instead he tells Lycaon that now that Patroclus has died, any Trojans whom Achilles meets will be killed, including Lycaon himself (99-106). Achilles refers in the same unemotional, matter-of-fact way to his *own* eventual death on the battlefield (108-113), which is almost unimaginable in the usual threats and boasts of such speeches.

Hearing these dispassionate, bizarre words, which are so unlike recogniz able battlefield behavior, Lycaon realizes that all is lost.

> ὣς φάτο, τοῦ δ' αὐτοῦ λύτο γούνατα καὶ φίλον ἦτορ·
> ἔγχος μέν ῥ' ἀφέηκεν, ὃ δ' ἕζετο χεῖρε πετάσσας
> ἀμφοτέρας· Ἀχιλεὺς δὲ ἐρυσσάμενος ξίφος ὀξὺ ...

> So he spoke, and in the other the knees and the inward
> heart went slack. He let go of the spear and sat back,
>   spreading
> wide both hands; but Achilleus drawing his sharp sword ...

> 21.114-16

174

.ine 114, which is formulaic, appears four times in the *Odyssey* but only here in he *Iliad*. While Lycaon throws away his sword and takes up a pose that clearly and simply shows that he will not attack,[46] Achilles draws his sword and kills the young man. The contrast between the one youth who lets go of his sword, and the other who stabs to death with his, creates a poignant image for the audience. Having killed Lycaon, Achilles throws him into the river nearby. He vaunts over the corpse partly by gloating that the dead youth will be eaten by fish and not lamented by his mother (122-127), which is a common motif in such vaunts. In the second part of the vaunt (128-135), Achilles repeatedly uses second person *plural* forms, casting Lycaon as just one member of an ever-increasing group of Trojans whom Achilles will kill and vaunt over.[47] This generalizing aspect of the vaunt parallels the references Achilles makes in his first speech to all the Trojans he plans to kill. Achilles' turn here displays the usual construction of "speech-attack-speech," but the content of his speeches and the explicit refusal of his victim to try to defend himself are all quite unusual. This combination of a typical structure with very surprising content sets off the oddity of Achilles' behavior in this scene and contributes to the general sense pervading Book 21 that Achilles is beyond the reach of the normal conventions of human behavior.

The turn structure in the Lycaon scene is basically regular, with the exception of Achilles' very brief first turn (failed attempt to cast his spear) that is essentially simultaneous with Lycaon's turn. In his turn, Lycaon physically and verbally supplicates Achilles rather than attacking his enemy. Achilles then has a more lengthy turn constructed in the common manner for a battlefield turn. However, the speeches that bracket his fatal attack on Lycaon show an unusual lack of emotion about the notion of being killed on the battlefield, whether it is himself or Trojan youths who are dying. They also generalize this particular encounter to any and all Trojans whom Achilles may meet. This generalizing strain in Achilles' remarks exists in tension with the various ways in which the narrative highlights the experiences of Lycaon in the first part of the episode and makes him vivid and meaningful to the audience. The audience is invited to participate in this encounter from Lycaon's perspective at the same time that Achilles sees Lycaon as a fungible representative of a large and indistinguishable class of victims. This contrast in perspectives shows the audience Achilles' own sense of disengagement from what is happening.

---

[46] Taplin 1992:224n35 points out that "this physical movement is made elsewhere only by those who have already been mortally struck."

[47] Forms of ὑμεῖς (129, 130); second person plural verb forms (128, 131 and each line thereafter).

In contrast, the turn sequence in the Asteropaeus episode immediately following the death of Lycaon is longer than in the Lycaon episode, creating a sense of crescendo leading up to the end of Book 21 and the meeting with Hector in Book 22. [48] The scene opens with an exchange of speeches. Then each repeatedly attacks the other, elongating the usual "each attacks once" component in the common pattern for such sequences. Finally, Achilles succeeds in killing Asteropaeus and vaunts over the corpse; normally, vaunts do not follow speech exchange between the two adversaries. [49] The lengthening of the usual "one turn each" sequence and of the "attack" segment of the meeting depicts Achilles' ferocity in this encounter, which very soon calls down the anger of the rivers of Troy on Achilles. Moreover, his passionate attack on Asteropaeus complements the strange detachment he feels when he kills Lycaon. Achilles feels different things during his *aristeia* but none of his reactions fit into typical battlefield patterns. All of them are extreme.

Once again, the narrative before the meeting says something about the Trojan whom Achilles is about to meet: we learn about Asteropaeus' genealogy, which includes the river Axius (140-143) and that Asteropaeus was inspired by the angry river Xanthus to meet Achilles bravely (144-147). Once the actual encounter begins, Achilles asks who Asteropaeus is (150-151) and Asteropaeus tells him (153-160). The subsequent physical attacks are unusually long and furious. First Asteropaeus throws two spears at once. He hits Achilles' shield with one of them and grazes his arm with the other (161-168). Then, Achilles throws his spear at Asteropaeus and misses (169-172, note especially κατακτάμεναι μενεαίνων "in a fury to kill him" [170]). Undaunted, Achilles unsheathes his sword (173-174). Again, the narrator emphasizes the ferocity of his relentless attack: ἆλτ' ἐπί οἱ μεμαώς, "[he] sprang upon him in a fury" (174). Meanwhile, Asteropaeus is trying repeatedly and fruitlessly to get Achilles' spear unstuck from the riverbank where it has landed (174-178). At length Achilles strikes Asteropaeus with the sword and kills him (179-182). Each warrior attacks his opponent more than once (or tries to) instead of the more usual "one attack each" that normally

---

[48] Fenik 1968:86 considers this pair of encounters an example of a general pattern in which "an event which receives its full development at one point is first stated briefly, then dropped, only to return again when it is then treated in full."

[49] Although Parks 1990:50 includes both speech exchange and vaunt in his model of "the total contest pattern," of which he cites this encounter with Asteropaeus as an example, in fact they rarely appear together.

ollows an exchange of challenge speeches. Now Achilles vaunts over the allen Asteropaeus (184-199). The content of this vaunt is much more in line with the usual structure of such speeches than what Achilles said to the dead ycaon: he boasts that his own descent from Zeus has proven more powerful han Asteropaeus' descent from the river Axius and asserts the power of eus over any and all bodies of water.

In the Asteropaeus episode, then, individual events in the scene take a asically normal form (the contents of speeches by each warrior, the individual attacks that each makes on the other). However, these individual vents are arranged in an unusual way so as to depict the extraordinary ury of Achilles as he attacks his enemy. Instead of each warrior getting one turn" composed of both speech and action, or two exchanges of "one turn ach" where the first exchange is of speech and the second of physical attacks, ne two warriors first exchange speeches and then attempt several physical ttacks on each other. Finally, Achilles' vaunt caps off the episode.[50] The reference to river ancestors in this speech leads smoothly into the conflict with the ver Scamander alongside wholesale fighting among the gods, which follows nortly afterwards (212-382). With the exception of an inconclusive encounter rith Agenor, who meets Achilles but is removed to safety by Apollo before he an be harmed (545-598), these encounters are the last that Achilles has with rojans before he meets Hector.

In the episode with Lycaon, in contrast, the usual turn structure for attlefield encounters appears virtually unchanged but the content of these urns is very unusual. The Lycaon episode exploits common forms to highght unusual content; the Asteropaeus scene arranges normal content in an nusual sequence. These contrasting narrative techniques are used to repre->nt different aspects of Achilles' feelings. Together, these two episodes depict ne magnitude of Achilles' alienation now that Patroclus is dead by means of oth his detachment as he kills Lycaon and his ferocity against Asteropaeus. Vhen Achilles' *aristeia* reaches its climax in his meeting with Hector, he feels oth extraordinary detachment and great ferocity. He will display both of nese qualities when he meets and kills Hector in Book 22.

⁰ A similar sequence appears in the meeting between Hector and Achilles in Book 20 (422-454): Achilles and Hector each take a speech turn; they attack one another; and then Achilles continues to attack, and afterwards vaunts (or more accurately challenges) even though Hector has been spirited away by Apollo. This sequence is not included as one of the lengthened series being discussed here because of Apollo's interruption.

Conversation Between Enemies

In the battle scenes discussed up to this point, more than the usual number of turns occurs, or the individual turns are arranged in an unusual order. However, there is never a series of more than two speeches without intervening action. These scenes, however unusual they may be, follow the typical pattern of battle scenes in which speech exchange is part of an ongoing fight, not the sole medium of exchange between the two speakers. Sometimes, on the other hand, two enemies may meet and exchange not simply a vaunt or a series of vaunts that accompany physical attacks, but a series of several speeches without any physical assaults intermingled. In other words, they may have a conversation. Given the rarity of conversation on the battlefield, such conversations draw attention to themselves simply because they exist, and the longer they are, the more attention they command. Indeed, in the books of the *Iliad* that Fenik 1968 focuses on as representative of battle scenes study (5, 11, 13, 16, and 17), there are 62 single speeches out of 151, or 41% single speeches. This is noticeably higher than the *Iliad's* overall percentage of single speeches (28%) and over three times the percentage of single speeches in the *Odyssey* (13%), where battle scenes are almost entirely absent. To put it another way, the cooperative exchange of conversation is in a basic sense antithetical to the hostilities of battle; when a conversation appears during a fight, the scene thereby transcends rather than simply lengthening or adapting the typical conventions of battle. This only happens in two scenes, both of which have paramount importance for the story as a whole.

Patroclus and Hector, Iliad 16   In Book 16 over half of the speeches are single (13 of 24). This is the highest percentage of single speeches in any book in either the *Iliad* or the *Odyssey*. Given this backdrop of single speeches especially predominant even for battle narrative, the one-on-one conversation that occurs at the end of the book between Hector and the dying Patroclus stands out particularly strongly. When Patroclus meets his doom at the end of Book 16, he is struck down by Apollo (788-806), wounded by Euphorbus (806-817), and finally killed by Hector (818-863). This means that the usual "attack" sequence, in which both enemies make some kind of attack on the other, does not occur here. Instead, Patroclus is wounded and trying to creep away when he is hit by Hector's spear (818-822). Both this sequence of events, and the conversation that takes place between Patroclus and Hector, dramatize not simply the fact of Patroclus' death but the process of dying.

After Hector attacks the reeling Patroclus, but before he vaunts over his
dying enemy, a simile describes the two heroes. As we have seen, in the typical
pattern in battlefield narrative, the narrative describes a warrior's vaunt over
his fallen enemy right after it describes the attack that occasions the vaunt.
Thus, this simile serves as an emphatic device: it focuses the audience's atten-
tion on the combat between Patroclus and Hector by pausing to dwell on it
after Hector's attack on his enemy, but before the speeches that the audience
would be expecting to follow the attack based on the typical sequences of
battlefield encounters.

> ὡς δ' ὅτε σῦν ἀκάμαντα λέων ἐβιήσατο χάρμῃ,
> ὥ τ' ὄρεος κορυφῇσι μέγα φρονέοντε μάχεσθον
> πίδακος ἀμφ' ὀλίγης· ἐθέλουσι δὲ πιέμεν ἄμφω·
> πολλὰ δέ τ' ἀσθμαίνοντα λέων ἐδάμασσε βίηφιν·
> ὡς πολέας πεφνόντα Μενοιτίου ἄλκιμον υἱὸν
> Ἕκτωρ Πριαμίδης σχεδὸν ἔγχεϊ θυμὸν ἀπηύρα·
> καί οἱ ἐπευχόμενος ἔπεα πτερόεντα προσηύδα·
> "Πάτροκλ' ... "

> As a lion overpowers a weariless boar in wild combat
> as on the high places of a mountain the two fight in
>   their pride
> over a little spring of water, both wanting to drink there,
> and the lion beats him down by force as he fights for his
>   breath, so
> Hektor, Priam's son, with a close spear-stroke stripped
>   the life
> from the fighting son of Menoitios, who had killed so many,
> and stood above him, and spoke aloud the winged words of
>   triumph:
> "Patroklos ... "

Iliad 16.823-830

In our simile, the two combatants are a lion and a boar (823). They fight each
other in a mountain glade, eager for combat (824). The lion beats the boar
through superior physical strength: two words using the root βια- "physical
strength, force" describe the victory of the lion over the boar (ἐβιήσατο χάρμῃ
[overpowers in wild combat], 823; λέων ἐδάμασσε βίηφιν [the lion beats him
down by force], 826). The two fighters are described in the dual, creating the

idea that they are closely matched in strength.[51] Indeed, even though the bo▪ of the simile loses its fight, it is a powerful foe. The boar is perhaps the mightie▪ animal found in battlefield similes beside the lion.[52] The boar in our simile ▪ described as ἀκάμαντα (weariless, 823) and the narrator emphasizes its deat▪ struggle (πολλὰ δέ τ' ἀσθμαίνοντα [as he fights for his breath], 826) rather tha▪ the condition of the victorious lion. Thus, this simile illustrates the victory ▪ the more powerful Hector over a beaten but nonetheless impressive Patroclus.

Viewed alongside other lion similes that have appeared in connectio▪ with Patroclus earlier in his *aristeia*, this simile forms part of a progression ▪ similes that trace the rise and fall of his fortunes on the battlefield. This simi▪ describing the mortally wounded Patroclus has several verbal echoes of a▪ earlier simile about two lions, which describes Hector and Patroclus fightir▪ over the body of Hector's charioteer Cebriones after Patroclus has killed hi▪ (756-758). These two similes share a location in a mountain glade (ὥ τ' ὄρε▪ κορυφῇσι, 757 = 824) and the eagerness of the two combatants to fight (μέγ▪ φρονέοντε μάχεσθον, 758 = 824). The conflict in both similes is over natur▪ resources (drinking water or food). In the earlier simile, however, both Hect▪ and Patroclus are described as lions. Similarly, in the narrative at that poin▪ Hector and Patroclus meet in a closely matched and inconclusive encounte▪ of equals.[53] The resemblance of these two similes, combined with the cruci▪ difference between them in the animals that fight, emphasizes the chang▪ that has taken place in the story between the first simile and the second. Th▪ dying Patroclus is no longer the mightiest warrior on the battlefield: he ha▪ been beaten in the battle of both narrative and simile.[54] At the same tim▪ Patroclus, despite his defeat, is still portrayed as a formidable warrior in bot▪ the simile and the narrative. Hector did not kill Patroclus alone, but struc▪ the third blow in a series. Even as Patroclus is dying, the narrative stresses h▪ power by calling him πολέας πεφνόντα Μενοιτίου ἄλκιμον υἱόν (the fightir▪ son of Menoitios, who had killed so many, 827).

---

[51] See Balthes 1983:41 on the dual in this simile and that of the two vultures at 16.428-430.

[52] Scott 1974:58-60.

[53] For Moulton, this simile "reverses in part the comparison at [16.]487 for the death of Sarpedo▪ (1977:105).

[54] Balthes 1983:45-46 argues that the two-vulture simile (16.428-430), the two-lion simi▪ (16.756-758) and the final lion-boar simile (16.823-826) mark the significant points in t▪ aristeia of Patroclus ("den Aufstieg, den Höhepunkt und das Ende in der Aristie des Patrokl▪ bezeichnen"). He notes that each of these similes is longer than the preceding one, ar▪ suggests that this simile progression demonstrates that the real crux of Book 16 is not t▪ encounter between Hector and Patroclus, but Patroclus' death.

Having fatally wounded his quarry, Hector now taunts Patroclus at ome length (830-842). He ridicules Patroclus for expecting to capture Troy, praises his own ability to defend his city, and finally, he scoffs at the send-off he imagines Achilles giving to his friend. While this is typical for a vaunt over a defeated enemy, Patroclus, unlike most dying heroes, replies to the vaunt of his killer, getting a conversation between the two men under way. The formulaic speech frame that introduces his reply follows a typical pattern for reply introductory formulas, with one important difference. Patroclus, unlike most other characters whose names appear in formulaic speech introductions, is identified with a vocative rather than a nominative. [55] What, if anything, does this vocative signify? The introduction to Patroclus' death statement contains both a vocative and a descriptive participle: τὸν δ' ὀλιγοδρανέων προσέφης, Πατρόκλεες ἱππεῦ (and now, dying, you answered him, o rider Patroclus; 843). Similarly, the other two speech introductions for Patroclus that give his name in the vocative—all during his *aristeia* in Book 16—also contain descriptive participles (βαρὺ στενάχων [groaning heavily], 16.20 and ἐπικερτομέων [in bitter mockery], 16.744). On the other hand, the verse τὸν δ' αὖτε προσέειπε Μενοιτίου ἄλκιμος υἱός (then in turn the strong son of Menoitios spoke to him, 11.837) is available to introduce a reply by Patroclus without any description of how he felt when he replied.

This strongly suggests that the presence of the vocative in the speech introductions for Patroclus in Book 16 is a function of the descriptive participles rather than a goal in itself, as many interpreters have argued.[56] If the vocative Πατρόκλεες were desired for its own expressive powers, we would expect to find the verse *τὸν δ' ἀπαμειβόμενος προσέφης, Πατρόκλεες ἱππεῦ (and now, taking your turn, you answered him, o rider Patroclus). [57] In fact this verse never occurs.[58] Moreover, the participle ὀλιγοδρανέων also precedes Hector's penultimate speech to Achilles (22.337), where the speaker's name appears in the

---

[55] Menelaus and Eumaeus are also referred to with vocatives in speech introductions in the *Odyssey*.

[56] Wilamowitz 1916:118-119; more recently Richardson 1990:170-172, whose overview of the controversy on this point is concise and helpful although I disagree with his strongly held view in favor of emotional expressiveness for such vocatives.

[57] Visser 1988:34 understands the verse-making of formulaic expressions with several semantic elements as follows: "[the poet] first placed the semantically most important elements . . . " [in our case, the participle] "and then adapted to this basic structure material whose semantic content is likewise indispensable, but whose prosodic scheme is variable [here the main verb of speaking and the designation of the speaker]."

[58] In contrast, the expression ἀπαμειβόμενος προσέφης does occur regularly in reply introductions for Eumaeus in the *Odyssey*.

more usual nominative and the verb in the third person. This further support
the idea that these vocative speech introductions for Patroclus are due to th
presence of emotive participles and not to their own emotional effect, becaus
other aspects of the death-scenes of Patroclus and Hector suggest that the dyin
Hector is meant to arouse at least as much sympathy as the dying Patroclus.[59]
This does not mean that *other* vocatives for Patroclus outside of speech intro
ductions may not convey the narrator's sympathy. It simply suggests that we
must consider not only the vocatives themselves, but the different narrative an
formulaic contexts in which they occur, when we think about this question.

Before Patroclus dies, he responds to Hector's vaunt (844-854). This speech
stands out for its awareness of the broader framework in which Patroclus
death takes place. Patroclus begins his speech with Hector's "now," in which he
is vaunting over a defeated foe (ἤδη νῦν, Ἕκτορ, μεγάλ᾽ εὔχεο, 844); he remind
Hector that he was the third in a series of adversaries who wounded Patroclu
(implying that this is not as impressive a feat as being solely responsible for killin
one's foe); and he ends by saying that death at the hands of Achilles awaits Hecto
(852-854). In this final speech, Patroclus describes an arc or a dynamic for Hecto
of victories followed by death that closely mirrors the one that book 16 depicts fo
Patroclus himself. The narrative focuses primarily on this dynamic for Patroclus
while the dying hero posits such a cycle for his victorious adversary.

Before Hector responds to Patroclus' final statement, a brief passag
describes the actual death of Patroclus. I will quote the verses here, becaus
a discussion of Patroclus' death is not complete without this passage; to avoi
redundancy, the content of this passage will be discussed in detail below in th
context of the death of Hector.

> ὣς ἄρα μιν εἰπόντα τέλος θανάτοιο κάλυψε·
> ψυχὴ δ᾽ ἐκ ῥεθέων πταμένη Ἀϊδόσδε βεβήκει,
> ὃν πότμον γοόωσα, λιποῦσ᾽ ἀνδροτῆτα καὶ ἥβην.
> <u>τὸν καὶ τεθνηῶτα προσηύδα φαίδιμος Ἕκτωρ·</u>

> He spoke, and as he spoke the end of death closed in upon him,
> and the soul fluttering free of his limbs went down into
> Death's house
> mourning her destiny, leaving youth and manhood behind her.
> <u>Now though he was a dead man glorious Hektor spoke to him:</u>

> 16.855-58

---

[59] These will be discussed further below, as will the similarities between Hector's death an
Patroclus'.

Here, we find an elaboration within the one-on-one conversation sequence, which itself is an elaboration of the usually single genre of the vaunt. In a one-on-one conversation, the most usual way to mark the transition from one speech to the next is with a single verse. Furthermore, verse 858 could stand alone—as far as clarity and structure are concerned—to introduce Hector's final speech. This elaboration in place of a single-verse transition between one turn and the next contributes to the appeal and the prominence of this moment in the poem. Hector questions Patroclus' assertion that Hector himself does not have long to live (859-861). He characterizes Patroclus' comments with the verb μαντεύεαι (prophesy, 859), showing his awareness if not his acceptance or understanding of Patroclus' striking vision of Hector's future. This verb, which is used four times in the *Iliad*,[60] appears only here for a human who is not a seer. This word choice draws out both the powerful nature of Patroclus' insights in his dying speech and the limitations of Hector's understanding of his own situation. He then removes his spear from the corpse and attacks Automedon (862-867).

Thus, the death of Patroclus includes several elaborations around what is essentially a typical battlefield motif of "A fatally wounds B, A vaunts over B, B dies."[61] We have seen more routine examples of this pattern in our discussion of the common patterns for the "vaunt" genre of single speech. Here, instead of just "A wounds B," we have "A fatally wounds B, simile describes A and B," where the particular content of the simile effectively plays off of the previous simile to reflect the progress of the story. In place of "A vaunts over B," the victor and his victim have a *conversation* consisting of three turns while the victim is dying. The death itself, unusually, takes place as an elaboration in between the last two speeches of the conversation. This conversation develops several motifs that are important to the progress of the story, chief among them the connections between the deaths of Patroclus and the death of Hector. Patroclus, at the moment of his death, clearly understands these connections, but Hector does not. Hector's blithe self-confidence contrasts ironically with Patroclus' prophesy of his impending death. Conversation provides a very effective framework for these contrasting characters. First, the mere presence

---

[60] Besides our passage, 1.107, 2.300, and 19.420 (addressed to the horse Xanthus).

[61] As Fenik 1968:216 acutely remarks on the death of Patroclus, "what the scene loses in plasticity and clarity it gains in grandeur and awesomeness. But this effect is not achieved with new, unparalleled motifs or bold new inventions. Instead, familiar, typical motifs are crowded together into a small space, one following quickly upon another. The poet uses this grouping and concentration of familiar material to create a special effect." One of these typical motifs, although Fenik does not say so, is the one-on-one conversation.

of a conversation at this point in a battlefield encounter calls attention to th
speakers and their words simply because it is unusual. Moreover, the inter
change of conversation dramatizes in a particularly vivid and effective wa
the contrasting viewpoints of the two characters and the poignantly incom
plete understanding that Hector has of his own future.

Hector and Achilles, Iliad 22   The death of Hector is one of the high points c
the *Iliad*, both because of its superlative pathos and vividness and because it link
together so many past and future deaths of Homeric heroes. As is well knowr
Hector's death is linked to Patroclus', in that Achilles sets out to kill Hecto
because he was responsible for Patroclus' death. Indeed, it shares many formula
and structural features with the end of Book 16. Hector's death is also connecte
to Lycaon and Asteropaeus' because Achilles kills them during his *aristeia*, whic
reaches its high point when he meets Hector. Hector's death in turn will lea
to Achilles' own after the events of the *Iliad*. Fittingly for such a pivotal par
of the story, the longest and most famous battlefield conversation in the *Ilia*
occurs when Hector meets his end in Book 22. Although the structure, conten
and imagery of many of the individual speeches in this episode have attracted
great deal of attention, neither the unusual presence of a conversation durin
a fight nor the unique length of this interchange have received much notice
This conversation is one of the longest in the *Iliad*, battlefield or not, and
includes many elaborations of various kinds. It contains both more turns tha
usual within a basically normal battlefield sequence and an extended one-or
one conversation. The norms of both conversation and battle types inform thi
scene, and we can appreciate its effects more fully if we view them against bot
of these two backdrops simultaneously.

The final encounter between Hector and Achilles begins when Hector, tricke
by Athena disguised as his brother Deiphobus (*Iliad* 22.226–247), stops his headlon
flight around Troy and confronts Achilles. In its first three turns, the encounte
between Hector and Achilles presents an orderly series of alternating turns of th
sort commonly found in battlefield encounters, although at more length tha
we usually find. Hector speaks first (249), thereby exerting some control over th
situation after he has fled from Achilles in terror (250–259, turn 1). Next Achille
speaks and throws his spear, which misses (261–274, turn 2);[62] finally Hector speak
and throws *his* spear, which strikes Achilles' shield but does not wound him (279
291, turn 3). The formulaic verse ἦ ῥα καὶ ἀμπεπαλὼν προΐει δολιχόσκιον ἔγχο

---

[62] The bT scholia comment on the verb ἠλεύατο (evaded) in verse 274: κινεῖ τὰς ἐλπίδας τῶ
ἀκροατῶν, ὡς τάχα ἂν περιγενησομένου τοῦ Ἕκτορος (it arouses hope for the hearers tha
Hector might perhaps escape).

(So he spoke, and balanced the spear far-shadowed, and threw it, 273 = 289 at the end of turns 2 and 3) appears twice in the same episode only here. This adds to the sense of elongation and elaboration that the unusually lengthy sequence creates. In addition, it creates the sense that the two adversaries are equally matched. Although the audience expects Hector to die, he is not portrayed as being at a disadvantage at the beginning of his fight with Achilles.

However, the tide is about to turn. When Hector's spear cast does not injure Achilles and he turns to Deiphobus for another spear, he finds no one there. At this point Hector realizes that he has been tricked, accepting that death is all but upon him. The soliloquy that he gives at this point is the only departure from the alternating turn structure that consistently governs the speeches and attacks in the encounter between Hector and Achilles. Both the disruption of typical conversational structures and the content of the speech itself emphasize the crucial moment at which Hector accepts the inevitability of his own death.

> Ἕκτωρ δ' ἔγνω ᾗσιν ἐνὶ φρεσὶ φώνησέν τε·
> "ὢ πόποι, ἦ μάλα δή με θεοὶ θάνατόνδε κάλεσσαν·
> Δηΐφοβον γὰρ ἔγωγ' ἐφάμην ἥρωα παρεῖναι·
> ἀλλ' ὃ μὲν ἐν τείχει, ἐμὲ δ' ἐξαπάτησεν Ἀθήνη.
> νῦν δὲ δὴ ἐγγύθι μοι θάνατος κακός, οὐδ' ἔτ' ἄνευθεν,
> οὐδ' ἀλέη· ἦ γάρ ῥα πάλαι τό γε φίλτερον ἦεν
> Ζηνί τε καὶ Διὸς υἷι ἑκηβόλῳ, οἵ με πάρος γε
> πρόφρονες εἰρύατο· νῦν αὖτέ με μοῖρα κιχάνει.
> μὴ μὰν ἀσπουδί γε καὶ ἀκλειῶς ἀπολοίμην,
> ἀλλὰ μέγα ῥέξας τι καὶ ἐσσομένοισι πυθέσθαι."
> ὣς ἄρα φωνήσας εἰρύσσατο φάσγανον ὀξύ . . .

And Hektor knew the truth inside his heart, and spoke aloud:
"No use. Here at last the gods have summoned me deathward.
I thought Deiphobos the hero was here close beside me,
but he is behind the wall and it was Athene cheating me
and now evil death is close to me, and no longer far away,
and there is no way out. So it must long since have been pleasing
to Zeus, and Zeus' son who strikes from afar, this way;
    though before this
they defended me gladly. But now my death is upon me.
Let me at least not die without a struggle, inglorious,
but do some big thing first, that men shall come to know of it."
    So he spoke, and pulled out the sharp sword . . .

22.296-306

185

His words here contrast noticeably with the self-confident tone of his reply to the dead Patroclus at the end of Book 16. Moreover, he realizes—as Patroclus did when he made his dying speech—that the gods have been instrumental in his defeat. He ends, as did Patroclus, with a comment about his future: Patroclus' last words predicted Hector's death at Achilles' hands (16.852-854); now Hector resolves that once his death has occurred, it will be a cause of future repute for him.

The regularity of the alternating turn structure elsewhere in this long series of speeches (three turns before this point, five turns afterwards) gives this exceptional speech added prominence. In fact, this soliloquy marks a decisive point in the episode: heretofore, the two heroes speak and attack one another as equals. After the soliloquy, Achilles fatally wounds Hector, and the remainder of their encounter takes place in the context of Hector's imminent death. Moreover, the presence of Hector's voice in particular here attracts the sympathy and the attention of the audience to him just before he sustains his fatal wound. The audience gets a vivid and moving glimpse of his thoughts at a brief transitional moment when he is still as strong physically as his adversary is, but he knows that his death is upon him. Although Hector draws his sword and is compared to a mighty bird of prey as he awaits the attacking Achilles (306-311), he expresses no doubt about his imminent death in his soliloquy and the audience could not have felt any either. By allowing the audience to experience Hector's thoughts directly, and by violating a consistent alternating turn structure to do so, the narrator gives great prominence and vividness to this crucial moment in the story and in particular to Hector's perspective on his own death.

Achilles now fatally stabs Hector in the neck, but in such a way as to avoid severing his windpipe (312-329).[63] He then vaunts over his dying foe, taunting him with the common vaunt motif that he will be eaten by wild animals, while the Greeks will give his victim Patroclus a proper burial (331-336). This vaunt, which in most fatal encounters would be the final speech in the episode, opens a conversation between Achilles and Hector. While very similar in structure to the conversation between Hector and the dying Patroclus, it consists of five turns where the conversation between the dying Patroclus and Hector consists of three turns.

Fatally injured by Achilles' spear, Hector begs for his life. The participle modifying Hector in the reply formula for his speech conveys that the situation is very grave: τὸν δ' ὀλιγοδρανέων προσέφη κορυθαίολος Ἕκτωρ (in his weak-

---

[63] This anatomically specific detail almost seems to be there in order to make possible the unusually long conversation between the two that now takes place.

less Hektor of the shining helm spoke to him, 337).[64] Hector begs Achilles to return his corpse to the Trojans (338-343), but Achilles is entirely unmoved by his appeal. In his reply, which is introduced by formulaic language of hostility τὸν δ' ἄρ' ὑπόδρα ἰδὼν προσέφη πόδας ὠκὺς Ἀχιλλεύς [but looking darkly at him swift-footed Achilleus answered], 344), Achilles not only refuses Hector's request for proper burial (345). He also wishes that his anger were such as to allow him to eat Hector's body himself (346-348). Certainly the animals will eat him, and he will not receive burial rites from his family (348-354). The fury that Achilles feels here surpasses what he had toward Asteropaeus in Book 21; the detachment that he showed in his response to Lycaon is absent when he is talking to the killer of his beloved Patroclus.[65] So Hector's doom is sealed.

The introduction of Hector's last speech before dying, in which he looks ahead to Achilles' own death, differs from the previous speech introduction in one crucial word.

τὸν δὲ <u>καταθνῄσκων</u> προσέφη κορυθαίολος Ἕκτωρ

Then, <u>dying</u>, Hektor of the shining helm spoke to him

22.355[66]

With these two speech introductions for the last two speeches of Hector, the narrator uses different formulaic participles with great effect to show Hector's death as a gradual but inexorable process.[67] In his final speech, Hector tells Achilles that his own death is coming and at whose hands (356-360), much as Patroclus did in his last speech to Hector (16.844-854). At the same time, Hector is clearly aware of the extreme and unique fury that Achilles feels towards him: while Patroclus only warns Hector that he too will soon die, Hector warns Achilles that the dead Hector may become a μήνιμα θεῶν (gods' curse, 358) to him when he himself dies at the hands of Paris and Apollo. The word μήνιμα, which appears twice in Homeric epic,[68] shows the strength of Achilles' rage by extending its effects to the world of the gods. Like Patroclus, the dying Hector shows an awareness of both his own weakness and the larger context in which

---

[64] Note that almost the identical verse appears before Patroclus' final speech in Book 16 (16.843). Hector, in contrast to Patroclus, is given two speeches before he dies, elongating and elevating his death.

[65] Hector himself, in contrast, shows only exultation, not fury, toward the dying Patroclus.

[66] Allen's i family of MSS reads τὸν δ' ὀλιγοδρανέων.

[67] See Mackay 1996:46-48 on the varied participles in the speech introductions for the dying Hector in this scene.

[68] Also at *Odyssey* 11.73, where Elpenor begs Odysseus to bury him and not to let him become a θεῶν μήνιμα.

his death occurs. In both cases, this awareness gives the sense that these deaths have an importance for the story overall that goes beyond the loss of this particular fighter.

After Hector's final speech, an extended passage appears before Achilles' brief final remarks to the just deceased corpse. As has been widely noted, these famous verses also appear when Patroclus dies, linking the two deaths.

> ὣς ἄρα μιν εἰπόντα τέλος θανάτοιο κάλυψε,
> ψυχὴ δ' ἐκ ῥεθέων πταμένη Ἄϊδόσδε βεβήκει,
> ὃν πότμον γοόωσα, λιποῦσ' ἀνδροτῆτα καὶ ἥβην.
> τὸν καὶ τεθνηῶτα προσηύδα δῖος Ἀχιλλεύς·

> He spoke, and as he spoke the end of death closed in
>   upon him,
> and the soul fluttering free of the limbs went down into
>   Death's house
> mourning her destiny, leaving youth and manhood
>   behind her.
> Now though he was a dead man brilliant Achilleus spoke
>   to him:

22.361-64 = 16.855-58

(with φαίδιμος Ἕκτωρ for δῖος Ἀχιλλεύς)

The anomalous scansion of ἀνδροτῆτα as ⏑⏑—⏑ suggests that λιποῦσ' ἀνδροτῆτα καὶ ἥβην is a very ancient formula dating from a period when ἀνδροτῆτα actually did have an initial short syllable because it was spelled *anr̥teta.[69] In response to the now dead Hector, Achilles tersely states his willingness to die whenever it is time for him to die (365-366). Throughout this scene, Achilles shows unparalleled fury, but here he shows for the first time the detachment that appeared in his encounter with Lycaon in Book 21. We saw that his response to Lycaon's plea for ransom included the bizarrely unconcerned comment that he, like Lycaon and many other Trojans, would die (21.110). He says essentially the same thing here. Killing Hector has lessened neither his rage nor his lack of interest in his own fate.

---

[69] See Watkins 1995:499 on the antiquity of this expression, which he dates to before 1400 BCE. Indeed, he asserts that the linkage between the deaths of Patroclus and Hector must also have existed at this date. For another ancient formula that occurs in a single very significant context, see Nagy 1974 passim on the connections between κλέος ἄφθιτον (deathless fame) and the Sanskrit expression ákṣiti śrávas. Finkelberg 1986, on the other hand, has argued that this is not a Homeric formula at all.

Having now reached the end of this long and varied sequence, let us review the overall turn structure and locations of the elaborations or variations in this scene:

Turn 1		A (Hector) addresses B (Achilles)—asks for ground rules about corpse of loser
Turn 2	i.	B responds to A—refuses A's request
	ii.	B throws his spear at A and misses; Athena returns it to him
Turn 3	i.	A challenges B
	ii.	A throws his spear at B, hits his shield without wounding him
Turn 4	i.	A speaks aloud to himself about imminent death—violates turn structure
	ii.	A draws his sword and awaits attack of B
Turn 5	i.	B examines A to find an unarmored place to attack him, spears him in the throat without severing his windpipe
	ii.	B vaunts over the dying A
Turn 6		A entreats B to accept ransom for his corpse ["weakened" participle in reply formula]
Turn 7		B refuses A's request
Turn 8		A responds to B re B's fate ["dying" participle in reply formula]; A dies
Turn 9		B responds to dead A [extended passage describing death of A introduces speech]

The first part of this scene (turns 1-3) displays common motifs and turn structures associated with battlefield encounters. Hector's soliloquy at 4 marks a change: after the fatal attack of Achilles following this speech, a sequence of five speeches in a one-on-one conversation appears. This represents an especially long elaboration on the single vaunt that we would expect to find here. In addition, the narrator skillfully varies the participles modifying the dying Hector in reply introductions for him so as to map out in detail his progress toward death. Finally, the passage describing the death itself between the penultimate speech in the series and the final one uses an expression of great antiquity that appears only in this scene and in the very similar death of Patroclus. The scene focuses on Hector as he grapples with his own death, treating him with both sympathy and nobility as he meets his end. This way of treating Hector is a key

part of the *Iliad's* unique approach to its subject, which underlines throughou
that the costs of war fall equally on both sides in a conflict.

Conclusions

The *Iliad*, unlike the *Odyssey*, most commonly contains conversations a
elaborations or expansions on single speech contexts. In the Epipolesis in Book
the normally single genre of the exhortation becomes a series of conversation
between Agamemnon and his men. This episode depicts Agamemnon a
ineffectual in his speaking and his leadership: when he uses praise, he consistentl
fails to say anything that changes the behavior of the men to whom he speaks
and no one to whom he gives a rebuke accepts the substance of his remarks
While Agamemnon is shown as an ineffective leader at the beginning of sustaine
fighting, the various heroes to whom he speaks behave in ways typical for then
Ajax remains silent; Nestor gives advice to his own men; Odysseus disputes wit
Agamemnon. Thus, the expansion here of the typically single genre of exhortatio
creates apposite portraits of several of the major Greek fighters. Exhortation, a
a genre most typically found on the battlefield, provides a particularly effectiv
lead-in to the fighting that is about to begin.

Once the fighting does get under way, conversations occur almost entirel
to dramatize the emotions and behavior of Achilles during his *aristeia* in Book
21 and 22. Other than the death of Patroclus, whose connections to the death
Hector and to Achilles himself have already been discussed, conversation in battl
shows us the tremendous fury and unique detachment that Achilles feels when h
returns to battle after Patroclus is killed. These scenes between Achilles and h
victims use conversation for several complementary effects. The speeches that th
victim makes, and the descriptions of him in the speech frames, depict the victir
in a sympathetic light and/or dramatize the scene from his point of view. Thi
implicitly casts Achilles as the unsympathetic figure in these interactions regarc
less of how he himself behaves. In addition, his own speeches and actions show h
rage to be so great that ultimately the gods refuse to sanction it, insofar as Thet
is sent down by Zeus to tell Achilles that he must cease maltreating the body c
Hector and return it to Priam for burial. In each of these scenes, conversatio
appears where a single genre of speech (usually a vaunt) would typically be foun
This departure from typical patterns emphasizes the content of the conversatior
Moreover, the interchange inherent in conversation provides a striking and effec
tive vehicle for portraying some of the most hostile and intense conflict in th
poem. In the *Iliad*, one-on-one conversation emphasizes the conflict that charac
terizes all the key relationships in the poem.

5

GROUP CONTEXTS I—ASSEMBLIES

L ET US BEGIN THIS DISCUSSION OF ASSEMBLY PATTERNS with a basic question. What is an assembly? How can we recognize a given scene as an assembly rather than as simply a group of people talking, or a council, or an mbassy? The ἀγορή, generally translated as "assembly," is a gathering of eople engaged in "civic debate,"[1] which means that the group of people has ome kind of identity *as* a group beyond the fact that they have been gathred together on a given occasion to discuss an issue that affects them. An ssembly occurs when someone decides to call one; heralds may be involved n summoning a group to assembly; it often takes place early in the morning; ll members of the group concerned are summoned to attend. The group sits own before the assembly begins, and the leader (or other speaker) stands efore speaking. The σκῆπτρον (staff, rod) may be held by the person speaking. Vhen an assembly ends, it is formally dissolved. Within the assembly itself, we nd particular sequences for speeches as well as unique speech introductions nd conclusions that are characteristic of, and restricted to, assemblies.

As with any multi-party conversation, formulaic speech conclusions escribing the reaction of the group—as distinct from the reaction of the ddressee—regularly occur. However, this kind of speech concluding language ccurs more frequently in assemblies than it does in more informal contexts, and he content is more specific. Indeed, conversation analysis work on conversation n institutional settings has shown that these exchanges tend to entail "procedures

---

[1] Mackie 1996:10. See Edwards 1992:311 for a list and very brief overview of important discussions to date of the assembly as a type scene. None of the references mentioned by Edwards agree on the exact elements of which a type scene consists. I have found the most useful treatments of the assembly type to be Arend 1933:116-121, Lord 1960:146-147, and Mackie 1996:21-27, all of which contributed to the typology that I describe here.

that are particular to specific institutional contexts."[2] For example, we regularl[y] hear in an assembly that a speaker stands up to make his remarks, and when he i[s] finished speaking, he sits down again. Then another speaker stands up and make[s] the next speech.[3] Outside of assemblies, on the other hand, the physical behavio[r] or location of the speaker is rarely described by the narrator during an ongoin[g] conversational sequence. In fact, formulaic speech conclusions that describe i[n] specific terms[4] how an individual or group responds to the previous speech i[n] the middle of an ongoing conversation characterize formal group settings of a[ll] sorts. In informal settings, on the other hand, separate language to describe ho[w] the hearer(s) respond to a speech is rarer, particularly in conversations betwee[n] two individuals. When such language does appear, it tends to describe a gener[al] response like approval or obedience, and/or to fall at the end of the conversatio[n] rather than in the middle.[5] So, as a formal, "institutional" kind of group conversa[-] tion, assembly is characterized partly by the convention that a would-be speake[r] stands to begin his turn and sits down to end it.

The regular presence of this kind of behavioral marker for individual turn[s] and speakers helps to keep the sequences of speakers orderly in a large group suc[h] as an assembly, for the simple reason that the person standing up is easy to distin[-] guish from his fellows and to identify as the speaker. This prevents confusion abou[t] who is speaking among the members of the group. From the pragmatic standpoin[t] this procedure gives the participants in the conversation a formal, regular mecha[-] nism with which to participate in ordering the turns in the conversation.[6] Mor[e] generally, the combination of speech and action in a given turn contributes to th[e]

---

[2] Drew and Heritage 1992:22. Here they define an "institutional setting" as one in which "som[e] core goal, task, or identity" motivates some or all of the participants; what is considered legitimate contribution is limited by the context; and there are particular procedures that a[re] characteristic of the institution in question. All of these attributes fit the different kinds [of] activities discussed in Chapters 5 and 6.

Gumperz (in Gumperz and Hymes 1972) offers a similar way of conceptualizing contexts lik[e] assembly under the name "speech event": "members of all societies recognize certain commun[i-] cative routines which they view as distinct wholes, separate from other types of discourse, cha[r-] acterized by special rules of speech and nonverbal behavior and often distinguishable by clear[ly] recognizable opening and closing sequences . . . these units often carry special names" (17).

[3] See Arend 1933:116 and 119 and Mackie 1996:24-25 on standing formulas in an assembly type-scen[e]

[4] That is to say, not simply "obeyed" or "approved" or "fell silent," but some particular actio[n] that the hearer(s) did upon hearing a given speech. Formulaic language to describe listene[r] response in laments and games will be discussed in Chapter 6.

[5] Appendix IV provides a complete list of formulaic speech conclusions.

[6] Hutchby and Wooffitt 1998:38 discuss the active engagement of participants in organizing convers[a-] tional sequences; see passim for the specific techniques speakers use to do this. Drew and Heritag[e] 1992:27 note that non-speaking participants in institutional conversations have a more prominen[t] role in governing the orderly sequence of turns than they do in non-institutional contexts.

formal tone of assemblies. Indeed, the regular combination of speech and action to form a turn within a conversation—as opposed to a non-conversational context like battle—distinguishes formal from informal contexts.[7] Although the σκῆπτρον (staff) does have a role to play in conferring or recognizing authority to speak in an assembly or council, and often appears prominently in assembly scenes, there is no formulaic language that pertains to any aspect of how the σκῆπτρον behaves during an assembly. This suggests that whatever the function of the σκῆπτρον may be, it does not play a crucial role in ordering the turns in an assembly.

For example, between speeches in an assembly we often find the following formulaic sequence:

> ἤτοι ὅ γ᾽ ὣς εἰπὼν κατ᾽ ἄρ᾽ ἕζετο· τοῖσι δ᾽ ἀνέστη
> [next speaker's name, either in a single verse or with some kind
>   of descriptive elaboration that may run to several verses]
> ὅ σφιν ἐϋφρονέων ἀγορήσατο καὶ μετέειπεν

> He spoke thus and sat down again, and among them stood up
> [next speaker's name and description]
> He in kind intention toward all spoke out[8] and addressed them.

The full-verse speech introduction ὅ σφιν ἐϋφρονέων ἀγορήσατο καὶ μετέειπεν is found with four of the six occurrences of Ἤτοι ὅ γ᾽ ὣς εἰπὼν κατ᾽ ἄρ᾽ ἕζετο· τοῖσι δ᾽ ἀνέστη.[9] In between these two verses, a speaker is always named, but the amount of information given about that speaker varies. At a minimum, we learn the speaker's name and his patronymic or other descriptive information, as when Nestor speaks in an assembly at *Iliad* 2.76-78:[10]

> ἤτοι ὅ γ᾽ ὣς εἰπὼν κατ᾽ ἄρ᾽ ἕζετο, τοῖσι δ᾽ ἀνέστη
> Νέστωρ, ὅς ῥα Πύλοιο ἄναξ ἦν ἠμαθόεντος,
> ὅ σφιν ἐϋφρονέων ἀγορήσατο καὶ μετέειπεν·

> He spoke thus, and sat down again, and among them rose up
> Nestor, he who ruled as a king in sandy Pylos.
> He in kind intention toward all spoke out and addressed them:

---

[7] Levinson 1992:70 considers the combination of speech with action in particular patterns to be one characteristic of a ritual.

[8] Adapted from Lattimore. He always renders "stood forth" for ἀγορήσατο in this verse. In fact, as my examination of the conventions of assembly will show, this translation is only accurate in the context of an assembly scene, where speaking and standing are in fact equivalent.

[9] Two verses together at *Iliad* 1.68/73, 2.76/78, 7.365/67, and *Odyssey* 2.224/28; ἤτοι ὅ γ᾽ ὣς εἰπὼν κατ᾽ ἄρ᾽ ἕζετο· τοῖσι δ᾽ ἀνέστη without ὅ σφιν ἐϋφρονέων ἀγορήσατο καὶ μετέειπεν at *Iliad* 1.101, 7.354.

[10] These verses are part of a longer passage athetized by Aristarchus (2.76-83).

The length of the identifying passage varies, however, depending on various contextual and aesthetic factors that I will discuss in more detail below. The importance of sitting as one aspect of appropriate behavior in assembly clearly emerges later on in this assembly scene from *Iliad* 2, after Odysseus heads the Greek army off from their eager rush to launch their ships for home. Here the narrator characterizes Thersites as a misbehaving speaker partly by his failure to sit down when everyone else has been seated (211-214).

Turn sequences for speeches in assemblies take many different forms. Often there are several different kinds of sequences within a given assembly. Some of these sequences are also found in one-on-one conversations, such as the alternating A-B-A-B structure itself (in *Iliad* 1 between Achilles and Agamemnon, for example). We also find sequences in assemblies in which the identity of one participant changes while the basic alternating turn structure continues, such as A-B, B-C or A-B, C-A (both of which also appear in *Iliad* 1). Several assemblies—as well as other formal group contexts (on which see Chapter 6)—open with a series of successive speeches by individuals to the group who has assembled. The assembly of Greeks and Trojans in *Iliad* 3, for instance, consists entirely of speeches to the group by various individuals. This kind of sequence does not appear in individual contexts, of course, since it is structurally impossible where there are just two speakers. It is also absent from more informal group discussions that do not display the specific formal conventions associated with assemblies: in these informal discussions, at most two speakers address a group in succession before an individual replies to one of the speakers. This extended "A speaks to group, B speaks to group, C speaks to group" sequence is restricted to formal contexts—assemblies, athletic games, and laments—where the procedures and aims of the conversation have very specific conventions governing them that are connected to the particular type of context. Indeed, conversation analysis has shown that "talk for an overhearing audience" characterizes institutional settings.[11]

Thus, the range of sequences that appear in assemblies includes the sequences that we find in informal conversations (whether one-on-one or group), but we also find turn sequences and speech framing formulas that are specific to assemblies and that mark a particular sequence *as* an assembly. Related group conversation types do not have these features. These related conversation types include councils (a small group of leaders rather than a large group discussing a particular issue), embassies (as in the famous scene in *Iliad* 9, where a formal delegation of Greek leaders is sent to Achilles), and informal group conversations that are not summoned or convened in the manner of an

[11] Drew and Heritage 1992:27.

assembly. *Iliad* 9 presents an instructive overview of a related group of multi-party conversation types, including assembly, council, embassy, and informal group conversation on a topic of public interest. By surveying the structure of the various conversations in *Iliad* 9, we can get a clear sense of how these different kinds of conversation work and how they differ from assemblies before we go on to discuss assemblies that depart from the normal assembly patterns.[12]

Assembly Patterns vs. Other Kinds of Deliberative Groups: Iliad 9

Assembly

As Book 9 opens, the Greeks are stricken with grief and panic, and Agamemnon calls an assembly to discuss the situation. In formulaic language, he tells the heralds to summon an assembly (φοίτα κηρύκεσσι λιγυφθόγγοισι κελεύων [went among his heralds the clear-spoken and told them], 10),[13] and the heralds then call all the Greeks together (11-12). At the start of the assembly, the downcast Greeks are seated, while Agamemnon stands up (13-14). A famous simile comparing Agamemnon's tears to a spring running down a rock face emphasizes his consternation (14-16). The grief-stricken Agamemnon tells the assembled Greeks that they should return home, since Zeus has turned against them and they will not be able to conquer Troy (17-28).

This speech arouses further consternation among the Greeks in the assembly, who sit silent and dismayed until at length Diomedes responds to Agamemnon's proposal.[14]

> ὣς ἔφαθ', οἳ δ' ἄρα πάντες ἀκὴν ἐγένοντο σιωπῇ.
> δὴν δ' ἄνεῳ ἦσαν τετιηότες υἷες Ἀχαιῶν·
> ὀψὲ δὲ δὴ μετέειπε βοὴν ἀγαθὸς Διομήδης·
> "Ἀτρεΐδη σοὶ πρῶτα μαχήσομαι ἀφραδέοντι,
> ἦ θέμις ἐστὶν, ἄναξ, ἀγορῇ· σὺ δὲ μή τι χολωθῇς."

[12] Lohmann 1970: Chapter V provides a detailed study of the content and structure of speeches in Book 9 as an illustration both of principles of ring composition and of the unity of the *Iliad* (213). My analysis, in contrast, focuses primarily on the sequence and framing of the speeches rather than on their content.

[13] κηρύκεσσι λιγυφθόγγοισι appears five times in this position in the verse, always with a form of the verb κελεύω (order) at the end of it (*Iliad* 2.50, 442; 9.10; 23.39; *Odyssey* 2.6). Mackie 1996:23 notes that this formula is never used to describe Trojan assemblies.

[14] Zenodotus wrote a couplet for 23-31, cutting off the last part of Agamemnon's speech and providing a more regular speech frame between his remarks and Diomedes' response: ἤτοι ὅ γ' ὣς εἰπὼν κατ' ἄρ' ἕζετο θυμὸν ἀχεύων / τοῖσι δ' ἀνιστάμενος μετέφη κρατερὸς Διομήδης (having spoken thus, he sat down, grieving in his spirit / and strong Diomedes stood up and spoke among them). This reading has not been accepted by modern editors.

> So he spoke, and all of them stayed stricken to silence.
> For some time the sons of the Achaians said nothing in
>   sorrow;
> but at long last Diomedes of the great war cry addressed them:
> "Son of Atreus: I will be first to fight with your folly,
> as is my right, lord, in this assembly; then do not be angered."
>
> 9.29-33

The speech frame between Agamemnon's initial turn in the assembly and Diomedes' reply consists of two full-verse formulas (29 and 31) and one verse that appears twice, both times in *Iliad* 9 (30). This passage allows us to imagine several different ways to make the transition from Agamemnon's speech to Diomedes' that provide varying amounts of length and emphasis to this moment in the episode. The simplest and briefest way to get from Agamemnon's words to Diomedes' answer would be the single verse formula τοῖσι δὲ καὶ μετέειπε βοὴν ἀγαθὸς Διομήδης (and Diomedes of the great war cry addressed them). A slightly more drawn-out version could pair this verse with the formulaic speech conclusion "they were stricken to silence" (9.29). A more emphatic but still entirely formulaic speech frame here could be achieved with 9.29 followed directly by 9.31. This would not only mention the silence of the audience after Agamemnon finished speaking (29), but would also draw their silence out by delaying the next speech until a certain amount of time had passed without anyone taking the next turn (31). In the passage as printed by modern editors, however, verse 30 literally extends the period of silence in the narrative—and emphasizes the reason for it—by saying why the Greeks were silent. Thus, the speech frame in 9.29-31 emphasizes the depths of the Greeks' emotions by describing it at length. This sets off both the gravity of the situation and the speech of Diomedes, when he does eventually give it.

Diomedes speaks at some length when he criticizes Agamemnon's suggestion (32-49). Now the Greeks shout their acclaim for Diomedes' proposal (50-51), whereupon Nestor rises to take the next turn (52). While agreeing with the content of Diomedes' speech, Nestor tells him that he is too young to bring his argument to fruition (53-59). Then he directs the Greeks to eat the evening meal and take up their stations for night guard duty (60-78). This disposition meets with the approval of the group: ὣς ἔφαθ', οἳ δ' ἄρα τοῦ μάλα μὲν κλύον ἠδ ἐπίθοντο (So he spoke, and they listened hard to him, and obeyed him, 79) and the assembly ends.

So, this set of three speeches displays most of the typical features of assembly scenes as well as emphatic elaborations on some of them. The ssembly is convened in the usual manner, with herald, seated group, and tanding leader Agamemnon giving the first speech. Following this opening peech, the narrator follows a typical pattern for group conversations of all orts by describing the group's reaction to the speech they have just heard, ut at more length and in more detail than usual. All the language in this laboration appears elsewhere in the *Iliad*. Diomedes addresses his response o Agamemnon in particular rather than to the group at large. After he speaks, nce again the group reaction is described, but this time it is a positive and ot a negative response. Finally, Nestor ends the assembly first by replying to iomedes directly and then giving instructions based on his age and authority. formulaic speech concluding verse states that the group obeyed these nstructions, and the assembly ends. Two of three participants stand up to nark themselves as the taker of the next turn; all speeches are followed by a escription of how the assembled Greeks responded to what the speaker said.

Council

Jext, Agamemnon consults a council of Greek leaders (89-178). The men whom e summons are called γέροντας (elders, 89), even though Nestor is the only one η the group who is really old. Traditionally, of course, old men are the source of ise council, which probably explains the use of the word here to describe men ho for the most part are of fighting age. The council, unlike an assembly, takes lace after a feast in which all the participants in the council take part (89-92). 1oreover, the first person to speak is the oldest and most authoritative person resent (Nestor), not the person who convened the council (Agamemnon).[15] lthough the social environment and composition of the council differ from η assembly, the passage that begins Nestor's first speech to the council shows ome similarities to what we have seen in assemblies.

> αὐτὰρ ἐπεὶ πόσιος καὶ ἐδητύος ἐξ ἔρον ἔντο,
> τοῖς ὁ γέρων πάμπρωτος ὑφαίνειν ἤρχετο μῆτιν
> Νέστωρ, οὗ καὶ πρόσθεν ἀρίστη φαίνετο βουλή·
> ὅ σφιν ἐϋφρονέων ἀγορήσατο καὶ μετέειπεν·
> "Ἀτρεΐδη κύδιστε ἄναξ ἀνδρῶν Ἀγάμεμνον ..."

> But when they had put away their desire for eating and drinking,
> the aged man began to weave his counsel before them

---

5 Both of these elements, council linked to feast and Nestor as first speaker, also appear when Agamemnon consults a group of leaders in *Iliad* 2. See Mackie 1996:26-27 for a useful description of the council type.

first, Nestor, whose advice had shown best before this.
He in kind intention toward all spoke out and addressed them:
"Son of Atreus, most lordly and king of men, Agamemnon . . . "

9.92-96

9.92 is formulaic, often effecting a transition from feasting to conversation.[16] The introduction of Nestor looks very similar to the introduction of a first assembly speaker, with some interesting differences: 93 briefly mentions the first speaker; 94 describes and names this person at slightly more length; and 95 is a formulaic reply introduction that is common in assembly scenes.[17] Although the structure here closely resembles common speech frame structures in assemblies (mention speaker / provide some details about speaker / reply introductory verse), the content of the description of the speaker differs compared to what we have seen in an assembly scene. Nestor is described in verses 93-94 in terms of the advice he had given to the Greeks on previous occasions. This passage, indeed, forms an instructive contrast with the previously quoted speech frame for Nestor from *Iliad* 2, where Nestor speaks in an assembly in response to a previous speech (2.76-78).

> ἤτοι ὅ γ' ὣς εἰπὼν κατ' ἄρ' ἕζετο, τοῖσι δ' ἀνέστη
> Νέστωρ, ὅς ῥα Πύλοιο ἄναξ ἦν ἠμαθόεντος,
> ὅ σφιν ἐϋφρονέων ἀγορήσατο καὶ μετέειπεν·

He [Agamemnon] spoke thus, and sat down again, and among
   them rose up
Nestor, he who ruled as a king in sandy Pylos.
He in kind intention toward all stood forth and addressed them

This description of Nestor focuses on his kingship—on his authority, in other words—and not on the quality of his advice. In the council, moreover, in contrast to the assembly, there is no reference to Nestor sitting or standing. This reinforces the idea that sitting and standing in connection with speaking is restricted to the formal, institutional nature of the assembly.

Nestor advises Agamemnon to try to appease Achilles for his dishonor with gifts and supplication (103-113). A regular reply formula precedes Agamemnon's response (τὸν δ' αὖτε προσέειπεν ἄναξ ἀνδρῶν Ἀγαμέμνων [Then in turn the lord of men Agamemnon spoke to him], 114), in which he

---

[16] 21x in the Homeric poems (7x *Iliad*, 14x *Odyssey*).

[17] The formula, though common in assembly scenes, is not restricted to them. Krarup 1941:23 notes that the formula regularly appears in both assemblies and groups.

lists the gifts and other perquisites that he is willing to offer (115-161). Once again, the transition to the next speech (reply by Nestor) consists of a simple reply formula (τὸν δ' ἠμείβετ' ἔπειτα Γερήνιος ἱππότα Νέστωρ [Thereupon the Gerenian horseman Nestor answered him], 162). Now Nestor names the men who will go to Achilles to put this proposal before him (163-172). The council ends with the pleasure of all those present (173),[18] and preparations for sending the embassy begin (174-178).

In terms of the turn structure and who the speakers are, this council is simply a conversation of three turns between Nestor and Agamemnon about what to do next. However, the speech frames at the beginning and end of the exchange, which allude to the presence of a silent but attentive group of men among whom the conversation takes place, make the discussion into a council instead of a simple one-on-one conversation.[19] None of the other men present take part beyond responding with approval to the course of action that Nestor and Agamemnon decide to follow. The somewhat indistinct presence of these other Greek leaders and the setting of a council give greater authority and seriousness to the conversation than it would have had if it had occurred between Agamemnon and Nestor alone. However, the council scene lacks the formal physical markers of speech that occur in assembly scenes. Therefore, we may say that a council is less formal than an assembly in that it lacks physical markers of any kind for the speakers. At the same time, it is more formal than a simple conversation in that Agamemnon summons a group whose presence and response—even though they do not speak—plays a role in structuring the conversation. This group and its reactions give authority and legitimacy to the decisions of a council that do not characterize an informal one-on-one conversation.

Embassy

Next, the embassy of Odysseus, Ajax, and Phoenix, together with the two heralds Odius and Eurybates, sets out for the hut of Achilles to try to persuade him to return to the fighting.[20] The embassy, like the assembly, apparently

---

[18] The verse that appears here, ὣς φάτο, τοῖσι δὲ πᾶσιν ἑαδότα μῦθον ἔειπεν (so he spoke, and the word he spoke was pleasing to all of them), is repeated but not formulaic according to my definition: it appears at *Odyssey* 18.422 in addition to this passage. However, there is a formulaic verse ὣς ἔφατ' [X], τοῖσιν δ' ἐπιήνδανε μῦθος (so X spoke, and his word pleased all the rest of them, 7x *Odyssey*). So, the idea here occurs regularly even if the specific language is infrequent.
[19] Here again, the association of a listening group with institutional contexts is useful (Drew and Hutchinson 1992:27).
[20] This discussion will not touch on the controversy about the dual verb forms in this scene. I will be concerned below with who speaks, and in what order.

requires the presence of heralds. The structure of verse 170 strongly implie
that heralds were a normal part of an embassy (κηρύκων δ' Ὀδίος τε κα
Εὐρυβάτης ἄμ' ἑπέσθων [and of the heralds let Odios and Eurybates go wit
them], 170). The partitive genitive κηρύκων implies that *some* heralds wi
certainly be going on the embassy. Indeed, the presence of these professiona
messengers marks the embassy as something more than a simple visit by
few concerned comrades to their friend. In the embassy, unlike either th
assembly or the council, every Greek leader who travels to Achilles' tent als
speaks to him, and as we will see below, the turn sequences in the embass
differ from those that we saw in either the assembly or the council.

When the visitors arrive, Achilles welcomes them with food and drink, an
all share a sacrificial meal (185-221). When the group has taken its fill (222, th
same formulaic verse that preceded the council at 9.92), Odysseus makes th
first appeal of the embassy (225-306).[21] A common reply formula introduce
the long response of Achilles (307), in which he rejects not only the offer, bu
perhaps the entire code of values on which the offer is based (308-429).[22] Clearl
at least on this first attempt, the embassy has failed entirely. Just as the Greeks a
the assembly that opens Book 9 were aghast when they heard that Agamemno
wanted to return home (9.29-31), the delegation from Agamemnon to Achille
sits quiet and appalled after hearing Achilles' response to their message.

> ὣς ἔφαθ', οἱ δ' ἄρα πάντες ἀκὴν ἐγένοντο σιωπῇ
> μῦθον ἀγασσάμενοι· μάλα γὰρ κρατερῶς ἀπέειπεν·
> ὀψὲ δὲ δὴ μετέειπε γέρων ἱππηλάτα Φοῖνιξ
> δάκρυ' ἀναπρήσας· περὶ γὰρ δίε νηυσὶν Ἀχαιῶν·

> So he spoke, and all of them stayed stricken to silence
> in amazement at his words. He had spoken to them very
> strongly.
> But at long last Phoinix the aged horseman spoke out
> in a stormburst of tears, and fearing for the ships of the
> Achaians:

> 9.430-33

Here, as in the assembly earlier in Book 9, an additional verse follows th
formula "they were all silent" that describes the emotions of the siler

---

[21] Edwards 1987:90 provides a short but helpful overview of the three different speakers in th
scene and how their respective characters are reflected in their speeches.

[22] Analyzing the contents of this speech is not my concern here. For such an analysis, see Marti
1989:146-205, with bibliography.

listeners. The embassy is amazed (ἀγασσάμενοι, 431), while the group at the assembly was grief-stricken (τετιηότες, 9.30). The basic structure, though, is the same: A gave a speech; listening group was silent because they felt/were [emotion]; finally, B replied. Our passage, like 9.30, lengthens the related typical structure "A gave a speech / listening group was silent / finally, B replied." By doing so, it calls the attention of the audience of the poem to the effect of the speech on the listeners. Furthermore, in 433, our passage contains a second additional verse after the "finally B replied" formula that describes the emotions of B. This is a particularly interesting elaboration from the structural standpoint, because it is rare for anything to intervene between a formulaic speech introduction and the speech itself. When an audience heard the reply introductory formula in 432, that would set up a strong expectation of hearing the beginning of a speech in the next verse. When they heard yet more description of the speaker instead, that surprising departure from the normal structures of speech frames would strongly draw their attention to this pathetic description of Achilles' old friend Phoenix, afraid and in tears, as he begs Achilles to pity his struggling comrades.

Phoenix, the next speaker, fails just as much as Odysseus does. Once again, a common reply formula introduces Achilles' response (606). He tells Phoenix that he ought to hate Agamemnon and invites Phoenix to spend the night if he wants to (607-619). After he finishes speaking, he nods to Patroclus to make up Phoenix' bed as a signal for the others to leave (620-622). At this point Ajax briefly attempts to persuade Achilles, but he too fails. A common reply formula introduces Achilles' answer (643), in which he gives a message for Agamemnon that he will not return to the fighting unless Hector reaches the Greek ships (644-655). Now the business of the embassy has been concluded: each member of the delegation has presented Agamemnon's offer to Achilles, and each has failed to persuade him to accept it. He refuses each man in a manner consistent both with the relationship he has to each and with the content of the specific appeal he is refusing. Finally, Achilles has given the delegation a message to take back to Agamemnon. And so, they leave (656-657).

This embassy differs from an informal or general group conversation because it is accompanied by heralds, who also are necessary to call an assembly and convey official messages of various other kinds. The essential business of an embassy, to formally convey a message to someone, extends in this scene over three pairs of speeches.[23] In each pair, one of the three

---

[23] We can imagine a less drawn out version of the same type in which one person presented the message of the embassy, and received one reply in response.

leaders who participate in the embassy repeat Agamemnon's offers of gifts to Achilles, and he declines. Each individual tries to persuade Achilles using different strategies that are consistent with his own personality and his relationship to Achilles, and Achilles responds differently to each. Elaborations of various kinds describe either the emotional response of Achilles' audience to what he says (430-433) or Achilles' own behavioral signals to the embassy that their business is finished (620-622). Achilles himself, however, responds only through speech. The narrator never describes Achilles' emotion, in contrast to the picture of the dejected and concerned members of the embassy after Achilles' comprehensive rejection of Odysseus' first offer. Just as Achilles himself rejects his comrades' appeals, the way he is described shows that he remains unmoved by them.

Informal Group Conversation

Finally, when the embassy returns to the Greek camp, the Greeks are eager to ask about the success of the mission. This conversation displays none of the various formal characteristics that we have seen in connection with the assembly, the council, and the embassy. It is simply a conversation in which there are more than two participants. When Agamemnon asks what happened on the embassy (673-675), Odysseus relays the message that Achilles has given him (677-692). A common reply formula introduces his speech (676). Once again, the Greeks fall silent with dismay at a piece of bad news; as in the assembly that began Book 9, it is Diomedes who finally breaks their silence.

> ὣς ἔφαθ', οἳ δ' ἄρα πάντες ἀκὴν ἐγένοντο σιωπῇ
> μῦθον ἀγασσάμενοι· μάλα γὰρ κρατερῶς ἀγόρευσε.
> δὴν δ' ἄνεῳ ἦσαν τετιηότες υἷες Ἀχαιῶν·
> ὀψὲ δὲ δὴ μετέειπε βοὴν ἀγαθὸς Διομήδης·

> So he spoke, and all of them stayed stricken to silence
> in amazement at his words. He had spoken to them very
> strongly.
> For a long time the sons of the Achaians said nothing, in sorrow,
> but at long last Diomedes of the great war cry spoke to them:

> 9.693-96[24]

---

[24] 694 was omitted by Zenodotus and athetized by Aristophanes and Aristarchus. Nevertheless it is printed in the major modern editions of the *Iliad* (although with editorial disclaimers of various kinds in van Thiel and West).

All the descriptive language here focuses on the grief and distress of the listeners rather than on the feelings of the next speaker.[25] Diomedes criticizes Agamemnon for sending the embassy in the first place and advises that the Greeks go to bed but be ready to fight at dawn (697-709). This proposal meets with the group's approval (710), and they retire for the night. In this conversation, although several people are present and make speeches, there are no references to any of the accompaniments of formal group conversations (heralds or the posture of the speaker when he makes his remarks). Hence, this exchange should be considered simply a group of people talking rather than as one of the more formal types of group conversation.[26]

In *Iliad* 9, which as a whole lacks any single or successive speeches, we have seen four different kinds of group conversations. The assembly is the most formal of these, since there are specific procedures not only for mustering an assembly but also for the marking of new turns while the assembly is in progress. A council is a more informal, smaller group summoned by a leader to give him advice. Although the turn structure of the speeches in a council scene may be the same as in a one-on-one conversation, the speech frames make it clear that the group who is present has a necessary if silent role to play in the scene. An embassy, in which a group of people and heralds formally takes a message from one person to another, is marked as formal by the presence of the heralds. In the last scene in book 9, although three different people speak, there are no formal markings of any kind, and we should view this sequence simply as a conversation in more than two people participate.

In any kind of group scene, whether formal or informal, the narrator often tells us how the listeners respond to a particular speech. In contrast to a conversation between two people, where the next speaker is always the same as the listener, in a group context the next speech alone is often not enough to tell us clearly how the audience responded to a speech. As we have seen, all of these group scenes feature such descriptions. Several of the listener responses that appear in Book 9 include silence, and follow the general pattern "A spoke; the group was silent; finally, B responded." Within

---

[25] Contrast 9.430-433, which describes the emotions of both the listeners as a group and specifically of Phoenix, the next speaker.

[26] Donlan 1979:64, in contrast, describes this conversation as a βουλή (council), but for the reasons I have given above, I disagree with this assertion.

this general pattern, different variations occur that distinguish each period of silence from the others and give each silent group its own individuality. Against the background of the typical patterns that characterize these different kinds of group conversations, we will now look at the structure, function, and effects of variations from these patterns.

Variations on Typical Assembly Patterns: Iliad 1 and 19

A number of assemblies take place in the *Iliad* and *Odyssey*. Within the *Iliad*, as Mackie notes, the Trojan assemblies are few in comparison to those of the Greeks, and they do not follow the same patterns of organization as the Greek ones do.[27] In the *Odyssey*, the only assembly takes place in Book 2.[28] The primary function of this meeting is to give a public, community "aspect to what has hitherto been presented as a domestic misfortune."[29] In fact, only the Greeks in the *Iliad* consistently hold assemblies that follow a specific pattern. At the same time, the noteworthy variations from typical assembly patterns also involve only the Greeks in the *Iliad*. These two phenomena are related: in an environment where a pattern has been strongly established, it can be effectively exploited as a recognizable point for the audience from which to depart in unusual directions.

The famous pair of assemblies in *Iliad* 1 and *Iliad* 19 both display unusual features of length and of turn structure, although they are unusual in different ways that are suited to their respective contexts. Both of these scenes exploit typical features of assembly scenes in order to depict the central concern of both assemblies, namely the disastrous conflict between Agamemnon and Achilles. Through the individual words and phrases that appear in regular formulaic verses and the contexts in which common turn structures appear (or fail to appear when we might expect to see them), Achilles is consistently depicted as the more sympathetic and less blameworthy of the two parties. Moreover, the development of the quarrel and its resolution in the context of assemblies forcefully emphasizes the considerable impact their disagreement has on the Greeks as a group. The specific nature and effect of the departures from common patterns in these two scenes will be the subject of the remainder of this chapter.

---

[27] Mackie 1996 passim, especially 21-26.
[28] See Nagler 1974:119-130 on the conventions of "convening" in the *Odyssey*.
[29] West in Heubeck et al. 1990a:128.

These two assemblies give us some of our most extensive glimpses of the character of Agamemnon. Although he is certainly a traditional character who appears in various Troy stories, he does not have a decisive role in the *Iliad* beyond his disastrous interactions with Achilles. Put another way, his situation does not change from the beginning of the *Iliad* to the end, in spite of how often he appears in the poem.[30] Agamemnon in the *Iliad* does the things that he does elsewhere in the traditional story cycle of the Trojan War (rule the Achaeans, dispute with Achilles).[31] However, in the particular telling that we find in the *Iliad*, his character is drawn in a certain way so as to create an effective foil for Achilles.[32] The interactions of Agamemnon and Achilles frequently take place in the public venue of the formal assembly. The public domain in which the two men regularly meet emphasizes the broader ramifications that their dispute has for all of the Greeks. It also brings to the fore the larger, abstract questions that the poem explores about the nature of power and what happens when the person in charge is not the best of the group.[33]

Although no critic has unmixed admiration for Agamemnon's behavior in these meetings (or for Achilles', for that matter), different readers entertain very different feelings about the culpability or justification of the behavior of each man both independently and in relation to his adversary in the quarrel. This seems to depend to some extent on individual feelings about what degree of allegiance is owed to one's official superior simply because he is one's superior, and on the other hand what the proper behavior of a superior toward his subordinates should be. Thus, some scholars are sympathetic to Agamemnon's attempts to exert control over a warrior superior in prowess to himself and are correspondingly critical of Achilles' failures of respect toward Agamemnon.[34] Meanwhile, others have seen Agamemnon as vain, arrogant, and overly concerned with his own possessions and standing,[35] and have validated Achilles' anger at the way he is treated by Agamemnon.[36] These

---

[30] See Kullmann 1960:91-93 for a concise and useful discussion of the traditions related to the character of Agamemnon. I am particularly indebted to this discussion for the idea that Agamemnon's fate does not change over the course of the *Iliad* even though he has many appearances in it.

[31] Also in the *Cypria*, although the relationship of the two disputes is unclear (Kullmann 1960:92).

[32] I find Whitman's reading of Agamemnon's character particularly effective in being both acute and sympathetic to the character's flaws and shortcomings (1958 passim, especially 161-164).

[33] Donlan 1979 treats this question, much more successfully for *Iliad* 1 than for the reconciliation in *Iliad* 19. He frames the problem underlying the quarrel partly in terms of the relationship between position authority (possessed by Agamemnon) and standing authority (of Achilles).

[34] E.g. Bowra 1930:15-19. Redfield 1994:12-15 offers an interpretation of Achilles' character that focuses on how its shortcomings interact badly with the character of Agamemnon.

[35] Whitman (supra note 32); Griffin 1980:70-71.

[36] Nagy 1979:227.

conflicting interpretations of the validity, so to speak, of each man's behavior for the most part are not based on what the narrator says. Instead, they rely mainly on the speeches of the characters themselves and on the interpreter's own opinions about what transpires.

Such analyses have focused primarily on the origins of the μῆνις in Book 1. The reconciliation of Agamemnon and Achilles in Book 19, although fascinating in its own right, has received much less attention. Some scholars who have studied it have done so merely in order to lambaste it supposed failings.[37] Others, more productively, have illustrated (if briefly) the points of similarity between Books 1 and 19.[38] Overall, the assembly in Book 19 has not received as much notice as one might expect, either on its own or its relationship to the assembly in Book 1. The following analysis will examine the conversational structures in the two assemblies in Books 1 and 19 as a window into the narrator's views about the behavior of Agamemnon and Achilles. I will argue that typical conversational structures are consistently manipulated in each of these two scenes so as to direct sympathy toward Achilles. In each scene, different kinds of variations from typical conversational patterns create specific effects that are appropriate to the different situations in the two assemblies. Moreover, the effects that are created in Book 19 have much greater impact if Book 19 is contrasted with Book 1.

Iliad 1

The Greek assembly called by Achilles to discuss the plague they are experiencing is the first conversation of any real length in the *Iliad*. It introduces the audience to Agamemnon and Achilles, or at least to their characters as portrayed in this telling of the story. In addition, the speeches and events in this assembly bring forward many of the key motifs that will recur throughout the poem. Both the order of turns in this episode and the formulaic speech frames between turns display unusual patterns for an assembly. Not only is this the longest assembly scene in the Homeric epic in terms of both the number of verses and the number of turns, but the bulk of it consists of a one-on-one conversation between Agamemnon and

---

[37] Page 1966:313-314 offers a particularly enthusiastic statement of this position.

[38] Lohmann 1970:173-174 discusses the points of thematic and narrative similarity among the four assemblies in *Iliad* 1, 2, 9 and 19, where he asserts that the first and last and the second and third, respectively, form ringed pairs within this progression.

Achilles. The assembly contains a total of 13 speeches, not counting the three speeches between Achilles and Athena. Of these, six speeches—nearly half—are between Agamemnon and Achilles. Although an alternating A-B-A-B sequence often forms a *part* of an assembly, nowhere else does an assembly serve essentially as a public forum for a showdown between two individuals. This unusual turn sequence in a formal, public context strongly emphasize both the personal conflict that lies behind this quarrel and the terrible effect it has on the Greeks as a whole. In other words, the combination of the turn sequence (characteristic of informal conversation) and the public context of this assembly juxtaposes private and public just as the quarrel itself does.

The speech frames in this assembly, particularly those associated with Achilles, depict his increasing anger and alienation in a crescendo that grows steadily as the scene progresses. The narrator accomplishes this through variations in single verse reply introductions and through expanded speech introductions and conclusions. Achilles, too, contributes to this crescendo effect: he uses three different full-verse vocatives for Agamemnon in three succeeding speeches addressed to the king, each of which is more abusive than the last.[39] These various methods of depicting emotion and giving emphasis all reach their highest point at the speech in which Achilles swears by the σκῆπτρον that the Greeks will miss him when he refuses to fight (1.225-244).[40] Moreover, speech introductions and conclusions on the one hand, and Achilles' vocatives on the other, complement one another in forming this crescendo over the course of the assembly. The order of turns and the formulaic speech frames in the assembly work together as a unit, primarily within the context of formulaic language and common turn sequences, to create a vivid and arresting picture of the strife between Achilles and Agamemnon building throughout this scene. Furthermore, the assembly setting for this clash of individuals highlights the public importance of the dispute.[41] We will now turn to the specifics of this process.

---

[39] For a detailed discussion of these vocatives, see Friedrich 2002.

[40] Combellack 1948:211 notes that only here in all the speeches in this assembly does anyone use the σκῆπτρον, and Achilles asks for it to be handed to him.

[41] Donlan 1979:57-59 casts this quarrel between Achilles and Agamemnon as a clash over authority, which is certainly an important aspect of their disagreement.

Chapter Five

Opening First of all, a chart of the sequence of turns and speakers in thi[s] assembly may prove useful as a prelude and framework for the following discussion. Underlines mark significant shifts in the tone or sequence of th[e] conversation.

turn	speaker	addressee	notes on speech framing language
1	Achilles	group	
2	Calchas	group	
3	Calchas	Calchas	
4	Calchas	Achilles	
5	Agamemnon	Calchas	first speech by Agamemnon; preceded by speech frame describing his anger
6	Achilles	Agamemnon	unique <u>vocative</u> for Agamemnon
7	Agamemnon	Achilles	
8	Achilles	Agamemnon	unique <u>vocative</u>
9	Agamemnon	Achilles	
10	Achilles	Athena	interlude between Achilles and Athena begins
11	Athena	Achilles	
12	Achilles	Athena	
13	Achilles	Agamemnon	return to Achilles and Agamemnon; unique <u>vocative</u>; after speech, Achilles throws down σκῆπτρον
14	Nestor	group	
15	Agamemnon	Nestor	
16	Achilles	Agamemnon	Achilles interrupts

Before Agamemnon enters the conversation at the fifth turn, no participants in the assembly are angry and no unusual speech framing language appears. Achilles stands, as is usual for the initial speaker in an assembly, thereby beginning both the assembly and his own turn as a speaker. Achilles' first speech is couched as a speech to the whole camp, although when he starts talking, he directly addresses Agamemnon in particular.

> τοῖσι δ' <u>ἀνιστάμενος μετέφη</u> πόδας ὠκὺς Ἀχιλλεύς·
> "Ἀτρεΐδη ... "

Achilleus of the swift feet <u>stood up among them and spoke forth:</u>
"Son of Atreus ... "

1.58-59

Although Calchas is worried initially (74-83), and his first speech is preceded by a multi-verse passage that describes him (69-72), no one is angry or upset in the first four turns of the conversation and the speech frames are correspondingly formulaic and regular throughout. This generally calm tone changes when Agamemnon begins to take part in the conversation.

Crescendo   Calchas' news infuriates Agamemnon, who now speaks for the first time. Before his speech here, the formulaic speech conclusion "X sat down, Y stood up" prefaces a description of Agamemnon as the next speaker. A speech introduction for him follows this description. The same formulaic pattern precedes Calchas' first speech. Whereas the earlier descriptive passage explained Calchas' mantic qualifications and accomplishments, this one describes the anger of Agamemnon (description indented for clarity).

> ἤτοι ὅ γ' ὣς εἰπὼν κατ' ἄρ' ἕζετο· τοῖσι δ' ἀνέστη
>   ἥρως Ἀτρεΐδης εὐρὺ κρείων Ἀγαμέμνων
>   ἀχνύμενος· μένεος δὲ μέγα φρένες ἀμφιμέλαιναι
>   πίμπλαντ', ὄσσε δέ οἱ πυρὶ λαμπετόωντι ἔϊκτην·
> Κάλχαντα πρώτιστα κάκ' ὀσσόμενος προσέειπε·
> "μάντι κακῶν οὐ πώ ποτέ μοι τὸ κρήγυον εἶπας ... "

He spoke thus and sat down again, and among them stood up
   Atreus' son the hero wide-ruling Agamemnon
   raging, the heart within filled black to the brim with anger
   from beneath, but his two eyes showed like fire in their blazing.
First of all he eyed Kalchas bitterly and spoke to him:
"Seer of evil: never yet have you told me a good thing ... "

1.101-106

The picture of Agamemnon in verses 103-104 focuses on his anger, which is portrayed at some length in strong and vivid language. Normally, in contrast, a personal description in this kind of formulaic context represents consistent aspects of the character's personality in a sort of elongated version of an epithet, rather than depicting his or her emotions at this particular moment of speaking (analogous to a context-specific participle). Hence, both the length of the description and the specific language it contains contribute to the emphasis it confers on this speech and on Agamemnon as he makes it.

In fact, the formulaic verse ὅ σφιν ἐϋφρονέων ἀγορήσατο καὶ μετέειπεν (He in kind intention toward all stood forth and addressed them) could appear instead of verse 105 to introduce Agamemnon's first speech. It is not necessary to provide Calchas' name in the speech frame here, because his identity as Agamemnon's addressee is clear from the vocative that Agamemnon uses at the beginning of verse 106. Moreover, ὅ σφιν ἐϋφρονέων ἀγορήσατο καὶ μετέειπεν can precede an address to one person in spite of the pronoun σφιν (them).[42] Verse 105 as it stands extends Agamemnon's wrath right up to the moment he begins speaking. Not only that, it casts Agamemnon in a bad light by focusing his wrath specifically on Calchas, the very person whose safety Achilles has previously guaranteed and whose power as a seer has been described at length. This speech framing passage as a whole makes clear that it was Agamemnon, not Achilles, who first became angry in the quarrel that leads to the events narrated in the *Iliad*. The content of Agamemnon's reply to Calchas reinforces this picture of his rage: he not only abuses Calchas, but also institutes a rather unappealing contrast between his wife Clytemnestra and Chryseis; he concludes by demanding a replacement for Chryseis without delay (106-120).

Even now Achilles is not angry, or at least not entirely or uncontrollably angry. The reply introduction preceding his speech to Agamemnon says that he simply "answered": τὸν δ᾽ ἠμείβετ᾽ ἔπειτα ποδάρκης δῖος Ἀχιλλεύς (then in answer again spoke brilliant swift-footed Achilleus, 121). On the other hand, his own words to Agamemnon show that he is not completely unaffected by what the king has said. He begins his speech with the first of his three successive unique vocatives for Agamemnon. This vocative, while not explicitly angry or abusive, subtly plays with the conventions and expectations associated with full-verse vocatives.[43]

---

[42] Compare its appearance at *Iliad* 1.73 followed by a vocative address to Achilles alone in 74.

[43] Friedrich 2002 is excellent on the appropriateness of the language in the three unique vocatives Achilles uses for Agamemnon in this scene and how they contribute to the sense of escalation in the conversation between the two.

Ἀτρεΐδη κύδιστε, φιλοκτεανώτατε πάντων

Son of Atreus, most lordly, eagerest for gain of all men[44]

1.122

Unlike Achilles' vocatives for Agamemnon later in the assembly, this verse is not *unambiguously* abusive: a desire for possessions is not necessarily bad. Beyond the unusual but ambiguous opening, Achilles' speech shows no particular animus toward Agamemnon personally: he says that the prizes have already been distributed, and so none is available to give to Agamemnon, but that he will be amply compensated when Troy is sacked (123-129).

Agamemnon does not appear angry at the opening of his reply. The repy introduction (τὸν δ' ἀπαμειβόμενος προσέφη κρείων Ἀγαμέμνων [then in answer again spoke powerful Agamemnon], 130) could include μεγ' ὀχθήσας (deeply disturbed) but does not. Moreover, Agamemnon addresses Achilles at the beginning of his speech as ἀγαθός (good, 131) and as θεοείκελ' Ἀχιλλεῦ (godlike Achilleus, 131). However, he accuses Achilles of deception (κλέπτε νόῳ [strive to cheat], 132) in a dismissive and presumptuous manner. Agamemnon states without apology that he will take someone else's prize if one is not given to him voluntarily, thereby reminding Achilles and the rest of the Greeks that he has the social standing among them to enforce his will in a way that Achilles does not (135-139). Finally, he gives orders that preparations be made for the return of Chryseis to her father (140-147).

Thus, this first pair of speeches involving Achilles and Agamemnon (turns 5 and 6, 122-147) shows both heroes feeling somewhat angry, or occasionally angry. The speech frames reinforce the language of the speeches themselves in depicting the two as disagreeing, but not yet entirely or irresistibly overcome with bad feeling. Agamemnon, unlike Achilles, has indeed shown great anger (103-120), but toward Calchas rather than Achilles. This pair establishes the beginning of an A-B-A-B structure. The appearance of an extended A-B-A-B turn sequence within a group conversational context, like the escalation of angry language in the speech frames and vocatives, occurs gradually rather than abruptly: at no point are normal rules of turn-taking violated. Instead, Agamemnon and Achilles simply take over the preponderance of the turns in a social context where this is not normally what happens. This pattern, as we will see, is in marked contrast to the assembly in Book 19, which achieves its effects by entirely avoiding one-on-one conversational sequences where

---

[44] Adapted from Lattimore.

an audience would expect them rather than by putting them into a context where they would not normally occur.

Achilles' next speech marks a noticeable increase in the tension between him and Agamemnon. Several factors contribute to this. First, the reply introduction for his reply to Agamemnon's assertion of his right to take another man's prize is τὸν δ' ἄρ' <u>ὑπόδρα ἰδὼν</u> προσέφη πόδας ὠκὺς Ἀχιλλεύς (Then <u>looking darkly</u> at him Achilleus of the swift feet spoke, 148).[45] The full-verse vocative that begins this speech (149) bears no resemblance to the courteous full-verse vocatives that are normally used for Agamemnon by other characters. Indeed, it makes no pretense of being anything but abusive.[46]

> ὦ μοι, ἀναιδείην ἐπιειμένε, κερδαλεόφρον
>
> O wrapped in shamelessness, with your mind forever
> on profit

This address begins with the interjection ὦ μοι (translated here simply as "O"), which in a full-verse vocative may give a tone of angry grief to abuse.[47] ἀναιδείην (shamelessness) is unambiguously disapproving; κερδαλεόφρον (with your mind forever on profit) is a more clearly negative but only slightly more frequently attested relative of φιλοκτεανώτατε (eagerest for gain of all men).[48] When compared to Achilles' previous vocative for Agamemnon, this one clearly shows the increase in his displeasure. He expresses the same idea of "out for gain" as in his previous address with a more clearly derogatory word. To strengthen the tone of disapproval, he adds the interjection ὦ μοι (generally associated with grief or disapproval, or both) and the unambiguously critical ἀναιδείην. On its own, Achilles' address here clearly indicates that he is angry with Agamemnon. If we consider the verse alongside his preceding full-verse vocative for Agamemnon, the change in tone gives additional depth and

---

[45] For an analysis of escalation in the speeches themselves, see Lohmann 1970:131-133.

[46] Friedrich 2002:3 attributes "indignation" to this verse.

[47] E.g. in Agamemnon's rebuke of Diomedes in Book 4, which begins ὦ μοι, Τυδέος υἱὲ δαΐφρονος ἱπποδάμοιο (Ah me, son of Tydeus, that daring breaker of horses, 370), on which see Chapter 4 (17-19); see also Menelaus' abuse of the Greeks at Iliad 7.96: <u>ὦ μοι</u>, ἀπειλητῆρες, Ἀχαιΐδες, οὐκέτ᾿ Ἀχαιοί (<u>Ah me!</u> You brave in words, you women, not men, of Achaia!).

[48] LSJ defines it as "greedy of gain" in the Iliad and "crafty" in the much later author Oppian (2nd c. CE), although Kirk 1985 ad loc. interprets it as "crafty" rather than "avaricious" (while noting the existence of both meanings). Leaf 1971 ad loc. says "greedy, or perhaps crafty." Holoka 1983:2n2 argues in favor of "greedy" rather than "crafty" and gives a useful overview of opinions on the meaning of these epithets. This range of interpretations suggests that the audience is meant to understand both meanings simultaneously, which would be consistent with Achilles' exceptional rhetorical skill.

shape to the scene as a whole. This progression in the language of Achilles' vocatives for Agamemnon also demonstrates his unique skill as a manipulator of language.

The speech itself, like the reply introduction and full-verse vocative that begin it, shows a noticeable increase in Achilles' anger. On the most basic level, it is much longer than Achilles' previous speech, and longer than any speech he has uttered thus far in the poem. He reminds Agamemnon that he did not come to Troy because he had any personal grievance against the Trojans (150-157), but rather for the sake of Agamemnon's τιμή (158-159). He very effectively neutralizes the normally positive associations of this word by positioning it between two clearly and emphatically negative vocatives for Agamemnon:

> ἀλλὰ σοί, ὦ μέγ' ἀναιδές, ἅμ' ἑσπόμεθ' ὄφρα σὺ χαίρῃς,
> τιμὴν ἀρνύμενοι Μενελάῳ σοί τε, κυνῶπα,
> πρὸς Τρώων·

> but for your sake,
> o great shamelessness, we followed, to do you favour,
> you with the dog's eyes, to win your honour and Menelaos'
> from the Trojans.

1.158-160

ὦ μέγ' ἀναιδές (o great shamelessness, 158) repeats the root in ἀναιδείην (149), with which Achilles abused Agamemnon in his previous speech. κυνῶπα (you with the dog's eyes, 159), which appears only here in extant Greek literature, has the same meaning as κυνῶπις (bitch [my translation]), a word used in the Homeric epics to refer particularly to shameless *women*.[49] Abusive as these expressions are, only here in the speech does Achilles attack Agamemnon personally. For the remainder of his remarks, he shows his displeasure without such attacks: he bemoans the possible seizure of his hard-won prize (160-168) and threatens to return home rather than remain without honor at Troy (169-171).

Agamemnon, apparently unmoved by this (τὸν δ' ἠμείβετ' ἔπειτα ἄναξ ἀνδρῶν Ἀγαμέμνων [then answered him in turn the lord of men Agamemnon], 172), replies in a speech whose very lack of emotion in the face of Achilles'

---

[49] The unique κυνῶπα may be due to the need to coin a male version of the word κυνῶπις (whose various Homeric occurrences are cited, with the name of the woman modified, in LSJ), but it seems likely that the word would nevertheless gain additional power as an insult by its clear connection to a female form of abuse.

rage slights Achilles' grounds for anger against him.[50] Agamemnon does not directly address Achilles with a vocative, the only time in the assembly that he does not acknowledge the person to whom he speaks by mentioning their name or title in the first verse of his speech. Instead he addresses Achilles with an imperative that conveys both disrespect for and lack of interest in him φεῦγε μάλ', εἴ τοι θυμὸς ἐπέσσυται (run away by all means if your heart drives you, 173). Consistent with this disrespectful beginning, in the body of the speech, Agamemnon repeatedly belittles Achilles both by discounting Achilles' strength and by repeatedly asserting his own intention to take Briseis away from Achilles, thereby asserting his own superiority over Achilles (178-187). This speech, predictably, makes Achilles so angry that he considers killing Agamemnon, but Athena appears and dissuades him from doing so (188-222).

Up to this point, there have been four turns between Achilles and Calchas; one transitional turn in which Agamemnon replies to Calchas; and four turns between Achilles and Agamemnon. Although the interlude with Athena interrupts Achilles' conversation with Agamemnon, it does not disrupt the turn sequence of the assembly within which it takes place: it is now Achilles' turn to reply, but he addresses Athena instead of Agamemnon (202-205).[51] He wants to know why she has come; she tells him not to physically attack Agamemnon (207-214); and he agrees, although he reasserts his anger against Agamemnon (216-218). He returns to the assembly with his anger unabated and Athena goes back to Olympus.

Climax   Now the turn structure becomes slightly irregular in such a way as to emphasize Achilles' anger. He has the last speech in the sequence of three turns with Athena (turn 12, 216-218), and then he takes the turn to reply to Agamemnon (turn 13, 225-244) that was left hanging when Athena appeared after turn 9. Although he is taking a turn that is rightly his, because there are two conversations going on at once, he has two turns in succession. This is just one of several ways in which the scene as a whole and Achilles' anger in particular come to a peak at this point. The speech introduction and full verse vocative that begin Achilles' delayed reply to Agamemnon show that if anything, Achilles is angrier than ever following the intervention of Athena. For this speech, the introduction, opening vocative, and conclusion combine

---

[50] Kirk 1985 ad 172-177 describes him, quite aptly, as "both sarcastic and complacent."

[51] See Pope 1960:121 for a brief discussion of Athena's participation in Achilles' mental processes at this point. Interestingly, he connects her actions here to her deception of Hector in Book 22, arguing that in both cases she acts as an externalized representation of a man's inner thoughts.

to produce the most intense, vivid, and highly developed portrait of the rage of Achilles to be found in the assembly in Book 1.

First, a couplet rather than a single verse introduces Achilles' reply to Agamemnon after Athena returns to Olympus.

> Πηλεΐδης δ' ἐξαῦτις ἀταρτηροῖς ἐπέεσσιν
> Ἀτρεΐδην προσέειπε, καὶ οὔ πω λῆγε χόλοιο·

> But Peleus' son once again in words of derision
> spoke to Atreides, and did not yet let go of his anger:

1.223-24

This is the only multi-verse speech introduction for Achilles in the assembly. This brings to mind the description of the angry Agamemnon before his first speaking turn in the assembly (101-105). In our passage, the multi-verse speech introduction magnifies and emphasizes anger at the moment when Achilles is angrier than at any other time in the assembly. This is conveyed through the word ἀταρτηροῖς (a rare word whose meaning is debated, 223)[52] and the clause οὔ πω λῆγε χόλοιο (did not yet let go of his anger, 224). When we compare the representations of Achilles and of Agamemnon at their angriest, it is noteworthy that—even at the height of Achilles' anger—the narrator describes his rage at less length than is given earlier to the fury of Agamemnon, for which preceding events give less justification.

Moreover, the description of Agamemnon's anger appears before a reply, where a single verse reply formula or the "X sat down, Y stood up and spoke" sequence is the most common way to make a transition from one speech to the next. So, the description of the strength of Agamemnon's anger stands out more than it would after a passage of narrative. In contrast, the two-verse introduction to Achilles' speech follows a passage of narrative. Contextual factors, such as the need to clarify the identity of both speaker and addressee given the disrupted turn structure, partly explain the expansion here. However, narrative clarity cannot fully explain the use of two verses instead of one, because a single verse containing the names of both Achilles and Agamemnon can be constructed along the lines of attested Homeric verses.

> *δὴ τότ' ἄρ' Ἀτρεΐδην προσεφώνεε δῖος Ἀχιλλεύς·

> Then great Achilles spoke a word to the son of Atreus

---

[52] For the word's rarity, see LSJ; on its dubious meaning, see Chantraine 1990.

This would be comparable to both *Iliad* 9.201 (αἶψα δὲ Πάτροκλον προσεφώνεεν ἐγγὺς ἐόντα [at once he called over to Patroklos who was not far from him], where Achilles is the unnamed speaker) and *Odyssey* 8.381 (δὴ τότ' ἄρ' Ἀλκίνοον προσεφώνεε δῖος Ὀδυσσεύς [Then great Odysseus spoke a word to Alkinoös]). Thus, although this couplet stands out less than the description of the angry Agamemnon, it nevertheless effectively uses length to draw the attention of the audience to Achilles' anger.

Like the passage preceding the speech, Achilles' own words show that he is now angrier at Agamemnon than he has been at any time before. Although the oath that forms the central section of his speech is nominally addressed to the whole group, his initial vocative is not to "Agamemnon and the other Greeks," for which a formulaic full-verse vocative is available. The formula Ἀτρεΐδη τε καὶ ἄλλοι ἀριστῆες Παναχαιοί [son of Atreus, and you other great men of all the Achaians] appears three times in the *Iliad*,[53] once used by Achilles himself. Achilles' real anger here is with Agamemnon alone, and the opening of his speech declaring his refusal to fight shows this.

> οἰνοβαρές, κυνὸς ὄμματ' ἔχων, κραδίην δ' ἐλάφοιο
>
> You wine sack, with a dog's eyes, with a deer's heart

1.225

This language abuses Agamemnon's manliness and courage in the strongest language of any of the three abusive full-verse vocatives that Achilles has employed in his confrontation with the king. οἰνοβαρές (wine sack) is another rare word used only here in the *Iliad*.[54] It is not obvious whether the insult is simply that Agamemnon is a drunk or whether it implies some additional slur, although the literal meaning is clear.[55] The phrase κυνὸς ὄμματ' ἔχων (with a dog's eyes) develops the same idea as the insult at 159 (κυνῶπα), but at greater length. This is similar to the evolution of the ambiguous φιλοκτεανώτατε (most eager for profit, 122) to the more obviously negative κερδαλεόφρον (with your mind forever on profit, 149) from the first to the second vocative that Achilles uses for Agamemnon. Moreover, it shows Achilles using length for additional emphasis in a manner that evokes the technique of the narrator. Only here is the word ἔλαφος (deer) applied to a person—elsewhere it refers

---

[53] 7.327, 7.385, 23.236 (where the speaker is Achilles).

[54] For a list of the unusually high number of words used only by Achilles, see the appendix in Griffin 1986 (57); see also Martin 1989, Chapter 4.

[55] See Friedrich 2002:5-6 on the appropriateness of οἰνοβαρές as a term of abuse for Agamemnon.

only to a literal deer, and it appears primarily in similes.[56] Achilles is able to use vocatives inventively to demonstrate his deep displeasure and disgust with Agamemnon. His ability to do this, and to create different vocatives of increasing ferocity and abusiveness, clearly demonstrate the exceptional language ability of his character.

In the body of the speech, Achilles continues to abuse Agamemnon personally, as he did with the vocative in 225. He impugns Agamemnon's courage (226-228) and he calls him more names (δημοβόρος βασιλεύς [king who feed on your people], 231). Finally he swears by the σκῆπτρον which governs the Greek assembly (234-239) that the Greeks will miss him when he does not fight and that Agamemnon will regret that he did not honor Achilles, ὅ τ' ἄριστον Ἀχαιῶν (the best of the Achaians, 244).[57] With the description of the σκῆπτρον, which as a whole is unenjambed with the surrounding speech, Achilles once again uses a technique that the narrator uses too: at a crucial moment in his speech—his oath about leaving the fighting—he includes an unenjambed digression to focus attention on the key moment by lengthening it. Indeed, the description has something in common with a simile, insofar as it has a connection to an aspect of the main thread of the narrative but is developed at some length for its own sake.[58]

Moreover, the σκῆπτρον figures in the narrator's description of Achilles immediately after his speech. Achilles does not merely sit down, as several characters have already done when they finished speaking. Instead, he expresses the depth of his disgust with the whole proceeding by first throwing the σκῆπτρον to the ground and then sitting down.

> ὣς φάτο Πηλεΐδης, ποτὶ δὲ σκῆπτρον βάλε γαίη
> χρυσείοις ἥλοισι πεπαρμένον, ἕζετο δ' αὐτός·
> Ἀτρεΐδης δ' ἑτέρωθεν ἐμήνιε· τοῖσι δὲ Νέστωρ
> ἡδυεπὴς ἀνόρουσε, λιγὺς Πυλίων ἀγορητής . . .

Thus spoke Peleus' son and dashed to the ground the sceptre studded with golden nails, and sat down again. But Atreides

---

[56] This may be seen as another example of Achilles' ability to use language in the same way that the narrator does, particularly if considered in combination with the very interesting and attractive suggestion of de Jong 1985 that the characters of Homeric epic do not know about the similes (263).

[57] Repeatedly using the future indicative (ἵξεται, 240; δυνήσεαι, 241; ἀμύξεις, 243) to show that this is not a possible but a definite event.

[58] Kirk 1985 *ad* 234-39.

> raged still on the other side, and between them Nestor
> the fair-spoken rose up, the lucid speaker of Pylos . . .

1.245-248

This passage also mentions Agamemnon, using the rare verb μηνίω to describe his anger.[59] This portrait of the two angry men at once, rather than one at a time as heretofore, gives extra vividness and point to the strong emotions of Agamemnon and Achilles just before Nestor intervenes. A much less emphatic and hence less effective, passage can be imagined here which would achieve the same narrative result (that is, "Achilles sat down, and Nestor got up"):

> ἤτοι ὅ γ᾽ ὣς εἰπὼν κατ᾽ ἄρ᾽ ἕζετο· τοῖσι δ᾽ ἀνέστη
> Νέστωρ ἡδυεπὴς, ὁ λιγὺς Πυλίων ἀγορητής[60]

> He spoke thus and sat down again, and among them stood up
> Nestor the fair-spoken, the lucid speaker of Pylos

1.245-247 as it stands adds detail and emphasis to the essentially formulaic idea of "X spoke and sat down, and Y got up to speak."

Various types of crescendos—of turn structure and of language—build to a climax as Achilles swears his oath. The turn structure itself has two speeches by Achilles in a row, although they are not "successive" in that they are not part of the same conversation; both the introduction and conclusion to the speech are longer and more elaborate than what is available from formulaic language; Achilles uses a more strongly abusive vocative for Agamemnon than any of the ones that he uses in other speeches in this assembly; and he gives further prominence and vividness to his speech by describing and swearing by the σκῆπτρον that he afterwards throws to the ground. All these effects work together to create an effective climax here. Throughout the crescendo leading to this moment, the structure and language of the conversation suggests that although both Agamemnon and Achilles are angry, Agamemnon is the more unjustified of the two in his behavior.

After this, Nestor gives the longest speech in the assembly in his attempt to patch things up between the arguing heroes (254-284) Agamemnon, depicted unemotionally in the reply introduction for him (τὸν

---

[59] Translated by Lattimore as "raged," this verb has the same root as the first word of the *Iliad* (μῆνις, "anger, wrath"). The simple verb appears eight times in the Homeric epics, but according to Cunliffe is used only here of outward display of anger. Nagy 1979:73-74 notes that μῆνις, when applied to mortals rather than gods, is restricted to Achilles' anger toward Agamemnon.

[60] This passage is an invention of mine cobbled together from phrases that appear in 1.247-248.

δ' ἀπαμειβόμενος προσέφη κρείων Ἀγαμέμνων [then in answer again spoke powerful Agamemnon], 285), ignores the part of the advice that applies to himself and begins to agree with Nestor in advising Achilles to moderate his behavior. He has just asked a question (291) when Achilles bursts in with the final speech in the assembly.

> τὸν δ' ἄρ' ὑποβλήδην ἠμείβετο δῖος Ἀχιλλεύς
> "ἦ γάρ κεν δειλός τε καὶ οὐτιδανὸς καλεοίμην ... "

> Then interrupting brilliant Achilleus answered him:[61]
> "So must I be called of no account and a coward ... "

> 1.292-293

Here, Achilles is so beside himself that he breaks the turn sequence by interrupting and leaving a question without an answer, very unusual events in Homeric epic.

Just as Achilles disrupts the turn sequence, the language in this verse departs from normal patterns. First, and most obvious, ὑποβλήδην (interrupting) is a *hapax legomenon*. In addition to the unique word ὑποβλήδην, the very common verb ἠμείβετο (took an answering turn) appears extremely rarely in this position in the verse. Normally, as we saw in the Introduction, it is found in the formula ἠμείβετ' ἔπειτα (then took an answering turn) which usually appears in the second half of the first foot through the first half of the third foot of a dactylic hexameter. The use of a formula for the speaker that begins at the bucolic diaeresis, which is rare in the context of speech introductions although common elsewhere, is related to this peculiar placement of the verb of answering. Of course δῖος Ἀχιλλεύς is a perfectly normal and regular Homeric formula,[62] but its function here as the entire noun-epithet formula in a speech introductory verse is anomalous. Finally, Achilles does not address Agamemnon at all, although he has always done so (if with increasing hostility) in his previous speeches. Instead, he refers to Agamemnon simply with second-person pronouns (e.g. σοί [you]; 294, 296, 299). Taken together, these unusual features of the turn sequence and speech introduction, as well as Achilles' own omission of a vocative "introduction" for his speech, show a man who is not only angry, but now also alienated from the very conventions of speech in the Homeric epics. Similarly, in the speech itself, Achilles refuses

---

[61] Adapted from Lattimore.
[62] 34x alone, 55x including its appearances as part of the longer formula ποδάρκης δῖος Ἀχιλλεύς (brilliant swift-footed Achilles).

to accept or obey further orders from Agamemnon (293-296), removing himself from the social structure that governs the Greeks as a group. Achilles' rejection of the usual conventions of conversation parallels and reinforces the end of the assembly[63] and Achilles' alienation from his fellow Greeks. He now physically marks out this alienation by physically leaving the Greek camp, an action that drives the events in the remainder of the *Iliad*.

This conversation between Achilles and Agamemnon, although it takes place in the formal public context of an assembly, displays many of the patterns of an extended conversation between two individuals. Normally assembly scenes do not include long interchanges between just two characters, so the very existence of such a conversation here attracts attention and interest. It emphasizes the private aspects of this quarrel, while the assembly context reminds us of the significant ramifications for the Greeks that the quarrel will have. This represents a surprising, pointed, and effective juxtaposition of two different typical patterns that do not normally appear together to create a specific effect for a particular context. Before Agamemnon enters the conversation, the speeches and surrounding languages are all calm. Agamemnon, however, is angry as soon as he begins to speak, and after that Achilles becomes angry also. The manipulation of speech-related formulas and of turn sequences during the rest of the conversation very effectively depict the increasing anger of Achilles, his unusually skilled use of the conventional naming patterns used by Homeric characters in order to abuse Agamemnon and the insulting disregard that Agamemnon shows toward him. Comparing the representations of Agamemnon and Achilles suggests that although both are angry and at fault, Agamemnon is more to blame for his anger than Achilles is for his.

Book 19, too, casts more blame on Agamemnon than on Achilles for the consequences of their quarrel, and it does this partly by its manipulation of conversation-related patterns. However, it strives for different effects, and accordingly handles typical conversational patterns differently. The picture of Agamemnon and of Achilles that emerges in the assembly of reconciliation in Book 19 can and should be appreciated on its own, but it gains a deeper resonance as well as a larger role in shaping the overall story if it is compared to the assembly in Book 1.

---

[63] Marked in a different way by the dual verb ἀνστήτην (stood up, 305), parallel to the beginning of the assembly with the verse τοῖσι δ' ἀνιστάμενος προσέφη ποδὰς ὠκὺς Ἀχιλλεύς [Achilleus of the swift feet stood up among them and spoke forth], 1.58). The dual form at 305 emphasizes that although this scene is ostensibly a group assembly, in fact only two people are really involved.

Iliad 19

After the assembly in Book 1, Achilles and Agamemnon do not meet again until the assembly reuniting the Greek forces in Book 19. In Book 19, in contrast to Book 1, the turn structure departs from usual assembly patterns not by containing a surprisingly large amount of alternating A-B-A-B conversation, but by not containing any. In fact, there is no speech in this assembly in which the speaker replies to the same person who addressed him. There is no other conversation in the poems that goes on as long as this assembly (seven turns) without a single pair of speeches featuring the same two people as speaker and addressee. Agamemnon consistently fails to address Achilles directly,[64] while Achilles repeatedly addresses Agamemnon using the honorific vocative that he so memorably refuses to use in the assembly in Book 1. This unusual turn structure suggests that although this assembly marks a reconciliation between Agamemnon and Achilles in their public personas and reintegrates Achilles into the Greek fighting force, the two men do not achieve any significant rapprochement on a personal level.[65] The structure and content of the conversation clearly imply that while Achilles is acting appropriately, Agamemnon behaves badly in not responding more directly and substantively to Achilles' apology.

Achilles begins the assembly by directly addressing Agamemnon (Ἀτρεΐδη, 56), in contrast to his final speech in the assembly in Book 1 when he was so angry and distraught that he did not address Agamemnon by name. He expresses regret for their conflict and the pain it has caused (59-66) and declares in so many words that he is no longer angry (νῦν δ' ἤτοι μὲν ἐγὼ παύω χόλον [now I am making an end of my anger, 67]). The Greeks respond to his speech with joy, but Agamemnon does not directly acknowledge Achilles in any way.

> ὣς ἔφαθ', οἱ δ' ἐχάρησαν ἐϋκνήμιδες Ἀχαιοὶ
> <u>μῆνιν</u> ἀπειπόντος μεγαθύμου Πηλεΐονος.
> τοῖσι δὲ καὶ μετέειπε ἄναξ ἀνδρῶν Ἀγαμέμνων
> αὐτόθεν ἐξ ἕδρης, οὐδ' ἐν μέσσοισιν ἀναστάς·
> "ὦ φίλοι ἥρωες Δαναοί, θεράποντες Ἄρηος ... "

> He spoke, and the strong-greaved Achaians were pleasured
>   to hear him

---

[64] Taplin 1992:206 notes this and suggests that "he [Agamemnon] is more interested in the picture he presents to the *laos* as a whole than to Achilleus."
[65] Here I differ from Donlan 1979, who says that in this assembly, "all the sore points in the Quarrel are smoothed over" (62).

> and how the great-hearted son of Peleus unsaid his <u>anger.</u>
> Now among them spoke forth the lord of men Agamemnon
> from the place where he was sitting, and did not stand up
>   among them:
> "Fighting men and friends, o Danaans, henchmen of Ares ... "
>
> 19.74-78

19.75, in adding enjambment with 74, features the thematically important word μῆνις (anger) in the verse-initial position to specify that the Greeks rejoiced because Achilles forswore his wrath. Yet 19.74 alone would achieve the same basic effect, namely "X spoke, and the Y's were happy." It is clear from Achilles' speech that the Greeks must be happy because he has renounced his quarrel with Agamemnon and returned to them. The additional verse stating this fact between Achilles' speech and Agamemnon's answer does not clarify the situation, but rather emphasizes what Achilles' feelings now are, particularly in light of the strong verse-initial position of the word μῆνις.

The next two verses (76-77) are a long-standing crux in the text and Agamemnon's demeanor as he delivers his speech is the subject of some disagreement, starting from the scholiasts and continuing on to the present day. The important question is, what is the position from which Agamemnon delivers his speech? I will suggest that if one accepts the reading of 19.76-77 as given above (which is what modern editors have done), the conventions of proper behavior in assembly, the bad personal relations between Agamemnon and Achilles, and the blame that is ascribed to Agamemnon for his behavior throughout this assembly explain quite clearly what has generally been seen as a problematic and difficult passage.

The major lines of interpretation are as follows. Zendotus rejected the reading I have given, and solved the supposed problem that these verses present by reading, in place of 76-77, τοῖσι δ' ἀνιστάμενος μετέφη κρείων Ἀγαμέμνων (standing up, strong Agamemnon addressed them; my translation).[66] If Agamemnon is indeed seated here, some ancient scholia on 19.77 suggest that he cannot stand because of the pain of his wound (διὰ τὴν τοῦ τραύματος ἀλγηδόνα, A). Others say that he remains seated to prevent his words from being heard on the grounds that they are humble (ταπεινοί, bT).

---

[66] Bolling 1925:185-186 is almost alone among modern interpreters Zenodotus in condemning the verse as I have given it.

Yet a third theory, held by various commentators,[67] argues that Agamemnon does stand up, but that he does not move from his standing position into the middle of the assembly. The suggestion that Agamemnon intends to be humble has not won noticeable adherents among modern critics, who have tended toward either the view of the A scholion on 19.77 or the idea that Agamemnon is standing, but not in the usual place for an assembly speaker. I suggest that none of these is correct, but that the literal meaning of the verses is meant: Agamemnon makes a speech from a sitting position. The problem is not the language, but previous approaches to making sense of it.

This apparently inexplicable behavior becomes intelligible, and in fact quite consistent with Agamemnon's character and the negative attitude that the narrator takes toward him, if we take into account typical assembly patterns and Agamemnon's behavior to Achilles. While Agamemnon's wound would give him an *excuse* for remaining seated, it seems probable that if he wished to, it would not be beyond his powers to rise to his feet and lean on his spear for support (if necessary) while speaking, since he was able to walk to the place of assembly (51-53). Given the importance of standing while speaking in an assembly, physical discomfort alone does not seem adequate to explain this lapse.[68] As for the idea that Agamemnon stands, but not in the center of the group, this seems improbable in light of the formulas that describe assembly behavior. The typical pattern, as we have seen, is that a speaker stands up, makes his speech, and sits down again. Moving into the center of the assembly space is not a regular element in this conversational type. Hence, it would be very surprising if the narrator were to try to make a point here by departing from an aspect of the assembly setting that is not firmly established as a typical part of such a scene. Indeed, if the narrator were to attempt such an effect, the audience would not have the means to understand it. Standing per se, not standing in a particular spot, marks someone as a speaker in an assembly. Therefore someone who is behaving unlike a usual assembly speaker would sit. This is what the Greek seems to say, in fact, if the reader is not feeling hounded by problems of interpretation to try to avoid such a conclusion. From the standpoint of formulas and the immediate context, then, the most plausible reading of 19.76-77 is that Agamemnon remains seated in his place while making his speech of apology.

---

[67] For a list of them see Edwards 1991:243. This view also appears in a bT scholion.

[68] This is the position of Arend 1933, who notes (118) that Agamemnon is capable of conducting an expiatory sacrifice in spite of his wound.

This action also makes sense in terms of Agamemnon's character and his interactions with Achilles earlier in the story. We can see it from Agamemnon's own point of view as one of several ways in which he shows disrespect for Achilles while ostensibly apologizing for his own role in their disastrous quarrel. For the audience, Agamemnon's actions here depict him in an unsympathetic light. In the speech itself, Agamemnon belittles or ignores Achilles on various levels, although Achilles' courteous address to him in the previous speech would seem to call for a more direct and self-deprecating response.[69] First, Agamemnon never directly acknowledges Achilles. Instead, he addresses his words to the Greeks as a group (ὦ φίλοι ἥρωες Δαναοί, θεράποντες Ἄρηος [fighting men and friends, o Danaans, henchmen of Ares, 78]). In addition, he does not respond to anything that Achilles said. Instead, he tells the story of the birth of Hercules as an explanation or justification for his own behavior (86-144). Unlike Achilles, he does not repudiate his earlier behavior; instead, he says that he is not responsible for it (86-87; 137-138).

Finally, after this lengthy story, Agamemnon does address Achilles after a fashion (139-144). That is to say, he uses second person singular verb forms in reference to an unnamed person who must be Achilles, but he never addresses Achilles by name.

> "ἀλλ' ὄρσευ πόλεμόνδε, καὶ ἄλλους ὄρνυθι λαούς.
> δῶρα δ' ἐγὼν ὅδε πάντα παρασχέμεν, ὅσσά τοι ἐλθὼν
> χθιζὸς ἐνὶ κλισίῃσιν ὑπέσχετο δῖος Ὀδυσσεύς.
> εἰ δ' ἐθέλεις, ἐπίμεινον ἐπειγόμενός περ Ἄρηος,
> δῶρα δέ τοι θεράποντες ἐμῆς παρὰ νηὸς ἑλόντες
> οἴσουσ', ὄφρα ἴδηαι ὅ τοι μενοεικέα δώσω."

> "Rise up, then, to the fighting and rouse the rest of
>   the people.
> Here am I, to give you all those gifts, as many
> as brilliant Odysseus yesterday went to your shelter
>   and promised.
> Or if you will, hold back, though you lean hard into the
>   battle,

---

[69] Indeed, Goffman 1981:199 asserts that someone who has made a mistake or a faux pas of this sort offers both reparations for the material harm that one's behavior has caused [here, the goods offered to Achilles] and "ritualistic acts" that repair the "expressive implications" of one's misbehavior [an apology]. Agamemnon shirks responsibility for both of these kinds of corrective action.

while my followers take the gifts from my ship and
bring them
to you, so that you may see what I give to comfort
your spirit."

n this passage, the bulk of Agamemnon's references to Achilles are imperative
'erb forms (ὄρσευ 'rise up', ὄρνυθι 'rouse', and ἐπίμεινον 'hold back'). One is
ιn indicative verb (ἐθέλεις 'you will'); two are dative pronouns (τοι '[to] you,
/our'). None are personal references of any kind. [70] Agamemnon's speaking
tyle here seems like a very minimal tip to a server in a restaurant: by giving
he bare minimum, one makes it clear that the small size of the token of respect
s deliberate rather than an oversight. Given that Agamemnon consistently
gnores Achilles in his speech, he may remain seated while uttering it for the
ame reason: his failure to stand up when speaking provides a non-verbal
ιnalogue for his studied avoidance of Achilles.[71] Thus, Agamemnon avoids
Achilles by addressing the Greeks as a group and by *not* addressing Achilles
ιimself by name, and he downplays the importance of the occasion (and thus
)f Achilles' anger towards him) by choosing to remain seated while making a
peech in an assembly. His wound gives him a plausible excuse for doing so,
)ut not a sufficient one. Formulas and typical patterns for assembly speakers
n the Homeric epics strongly suggest that what Agamemnon does here is to
·it rather than to stand in the same spot that he had been sitting. If we view
.9.76-77 against the background of the typical assembly, we need resort
ιeither to emendation nor to involved explanations to be able to understand
he verses. They make cogent sense as they are.

Agamemnon's vocative address to all the Greeks at verse 78 bears further
·tudy, aside from its obvious disrespect for and avoidance of Achilles, because
here are two different full-verse vocative formulas for the Greeks as a group.
)ne stresses their wisdom, while the one used here describes their valor
ιn battle.

---

[70] As Lohmann notes (1970:76n133), this passage is the only time in the assembly that
Agamemnon speaks directly to Achilles, indeed the only time he does so in the entire *Iliad* after
1.187. On the other hand, Achilles consistently uses the honorific vocative for Agamemnon. In
fact, as Lohmann goes on to say, Agamemnon never addresses Achilles in the poem after this
point—Achilles addresses him twice in Book 23 without receiving an answer.

[71] Austin 1975 (126 and 272n37) has a similar overall view of Agamemnon's behavior and defends
19.77 as printed by Allen. While Achilles recognizes his own responsibility, Austin writes,
Agamemnon "offers only an ersatz apology which attempts to camouflage more than it reveals"
(126). In the accompanying endnote, Austin continues, "I, for one, would be sorry to lose the line
since it harmonizes so well with the self-pitying and paranoid character of Agamemnon as shown
through the poem, and particularly here in his speech of flagrant self-exculpation" (272).

ὦ φίλοι, Ἀργείων ἡγήτορες ἠδὲ μέδοντες[72]

Friends, who are leaders of the Argives and keep
their counsel

ὦ φίλοι ἥρωες Δαναοί, θεράποντες Ἀρῆος[73]

Fighting men and friends, o Danaans, henchmen of Ares

Each of these verses appears in both battle scenes and assemblies and is spoken
by various characters. There is no clear and obvious pattern that explains why
one verse is used rather than the other in every case.

However, an interesting contrast does emerge between the two charac-
ters who use both expressions, namely Nestor and Agamemnon. Agamemnon
uses ὦ φίλοι, Ἀργείων ἡγήτορες ἠδὲ μέδοντες once in a scene explicitly said
to be an assembly (9.17). However, in Book 11 (11.276), Ἀργείων ἡγήτορες
ἠδὲ μέδοντες begins a speech urging the Greeks to protect the ships during
one of the most desperate moments in the battle. When Agamemnon calls
the Greeks ἥρωες Δαναοί, θεράποντες Ἀρῆος, on the other hand, he is either
urging them to leave the battle entirely and go home (2.110) or in our passage
he is speaking in a council whose purpose is to reconcile him and Achilles. In
other words, he uses these two vocatives with at best indifferent relevance
to the context in which he is speaking. Nestor, who unlike Agamemnon is a
skilled speaker,[74] uses his words to better effect. When he emphasizes the wise
counsel of the Greeks by addressing them as ὦ φίλοι, Ἀργείων ἡγήτορες ἠδὲ
μέδοντες (friends, who are leaders of the Argives and keep their counsel), he is
speaking in the assembly at which Agamemnon's dream is discussed (2.79) or
asking about the results of the night foray of Odysseus and Diomedes (10.533).
If he calls the Greeks warriors, he means what he says: at 6.67, he urges the
Greeks to fight in such stirring language that the Trojans nearly retreat behind
the city walls in fear (6.72-74).

Returning now to the assembly, when Achilles answers Agamemnon's
ill-worded apology, he begins his remarks with the regular, honorific full
verse vocative that he so conspicuously refused to utter in Book 1. Moreover
his promise to return to the fighting is introduced with τὸν δ' ἀπαμειβόμενο
προσέφη πόδας ὠκὺς Ἀχιλλεύς (Then in answer to him spoke Achilleu

---

[72] *Iliad* 2.79, 9.17, 10.533, 11.276, 11.587, 17.248, 22.378, 23.457.
[73] *Iliad* 2.110, 6.67, 15.733, 19.78.
[74] Martin 1989:101-119 discusses the speaking styles of these two characters in detail.

f the swift feet, 145), which could include a participle expressing anger or displeasure but does not. Achilles addresses Agamemnon as Ἀτρεΐδη κύδιστε, ἄναξ ἀνδρῶν Ἀγαμέμνον at 146 (son of Atreus, most lordly and king of men, Agamemnon). Then he briefly says that he is uninterested in the offered gifts and simply wishes to return to the fighting (147-153).

Odysseus rather than Agamemnon replies to this proposal. He gives directions for how Agamemnon is to appease Achilles, telling him to swear an oath that he never slept with Briseis and to give Achilles a festive meal (156-183). Now Agamemnon answers Odysseus as the previous speaker, directly and politely addressing him, which he did not do in the case of Achilles:

> τὸν δ᾽ αὖτε προσέειπεν ἄναξ ἀνδρῶν Ἀγαμέμνων
> "χαίρω σεῦ, Λαερτιάδη, τὸν μῦθον ἀκούσας . . . "

> Then in turn the lord of men Agamemnon answered him:
> "Hearing what you have said, son of Laertes, I am pleased
>   with you . . . "

19.184-185

In the body of Agamemnon's speech, he agrees to Odysseus' proposal and refers to Achilles, but in the third person and with an imperative (αὐτὰρ Ἀχιλλεὺς / μιμνέτω [Let Achilleus / stay here], 188-189). He avoids Achilles in another way by making it Odysseus' job to select the prizes for Achilles 192-195).

As if to emphasize Agamemnon's omission in repeatedly failing to respond to Achilles although Achilles has spoken to him, when Achilles agrees to the arrangements proposed, he again addresses Agamemnon using the most common formulaic full-verse vocative for him rather than saying anything abusive (19.199).[75] Even now Agamemnon will not speak to him. The final speaker in the assembly is Odysseus, who begins his "reply" to Achilles with a full-verse vocative: ὦ Ἀχιλεῦ, Πηλῆος υἱέ, μέγα φέρτατ᾽ Ἀχαιῶν [son of Peleus, Achilleus, far greatest of the Achaians], 216.[76] If the verse is read μέγα φέρτατ᾽ Ἀχαιῶν (far

---

[75] Whallon 1961:105 interprets this use of the "full reverential title" for Agamemnon in light of his indifference to anything but resuming the battle. Friedrich 2002 views Achilles' vocatives for Agamemnon in Book 19 in the context of the unusual ones in Book 1: "the resumption of the typical formula for the address signals that Achilleus' quarrel with Agamemnon is over" (5).

[76] The individual words that make up this verse are the subject of some disagreement in the MSS., but there is certainly a full-verse vocative here, which is the main point at issue.

greatest of the Achaians) and not φίλτατ᾽ (dearest) with some manuscripts,[77] it is possible to imagine Agamemnon refusing to address Achilles throughout this scene simply in order to avoid calling him μέγα φέρτατ᾽ Ἀχαιῶν.[78]

In stark contrast to Achilles' courteous behavior toward Agamemnon throughout this assembly scene, the king not only does not use a vocative in addressing Achilles, he never addresses him at all.[79] Achilles takes the initiative in apologizing for his own anger, and repeatedly addresses Agamemnon with an honorific full-verse vocative. This vocative gains additional point if it is compared with his creativity in devising ever-more abusive vocatives for Agamemnon in the assembly in Book 1. Agamemnon, on the other hand, makes a minimal and indirect apology, which he makes even more disrespectful by saying it from a sitting position. At the same time, he delegates most of the responsibility for implementing his reparations, and he refuses to speak directly to the man he has offended. Odysseus has the role of intermediary, replying to Achilles' speeches to Agamemnon when Agamemnon himself does not do so. Despite the surface reconciliation achieved here, the two men never meet on a friendly footing after this: in Agamemnon's one other appearance in the remainder of the poem (during the funeral games for Patroclus), Achilles twice addresses Agamemnon without receiving an answer. The structure of the conversation and the behavior of Achilles and Agamemnon make it quite clear that Agamemnon is to be blamed for his ungracious failure to take responsibility for his own behavior, while Achilles has acted appropriately and generously.

Conclusions

The formal assembly has several characteristics that distinguish it from other, less formal modes of group conversation. The assembly is summoned by heralds. Speakers mark their turns by standing up when they start to talk and sitting down when they finish. This performs the pragmatic function of maintaining an orderly turn sequence. In addition, this prescribed behavioral component of speaking gives a more formal air to the assembly that is lacking in descriptions of related but less formal modes of group conversation such as councils. Turn structures of the speeches themselves are fluid and encompass

---

[77] This is the reading of Allen's i family and of one other MS.

[78] We may remember at this point that Agamemnon tells Achilles in Book 1 (186) that Agamemnon himself is the stronger of the two.

[79] Lohmann 1970:76n133 notes the contrast between Achilles' consistent direct address to Agamemnon and Agamemnon's consistent avoidance of Achilles, which he describes as "circle" (Zirkel) effect.

a wide range of alternatives, some of which are found in other conversational contexts and some of which are restricted to assemblies. All of these features are consistent with linguistic work on conversations in institutional settings.

This basic pattern applies to the Greek assemblies in the *Iliad*. Trojan assemblies are rare and do not follow the same kinds of patterns as Greek ones do. There is only one assembly in the *Odyssey*, where the assembly is not a commonly represented way of conducting public business. Two Greek assemblies in the *Iliad*, both with crucial importance for the story as a whole, display unusual features of both length and turn structure. By using the assembly form in particular to set off the beginning and the (ostensible) end of the quarrel between Agamemnon and Achilles, the narrator effectively demonstrates the significance of this quarrel not only for Achilles and Agamemnon, but also for all the men whom they lead.

The specific effects created differ in the two assemblies. In Book 1, the origin of the quarrel between Agamemnon and Achilles, the public forum of an assembly becomes essentially a showdown between two individuals, insofar as the majority of the turns in a long assembly take the form of a one-on-one conversation. Normally, assemblies include a wider range of participants and avoid prolonged exchanges between just two people. This confrontation steadily escalates, leading up to a climactic speech by Achilles in which he refuses to fight any more on behalf of the Greeks. Close examination of the speech frames in this conversation demonstrates that although the narrator depicts both characters as at fault for their anger, Agamemnon is consistently described in such a way as to make him more at fault. This directs the sympathy of the audience toward Achilles. Achilles himself demonstrates unique command of the typical forms of speech among Homeric heroes—and plays an important role in creating the escalation that shapes the scene—when he invents a series of unique abusive vocatives for Agamemnon that become more and more creative and more and more abusive.

In Book 19, typical conversation patterns are manipulated in a different way to create a different effect. There are *no* exchanges in which a speaker answers the same person who spoke to him. In particular, Agamemnon refuses to address Achilles throughout the assembly in which he and Achilles are supposedly reconciled. Achilles, in contrast, repeatedly gives Agamemnon the respectful full-verse vocative that he refused to use in Book 1. This, too, directs the audience's sympathy toward Achilles, again through a subtle manipulation of the typical patterns of conversation and of assembly in particular. By taking account such these patterns when we interpret this assembly, we can make sense of a crux that has troubled commentators since Hellenistic times.

6

GROUP CONTEXTS II—ATHLETIC GAMES, LAMENTS

T HIS CHAPTER DIFFERS somewhat from the previous chapters in its organization and goals. Chapters 1-5 discussed various forms of lengthening and elaboration that occur in connection with repeating conversational types (one-on-one conversations, single speeches, and formal assemblies). The conversational types that were studied in these chapters all occur sufficiently often that it is clear what the repeated, "normal" pattern is for each. As a result, it is equally clear when elaborations or variations occur. The purpose of this chapter, on the other hand, is to explore the similarities between the typical form of the assembly and the typical patterns for other contexts in which formal group conversations take place, namely athletic competitions and laments. These two types, unlike assemblies or the other kinds of conversations that we have discussed so far, are not repeating modes of conversation. In fact, we have just one clear example of each (both in the *Iliad*) in which a series of speeches occurs that is long enough to constitute a sequence of speeches.[1] One example does not constitute a clear or a repeated "type" for either games or laments. For this reason, it is not possible to talk about expansions or elaborations on a basic conversational *type* for either of these genres of group speech.[2] Without a set of several examples, it is not possible to identify these patterns with certainty as types, just as it is usually not possible to identify rarely occurring phrases as formulas. In the case of both types and

---

[1] The game or competition is certainly a type (see Scott 1997:216-218 for a description of it), but conversation is not a regular element of it. Hence, although the competition is a type, it is not a conversational type.

[2] Alexiou 1974 constructs a typology of lament based on repeated examples of laments in the Homeric epics, which I will draw on extensively in the discussion that follows. However, for lament specifically as a conversational genre, we have only *Iliad* 24 in which several laments appear in succession.

ormulas, one or a few examples of what seems to be a regular pattern may well be a Homeric type or a formula, but it is simply not possible to be sure.

However, this does not mean that the games in *Iliad* 23 and the series of aments for Hector in *Iliad* 24 have nothing to tell us of wider relevance for he Homeric poems. Regular patterns do characterize the funeral games for ?atroclus in *Iliad* 23 and the series of formal laments for Hector in *Iliad* 24. [hese patterns are clear and regular enough that the genres of speech they :haracterize can be called "types," as long as we use that term with the under-standing that these types are not as firmly and clearly established as the kinds of conversations discussed in Chapters 1-5. They repay study as conversational sequences in spite of the fact that the sequences do not repeat with the same order and social context elsewhere in the Homeric poems. The similarities between assembly scenes and these two very different types of group activi-ties give us a new understanding of the underlying unity of different kinds of ormal group contexts that involve speech. The same similarities that unite assembly, games, and lament, moreover, have been documented by linguistic research in connection with institutional settings of conversation,[3] suggesting that the conventions depicted for these activities in Homeric poetry reflect at east to some extent a social reality,

Athletic Games

will argue in this chapter that all formal conversational contexts in Homeric epic use behavior in some way as a regular accompaniment to speech. This regular link between behavior and speech, in fact, marks them as formal modes of conversation. In an assembly, as we have seen in Chapter 5, formulaic language is available to describe the most consistent aspects of such a scene. First, the gathering is assembled by heralds. The group as a whole is seated when an assembly begins. While the assembly is in progress, ndividual speakers usually stand up to mark the start of their turn as a speaker, and sit down to end their turn. Such behavioral accompaniments to speech regulate the order of turns and the progression from one speaker to the next, both for the internal audience in the poem (who needs to know when someone else can speak, or when they should respond) and also for the external audience. An assembly may also be formally dissolved. Thus, an assembly as a whole has a formal beginning (the group is called by a leader

---

[3] In particular Drew and Heritage 1992 passim.

and sits down), is clearly regulated turn by turn while it is in progress (by sitting and standing), and is dissolved when it is over. Athletic games display the same features of overall organization: they take place within a broad context of rules and order. This allows conflict in the games themselves to unfold within firm and reliable limits of stability. The basic idea that funeral games represent a more orderly, less dangerous replay of battle is not a new one.[4] This discussion extends that connection to the structure and function of conversation in funeral games, which combine elements of both the battlefield and the assembly. This allows us to see the interaction of contest and order at the level of both the structure of the type and the social interactions that take place during athletic games.

Individual speeches, turns, and turn sequences in athletic games have important similarities to battlefield speech genres. In addition to the implicit equation between speaking and competing as modes of activity presented in Chapter 4, the games also resemble battle scenes because they do not include conversation as a normal element of the type. Instead, the very existence of a conversation in funeral games highlights that particular moment in the games. While the emphatic function of conversation in games resembles what we find in battle, the specific notions that are emphasized differ: conversation in battle contexts, as we have seen, emphasizes key aspects of conflict, while conversation in games appears primarily to emphasize peaceful resolutions of disputes about various events in the competition. In particular, conversation dramatizes moments when the spirit of competition threatens the essentially cooperative spirit of the games, but the conflict is successfully defused. The funeral games of Patroclus, as has been shown, depicts resolution as the events of the *Iliad* draw to a close;[5] the important role that conversations play in achieving this effect will be the focus of the following discussion.

Iliad 23: The Funeral Games of Patroclus

This section will use the funeral games of Patroclus in *Iliad* 23 as a basis for a study of the typical patterns governing funeral games, with the proviso given at the beginning of the chapter that we cannot be sure of the extent to which such patterns can be generalized since *Iliad* 23 offers the only fully developed

---

[4] See Redfield 1994:204-210 for a valuable discussion of the structural similarities between the two.

[5] Richardson 1993:164-166 provides a particularly helpful discussion of this point, along with the ring compositional links between our introduction to the Greek forces in the Catalogue of Ships in Book 2 and our farewell to them during the funeral games.

xample of funeral games. After exploring these typical patterns, including
heir links to the conventions governing conversational types that have been
tudied in previous chapters, I will examine the role of conversation in creating
mphasis and shaping the funeral games of Patroclus into our final picture of
he Greek forces in the poem, restored to harmony among themselves while at
he same time preserving a strong sense of honor and competition.

;ames and Assembly

he similarities between assemblies and athletic games exist at the level of
road, organizational principles. One of these similarities is the notion of the
roup being seated at the start of the business for which they have gathered
ogether. When the games in honor of Patroclus begin after the Greeks finish
utting out his funeral pyre, a leader—here the chief mourner, Achilles—
ollects the group together, who are then seated (23.257-258).

> αὐτὰρ Ἀχιλλεὺς
> αὐτοῦ λαὸν ἔρυκε καὶ ἵζανεν εὐρὺν <u>ἀγῶνα</u>,

> But Achilleus
> held the people there, and made them sit down in a wide
> <u>assembly</u>,

lthough some critics believe that ἀγών means any type of assembly,[6] in fact,
his word is never used for an assembly of the kind discussed in the previous
hapter. Besides the expressions θεῖος ἀγών (divine assembly)[7] and νεῶν
γών (place where the ships are assembled),[8] the ἀγών in Homer is limited
ɔ games.[9] In Iliad 23, it is used both for the people themselves gathered
ogether and also for the place where this happens. Most of the time, both
enses can apply at once, as in the repeated phrase ἐν ἀγῶνι καθήμενοι
23.448, 23.495), which could mean "sitting in [the place of] assembly" as
ɣell as "sitting in [the group of] assembled [spectators/competitors]."
ccasionally it is clear that ἀγών refers specifically to people, as at 23.258
bove. The accusative ἀγῶνα after ἵζανεν must mean that Achilles caused
he Greeks to be seated, because the transitive force of this construction
aakes no sense unless ἀγῶνα means "people gathered together." So, there

---

[6] E.g. Lattimore (at least implicitly), who translates this word as "assembly."
[7] Twice in the *Iliad* (7.298, 18.376).
[8] Five times in the *Iliad* (15.428, 16.239, 16.500, 19.42, 20.33).
[9] Sixteen times in *Iliad* 23 and 24, and once in *Odyssey* 24 to refer to the funeral games of Achilles (86); five times in *Odyssey* 8, when the Phaeacians hold games during Odysseus' stay there.

is a particular word that can refer to both the collected people and the place they gather in the context of games, just as the word ἀγορή can mean both the people at an assembly (e.g. *Iliad* 2.144) and the place where they hold their assembly (e.g. *Iliad* 11.807).

Moreover, just as standing up marks the start of a turn in assembly, the most common formulaic speech introduction in *Iliad* 23 is στῆ δ’ ὀρθὸς καὶ μῦθον ἐν Ἀργείοισιν ἔειπεν (<u>he stood upright</u> and spoke his word out among the Argives).[10] This verse appears when Achilles announces a new competition in the funeral games, and is not used in other contexts.[11] This makes sense in funeral games for some of the same reasons I mentioned in connection with assembly turn regulation: standing up clearly identifies the start of a new portion of the funeral games, so that the rest of the group knows to whom to listen next and also that the next part of the games is now taking place. Thus, order is maintained in a possibly disorderly situation. Other speakers regularly stand up during these games before speaking, too, but there is no formulaic speech introduction to introduce these other speakers. Finally, after the funeral games, the first words of Book 24 are λῦτο δ’ ἀγών (and the games broke up, 24.1), evoking the end of the assembly in Book 1 (λῦσαν δ’ ἀγορήν [they dissolved the assembly], 305). In broad, formal outlines, the procedures for funeral games closely resemble those for assemblies: the group is gathered together by a leading individual; they sit down; standing regularly precedes a new speech; and at the end of the meeting the group is dissolved. Both activities, in broad outline, involve a group of people who has some identity as a group engaged in a cooperative activity important to all of them.

Games and Battle

At the level of individual turns, however, athletic games in many respects are more like battles than like assemblies. In an assembly, speaking is the only activity. Speaking turns in an assembly occur one after the other, generally without anything happening between one turn and the next except for reaction by the assembled group. In contrast, both action and speech may

---

[10] Seven times, all in *Iliad* 23: 271, 456, 657, 706, 752, 801, 830. Arend 1933:120-121 includes the formula in a brief but useful discussion of various similarities between *Iliad* 23 and assembly scenes, in which he includes the elements of sitting down, the scepter, and the presence of a herald.

[11] With one exception that I will discuss further below.

ccur within a given set of turns in the funeral games, and extended speech-
nly exchanges rarely take place.[12] While standing up in an assembly always
teans that the person wishes to speak, participants in the funeral games for
atroclus stand up for various reasons. Achilles, as we have seen, regularly
:ands up to introduce a new contest. In addition, competitors who wish to
ompete in a particular contest indicate their interest by standing up after the
ontest has been announced. The particular verb that usually appears when
omeone stands up to show that he wants to compete in an athletic contest is
form of ὄρνυμι "rouse oneself, stir oneself up, rise from a sitting position."[13]
ometimes we find forms of ἵστημι "stand" for one competitor in a particular
ontest, and ὄρνυμι for the other, showing that the two verbs indicate the
ame activity for competitors who want to show their interest in competing.[14]
t other words, would-be competitors stand up to indicate that they want
"turn" not to speak, but to do, to compete. This function of standing as a
relude both to speech and to action implicitly equates speech and action
s modes of activity in the funeral games. We have also seen this kind of
ssociation between speech and action on the battlefield, where individual
:urns" may consist of both speech and action and where a warrior may attack
1 enemy both by threatening him and by shooting at him. When the purpose
f a given turn is explicitly competitive rather than cooperative—whether in
attle or in games—it may contain both speech and action.[15]

Although game participants mark themselves as taking a turn when they
.and up, there is no corresponding way to indicate that a turn is over, as there
for assembly speakers. In assemblies, in contrast, the formula "X stood up"
efore a speech generally follows a formula mentioning previous speaker Y,
ho sat down after finishing a turn at speaking. This has to do with two unique
ipects of game turns: first, if the "turn" that is indicated by the person who
ands up is a shot at competition, it is not only permitted but necessary that
ore than one person at a time should take a turn. So, standing up identifies

---

[2] In the terminology of Hymes, assembly is a speech event while battle is a situation associated
with speech (Gumperz and Hymes 1972:56).

[3] Used ten times in this sense in *Iliad* 23, including four examples of a formulaic speech
concluding verse ὣς ἔφατ', ὦρτο δ' ἔπειτα [nominative name/epithet] (so he spoke, and pres-
ently there rose up [subject]: 708, 811, 836, 859).

[4] For example, at 23.708, Ajax "rose up" (ὦρτο) while his competitor Odysseus "stood up"
(ἀνίστατο, 709).

[5] Of course, one-on-one conversations or assemblies may be competitive, but unlike battlefield
vaunts or athletic competition, this competitiveness is a function of the specific conversation
rather than the genre itself.

someone as a turn-taker in a particular contest, but does not limit the entire turn to this person. Because it is not necessary to limit a game turn to one individual, it does not matter if turns overlap, and so it is not as important in funeral games as it is in assemblies to indicate where a particular turn ends. Secondly, even when standing marks the start of a speaking turn rather than a competitor turn (as when Achilles stands before announcing a new competition), the speech it introduces usually does not lead to conversation. Achilles, like a speaker in an assembly, does exclude others from taking a turn when he stands up before announcing a new competition. He not only identifies himself as a turn-taker by standing, he also signals that he alone is taking a turn. But Achilles, unlike a speaker in assembly, has a unique type of turn because he is the leader of the funeral games. No one else can announce new competitions, whereas many people can take a turn at speaking in an assembly. For the most part, after Achilles announces a new competition, the next turn is not another speech but the self-identification of competitors. Again, such a mixture of speech and action within a larger exchange recalls the battlefield, particularly since the only repeating speech element of the "competition" type is a single kind of speech (announcement that a competition will begin). The overall structure and the orderly rules governing the competition in games closely resemble the essentially cooperative conversational type of the assembly. Individual turns, which emphasize the spirit of competition more than the spirit of cooperation, resemble those found in combat situations. This combination of elements produces an activity that successfully mixes cooperation and competition.

Elements of the Game Type

Thus far, I have discussed the resemblances of the conversational turn sequences in game scenes to those found for the assembly and for the battlefield. Before turning to the role of specific conversations in the various contests in the funeral games for Patroclus, I will briefly list the elements of the "competition" type.[16]

- list of the prizes to be awarded, in order

- leader of the competition stands up[17]

---

[16] This list is based on Scott 1997:217-218. Minchin 2001:43-44 offers a very similar overview the type, although she provides more detail about the preparations for and accomplishments of the contest itself.

[17] Scott 1997 does not include this as an element of the type, but as it occurs in all of the competitions except one, I have added it to his list.

- leader announces the competition to be held
- competitors rise to indicate their interest in competing
- description of the contest
- awarding of prizes

These elements appear in this order in all of the competitions in the funeral games for Patroclus except for the final spear throwing competition (884-897), which does not take place at all when Achilles decides to award the prize outright to Agamemnon without even holding the competition. Conversation does not have an important role in the "competition" type, and speech of any kind has only a very minor role. Some contests contain a speech or conversation, such as the boast of Epeius during the boxing match (667-675) or the discussion at the finish of the foot-race about awarding a special prize to Antilochus (782-796). A competition may have no speech at all except for Achilles' announcement that the competition will take place (e.g. the throwing contest, 826-849).

The chariot race, which is the first contest to take place in the funeral games, develops these various typical motifs at the greatest length. It achieves its status as the longest and most elaborate competition partly by including a lot of conversations at points in the action that do not feature speech, let alone conversation, in other examples of the competition type in *Iliad* 23. All of these conversations take place once the competition is actually under way. Most of them focus the audience's attention on issues of fair play and proper behavior rather than on the skill of the athletes.[18] Through these conversations, the games depict the Greeks—and Achilles in particular—as able to negotiate differences of opinion and resolve them successfully instead of being consumed by them.

Conversations in the Chariot Race

The first conversation in the chariot race occurs between two spectators, and it threatens to turn into a competition of its own until Achilles puts a stop to it. After some sharp words between the competitors Menelaus and Antilochus about Antilochus' sneaky driving technique while the race is in progress, the scene shifts to the spectators. The spectators are seated ἐν ἀγῶνι (in their assembly, 448), but Idomeneus sits higher up than the other spectators and so he can see the racecourse better than they can (450-455). He rises from his seat and speculates about who is in the lead.

---

[18] Scott 1997:221.

στῆ δ' ὀρθὸς καὶ μῦθον ἐν Ἀργείοισιν ἔειπεν·
"ὦ φίλοι, Ἀργείων ἡγήτορες ἠδὲ μέδοντες,
οἶος ἐγὼν ἵππους αὐγάζομαι ἦε καὶ ὑμεῖς;"

[Idomeneus] rose to his feet upright and spoke his word out
to the Argives:
"Friends, who are leaders of the Argives and keep their
council:
am I the only one who can see the horses, or can you also?"

23.456-458

Only here does the formulaic verse στῆ δ' ὀρθὸς καὶ μῦθον ἐν Ἀργείοισιν ἔειπεν (he rose to his feet upright and spoke his word out to the Argives) precede anything other than an announcement of a new competition. Indeed Idomeneus' speculations about which competitor is leading and his suggestion that the others should stand up too and look (458-472) precede a sequence that has some elements in common with the first part of the "competition" type, both in content and in structure: not only does he stand up before speaking, but he solicits the participation of others in a way that may lead to competition among them. Ajax responds to this speech, berating Idomeneus for speaking foolishly (λαβρεύεαι, 474 and 478) and telling him that of course the same horses as before are in the lead (474-481).[19] Idomeneus now becomes angry in his turn. He proposes a wager between himself and Ajax about what chariot is ahead (483-487) and suggests that they bet a tripod or a cauldron, both of which are prizes that would be suitable for competitors in the games.

This conversation about the competition now runs the risk of becoming a full-fledged competition in "competition" with the chariot race. Ajax rises to take up Idomeneus' challenge, just as he might have done if he were showing his intention to compete in a contest that had been formally announced by the leader of the games. But for the timely intervention of Achilles, a contest other than the chariot race would have broken out (488-491).

ὣς ἔφατ', ὄρνυτο δ' αὐτίκ' Ὀϊλῆος ταχὺς Αἴας
χωόμενος χαλεποῖσιν ἀμείψασθαι ἐπέεσσι·
καί νύ κε δὴ προτέρω ἔτ' ἔρις γένετ' ἀμφοτέροισιν,
εἰ μὴ Ἀχιλλεὺς αὐτὸς ἀνίστατο καὶ φάτο μῦθον·

[19] The speech introduction at 23.473 is not formulaic, but it does appear at *Odyssey* 18.321 as well as in our passage: τὸν δ' αἰσχρῶς ἐνένιπε [name/epithet] (at 23.473, Swift Aias, son of Oileus spoke shamefully to him in anger).

So he spoke [sc. Idomeneus], and swift Aias, son of Oïleus,
> was rising

up, angry in turn, <u>to trade</u> hard words with him. And now
the quarrel between the two of them would have gone still
> further,

had not Achilleus himself <u>risen up</u> and spoken between them:

The progression here resembles the "competition" type in some ways: it includes the typical contest elements "leader stands (Idomeneus' first speech) / announces contest / contestants rise (Ajax after second speech of Idomeneus)." However, unlike the typical pattern for introducing a competition, this exchange between Ajax and Idomeneus includes conversation in which the announcer and the would-be competitor get into an argument. Moreover, it presents the person who speaks first as a possible competitor, which Achilles never is. At the same time, the narrative depicts this budding competition as a conversational exchange, since Ajax's aborted reply is referred to in verse 489 with the verb ἀμείψασθαι.

A wrangle is now on the verge of breaking out between Ajax and Idomeneus when Achilles, as the leader, takes the next turn. He stands up and speaks to the disputing men, thereby preventing them from fighting or from making a bet about who will win the race. We have seen in the chapters about one-on-one conversations that conditional speech introductions regularly emphasize the strength of some feeling that the subsequent speech averts or tames.[20] Here, the strong feeling that Achilles averts is the competitive impulse: the desire to be right, to be strongest, to gain the upper hand over others. Both the conversation itself and the conditional structure it contains before Achilles' speech highlight the spectators' feelings about competition. These features in turn give greater impact to Achilles' success in defusing these feelings. Although Achilles has calmed this particular group of unruly spectators, the chariot race includes several more instances of disagreements breaking out that threaten the stability of the games. Again and again, we will see conversation illustrating both the strength of the competitive urges that the chariot race elicits and the success of the Greeks in managing and resolving these impulses. Given that conversation in the *Iliad* often illustrates the strength and power of unchecked or destructive competitive impulses, this

---

[20] The comments of Lang 1989 about the difference between affirmative and negative protases are particularly useful here: see e.g. 6 for her characterization of conditions with negative protases as reporting "what happened to prevent an expected result."

technique is particularly effective in creating a sense of resolution and closure for the Greeks as a group in these games.

New difficulties arise in the chariot race after the contestants have all finished the race and the prizes are to be awarded. Several conversations occur in the course of these disagreements. First, Antilochus refuses to accept Achilles' decision to give second prize to Eumelus even though Eumelus came in last place. A conversation takes place in which he and Achilles discuss the issue (536-562). Then a second dispute arises almost immediately between Antilochus and Menelaus over which of them is really entitled to Antilochus' prize (566-611). The overall organization of this conversation and its turn sequences resembles a battlefield exchange. That is to say, conversation about a particular activity alternates with the activity itself, namely the distribution of the prizes. This gives a competitive edge to the idea of distributing prizes even though in theory, this should be a celebratory, consensus-based part of a contest. Once again, conversation is used to bring forward both the strength of the competitive feelings of the participants and the underlying group harmony that makes it possible to resolve or defuse these feelings.

This extended interchange about the two prizes, which is the longest one in the funeral games, highlights the orderly division of goods and the resolution of differences of opinion just by existing in the first place. Most contests in the funeral games do not feature disputes about prizes. The usual element of the competition type at this point is simply "prizes are distributed." This sometimes happens in just one verse,[21] and it need not entail any direct speech even if there is a draw or other reason to adjust the distribution of prizes.[22] Moreover, several individual speeches in this conversation about the prizes in the chariot race have speech frames that call particular attention to the feelings and behavior of the speakers at points where feelings about competition and status run especially high. These speech frames contain a verse(s) describing the feelings or behavior of the person about to speak followed by the formula καί μιν φωνήσας ἔπεα πτερόεντα προσηύδα or a very similar verse.

After Achilles proposes to give the second prize to Eumelus even though he came in last (536-538), Antilochus rises to say that he will be very angry if this is done. Instead, he says, Achilles should give Eumelus an additional prize from his own stores if he wants.

---

[21] E.g. 699 for awarding the boxing prizes.
[22] In the close combat, we learn in 822-823 that the crowd called for a draw and an equal distribution of prizes, but no direct speech appears.

"ὦ Ἀχιλεῦ, μάλα τοι κεχολώσομαι, αἴ κε τελέσσῃς
τοῦτο ἔπος· μέλλεις γὰρ ἀφαιρήσεσθαι ἄεθλον . . . "
     ὣς φάτο, <u>μείδησεν</u> δὲ ποδάρκης δῖος Ἀχιλλεὺς
χαίρων Ἀντιλόχῳ, ὅτι οἱ φίλος ἦεν ἑταῖρος,
καί <u>μιν ἀμειβόμενος ἔπεα πτερόεντα προσηύδα·</u>

"Achilleus, I shall be very angry with you if you accomplish
what you have said. You mean to take my prize away from me . . . "
     So he spoke, but brilliant swift-footed Achilleus,
     favouring
Antilochus, <u>smiled</u>, since he was his beloved companion,
<u>and answered him and addressed him in winged words</u>:

23.543-544, 555-557

chilles, whose own anger at losing a prize he earned has fueled much of the
lot of the *Iliad*, reacts favorably to this appeal. One can imagine a functionally
quivalent but less effective passage as follows:

*τὸν δ' ἐπιμειδήσας προσέφη πόδας ὠκὺς Ἀχιλλεύς,
χαίρων Ἀντιλόχῳ, ὅτι οἱ φίλος ἦεν ἑταῖρος·

Swift footed Achilles, smiling, addressed him,
favouring Antilochus, since he was his beloved companion,

he change of epithets seems insignificant: both refer to Achilles' swiftness
f foot.[23] The important difference between this hypothetical couplet and
ie passage in our text is the increased prominence of Achilles' emotions
sulting from the additional verse to describe them. His feelings here, and
is role in the dispute, contrast strongly with his feelings on the previous
ccasions when we have seen him involved in conversations about disputed
roperty. He is now the unruffled distributor of prizes, not the irate recipient
r non-recipient). Achilles tells one of his companions to fetch additional
fts for Eumelus from his tent; this is done, and Eumelus accepts his prize
ith pleasure (563-565). This portrayal of Achilles calming Greeks who are
cercised about the allocation of prizes, evoking his very different demeanor
out the distribution of his own prizes in Book 1, ends the first movement
f this conversation. By showing Achilles in this way, the episode provides a
ear and effective closure to the conflict surrounding him that has troubled
ie Greeks for much of the poem.

---

[3] If that is what ποδάρκης means; see Chantraine 1984.

Chapter Six

Similar concerns now arise for other competitors. Menelaus, th winner of the third prize, becomes angry. He rises to speak (566), saying tha Antilochus had beaten him unfairly to win (570-585). Antilochus gives wa before the wrathful Menelaus and offers to hand over the mare that he wa awarded for his prize (587-595). The pleasure of Menelaus at this deferenti treatment is described at some length and includes a simile. The thrust of 59 601, however, is simply that Menelaus replied to Antilochus:

> ἦ ῥα, καὶ ἵππον ἄγων μεγαθύμου Νέστορος υἱὸς
> ἐν χείρεσσι τίθει Μενελάου· τοῖο δὲ θυμὸς
> <u>ἰάνθη</u> ὡς εἴ τε περὶ σταχύεσσιν ἐέρση
> ληΐου ἀλδήσκοντος, ὅτε φρίσσουσιν ἄρουραι·
> ὣς ἄρα σοί, Μενέλαε, μετὰ φρεσὶ θυμὸς <u>ἰάνθη</u>.
> <u>καί μιν φωνήσας ἔπεα πτερόεντα προσηύδα·</u>

> He spoke, the son of Nestor the great-hearted, and leading
> the mare up gave her to Menelaos' hands. But his anger
> <u>was softened</u>, as with dew the ears of corn are softened
> in the standing corn growth of a shuddering field. For
>   you also
> the heart, o Menelaos, <u>was thus softened</u> within you.
> <u>He spoke to him aloud and addressed him in winged word:</u>

The passage highlights Menelaus' pleasure by describing it in terms of dew o ears of wheat that are blowing in the breeze, a vivid and peaceful image tha both adorns the scene and contributes to the sense of calm that succeeds th conflict over the prize.

The simile and the speech frame as a whole emphasize the swift actio that Antilochus takes to placate Menelaus (in contrast to Agamemnon inaction in a similar situation) and its beneficial, calming effect on th offended person. As it turns out, Antilochus' gesture alone is enough to cal Menelaus, and he refuses to take the mare (602-611). Menelaus gives her to th companion of Antilochus to lead away, and Menelaus gets a cup instead (61 613). Thus, this disagreement contrasts strongly with the disastrous argume between Achilles and Agamemnon over prizes that begins the poem and h such a far-reaching effect. Here, both participants go further than is necessar to resolve their dispute, whereas neither Agamemnon nor Achilles was willir to go far enough to resolve theirs until it had already done enormous damag As this passage makes clear, in these games, conflict is not avoided; instead, is repeatedly confronted and defused in an orderly and productive manne

1e poem draws to a close partly by dwelling at length on this process and 1plicitly contrasting it to the conflicts that bedevil the Greeks through most the *Iliad*.

No one argues about Meriones' fourth prize, which he receives ithout any accompanying disputes or speeches (614-615). Achilles awards 1e fifth and final prize for the chariot race, which has gone unclaimed 7 any contestant, as a sort of honorary prize for Nestor since he is now 0 old to compete (618-623). Nestor is delighted to accept this award, hich we learn not only from the narrator in the introduction to Nestor's 1eech (624-625) but also from Nestor's own words (626-650). Here, too, 1 expanded speech frame emphasizes reciprocity, both the actual giving the gift and the joy of the recipient, although the narrative could have 10ceeded smoothly if a single verse "Nestor answered him" reply intro- 1ction were used instead.

> ὣς εἰπὼν ἐν χερσὶ τίθει· ὁ δ' ἐδέξατο <u>χαίρων</u>,
> <u>καί μιν φωνήσας ἔπεα πτερόεντα προσηύδα·</u>

He spoke, and put it in the hands of Nestor, who took
>   it <u>joyfully</u>
> <u>and spoke in answer and addressed him in winged words</u>:

23.624-625

1ce again, the full-verse introductory formula καί μιν φωνήσας ἔπεα :ερόεντα προσηύδα appears in combination with another verse or verses 1at describe the pleasure of one of the participants in the games at an orderly stribution of prizes, bringing this notion to the fore at the end of the process awarding the prizes for the chariot race.

Thus, the conversations that occur during the chariot race and the 1ecific speeches that are introduced by multi-verse speech frames in 1rticular repeatedly show the heroes successfully adjusting differences of 1inion about prizes and reputation, sometimes after heated disagreements 1d angry words. The expanded speech frames emphasize the importance these issues specifically by highlighting the strength of the emotions that 'e stirred up by them. This calls the audience's attention not only to the 1werful feelings surrounding the equitable allotment of goods, but also to e consistent success of Achilles in particular at facing these conflicts and solving them. This success, in turn, contrasts with Achilles' own angry and 1tractable behavior earlier in the *Iliad* when he fails to get the prizes he els he deserves. Achilles appears throughout the chariot race as a strong

243

and effective force for order, equity, and conflict resolution.[24] This dram
tizes his character's evolution over the course of the poem and—given th
central role in the *Iliad* of Achilles' feelings about prizes and conflict ov
them—brings the poem toward its conclusion. It is largely through conve
sations that these ideas emerge, conversations that distinguish the chari
race from the other contests in the funeral games. This technique deriv
even more impact from the contrasting functions of conversation in th
funeral games, where they emphasize moments when conflicts are succes
fully resolved, with the function of conversation in most other contex
in the poem, where they draw out various aspects of unresolved and/
ongoing conflicts.

What have we learned about the structure of games? In the funer
games in *Iliad* 23, the overall structure with its formal markers for beginnin
turn-taking, and ending resembles that of an assembly. Within this structur
however, individual turns and speeches differ from those that occur in form
assemblies because they rarely make a conversation. Instead, speech ar
action can each constitute a "turn," and both may be combined in one interd
pendent structure within a given turn. These aspects of speech representatic
in the funeral games in *Iliad* 23 resemble battlefield scenes more than asser
blies, where conversation forms the essence of the scene and where actic
other than various formal accompaniments to speech rarely occurs. So, we ca
say that the representation of speech and conversation in Patroclus' funer
games combines the formal structures of assembly with the competition ar
speech-plus-action turn patterns found on the battlefield. That is to say, opp
nents strive against one another in an agonistic, competitive manner with
a larger framework of rules and order that prevents the competitive aspe
of the situation from getting out of control. Because conversation is rare
games scenes, when it does occur it creates emphasis simply by being there,
we have seen at length in the chariot race in Patroclus' funeral games. In th
competition, several different conversations consistently highlight confli
over the equitable distribution of goods in order to show these conflic
being resolved. Because conflict over prizes is one of the main themes of th
Iliad, this provides an effective sense of closure in our last view of most of th
important Greek heroes.

---

[24] Taplin 1992:253 notes that "it is one of the main poetic functions of the funeral games to sh
Achilleus soothing and resolving public strife, instead of provoking and furthering it."

aments

ike funeral games, formal laments may be seen as a conversational[25] type
ith very specific, formalized conventions of sequence and framing similar
ɔ those found in assemblies. At the level of turn sequence, we saw in
hapter 5 that the possibility of a series of speeches by several individuals
ɔ the group as a whole is restricted to formal assemblies. When a sequence
f several laments occurs, this same order appears. In both assembly and
ıment, formulaic speech conclusions that describe the behavior of either
ıe speaker or the listeners, or both, regularly follow all or most of the
ɔeeches in a particular conversation. Ordinarily, speech conclusions appear
t the end of a conversation or after a single speech. The regular behavioral
ccompaniment to speaking in a formal lament includes both weeping on
ıe part of the speaker and responsive lament by the speaker's companions.[26]
hese companions and their prescribed behaviors always accompany a formal
ıment. The same basic sequence characterizes not only the three laments
y Hector's female relatives that close the *Iliad*, but also the various single
ıments that appear earlier in the *Iliad*:[27]

- formulaic speech introduction: τῇσιν δ' αὖτε or ἔπειτα [name of
  lamenter] ἐξῆρχε γόοιο

- lament

- formulaic speech conclusion: ὣς ἔφατο κλαίουσ', ἐπὶ δὲ στενάχοντο
  γυναῖκες

ll of these elements are not necessarily found in this identical form in every
ıment, but this basic structure and often these formulas usually accompany
ıments. As in assemblies, the regular structure of an individual turn in a formal
ıment sequence includes not only the speech itself, but also specific actions before
ıd after the speech that are related to the context in which the speech occurs.

---

5 The *Odyssey* clearly demonstrates that lament is a kind of conversation: when the soul of
Agamemnon describes the death and funeral of Achilles in Book 24, he says Μοῦσαι δ' ἐννέα
πᾶσαι ἀμειβόμεναι ὀπὶ καλῇ / θρήνεον (all nine Muses taking turns with one another in sweet
singing / mourned, 60-61).

6 Alexiou 1974:6 remarks that "the archaeological and literary evidence, taken together, makes
it clear that lamentation involved movement as well as wailing and singing." Unfortunately
this movement is not referred to in formulaic speech frames, but it supports the basic idea
that lament is a genre of formal conversation akin to assembly in its use of particular kinds of
ritualized behavior as an accompaniment to speech.

7 Primarily for Patroclus. These will be discussed below.

This pattern underlies not only the elaborate series of laments for Hector that closes the *Iliad*, it also shapes the speeches that Hector's parents and wife make at the end of Book 22 when they see him fall at the hands of Achilles. These speeches, although clearly resembling laments in most particulars, are not developed as fully as the series of speeches in Book 24. This gives a vivid sense of immediacy and rawness to the grief of Hector's family when they first learn of his death. In addition, a series of speeches about the dead Patroclus, which for the most part take the form of laments, create an interlocking complementary structure with the laments for the dead Hector over the last several books of the poem. This constitutes yet another way in which the *Iliad* links the two deaths. Largely through these laments, the *Iliad* dwells at length on the grief that people on both the Greek and the Trojan sides feel when their loved ones are killed, thus conveying that sorrow and loss are an inevitable part of war that affects all sides equally.[28]

Some of these laments for Patroclus have been used by neoanalysts to argue that Patroclus' death is a superficially adapted version of Achilles' death which has an uneasy or problematic relationship to its Iliadic context. However, if we closely examine the structures found in speeches about the dead Patroclus, it becomes clear that the speech most extensively used to support this neoanalytical argument shows significant differences from typical lament patterns and is not really a lament at all. In other words, speeches lamenting Patroclus' death do not seem to be taken from some other part of the Troy tale without regard to their suitability for the *Iliad*, but to be well integrated into their own contexts. If we look for lament patterns outside of the well-known series about Hector in Book 24, we find them creating added layers of meaning and connection through the last section of the *Iliad*. Many of these laments, among the most beautiful and moving speeches in the *Iliad*, have been extensively studied before for their individual pathos and artistry; this analysis will draw out the connections among different examples of lament in order to show their significance as a consistent force in shaping the end of the poem into a depiction of the costs of war for Greek and Trojan alike.

Iliad 24: The Funeral Rites of Hector

We can see the typical characteristics of formal lament most clearly and consistently in the series of laments that the Trojans make for the dead Hector after Priam fetches his body back from Achilles (*Iliad* 24.723-776), so this makes a good starting point for a discussion of lament as a type even though the

---

[28] The *Chanson de Roland* provides a parallel for a traditional story that is told with a lot of lament in order to draw out not simply the heroism but also the bereavement and sadness of war (Duggan 1973:171-183, especially 175-176).

scene forms the conclusion of the *Iliad*.[29] While offering an example of what appear to be the typical sequences and speech frames for the genre of lament, these speeches also display some unusual features that contribute to the sense of closure that this scene gives to the poem as a whole.

The special, formal nature of this series of laments for Hector emerges in several ways. First of all, this is the longest series of successive laments in the Homeric epics for the same individual.[30] In addition, professional singers are present to mourn for Hector, whereas other laments are performed only by the friends, relatives, and comrades of the dead person. These professionals, too, lament in a responsive fashion, although the narrative does not present any of their laments in direct speech. Instead, they appear as a kind of prelude or backdrop for Andromache, who leads off the laments that are sung by Hector's relations.

οἱ δ' ἐπεὶ εἰσάγαγον κλυτὰ δώματα, τὸν μὲν ἔπειτα
τρητοῖς ἐν λεχέεσσι θέσαν, παρὰ δ' εἷσαν ἀοιδοὺς
<u>θρήνων ἐξάρχους</u>, οἵ τε στονόεσσαν ἀοιδὴν
οἱ μὲν ἄρ' ἐθρήνεον, <u>ἐπὶ δὲ στενάχοντο γυναῖκες</u>.
τῇσιν δ' Ἀνδρομάχη <u>λευκώλενος</u> ἦρχε γόοιο
<u>Ἕτορος ἀνδροφόνοιο κάρη μετὰ χερσὶν ἔχουσα·</u>
"ἆνερ..."

And when they had brought him inside the renowned house,
    they laid him
then on a carved bed, and seated beside him the singers
who were to <u>lead the melody in the dirge</u>, and the singers
chanted the song of sorrow, and <u>the women were mourning
    in response</u>.[31]
Andromache <u>of the white arms</u> led the lamentation among them,
<u>and held in her arms the head of manslaughtering Hektor</u>:
"My husband..."

                                            24.719-725

---

[29] The following discussion will be concerned primarily with the order of laments and the speech frames that link them together into a series. Those interested in the content of the laments themselves are referred to Lohmann 1970:108-112 and Alexiou 1974:132-134; see also the overview of this series of laments in Richardson 1993:349-352, and his comments on the contents of the laments themselves *ad locc.*

[30] Edwards 1986b points out that these laments are longer and more elaborate than the laments in other funerals described in the Homeric epics (85).

[31] Adapted from Lattimore, who consistently translates ἐπί as "beside" or "around" in lament formulas. It seems to me that ἐπί represents the responsive nature of the wailing in these contexts, not the location of the wailers.

This opening, in fact, represents the πρόθεσις (laying out) of Hector, including not only the laying-out itself but also the lamentations that formed a part of this mourning ritual.[32] From the brief description in 721-722, it appears that while the professional singers are present, they sing a lament and the women respond.[33] This general procedure, although it contains several words that appear only here in the *Iliad*,[34] mirrors quite closely what we find when female relations rather than professionals lead the lament. Although the noun ἔξαρχος is not found elsewhere in the *Iliad*, the root ἐξαρχ- appears regularly in formulaic introductions for laments. So, not only the responsive interchange between the professional singers and the women but also the language that the narrator uses to describe the scene closely matches that which we find elsewhere for formal laments sung by non-professional mourners.

As the wife of the dead man, it is not surprising that Andromache should make the first lament for Hector among his female relations. Her lament gains in power and impact not only from being first in this series, but also from vivid description of her appearance and demeanor as she begins to speak. Andromache, alone of the three women who address the corpse, receives an epithet in the formulaic introduction to her lament (λευκώλενος [white-armed], 723). Furthermore, an additional verse between the speech introduction and the lament itself describes Andromache holding Hector's head in her arms (724).[35] The unusual position of this verse between the speech introduction and the speech strongly highlights her action; in a different way, the surprising appearance of an epithet in the introduction itself does the same thing.[36] Together, these departures from the common patterns for lament introductions create a vivid, moving picture of the grief-stricken young wife as she bids farewell to her husband not only with words but also with a final embrace.

After Andromache, Hecuba takes her turn to lament for her dead son. In contrast to the introduction for Andromache's lament, the language between

[32] Alexiou 1974:12.

[33] Whether there is a difference in the *Iliad* between the θρῆνος of the professionals and the γόος of the female relations is debated. Nagy 1979:112 suggests that the use of indirect speech to represent professional mourners' laments, versus direct speech for relatives, indicates a genre distinction between θρῆνος and γόος.

[34] Richardson 1993:351 cites ἀοιδός (singer), θρῆνος (lament), θρηνεῖν (to lament), and ἔξαρχος (leader). This last, Richardson says, along with the verb ἐξάρχειν (to lead) "are virtually technical terms for leading a group of singers or dancers."

[35] This is a regular accompaniment to formal lament (Alexiou 1974:6); the combination of specific behavior with speaking characterizes lament as a formal genre of speech.

[36] Edwards 1987:314 says, "it is hard not to think that the change of the adjective is intended to evoke more vividly the picture of her bare arms around the corpse."

the end of Andromache's lament and the beginning of Hecuba's closely follows typical patterns (746-748).

ὣς ἔφατο κλαίουσ', ἐπὶ δὲ στενάχοντο γυναῖκες.
τῆσιν δ' αὖθ' Ἑκάβη ἁδινοῦ ἐξῆρχε γόοιο·
"Ἕκτορ, ἐμῷ θυμῷ πάντων πολὺ φίλτατε παίδων ... "

So she spoke in tears, and the women were mourning in response.
Now Hekabe led out the thronging chant of their sorrow:
"Hektor, of all my sons the dearest by far to my spirit ... "

The women who are with Andromache and Hecuba play a necessary part in these laments, as we can see from both ἐπὶ δὲ στενάχοντο γυναῖκες in the conclusion for Andromache and τῆσιν in the introduction for Hecuba. The structure of these formulas shows that the conversation or interchange in formal lament is not between the chief mourners and one another, but between each individual chief mourner and the group of women who respond to her lament.[37] It is these women who respond after Andromache laments, and the women to whom Hecuba addresses her lament as well. At the same time, the laments themselves are "addressed" to the dead Hector, in that the vocative forms in them refer to him. So, laments display their formal, stylized nature partly in the complete separation of the audience for a given speech (the women) and the addressee of the speech (the dead person). In one-on-one conversations, the audience and the addressee are always the same. In group conversations, they may overlap to a greater or lesser degree. Only in laments are they totally distinct.[38] This contributes to the formality that distinguishes lament from other ways of expressing grief.

The notion of the women's responsive role appears in a slightly less developed way following the lament of Hecuba, since the usual conclusion for lament has an unusual expression in the second half of the verse (24.760-762).

ὣς ἔφατο κλαίουσα, γόον δ' ἀλίαστον ὄρινε.
τῆσι δ' ἔπειθ' Ἑλένη τριτάτη ἐξῆρχε γόοιο·
"Ἕκτορ ἐμῷ θυμῷ δαέρων πολὺ φίλτατε πάντων ... "

---

[37] Drew and Heritage 1992:27 discuss "talk for an overhearing audience" as characteristic of institutional talk settings.
[38] This is consistent with various observations about institutional talk: its turn structures vary noticeably from those found in regular one-on-one settings, and in a given setting, there may be particular turn structures that distinguish that particular activity or setting from other institutional settings (Drew and Heritage 1992:25-26).

> <u>So she spoke, in tears</u>, and wakened the endless mourning.
> Third and last Helen led the song of sorrow among <u>them</u>:
> "Hektor, of all my lord's brothers dearest by far to my spirit . . . "

Although 760 does not have the concluding half-verse ἐπὶ δὲ στενάχοντο γυναῖκες (and the women mourned in response), the passage between the laments of Hecuba and Helen nevertheless includes the key behavioral and responsive elements of formal lament. ὡς ἔφατο κλαίουσα tells us that Hecuba wept as she lamented, and τῇσι refers to the assembled women who are the audience for the lament of Helen. The expression γόον δ' ἀλίαστον ὄρινε (wakened the endless mourning, 760) strongly implies the assembled women as the people in whom this mourning was awakened, but they are not mentioned explicitly as they would have been by the more common phrase ἐπὶ δὲ στενάχοντο γυναῖκες. Even so, this expression conveys the idea of a responsive group wailing in response to Hecuba's speech.

Helen gives the last lament for Hector (762-775).[39] When she has finished her speech, the scene shifts to Priam and the funeral rites of pyre and burial that men perform. The conclusion to her lament effects a transition from the women's laments to the men's funeral rites by making the entire Trojan people, rather than just the womenfolk, the responsive mourners for her lament.

> ὡς ἔφατο κλαίουσ', ἐπὶ δ' ἔστενε δῆμος ἀπείρων.
> λαοῖσιν δ' ὁ γέρων Πρίαμος μετὰ μῦθον ἔειπεν·
> "ἄξετε νῦν Τρῶες ξύλα ἄστυ δέ . . . "

> So she spoke in tears, and the vast populace grieved with her.
> Now Priam the aged king spoke forth his word to his people:
> "Now, men of Troy, bring timber into the city . . . "

> 24.776-778

Helen weeps as she laments, as we are told in the formulaic beginning of verse 776, but unlike Hector's other mourners, her "audience" is not limited to the women of Troy. The "vast populace" who groans aloud in response to her lament is also the addressee of Priam's next speech. He speaks immediately after the formal laments by the women have ended, and he addresses the group to whom the last speaker was talking rather than—as is usual in other

---

[39] Richardson 1993:350 rightly contrasts Helen's position as a chief mourner, which is surprising, with that of Hector's mother and wife, "and it is surely significant that she, who was the cause of the war, should speak thus so near the poem's end."

onversational situations—the last speaker. The sequence and arrangement f the speeches here touches Priam's speech with the idea of lament. In fact, he speech that Priam makes here is the last speech in the poem. He gives nstructions for bringing wood into the city along with assurances that the reeks will not harm the Trojan people while they conduct funeral rites for ector (778-781). This means that a series of laments for Hector are the final vords that the audience hears in the mouths of the characters rather than of ne narrator. This essentially concludes the poem with the grief of the Trojan vomen, instead of (e.g.) the contests of the Greek men, ending the tale on a orrowful rather than a triumphant or victorious note.

This scene displays the basic features of formal lament. A series of peeches occur that are nominally addressed to the dead person, insofar s the vocatives they contain refer to him. Like assembly, laments feature a eries of speeches by different characters to the same addressee. However, he group of people present are the ones who respond to a speech of lament, he dead person obviously being prevented by his condition from doing so. his response by the listening group forms an important and regular element f a lament, as shown by the formulaic expression that refers to it. Both the steners and the person speaking the lament weep. Thus, lament alone of the onversational genres we have studied has a complete separation between the erson addressed in a speech and the person(s) who responds to the speech. his separation contributes to the formality of the occasion; the importance f the listening audience in lament, assembly, and athletic games links all of hese together as formal genres of speech. Moreover, since their common ttributes have been documented linguistically as characteristic of institu- ional speech, it seems probable that the specific behavioral and sequential haracteristics of these different kinds of conversation reflect at least to some legree a social reality in how they were conducted.

Iliad 22: The Death of Hector

he formal laments in *Iliad* 24 take place within the larger context of funeral ites, including professional singers and the construction of a funeral yre on which Hector is cremated after the laments over his body. The ame conventions that apply to the laments themselves in *Iliad* 24, namely he invariable practice of weeping while lamenting and the responsive ccompaniment of a group of mourners, also occur with the laments for Hector mmediately after his death. These are less formal insofar as they do not ake place as part of his funeral rites, and they sometimes lack the formulaic

Chapter Six

speech frames for lament that appear regularly in Book 24. Nonetheless, th
speeches themselves display the conventions of lament for the behavior of
both lamenter and responsive group. Thus, the audience experiences Hector'
death twice. They also experience it in different ways, first with the despairin
shock and immediacy of the moment of death itself, and then in a calmer an
more elaborate way during Hector's funeral. This double treatment of Hector'
death gives it great importance in structuring the end of the poem, and thus i
creating the feeling of sorrow and loss that characterizes the poem as a whol

When Achilles begins dragging the body of Hector around the city o
Troy, Hector's parents and the assembled Trojans are stricken with grie
The language of the passage that describes their emotions does not use th
specific words for "grief" or "wail" that we saw repeatedly in Book 24. No
does Priam ever address Hector in the second person when he expresses hi
misery, as we saw each of the mourners do in Book 24.[40] Nevertheless, whe
Hector's parents witness his death and first give voice to their grief, we hav
the lament-like scenario of weeping speaker accompanied by mourning grou
of people. As the scene goes on, each new speech has more of the characte
istics of a formal lament, starting with the quasi-lament of Priam—section
of which are quoted below—and culminating in the full-fledged lament o
Andromache that concludes the scene. This gives a sense that the members o
Hector's family are in the process of internalizing his death as the scene goe
on; by the end of Book 22, his parents and wife have accepted the fact of hi
death and are speaking in the typical formal patterns of lament.

> <u>ᾤμωξεν</u> δ' ἐλεεινὰ πατὴρ φίλος, <u>ἀμφὶ δὲ λαοὶ</u>
> <u>κωκυτῷ τ' εἴχοντο καὶ οἰμωγῇ</u> κατὰ ἄστυ . . . .
>
> . . . πάντας δὲ λιτάνευε κυλινδόμενος κατὰ κόπρον,
> ἐξ ὀνομακλήδην ὀνομάζων ἄνδρα ἕκαστον·
>
> " . . . τῶν πάντων οὐ τόσσον ὀδύρομαι ἀχνύμενός περ
> ὡς ἑνός, οὗ μ' ἄχος ὀξὺ κατοίσεται Ἄϊδος εἴσω,
> Ἕκτορος· ὡς ὄφελεν θανέειν ἐν χερσὶν ἐμῇσι·
> τώ κε κορεσσάμεθα κλαίοντέ τε μυρομένω τε
> μήτηρ θ', ἥ μιν ἔτικτε δυσάμμορος, ἠδ' ἐγὼ αὐτός."
> <u>ὡς ἔφατο κλαίων, ἐπὶ δὲ στενάχοντο πολῖται·</u>
> <u>Τρῳῆσιν</u> δ' Ἑκάβη ἁδινοῦ ἐξῆρχε γόοιο·
> "τέκνον ἐγὼ δειλή . . ."

[40] Alexiou 1974:171-172 discusses the importance of the "I/you" contrast as a regular feature o
Greek laments, as well as other genres such as hymns.

252

...and his father beloved <u>groaned</u> pitifully, and <u>all his people</u>
    <u>about him</u>
<u>were taken with wailing and lamentation</u> all through the city . . .

. . . he implored them all, and wallowed in the muck
before them calling on each man and naming him by his name:

" . . . But for all of these [sons] I mourn not so much, in spite
    of my sorrow,
as for one, Hektor, and the sharp grief for him will carry me
    downward
into Death's house. I wish he had died in my arms, for that way,
we two, I myself and his mother who bore him unhappy,
might have so glutted ourselves with weeping for him and
    mourning."
    <u>So he spoke, in tears, and in response mourned the citizens.</u>
<u>But for the women of Troy</u> Hekabe led out the thronging
chant of sorrow: "Child, I am wretched . . . "

22.408-409; 414-415; 424-431

While some typical features of a lament (weeping individual and a mourning group in accompaniment) are present here, the passage preceding Priam's speech does not explicitly identify his words as a lament. At the opening of his speech, Priam directly addresses the surrounding group (416-417). Most of Priam's speech concerns the immediate necessity of journeying to the Greek camp to ransom Hector's body from Achilles (416-423). This section of the speech is neither to Hector nor about him in the normal manner of a Homeric lament.[41] At the end of the speech, however, Priam is bewailing the loss of his son (although he never addresses him directly). Thus, the speech does not consistently maintain the distinction between the audience of a lament (the other mourners) and its addressee (the dead person) that characterizes laments elsewhere. Nevertheless, the conclusion of the speech identifies it as a lament. Just as the speech itself does not display some of the important features of a lament, yet has strong affinities with lament toward the end, the speech framing language that surrounds Priam's speech only identifies it as a lament in the conclusion (429). This conclusion adapts the usual formula that follows laments to accommodate a male mourner rather than the more usual female. The participle "weeping" has the same metrical shape whether

---

[1] Ibid. 133, where Alexiou notes that this is a traditional structure in laments.

it is masculine or feminine (κλαίων vs. κλαίουσ', where the final α is elide before the initial vowel in ἐπί). Similarly, πολῖται has the same metrical shap as γυναῖκες (women), the usual subject of the verb στενάχοντο. A series ɔ laments for a dead person in which one of the mourners is a *male* relative an the rest are female relatives is unprecedented; it seems that Priam speaks her as one of those most closely affected by Hector's death, but that his speec is not presented as a full-fledged lament because that would be inconsister with the lament type.[42]

After Priam finishes, Hecuba begins to speak. Her speech is bot preceded and followed by formulaic speech frames for lament. In contras to Priam, whose "chorus" of mourners are men like himself, Hecuba noᵥ makes a lament among the Trojan women. The introduction to her lamer uses a dative proper noun to emphasize this difference, rather than the usɑ pronoun τῇσι (them), which in this context would not clearly identify th women who mourn with her. Her speech, unlike Priam's, consists entirel of direct address to Hector and the traditional comparison between her ow condition and his (431-436). The most unusual feature of Hecuba's lamen is the lack of a responsive audience in the speech conclusion that follow her lament, although the Trojan women appear as her audience before sh begins. With this exception, Hecuba's speech—unlike Priam's—displays th typical features of formal lament.

After she finishes, however, the most usual speech concluding formul for laments is changed. The resulting verse turns the audience's attention t Andromache in an extremely effective and moving manner.

> "ἦ γὰρ καί σφι μάλα μέγα κῦδος ἔησθα
> ζωὸς ἐών· νῦν αὖ θάνατος καὶ μοῖρα κιχάνει."
> <u>ὣς ἔφατο κλαίουσ', ἄλοχος δ' οὔ πώ τι πέπυστο</u>
> Ἕκτορος· οὐ γάρ οἵ τις ἐτήτυμος ἄγγελος ἐλθὼν
> ἤγγειλ' ὅττι ῥά οἱ πόσις ἔκτοθι μίμνε πυλάων . . .

> "since in truth you were their high honor
> while you lived. Now death and fate have closed in upon you."
> <u>So she spoke in tears, but the wife of Hektor had not yet
> heard</u>: for no sure messenger had come to her and told her
> how her husband had held his ground there outside the gates . . .

> 22.435-439

---

[42] Alexiou 1974 repeatedly cites the speeches of Hecuba and Andromache in Book 22 as laments but not that of Priam. The situation of Achilles in relation to Patroclus (discussed below) is nc a true parallel because no family members of Patroclus are present to mourn for him.

he conclusion to Hecuba's speech begins with the usual formula that follows
lament, but the narrator goes on to depict the as-yet ignorant widowed
ndromache in the second half of the verse instead of mentioning the
esponsive lamenting of the Trojan women. The narrator here uses the part
f the verse that normally refers to the response of an audience to a lament to
ay that Andromache is *not* there, and does not know of her husband's death.
s a result of her ignorance, Andromache does not form part of the responsive
lourning group, as the wife of a dead man typically would. Andromache does
iment for Hector when she learns of his death. However, the narrator does
ot put her lament immediately after Hecuba's, as the turn sequence and
prmulas leading up to this point lead the audience to expect. Instead, the
arrator emphasizes her emotions on the death of her husband by devoting
significant amount of time to describing them. First, her happily ignorant
omesticity immediately before she hears the news of Hector's death sets
p a poignant contrast to the scene of death and misery outside the walls of
roy (437-459). When her emotions are finally described (460-475), they gain
dditional intensity from the disparity with what came immediately before.
ather than analyze the construction of this passage myself, I will quote from
egal's superb discussion of it.

> By so withholding Andromache's lament until line 476, Homer
> accomplishes two specific purposes. First, he gives her grief a
> special prominence, a prominence which book 6 has both justified
> and rendered necessary. Second, he avoids too obvious an anticipa-
> tion of the similar threnodic scene in book 24. He reserves for the
> end of the poem that more stylized, more ritualized, and hence
> more solemn effect . . . Here in book 22 the agony of loss still has
> its rawest edges. We are kept as closely as possible to the shock and
> horror of the event. Accordingly, the structure is less symmetrical,
> more angular; and the language too veers sharply and suddenly
> away from the grooves of formulaic expectation.[43]

When Andromache does at length make her lament for Hector, the
arrator uses a unique expression to introduce her speech: ἀμβλήδην <u>γοόωσα</u>
ετὰ Τρῳῇσιν ἔειπεν (lifted her voice among the women of Troy <u>in mourning</u>,
76). The same root appears in the participle γοόωσα as we see in the genitive

---

[43] Segal 1971:37. Readers desiring a detailed analysis of the description of Andromache's grief,
which I note here primarily for its length and interruption of the formal patterns of ritual
lament, are referred to Segal's article.

noun γόοιο (lament) in the formulaic introduction for laments (e.g. 24.72 for Andromache's lament). Also, Andromache makes her speech with a grou of women (μετὰ Τρῳῆσιν, among the women of Troy), but when she actuall speaks, she begins by addressing Hector directly (477). So, her speech is clearl a lament, given who the audience and addressee are and the distinction tha is made between them. At 38 verses, the speech that she makes here is longe than any of the other laments for Hector in either Book 22 or Book 24.[44] Th main importance of Hector's death for the *Iliad* when it occurs, in other word: lies in the bereavement of his wife, and only secondarily in the destruction c his city. We are so used to the *Iliad* that it is easy to forget how extraordinar and affecting it is for a Greek poem to give this particular cast to the story c the Greek defeat of the Trojans.

In the more formal series of laments in Book 24, Andromache is give pride of place by going first among the mourners. Here, in contrast, the new of Hector's death is fresh and the scene is one of confusion and raw emotior Accordingly, the narrator heightens the impact of Andromache's first reactio to her husband's death by placing it after the laments of Hector's parents an a detailed description of her emotions as a newly bereaved wife. Finally, he lament and Book 22 as a whole come to an end with the most common formu laic lament conclusion (ὣς ἔφατο κλαίουσ', ἐπὶ δὲ στενάχοντο γυναῖκες [s she spoke, in tears; and the women joined her in mourning], 515). Whateve the date and origin of the book divisions,[45] for our modern appreciation of th scene if not necessarily for any ancient audience, the poem very effectivel highlights the lament of Andromache and brings the family expressions c grief to a peak by ending the book with this image of the weeping wife and he mourning companions.

In Book 22, the very first speech about the dead Hector (by Priam) onl resembles a lament in some respects. It does not separate the addressee fror the audience, for example, which other laments in the poem consistently dc Nor does it directly address the dead man. As the scene progresses, howeve: the speeches of other family members more clearly and fully demonstrate th characteristics of the formal lament. Hecuba's speech displays virtually al of the conventions of lament, except for a reference to a responsive choru at the end. The lament of Andromache derives special emphasis from it delayed position after the speeches of Hector's parents, and it displays all c the conventions of formal lament that we see in all three laments in Book 24

---

[44] Indeed, the entire series of laments in Book 24 comprises 59 verses.

[45] Heiden 1998a has recently argued that the book divisions in the *Iliad* are not only useful i "assist[ing] appreciation" (79), but could also be useful in oral performance.

Overall, the scene gives a sense that the fact of Hector's death sinks in gradually for the members of his family: Priam, in the immediate flush of grief, does not give a formal lament; Hecuba, with a bit more time to process that her son has been killed, gives a speech with most of the features of formal lament, while Andromache, the last speaker, makes the longest and most formal lament not only of the three in Book 22, but of any in the *Iliad*. This progression only emerges clearly against the backdrop of the typical patterns for formal lament.

If we compare the series of laments for Hector immediately after his death in Book 22 with those that appear in Book 24 in connection with his funeral rites, we see that the series in Book 24 is more formally arranged and presented in several respects. All of the laments in the series in Book 24 display the same set of formal criteria; the dynamic there is a gradual broadening of the responsive group of lamenters rather than (as in Book 22) a progressive heightening of the expression of grief from unadorned sadness to full-blown lament. At first, the mourners are women, as is usual in such contexts. By the final lament of Helen—who has caused the whole situation, in some sense—the group of mourners has been extended to include all the people of Troy, which will soon fall to the Greeks now that Hector is dead. These two scenes both use the typical features of formal lament to create an overall dynamic for a scene of mourning for Hector, but each scene does this in a different way that is well suited to the particular circumstances of that particular point in the story. Book 22 uses the conventions of lament to depict the gradual process of the loved ones taking in the fact of someone's death; in Book 24, the narrator creates a sense of closure by gradually broadening the impact of Hector's death from his immediate family to his entire city, which is now destined to fall, taking Achilles with it. Neither of these effects would be as successful as they are without a typical pattern as the basis for them.

Achilles and Patroclus: Iliad 18, 19, 23

There are two sets of laments for the dead Hector, one somewhat informal series at the point when his family first learns of his death, and a second, more formal group that takes place in the broader context of his funeral rites. In the same way, informal laments for Patroclus occur after Achilles and then Briseis first learn of Patroclus' death (Books 18 and 19), and Achilles laments for Patroclus again in the more formal context of the funeral games in Book 23. Indeed, after the death of Patroclus in Book 16, the narrative moves back and forth between laments for Patroclus and laments for Hector, one of the ways in which the poem highlights the interconnectedness of their deaths and the more general idea of the terrible emotional costs of war for both sides. Patroclus' death, moreover, is linked both to Hector's death and also—after the end of the *Iliad*—to the death of Achilles. In many of these speeches, the lamenter sees the death of Patroclus primarily in terms of the death of Achilles rather than on its own terms. Indeed, it has often been suggested that the primary importance of Patroclus' death is not the death of Patroclus himself but the death of Achilles to which it will inevitably lead.[46] However, the position of some neoanalysts that many passages having to do with Patroclus' death have been taken over with minimal changes from passages describing Achilles' death in the epic cycle[47] is an overstatement, as a close examination of the use of lament features in the relevant speeches will show. While it is clearly true that much of the emotion that people feel about Patroclus' death stems from its almost certain result of Achilles' demise, it is not therefore the case that Patroclus' death stands in for Achilles'.

Iliad 18

The connection between the two deaths emerges clearly from the very first speech that follows the death of Patroclus. This speech, moreover, has often been cited by neoanalysts as belonging more naturally to a scene in which Achilles rather than Patroclus is the dead person. Achilles himself does not speak when he learns the sad news from Antilochus. Instead, he wails with inarticulate sorrow and rolls in the dust, an informal but extremely effective and affecting way of showing his emotion. Both the Trojan women who are his captives and his own comrades join him in his grief (18.22-34). The cries of Achilles attract the attention of his mother Thetis, in her home beneath the sea, and she and her sister Nereids mourn the sad event that has taken place. The catalogue of Nereids before Thetis speaks (39-49) heightens the sense of grief both by adding length to the scene and also by giving an identity to the group of women who shares Thetis' emotion.[48] Although the group of women accompanying another woman singing a γόος (18.51) suggests that this speech is a lament, in several important respects it differs from the common patterns in laments for Hector.

[46] See Nagy 1979:111-115 for a wide-ranging and illuminating discussion of the interconnectedness of these two heroes.

[47] See Kakridis 1949 (Chapter III) for sources for Patroclus in the *Iliad*.

[48] For the neoanalyst view that this catalogue (and indeed, the speech itself) is more appropriate for a scene of the death of Achilles, see e.g. Reinhardt 1961:367-368. Minchin 2001:83-84, on the other hand, argues that the poet invented the names in this catalogue and discusses the particular associations of several of the invented names it contains.

... ἄλλαι θ' αἳ κατὰ βένθος ἁλὸς Νηρηΐδες ἦσαν.
τῶν δὲ καὶ ἀργύφεον πλῆτο σπέος· αἳ δ' ἅμα πᾶσαι
στήθεα πεπλήγοντο, Θέτις δ' ἐξῆρχε γόοιο·
"κλῦτε κασίγνηται Νηρηΐδες, ὄφρ' ἐῢ πᾶσαι
εἴδετ' ἀκούουσαι ὅσ' ἐμῷ ἔνι κήδεα θυμῷ.
ὤ μοι ἐγὼ δειλή, ὤ μοι δυσαριστοτόκεια ..."

... and the rest who along the depth of the sea were the
    daughters of Nereus.
The silvery cave was filled with these, and together all
    of them
beat their breasts, and among them <u>Thetis led out the
    threnody</u>:
"Hear me, Nereids, my sisters; so you may all know
well all the sorrows that are in my heart, when you hear of
    them from me.
Ah me, my sorrow, the bitterness in this best of child-bearing ..."

18.49-54

Thetis does not mention Patroclus, the dead man, and she cannot address Achilles directly—the person for whom she is in fact expressing grief and sorrow—because he is still alive. Nor is Patroclus present physically, a feature of all the other laments in the *Iliad*.[49] Hence, in this speech, Thetis addresses the people who are mourning with her when she describes her own grief, an unusual thing to do in a lament.[50] Thus, in two important respects, this speech does not follow the conventions of lament: it does not address the dead person in the second person (nor does it address Achilles this way in lieu of Patroclus), and it does directly address the women who accompany the speaker. Similarly, there is no reference in the conclusion to Thetis' speech to either her own weeping or the responsive laments of her sisters. Instead, the verse following the lament simply says that after she spoke, she and her sisters left her cave (65-66). When Thetis later reaches Achilles, a sad conversation between them rather than a lament for Patroclus follows.[51]

---

[49] Hector is visible to his parents and Andromache in Book 22 even though his corpse is in the possession of the Greeks.

[50] Here I differ from Edwards 1991 *ad loc.* (on 18.54), where he says that "the first laments for Hector begin in the same way."

[51] Kakridis 1949:67-70 brings out effectively the lament-like aspects of this interaction, although it is not necessary to follow him in considering this to *be* a lament to appreciate these evocations of the notion of lament.

Thus, in both the speech itself and the speech conclusion to it, the traditional separation in laments between the addressee and the audience break down, and the speaker never uses direct address to refer to the person who has died. As we saw above, this is one of the most significant features of lament and one that marks it as a formal genre of speech. This speech alludes to the genre of lament insofar as the narrator uses a lament introductory formula to precede the speech, and the speaker is sad because someone close to her has died. However, in several important respects, this speech is *not* a lament even though it is often referred to as one: the audience and the addressee of the speech are the same, and the dead person is not mentioned in the speech itself. A desire to connect the deaths of Achilles and Patroclus should not lead us into thinking wrongly that this speech is a lament for Achilles. In fact, it follows only a few of the conventions of formal lament. Kakridis[52] argues that this scene is derived from one representing the death of Achilles and the laments of his mother and aunts on that occasion. Given the many significant ways that this speech does not follow the conventions of lament, I suggest that Kakridis overstates the similarity of the speech of Thetis to a lament in his desire to demonstrate the link between *Iliad* 18 and a scene of the death of Achilles in another part of the epic cycle. The less this speech resembles lament, indeed, the more improbable it becomes that the passage has links to any specific version of the death of Achilles. Just as Thetis' speech evokes or alludes to lament, the death of Patroclus evokes the death of Achilles but is not, itself, the death of Achilles.

Achilles laments for Patroclus later in Book 18, after Patroclus' corpse has been returned to the Greek camp. While the Trojans eat their supper after holding an assembly, Achilles and his comrades spend the night in lamentation for Patroclus. Here Achilles is the only mourner to lament in direct speech but in spite of the lack of a series of speeches, it is clear that his speech is a lament.

αὐτὰρ Ἀχαιοὶ
παννύχιοι Πάτροκλον <u>ἀνεστενάχοντο γοῶντες,</u>
<u>τοῖσι δὲ Πηλεΐδης ἁδινοῦ ἐξῆρχε γόοιο,</u>
χεῖρας ἐπ' ἀνδροφόνους θέμενος στήθεσσιν ἑταίρου,
πυκνὰ μάλα στενάχων ὥς τε λὶς ἠϋγένειος,
ᾧ ῥά θ' ὑπὸ σκύμνους ἐλαφηβόλος ἁρπάσῃ ἀνὴρ
ὕλης ἐκ πυκινῆς· ὃ δέ τ' ἄχνυται ὕστερος ἐλθών,
πολλὰ δέ τ' ἄγκε' ἐπῆλθε μετ' ἀνέρος ἴχνι' ἐρευνῶν,
εἴ ποθεν ἐξεύροι· μάλα γὰρ δριμὺς χόλος αἱρεῖ·

---

[52] Ibid. 65–75.

ὡς ὃ βαρὺ στενάχων μετεφώνεε Μυρμιδόνεσσιν·
"ὢ πόποι . . . "

> Meanwhile the Achaians
> mourned all night in lamentation over Patroklos.
> Peleus' son led the thronging chant of their lamentation,
> and laid his manslaughtering hands over the chest of his dear
> friend
> with outbursts of incessant grief. As some great bearded lion
> when some man, a deer hunter, has stolen his cubs away
> from him
> out of the close wood; the lion comes back too late, and is
> anguished,
> and turns into many valleys quartering after the man's trail
> on the chance of finding him, and taken with bitter anger;
> so he, groaning heavily, spoke out to the Myrmidons:
> "Ah me . . . ."

> 18.314-324

his passage begins by describing the group of grieving comrades among whom chilles laments for Patroclus (314-315). The verb στενάχομαι (mourn), which regularly ppears in formulaic lament conclusions to describe the responsive mourning of an ccompanying group, is used in verse 315 in compound form for the activity of the chaeans. This portrays them as the responsive chorus for the lament of Achilles. erse 316 is a formulaic introduction for laments, with a masculine dative pronoun istead of a feminine one to suit the Achaeans as the audience for the lament.

The formulaic lament introduction at 316 does not introduce the lament self, as the audience would expect. Instead, an extended passage describing chilles' grief follows it. First, a verse in adding enjambment (317) tells us that chilles touches the body of his dead friend while he laments. An almost iden- cal description precedes Andromache's lament for Hector (24.723-724). While ndromache embraces her husband, putting her arms around him in a physical esture of wifely affection, Achilles only places his hands on Patroclus' corpse ithout embracing him. This laying on of hands is one of the physical gestures hat are part of the ritual of mourning along with the lament itself.[53] The

---

[53] Alexiou 1974:6. In addition to the passages mentioned above, Alexiou points to the opening of the *Choephoroi* (restored from a scholion to a similar verse in Euripides' *Alcestis*), where Orestes laments that he has not been able properly to discharge his responsibilities to his dead father: οὐ γὰρ παρὼν› ὤμωξα σὸν πάτερ μόρον, / οὐδ' ἐξέτεινα χεῖρ' ἐπ' ἐκφορᾷ νεκροῦ (for I was not present to mourn your death, father, nor did I stretch out my hand at the *ekphora* of your corpse, 8-9).

description of this accompanying piece of ritual makes the laments part of a larger and more vivid process than the speeches alone would.

After this, a simile extends the moment even further. Verse 316 has prepared the audience to expect a speech, but it does not appear. This unful filled expectation focuses attention especially strongly on the intervening simile. In one way, the simile heightens the impact of the moment simply by making it longer. Moreover, Achilles, the pre-eminent warrior of the *Iliad*, is described here in terms of a lion.[54] However, instead of the proud and fero cious animal to which warriors are often compared on the battlefield, this lion is a parent inconsolable with grief for the cubs it lost to a hunter. The compar ison draws out the details of the scene, all of which parallel the situation of Achilles and Patroclus: the lion is too late to stop the hunter (320), but tries to find him after the fact in his grief and anger for the cubs (321-322). Here the lion is a symbol of grief rather than power, just as the strength of the form dable Achilles has not sufficed to protect his dearest friend. Like the lion in the simile, his strength only makes his grief more poignant.

Thus, the introduction to this lament is extended with both a single verse in adding enjambment, in a pattern which appears elsewhere[55] and with simile. Both of these additions call attention to themselves because of where they are located: the audience would have their attention firmly fixed on these verses because the verses violate the expectation of hearing the lament itself after the formulaic lament introduction. This produces an especially vivid and emphatic focus on the grief of Achilles before his first, pain-wracked lament for his dead friend. This dramatizes that he has changed from the angry and defiant hero of the earlier part of the poem to the grief-stricken sorrowful figure who has lost his dearest friend. The lament itself, while clearly a lament, is unusual in its arrangement: Achilles begins by lamenting both his own failure to bring Patroclus home to his father Menoetius and the fact that he himself will never come home (324-332). Only in verse 333 does he directly address the dead Patroclus. When he does speak to him, he does not mention his grief at Patroclus' death. Rather, he describes the funeral rites that he will hold for Patroclus and the sacrifice of Trojan youths that he will make to avenge his anger for Patroclus' slaying (333-342).

---

[54] Moulton 1977:105-106 has an excellent discussion of this simile and its similarity to various other similes. This motif reappears later in the poem, in the simile comparing Achilles' grief at the funeral pyre of Patroclus to that of a father whose son has died young (23.222-225). For the consistent use of father-son imagery in connection with the relationship between Achilles and Patroclus, see Moulton 1977:99-106.

[55] For Achilles himself at 23.18 (on which see below) as well as for Andromache at 24.724.

This lament does not lead to further laments by other comrades. Instead, after Achilles finishes speaking, he and his companions bathe the corpse and lay it on a bier (343-353). Following this, a couplet very similar to 314-315 tells us that the Myrmidons lamented with Achilles throughout the night (354-355), and this vignette of the lamenting Achilles comes to an end. This speech displays all of the conventional features of formal lament except for a formulaic conclusion describing responsive lament by a group. This group lamenting does take place, but it is delayed until after the body has been washed. Moreover, the lament gains particular distinction from the simile that is woven into the introductory formula. The simile, which appears in addition to the traditional introduction for a lament rather than instead of it, draws on common battlefield imagery in an unusual context to create a particularly apposite image of Achilles' grief when he first "meets" the corpse of his dead friend and laments over it.

Although the component of the lamenting group does occur in this scene, the primary focus is very much on Achilles rather than on a group of mourners, as befits the bitter and overwhelming grief of his first confrontation with the dead body of his friend. Unlike Hector, who has several loving relatives who are all grief-stricken by his death, only Patroclus' absent father Menoetius is said to have an affection for him that resembles that of Achilles. As a result, Achilles has a distinctive role as "head mourner" for Patroclus, while the father, son, brother, and husband Hector is lamented over by many of his relatives. In Book 19, however, Achilles is joined by others in lamenting for Patroclus in a series that more closely resembles those that we saw for Hector. This broadens the impact of Patroclus' death to include associates of Patroclus' beyond Achilles. Similarly, Briseis' lament and the response of the group around her provide an opportunity to explore the broader impact of war itself on the wives, parents, and comrades who are bereaved by the death of warriors they love during a peaceful interlude before Achilles returns to the battlefield to cause the deaths of many more warriors.

Iliad 19

The impetus for this set of laments for Patroclus is Briseis' return to Achilles after the assembly at which the disagreement between him and Agamemnon is resolved. When Briseis reaches Achilles' tent and sees the corpse of Patroclus, she addresses him in tears. The introduction to her speech is not based on the common formulaic lament introduction and it does not include a reference to a responsive audience among whom she speaks. In other respects, her speech can be confidently identified as a lament.

Βρισηῒς δ' ἄρ' ἔπειτ', ἰκέλη χρυσέη Ἀφροδίτη,
ὡς ἴδε Πάτροκλον δεδαϊγμένον ὀξέϊ χαλκῷ,
<u>ἀμφ' αὐτῷ χυμένη λίγ' ἐκώκυε</u>, χερσὶ δ' ἄμυσσε
στήθεά τ' ἠδ' ἁπαλὴν δειρὴν ἰδὲ καλὰ πρόσωπα.
εἶπε δ' ἄρα <u>κλαίουσα</u> γυνὴ ἐϊκυῖα θεῆσι·
"Πάτροκλέ μοι δειλῇ πλεῖστον κεχαρισμένε θυμῷ ...
... τώ σ' ἄμοτον κλαίω τεθνηότα, μείλιχον αἰεί."
ὣς ἔφατο κλαίουσ', ἐπὶ δὲ στενάχοντο γυναῖκες,
Πάτροκλον πρόφασιν, σφῶν δ' αὐτῶν κήδε' ἑκάστη.

And now, in the likeness of golden Aphrodite, Briseis
when she saw Patroklos lying torn with sharp bronze, <u>folding him in her arms cried shrilly above him</u> and with her hands tore
at her breasts and her soft throat and her beautiful forehead.
The woman like the immortals <u>mourning</u> for him spoke:
"Patroklos, far most pleasing to my heart in its sorrows ...
... therefore I weep your death without ceasing. You were
    kind always."
So she spoke, lamenting, and the women sorrowed in
    response
grieving openly for Patroklos, but for her own sorrows each.

19.282-287; 300-302

Like Achilles, Briseis touches the corpse, but she embraces it (like Andromache embraces the dead Hector) rather than simply putting her hands on its chest. The verbs that describe her wailing appear elsewhere for mourning women (ἐκώκυε, 284,[56] and κλαίουσα, 286). The introduction for her lament includes no pronoun for her addressee(s), so it is not clear here whether a group or Patroclus himself is envisioned here as the (grammatical) object of her speech.

When she speaks, she addresses the corpse directly, as do the relatives of Hector when they mourn for him. Briseis, unlike Thetis, laments for Patroclus himself and the grief that his loss will cause her. She follows the typical lament pattern of directly addressing his corpse at the beginning and the end of her

---

[56] This verb is used with a lament at e.g. *Iliad* 22.407 (Hecuba immediately after the death of Hector).

ament, and she gives a narrative description of her own life in between. In addition, the formulaic conclusion for laments at 301 brings in the responsive group that usually accompanies lament. Moreover, an additional verse (302) describes the feelings of this lamenting chorus in more detail than we find elsewhere, giving them a particularly prominent role here in spite of their absence from the narrative before the lament begins. Briseis, in essence, assumes the role of a female relation of Patroclus, and gives a formal lament that follows all the conventions of the genre except for the explicit mention of a responsive group before the lament begins.

Achilles, however, maintains his position as the chief mourner and most bereaved person. So, he laments here also, even though he already lamented for Patroclus when the body was first returned to him. After Briseis' lament, the leaders of the Greeks beg Achilles to eat, but he refuses and most of the leaders leave (303-309). A few men stay with Achilles, however, and form a chorus for his lament for Patroclus.

> μνησάμενος δ' ἀδινῶς ἀνενείκατο φώνησέν τε·
> "ἦ ῥά νύ μοί ποτε καὶ σὺ δυσάμμορε φίλταθ' ἑταίρων . . .
> . . . ἤδη γὰρ Πηλῆά γ' ὀΐομαι ἢ κατὰ πάμπαν
> τεθνάμεν, ἤ που τυτθὸν ἔτι ζώοντ' ἀκάχησθαι
> γήραΐ τε στυγερῷ καὶ ἐμὴν ποτιδέγμενον αἰεὶ
> λυγρὴν ἀγγελίην, ὅτ' ἀποφθιμένοιο πύθηται."
> ὣς ἔφατο κλαίων, ἐπὶ δὲ στενάχοντο γέροντες,
> μνησάμενοι τὰ ἕκαστος ἐνὶ μεγάροισιν ἔλειπον.

> Remembering Patroklos he sighed vehemently for him, and
>   spoke aloud:
> "There was a time, ill-fated, o dearest of all my companions . . .
> . . . for by this time I think that Peleus must altogether
> have perished, or still keeps a little scant life in sorrow
> for the hatefulness of old age and because he waits ever from me
> the evil message, for the day he hears I have been killed."
> So he spoke, mourning, and the elders lamented in response,
> remembering each those he had left behind in his own halls.

> 19.314-15; 334-39

Here, as in Briseis' lament, the introduction to Achilles' speech uses language that is similar to formulaic lament introductions, but it does not explicitly identify the speech as a lament. The adjective ἀδινός (incessant, shrill) modifies the lament itself in language regularly found in lament introductory formulas (ἀδινοῦ ἐξῆρχε γόοιο, led out the incessant lament), but here it takes the form of an adverb and describes the manner of Achilles' speech. The introductory verse, like that for Briseis' speech, uses a common verb of speaking (ἀνενείκατο φώνησέν τε, sighed and spoke) rather than the technical term for leading a lament (ἐξῆρχε γόοιο, led out lament). It includes no pronoun for the addressee, leaving open the question of who exactly is being addressed. The speech itself is a direct address to the dead Patroclus, as we expect for a lament.[57] Here, as for Briseis' lament, the formulaic conclusion gives a particularly prominent role to the responsive community of mourners who were absent from the introductory language. These mourners, like the captive women who lament with Briseis, remember their own loved ones as they lament for Patroclus. The aorist participle μνησάμενος "remembering" appears twice in the verse-initial position at the beginning (314) and the end of this lament (339, with the nominative plural ending -οι). This highlights the connection of memory with lament.

Thus, this lament for Patroclus brings in more people to grieve for him alongside Achilles. The contents of these various laments, and the stress that the speech frames lay on the thoughts of the lamenters, draw attention to the impact that the death of a warrior has on the range of people with whom the warrior is connected. Such connections, which led to Patroclus' presence on the battlefield in the first place through his relationship to Achilles, become increasingly prominent during the last section of the poem. They finally assume center stage in Book 24, where they provide a way for Priam and Achilles to make a connection to each other and—in a very different context—draw together the whole community of Troy through their grief for the dead Hector to conclude the *Iliad*.

Iliad 23

Thus far in our exploration of the sorrowful speeches about the dead Patroclus, we have seen one speech by Thetis that evokes lament without actually being one (18.52-64); a lament by Achilles amid the Achaeans when Patroclus' corpse is brought home (18.324-342); and further laments by Briseis and then by Achilles when Briseis returns to Achilles' tent and sees the corpse of Patroclus (19.287-300). Finally, in Book 23, Patroclus is buried with full funeral honors, which start with another lament by Achilles. This lament follows almost

---

[57] For similarities between the content of the laments of Briseis and of Achilles in this scene, see Lohmann 1970:102-105. See especially 105 for broader issues of repetition and comparison that these two speeches evoke.

mmediately after Andromache's lament for Hector at the end of Book 22, emphasizing the manifold connections among the characters involved in these two related deaths and the universality of sorrow and lament in war. ust after Hector dies for having killed Patroclus, Patroclus' corpse receives its final funeral rites. As Book 23 opens, most of the other Greeks return to their ships after the fighting over Hector's body has ended, but Achilles tells the Myrmidons to stay with him and mourn for Patroclus (4-11). Achilles leads a lamenting group of Myrmidons (οἱ δ' ᾤμωξαν ἀολλέες, ἦρχε δ' Ἀχιλλεύς [all of them assembled moaned, and Achilleus led them], 12). Accompanied by Thetis, they slowly drive their chariots around the corpse (12-16).

The introduction to Achilles' speech at this point is identical to the beginning of the introduction to his first lament for Patroclus.

> τοῖσι δὲ Πηλεΐδης ἀδινοῦ ἐξῆρχε γόοιο
> χεῖρας ἐπ' ἀνδροφόνους θέμενος στήθεσσιν ἑταίρου·
> "χαῖρέ μοι ὦ Πάτροκλε καὶ εἰν Ἀΐδαο δόμοισι"

> Peleus' son led the thronging chant of their lamentation,
> and laid his manslaughtering hands over the chest of his dear
>   friend:
> "Good-bye, Patroklos. I hail you even in the house of the
>   death god."

$$23.17\text{-}19 \ (17\text{-}18 = 18.316\text{-}317)$$

Once again, the added verse after the formulaic lament introduction gives a fuller and more moving picture of the grieving Achilles than the introduction alone would. A simile appeared in Book 18 after this additional verse, but the lament itself directly follows the couplet here. There is no reason why a simile could not have appeared in Book 23 as well as in Book 18. But the appearance of the simile when Achilles first grieves for Patroclus, and when his grief is presumably sharpest and strongest, gives that episode special prominence compared to the more formal context of the funeral rites for Patroclus. This progression, in which the grieving person (or people) becomes more able to voice his sorrow in the formal terms of lament as he gradually takes in the reality of his loved one's death, resembles what we saw when we compared the laments for the just-killed Hector in Book 22 with the more formal and orderly speeches during his funeral at the end of Book 24.

By this point, although Achilles has not recovered from his grief (and in fact he refuses to eat just after this lament), his grief is somewhat more under control than it has been. He opens his speech here not with expressions of

267

grief but with a salutation to the corpse when he says χαῖρέ μοι ὦ Πάτροκλε (contrast the opening words of his first lament at 18.324, ὦ πόποι [ah me]) Moreover, this lament forms part of the funeral rites for Patroclus rather than standing on its own. For this reason too, less elaboration than in Book 18 seems appropriate. The lament itself is short, given that Achilles has already expressed his grief for Patroclus twice before: he merely bids Patroclus farewell and tells him that he has done all the things he promised the corpse that he would do.

If we look at the various laments for Patroclus (by Achilles in Books 18, 19, and 23 and by Briseis in Book 19), we can see that all of them are addressed at least partly to Patroclus himself; all take place with a group of accompanying mourners, although this group may not be mentioned in both the introduction and conclusion of the lament; and all maintain the distinction between the audience of the lament (the group) and the addressee of the lament (the dead person). Thetis' speech at the beginning of Book 18, on the other hand, although it is often considered a lament resembles formal laments only in naming the speech as a γόος at the beginning and in giving Thetis a group of women to whom to speak. Her speech itself conforms very little to the traditional structures of formal lament This casts grave doubt on the neoanalyst contention that Patroclus' death is a rehash or a reworking of Achilles' death as depicted in other parts of the epic cycle. While much of the interest in Patroclus' death lies in its connection to the death of Achilles, Patroclus and Achilles are not interchangeable and the laments for Patroclus should be evaluated on their own terms.

These laments for Patroclus adhere to the basic conventions of the lament as a formal speech genre that we saw in the more developed lament sequences for Hector. In fact, the genre of lament is restricted in the *Iliad* to Patroclus and Hector, yet another way that these two heroes are linked together and that the poem universalizes the sorrow of war to both sides of the conflict. For both Patroclus and Hector, speeches by dear friends or relatives immediately following the death of the relevant hero have a ragged immediacy that stems partly from the fact that these speeches do not include all the typical attributes of a lament. A later speech or series of speeches, by following lament patterns more fully, have a calmer and more formal tone. Individual laments regularly achieve special effects of pathos or vividness by using the common patterns of lament in unusual ways Moreover, the laments for each hero interlock with one another over the last uarter of the poem, thereby strengthening its shape and cohesion: Hector's eath at Achilles' hands follows the first laments for Patroclus and precedes is funeral. Laments for Hector, the most developed and formal of all, bring he poem to a close after Patroclus' funeral has taken place. Thus, the genre f lament plays a significant role both in setting apart Hector and Patroclus nd in linking them together. Indeed, it shapes the last section of the poem nto a subtle and highly effective depiction of war primarily as a source of orrow for those on both sides. Of course, it is also a source of honor and rizes and so forth, but the consistent emphasis on lament and grieving in he last part of the *Iliad* depicts loss for both winners and losers as the main ffect of war.

Conclusions

lthough athletic games and formal laments do not appear often enough to ave the same secure status as types that other kinds of conversations do, hey show patterns that are clear and consistent. Not only do they follow articular patterns, albeit patterns that appear less often than those of more ell established types, they also manipulate these patterns to create effects in he same manner that we have observed in previous chapters. Athletic games, ormal laments, and assemblies share turn sequences and turn structures hat appear to be associated with formal contexts. These include successive peeches to a group at the level of turn sequence; turns that are composed of oth speech and action; and speech turns that are regularly accompanied by ome kind of behavior. To a great extent, these patterns are consistent with haracteristics of institutional talk that have been documented by linguistic esearch, suggesting that the specifics of behavior and sequence described in hese poetic representations reflect at least to some degree actual practices in ssembly, games and lament.

Each of these genres regularly adapts these conventions to create esthetic effects that dramatize themes important to the poem overall. In he funeral games for Patroclus, conversation appears at moments when he Greeks in general and Achilles in particular successfully negotiate and esolve conflicts about status and prizes. This contrasts markedly with chilles' behavior and the use of conversation elsewhere in the *Iliad*, thereby roviding an effective resolution to the theme of conflict and status among he various Greeks. Laments for Hector and for Patroclus in the last third of he poem bring forward the idea that the main characteristic of war is the costs it exacts from the loved ones of the dead warriors on both sides. This idea of war, an extraordinary one in a Greek poem depicting a Greek victory, characterizes the outlook of the *Iliad* and gives it much of its superb force and power.

The Conclusion will discuss the characteristics and aesthetic significance of conversation, and will speculate on what this means for the composition, transmission, and writing down of the Homeric epics.

CONCLUSIONS

ACH CHAPTER OF THIS BOOK has examined the aesthetic and poetic effects of a different type of conversation. In the first two chapters, we saw that one-on-one conversations in the *Odyssey* consistently highlight the conflict that the main characters in the poem feel between revealing themselves and/or believing what other characters say about their own identities, and maintaining a cautious skepticism or concealment in order to guard against the adverse effects of too much openness. Odysseus feels this conflict the most strongly and consistently, but Penelope and Telemachus also feel it. Indeed, an involvement in and awareness of this tension may be said to characterize the members of the Odysseus family as kin. This tension and its eventual resolution in Odysseus' happy reunions with the various members of his family are one of the main themes of the poem. An abiding interest in this tension and its effects characterizes the *Odyssey*'s attitude toward its traditional characters and events. In the *Odyssey*, conversation dramatizes tensions that are ultimately resolved between characters who care deeply for each other.

One-on-one conversation in the *Iliad*, on the other hand, consistently depicts characters who are enemies or who, although ostensibly comrades or even spouses, have relationships characterized mainly by conflict and hostility rather than affection. This effect emerges in several ways. First of all, one-on-one conversations off the battlefield occur very rarely in the *Iliad*: there are few scenes of characters involved in peaceful and harmonious interchange, and those that do occur take place between enemies or characters who are somehow at odds with each other. Moreover, the majority of one-on-one conversations take place in various battle contexts where such exchanges are not usually found. The very presence of a conversation on the battlefield calls attention to itself because it is not part of the usual conversational types in battle. Similarly, the content of these conversations emphasizes moments in the poem where the conflict is particularly intense or important to the story.

271

Conclusions

In particular, one-on-one conversations occur at several key points in the *aristeia* of Achilles to depict his implacable hatred for the Trojans and the furious rage he feels toward Hector before killing him, often from the perspective of a sympathetic Trojan victim. This approach to one-on-one conversation emphasizes the isolation of the characters in the *Iliad* and the primacy of conflict and tension in their relationships with each other.[1]

In addition to conversations between two people, the *Iliad* also focuses several types of formal group conversations that are either entirely or mostly absent from the *Odyssey*. This implies that the *Iliad*, more than the *Odyssey*, is interested in the relationships and power dynamics that take place among groups of people as well as in the relationships between individuals that emerge through one-on-one conversation. All of these group conversational genres have certain features in common that characterize them as formal (or institutional, in linguistic terms). These include common or required behavioral accompaniments to speaking and a listening group to whom a given speech is not directly addressed but whose presence is required to give the speaker's remarks legitimacy and authority. Specific types of formal group conversations include assembly, funeral games, and lament.

In different ways, each of these group contexts dramatizes a key theme of the *Iliad*. The disastrous quarrel between Achilles and Agamemnon that drives much of the action of the poem takes place largely in public assemblies thereby emphasizing the effect that their disagreement has on the whole Greek community as well as the power struggle that underlies the quarrel itself. Although the type of funeral games does not appear repeatedly in the *Iliad*, it is nevertheless clear what the key elements of the type are. As a result, we can see that the funeral games for Patroclus include conversations at points where the type would not normally feature a conversation in order to depict the Greeks—and especially Achilles, as the presider over the games—successfully resolving tensions that arise about awarding prizes in the competitions. This provides an effective sense of closure for the Greeks as a community, which for most of the poem fails very conspicuously to resolve just such tensions as these. Finally, the formal laments for Hector and for Patroclus that appear throughout the last third of the poem play a key role in conveying the poem's perspective on war, loss, and sorrow. Largely by means of these laments, the poem suggests that the most important of war's many effects is bereavement

---

[1] Here it will be clear that I disagree, at least as far as the *Iliad* is concerned, with Feeney's statement that "the world of the *Aeneid* is lacking in the homeric style of open, co-operative and sustaining speech" (1983:213).

and sadness, and that the grieving and the dead on both sides in a war deserve our sympathy equally.

So, conversation is used to create a range of different effects in various contexts in the two Homeric epics. However, basic similarities of structure, aesthetics, and narrative strategy underlie all of these individual examples. The conversations studied in this book are based on consistent types of conversation that can be described in much the same way as other types. These types are characterized by sequences of speakers and formulaic speech frames that depend on the particular kind of conversation. Many conversations in the Homeric epics follow the patterns of these types; many others extend or vary the typical patterns in order to create emphasis and dramatize important themes of the poem in question. These variations follow a consistent pattern. First of all, they assume a familiarity with the typical pattern, in relation to which the extension or variation derives its force. The variations in typical conversational structures tend to have consistent features of their own. The specific ways in which the typical features vary from their usual patterns reflect the basic aesthetic principles laid out in the Introduction: notable effects arise from a gifted use of the traditional and/or formulaic, not from invention; length conveys emphasis.

Indeed, conversation in each poem plays a central role in shaping the key themes of the story overall. In the *Odyssey*, conversations between Odysseus and his family and household both develop and portray for the audience the complex tensions between the impulse for openness and the self-preserving desire to conceal one's identity and doubt other people's veracity. This view of human relationships in general, as fraught and complex but ultimately satisfying and harmonious, may be said to characterize the *Odyssey* as a whole. On the other hand, the *Iliad* uses conversation to portray interpersonal connections as fleeting, when they occur at all, and as characterized in general by conflict, hostility, and power struggles of various kinds. As one of the most basic kinds of human interaction, conversation is an appropriate vehicle for exploring the nature of these relations. As one of the most common and widespread types in the Homeric epics, it is a very powerful narrative tool for shaping the tone and themes of the poems.

Two features of the poems overall emerge most clearly from this analysis. First, each poem displays a compelling and consistent unity: the regular structure of conversational types, the ways in which conversations vary from these regular structures, the effects to which these variations are put, and the significance of these variations for the artistic and aesthetic shape of the poems are both widespread and consistent in their various appearances. These structures and aesthetic strategies, in particular type scenes and the expansion aesthetic, are characteristic of oral poetry. In addition, in several instances, conversations and the formulas that comprise them make strong linkages between one part of the poem and another part that may be quite distant (for instance, the two assemblies in *Iliad* 1 and 19, or the various scenes between Penelope and Odysseus in the last third of the *Odyssey*). The aesthetic effects of conversation, in other words, are not only consistent throughout the poems, but link together widely distant parts of the poems. This strongly underlines the overall unity of the poems. Secondly, the consistency of these aesthetic effects and of the underlying vocabulary of what a conversation "normally" looks like implies the existence of an audience for the poems who was versed in these effects and for whom they were intended to make sense. What is the significance for our conceptions of the origins of the Homeric epics of unified poems of great length that seem to be addressed to an audience versed in the tools and techniques of such poems?[2]

This above all seems to me to suggest a synchronic unity for the poems, in substantially the form in which they now exist, at a time and in a compositional context in which the existence of an audience would have played an important role in shaping the poems.[3] Moreover, this audience must not only have participated actively in giving rise to the poems as they have come down to us; they must have been able to understand the specific social and linguistic features of the conversations that are represented in the poems. These conversations, as we have seen, reflect identifiable attributes of conversations in particular contexts as they have been documented by linguistic research. This suggests that the actions and conventions that characterize conversations in different contexts are not simply an artistic creation, but a reflection of what people actually did when they engaged in these activities.[4] It has been suggested that social practices and conventions in oral poetry, unlike (e.g.) archaeological artifacts or place names, are highly responsive to the expectations and realities of the audience of the poetry.[5] Accordingly, social structures in the poems should represent actual systems familiar to the audience of a particular time, not an artistic composite or a picture of a vanished and alien culture. Given the consistency

---

[2] Although similar features characterize both the *Iliad* and the *Odyssey*, I take no position on whether, if one poet was responsible for each poem, it is also the case that one poet was responsible for both.

[3] This is a prominent feature of a wide range of oral poetry: Finnegan 1977:54-55.

[4] Alexiou 1974 passim, for example, documents the linkages between Greek laments in literature and in reality.

[5] Morris 1986.

and specificity of conversational conventions in the *Iliad* and the *Odyssey*, it seems probable that these conventions are based on actual behaviors familiar to an audience at a given time.[6] This in turn implies the existence of an audience, synchronically, to whom these poems were orally addressed. There are, of course, problems with this view.[7] Nevertheless it seems to me to fit best with the poems as they have been transmitted to us.

I do not believe that any theory of composition and transmission of the Homeric epics can be definitely proven based on the current state of our knowledge. Among the various possibilities, it seems to me that the poems themselves reflect not only an oral sensibility, but a set of particular conventions for conversations in various social contexts that are likely to stem from social practices of a particular time, although there is no way to know what exactly what time that was. This evidence suggesting that the poems as we have them arose at one particular time, rather than over many generations, is not disproved by any of the usual arguments against a synchronic unity for the poems: the writing down of the poems need not coincide with or have been caused by the status of written texts as definitive, canonical, or authoritative; there are parallels of oral poems that are similar in length; we don't know enough about the technology of writing at this time to rule out on that basis the idea that the poems were written down at a comparatively early date.

More positively, scholars working in various cultures and disciplines have noted that a particularly talented singer who is stimulated by a receptive audience often produces poems that are distinguished by the same qualities that characterize our *Iliad* and *Odyssey*: they tell the same stories as other poets do, and they use the same traditional techniques, language, and characters, but they tell their tales at much greater length than other less gifted poets. These artists create nuanced tales imbued with emotion, with subtle and pervasive thematic unity, and above all with highly appropriate and effective use of the traditional language and stories that in the hands of other artists simply relate that Odysseus spoke to Penelope or that Hector was killed in fighting at Troy. In the hands of a master, these events become the kernel of superbly moving and unified tales that achieve their effects by means of, not in spite of or beyond, the typical scenes and sequences on which they are based.

---

[6] There is no way to know when this time was exactly, but presumably sometime in the archaic period. Janko 1982 and Morris 1986 both proposed the eighth century B.C.E., a date recently questioned by Graziosi 2002.

[7] See most notably Nagy, e.g. 1992, which cogently states the diffusion-evolutionary model of Homeric composition and transmission and the objections to synchronic views of the poems' unity.

APPENDICES

APPENDIX I

BREAKDOWN OF DIRECT SPEECHES IN THE ILIAD AND THE ODYSSEY BY TURN TYPE AND BY TYPE OF SPEECH INTRODUCTORY FORMULA

T HE FOLLOWING TWO TABLES CATEGORIZE AND TOTAL i) the speeches and ii) the speech introductions in the *Iliad* and the *Odyssey* book by book. The category names at the left side of the chart—reply position, initial position, single speech, and successive speech—indicate the type of speech as described in the Introduction. Totals are given for each of these types of speech for each book of the *Iliad* and *Odyssey* (extending horizontally across the chart) and for each poem overall (at the right side of the chart). At the bottom of the chart, totals are also given for each book of the number of speeches of all kinds, the number of single speeches, the number of verses of direct speech, and the total number of verses in the book. These overall figures give a general sense of how much speech there is in each book and how much of the speech takes place within a conversation.

Within each speech type (except successive, which is very rare), I have given the number of speech introductory formulas for that particular kind of speech, again according to the categories developed in the Introduction (reply formula, a subcategory of reply for reply formulas that use a verb containing the root -μειβ-, group reply formula, flexible formula, context-specific formula, initial formula, group initial formula, partial verse formula, no formula). Totals for each type of speech introductory formula within each speech type are given book by book horizontally across the chart, and are totaled for each poem at the right side of the chart.

The same formula types are given beneath each speech type. Although all types of formulas introduce all types of speeches (with the exception of reply formulas that use a verb containing the -μειβ- root, a category which is restricted to "reply position"), these data show that different kinds of formulas appear at vastly different rates for different types of speeches. Moreover, partial verse formulas and non-formulaic speech introductions also appear at different rates depending on the type of speech.

In the *Odyssey* table, the tale of Odysseus in Books 9-12 is considered to be one long speech. His tale represents one (or rather two, counting the interruption in Book 11) turns in a normal conversational sequence among the Phaeacians. I plan to treat the conversations reported within Odysseus' tale in a separate study.

ILIAD Totals	Book 1	2	3	4	5	6	7	8	9	10	11	12
reply position	23	6	12	14	14	10	14	9	11	25	8	
reply formula	14	1	4	9	12	5	6	7	6	18	6	
reply w/ -μειβ- root	11	1	1	3	5	3	1	4	4	10	3	
group reply		1	1				1	1	3	3		
variable formula	1			1			1			1		
context-spec.	2	3		1	1		2					
initial												
group initial	1											
partial verse	1	1	4	1	1	3	3		1	2	1	
no formula	4		3	2		2	1	1	1	1	1	
initial position	6	3	5	7	10	7	7	8	5	9	7	
reply formula									1			
group reply												
variable formula				2								
context-spec.	1		1		3	2	2	2	1		1	
initial					2		1			1	1	
group initial	1			1	1	2	2		1			
partial verse			3	1	2	1	1	2		3	3	
no formula	4	3	1	3	2	2	3	3	3	4	2	
single speech	6	8	10	5	13	4	4	5	0	5	11	
reply formula												
group reply		1	1									
variable formula		1		1						1		
context-spec.		4	1	3	3	1	3	1			7	
initial												
group initial		1	0									
partial verse	4	2	6		3	1	1	1		1	3	
no formula	2		2	1	7	2		3		3	1	
successive speech	1	1	1	1	2	2	1	3	1	2	1	
number of speeches	36	18	28	27	39	23	26	25	17	41	27	1
number of single sp's	6	8	10	5	13	4	4	5	0	5	11	
verses of direct sp	373	283	242	242	334	323	244	268	588	292	320	12
total verses	611	877	461	544	909	529	482	565	713	579	848	47

13	14	15	16	17	18	19	20	21	22	23	24	TOTAL
11	18	12	7	7	13	10	8	13	14	14	25	299
9	13	7	5	5	13	8	5	4	9	3	18	188
2	6	3	1	1	6	5	3	1	1	1	9	85
	1					1						12
1		3								3	1	12
	1	1				1		3	1		2	18
												0
								1				2
	1						1	3	1	4	3	31
1	2	1	2	2			2	2	3	4	1	36
7	5	5	4	8	6	4	8	9	6	7	11	155
	1									1		3
						1						1
		1	1			1		1				6
	2	2	1	1	5		2	2	2	3	3	36
1								1	1		1	9
			1	1		1			1			12
5	2	1	1	1			3	3		3	6	42
1		1	1	5	1	2	2	3	2		1	49
9	4	16	13	16	4	4	3	5	5	19	9	187
			1									1
										1		3
	1			1			1					6
7	1	8	4	9	2	1	2	2	2	6	1	70
												0
											1	2
1	1		3	2	1			1	1	3	2	38
1	1	9	5	4	2	3		2	2	9	5	70
	1	1		3	2	1	2	4	2	3	2	37
27	28	34	24	34	25	19	21	31	27	43	47	678
9	4	16	13	16	4	4	3	5	5	19	9	187
254	247	292	256	273	266	272	229	270	277	347	453	7067
837	552	746	867	761	617	424	504	611	515	897	804	15724

Appendix I

ODYSSEY Totals	Book 1	2	3	4	5	6	7	8	9	10	11	12
reply position	15	12	14	26	6	2	8	11	1		6	
reply formula	14	7	11	19	3	1	6	7	1		4	
reply w/ -μειβ- root	4	1	3	8	2			5	6		4	
group reply		1	1	1			1				1	
variable formula		1		1	2							
context-spec.		3			1		1	1				
initial												
group initial											1	
partial verse			1	2		1	1	1				
no formula	1	1	1	2				2				
initial position	4	4	4	7	4	2	4	5				
reply formula												
group reply								1				
variable formula							1	1				
context-spec.		1		3				2				
initial		1										
group initial	2	1	1		1		2					
partial verse		1		3	2	1		1				
no formula	3	2	2	1	1	1	2					
single speech	1	4	2	4	9	6	3	7				
reply formula				1								
group reply		1		1				1				
variable formula	1							1				
context-spec.		1		1	6	1	1	4				
initial												
group initial			2				1					
partial verse		1			1	2		1				
no formula		1		1	2	3	1					
successive speech					1	1		1				
number of speeches	20	20	20	37	20	11	15	24	1		6	
number of single sp's	1	4	2	4	9	6	3	7				
verses of direct sp	275	288	331	617	210	174	193	247	566	574	631	453
total verses	444	434	497	847	493	331	347	586	567	574	640	453

13	14	15	16	17	18	19	20	21	22	23	24	TOTAL
18	11	24	23	32	19	26	16	14	19	18	19	340
12	10	17	18	23	10	20	8	6	12	13	13	235
10	9	3	5	10	3	12	3	0	4	4	7	103
				1	3		4	2			2	17
3										1	1	9
1		1	2	1			1	3	3	2	2	22
												0
1		1	1		1							5
	1	5	1	3	3	6	1	1	3		2	32
1			2	4	3		2	2	1	2		24
5	4	8	7	14	6	7	5	5	9	3	8	115
											1	1
		1	1				1					4
1	1	1	1						1		1	8
2		1	3	4	1	2	1	1	4	2	1	28
			1	1							1	4
1		1	1	2	1	2					1	16
1	1	2		1	3	1	2	3	2	1		25
1	2	3		5	2	2	2		2		3	34
1	2	1	3	2	5	0	6	3	9	2	3	73
									1			2
							1					4
					1							3
1					3			1	1		1	21
												0
									2			5
		2		1		1	1	3	1	1	15
	2		1	2			4	1	2	1	1	22
		1		3	2	1	1	4			2	17
24	17	34	33	51	32	34	28	26	37	23	32	545
1	2	1	3	2	5	0	6	3	9	2	3	73
257	409	348	322	373	254	423	222	227	208	224	350	8176
440	533	557	481	606	428	604	394	434	501	372	548	12111

APPENDIX II

ALL PARTICIPLES THAT APPEAR IN REPLY FORMULAS OF THE TYPE τὸν/τὴν [PARTICIPLE] προσέφη [NOMINATIVE NAME/EPITHET]

The verses that contain participles other than ἀπαμειβόμενος with the main verb προσέφη are given below in order of frequency of the participle.

Initial half-verses that appear three times or more

τὸν δ' ἄρ' <u>ὑπόδρα ἰδὼν</u> προσέφη [nominative name/epithet, subject]
20x (13x *Iliad*, 7x *Odyssey*)
Then <u>looking darkly</u> at him, [subject] answered him

τὸν δὲ <u>μέγ' ὀχθήσας</u> προσέφη [nominative name/epithet, subject]
13x (10x *Iliad*, 3x *Odyssey*)
<u>Deeply disturbed</u>, [subject] answered him

τὸν δ' <u>ἐπιμειδήσας</u> προσέφη [nominative name/epithet, subject]
4x (3x *Iliad*, 1x *Odyssey*)
[subject] answered him, <u>laughing</u>

τὸν δὲ <u>βαρὺ στενάχων</u> προσέφη [nominative name/epithet, subject]
3x *Iliad*
Then <u>groaning heavily</u>, [subject] answered him

τὸν δ' <u>ἐπικερτομέων</u> προσέφη [nominative name/epithet, subject]
3x (2x *Iliad*, 1x *Odyssey*)
[subject] spoke <u>in bitter mockery</u> over him

τὸν δ' <u>ὀλιγοδρανέων</u> προσέφη [nominative name/epithet, subject]
  3x *Iliad*
In his <u>weakness</u> [subject] answered him

τὸν δ' <u>οὐ ταρβήσας</u> προσέφη [nominative name/epithet, subject]
  3x *Iliad*
Then [subject] answered, <u>not frightened</u> before him

nitial half-verses that appear once[1]

<u>τὸν καὶ φωνήσας</u> προσέφη κρείων Ἀγαμέμνων, *Iliad* 14.41
Now powerful Agamemnon spoke aloud and <u>addressed him</u>

<u>καί μιν φωνήσας</u> προσέφη πολύμητις Ὀδυσσεύς, *Odyssey* 14.439
Then resourceful Odysseus spoke to him and <u>addressed him</u>

τὸν δ' <u>ἀναχωρήσας</u> προσέφη πολύμητις Ὀδυσσεύς, *Odyssey* 17.453
Now resourceful Odysseus spoke, as he <u>drew back</u> from him

τὸν δ' <u>ἐπιθαρσύνων</u> προσέφη ξανθὸς Μενέλαος, *Iliad* 4.183
Then <u>in encouragement</u> fair-haired Menelaos spoke to him

τὸν δὲ <u>καταθνήσκων</u> προσέφη κορυθαίολος Ἕκτωρ, *Iliad* 22. 355
Then, <u>dying</u>, Hektor of the shining helmet spoke to him

τὸν καὶ <u>νεικείων</u> προσέφη ξανθὸς Μενέλαος[2], *Iliad* 23.438
But Menelaos of the fair hair called to him <u>in anger</u>

τὸν δὲ <u>παρισταμένη</u> προσέφη γλαυκῶπις Ἀθήνη, *Odyssey* 24.516
Then <u>standing close beside</u> him gray-eyed Athene said to him

τὸν δὲ <u>χολωσαμένη</u> προσέφη λευκώλενος Ἥρη, *Iliad* 24.55
Then <u>bitterly</u> Hera of the white arms answered him, saying

---

[1] This appendix, unlike other data in this study, includes participles that only appear once. This is because the basic verse in which the participles appear is so common, and the idea of slotting in different participles depending on the context seems so ingrained in the poetry, that even if a given participle appears only once it seems to me that the verse is still a formula. This is a judgment with which some readers may not agree, but as it affects only a handful of verses, it is not an important point from the standpoint of numbers.

[2] Cf. καί μιν νεικείων ἔπεα πτερόεντα προσηύδα at *Odyssey* 18.9.

APPENDIX III

FULL-VERSE CONTEXT-SPECIFIC INTRODUCTORY FORMULAS

All context-specific speech introductory formulas that occur at least three times in the Homeric epics (presented in order of frequency, with most frequent first) are given below.[1]

Implied subjects whose names would be given in a different verse if the formula appeared in a longer passage of Greek are given in parentheses in the English translations. Varied nouns or pronouns are noted in square brackets. Where either a masculine or a feminine gender is possible (e.g. with participles modifying the subject, or with the accusative pronoun μιν), all possible genders are given in the Greek, but only the masculine possibility is translated into English to simplify presentation. The main verb of speaking is highlighted.

Formulas Appearing Ten Times or More

> ὅ σφιν ἐϋφρονέων <u>ἀγορήσατο καὶ μετέειπεν</u>
> 15x (9x *Iliad*, 6x *Odyssey*)
> He in kind intention toward all <u>spoke publicly and addressed them</u>

> ἀγχοῦ δ' ἱστάμενος (or -η) ἔπεα πτερόεντα <u>προσηύδα</u>
> 13x (9x *Iliad*, 4x *Odyssey*)
> Speaking in winged words he stood beside him and <u>spoke to him</u>

> καὶ or δὴ τότε [accusative, direct object] <u>προσέφη</u> [nominative name/epithet, subject]
> 12x (4x *Iliad*, 8x *Odyssey*)
> And now [subject] <u>spoke to</u> [object]

---

[1] In Appendices III and IV, formulas that appear in the mouth of a character-narrator rather than the primary narrator are not included in the tallies. Such formulas will form part of a study I am currently writing on the range of speech representational strategies in the Homeric poems.

ὀχθήσας δ' ἄρα εἶπε πρὸς ὃν μεγαλήτορα θυμόν
11x (7x *Iliad*, 4x *Odyssey*)
And troubled, he spoke then to his own great-hearted spirit

αἶψα δὲ [accusative, direct object] ἔπεα πτερόεντα προσηύδα
10x (3x *Iliad*, 7x *Odyssey*)
(he) swiftly uttered winged words to [direct object]

ἔν τ' ἄρα οἱ φῦ χειρὶ ἔπος τ' ἔφατ' ἔκ τ' ὀνόμαζε
10x (6x *Iliad*, 4x *Odyssey*)
S/he clung to his hand and called him by name and spoke
to him[2]

Formulas Appearing between Five and Ten Times

ὧδε δέ τις εἴπεσκεν ἰδὼν ἐς πλησίον ἄλλον
9x (3x *Iliad*, 6x *Odyssey*)
And thus they would speak to each other, each looking at the
man next to him

τοῖσιν δ' [nominative, subject] ἀγορήσατο καὶ μετέειπε
7x *Odyssey*
[subject] spoke publicly and addressed them

στῆ δ' ὀρθὸς καὶ μῦθον ἐν Ἀργείοισιν ἔειπεν
7x *Iliad*
He stood upright and spoke his word out among the Argives

χειρί τέ μιν κατέρεξεν ἔπος τ' ἔφατ' ἔκ τ' ὀνόμαζε
6x (4x *Iliad*, 2x *Odyssey*)
(s/he) stroked him with her hand and called him by name
and spoke to him

στῆ δ' ἄρ' ὑπὲρ κεφαλῆς καί μιν πρὸς μῦθον ἔειπεν
6x (2x *Iliad*, 4x *Odyssey*)
(he) stood over his head and spoke a word to him

---

[2] Generally used between a man and a woman, so gender is used in translation. The same applies
to χειρί τέ μιν κατέρεξεν ἔπος τ' ἔφατ' ἔκ τ' ὀνόμαζε below.

καί ῥ' ὀλοφυρόμενος/η ἔπεα πτερόεντα <u>προσηύδα</u>
  6x (3x *Iliad*, 3x *Odyssey*)[3]
So in sorrow for himself he <u>addressed</u> him in winged words

<u>ἤϋσεν</u> δὲ διαπρύσιον [dative plural, indirect object] γεγωνώς
  6x *Iliad*
He lifted his voice and <u>called</u> in a piercing cry to [indirect
  object]

Formulas Appearing Three to Five Times

[nominative, subject][4] δ' <u>ἐνένιπεν ἔπος τ' ἔφατ' ἔκ τ' ὀνόμαζε</u>
  5x *Odyssey*
[subject] <u>scolded him with a word and spoke out and named him</u>

ὧδε δέ τις <u>εἴπεσκε</u> νέων ὑπερηνορεόντων
  5x *Odyssey*
And thus <u>would go the word</u> of one of the arrogant young men

τὸν δ' αὖτε (or προτέρη) ψυχὴ <u>προσεφώνεε</u> [genitive singular
  patronymic][5]
  5x *Odyssey*
The soul of [the son of X] <u>answered</u> (or, was first to speak)

[nominative, subject] [dative plural, indirect object] <u>ἐκέκλετο</u>
  μακρὸν ἀΰσας
  5x *Iliad*
[subject] in a great voice <u>cried out</u> to [indirect object]

αἶψα δὲ [accusative, direct object] <u>προσεφώνεεν</u> ἐγγὺς ἐόντα
  5x (3x *Iliad*, 2x *Odyssey*)
And at once (he) <u>called over</u> to [direct object] who was not
  far from him

---

[3] This total does not include six uses by Odysseus, with elided με in place of ῥα, in the tale of his
  wanderings.
[4] Plus two examples in the *Odyssey* of an accusative instead of a nominative beginning the
  verse.
[5] These are lumped together as "speech introduction for dead soul" rather than being separated
  into the subcategories of "response by dead soul" (with δ' αὖτε) and "initial speech by dead
  soul" (with προτέρη).

αὐτίκα [accusative, direct object] ἔπεα πτερόεντα <u>προσηύδα</u>
    4x *Iliad*
But immediately (he) <u>spoke</u> in winged words to [object]

καὶ or δὴ τότε [nominative, subject] <u>προσεφώνεε</u> [accusative,
    subject]
    4x *Odyssey*[6]
Then [subject] <u>talked to</u> [object]

κινήσας δὲ [or ῥα] κάρη προτὶ ὃν <u>μυθήσατο</u> θυμόν
    4x (2x *Iliad*, 2x *Odyssey*)
(he) stirred his head and <u>spoke</u> to his own spirit

[dative singular pronoun, object] δ' ἐπὶ μακρὸν <u>ἄϋσε</u>
    [nominative name/epithet, subject]
    4x *Iliad*
And [subject] <u>cried aloud</u> to [object] in a great voice

τοῖσι δὲ [nominative, subject] <u>ἁδινοῦ ἐξῆρχε</u> γόοιο
    3x *Iliad*
[subject] <u>led the thronging chant</u> of their lamentation

καί μιν λισσόμενος ἔπεα πτερόεντα <u>προσηύδα</u>
    3x *Odyssey*
And (he) <u>spoke</u> to him in winged words and in supplication

[compound dative, indirect object] <u>ἐκέκλετο</u> μακρὸν ἀΰσας
    3x *Iliad*
He <u>called out</u> in a great voice to [indirect object]

[nominative, subject] δ' ἔκπαγλον <u>ἐπεύξατο</u> μακρὸν ἀΰσας
    3x *Iliad*
And [subject] <u>vaunted</u> terribly over him, calling in a great voice

τοὺς ὅ γ' ἐποτρύνων ἔπεα πτερόεντα <u>προσηύδα</u>
    3x *Iliad*
<u>Calling out</u> to these in winged words he rallied them onward

τεύχεά τ' ἐξενάριξε καὶ εὐχόμενος <u>ἔπος ηὔδα</u>
    3x *Iliad*
(he) stripped off his armor and <u>spoke</u> exulting over him

---

[6] One additional example in the *Odyssey* where the subject and object are reversed in position.

APPENDIX IV

FULL-VERSE SPEECH CONCLUDING FORMULAS

All speech concluding formulas that occur at least three times in the Homeric epics (presented in order of frequency, with most frequent first) are given below. The main verb (other than or in addition to "so s/he spoke" is <u>highlighted</u>.

Formulas Appearing Ten Times or More

> ὣς οἳ μὲν τοιαῦτα πρὸς ἀλλήλους <u>ἀγόρευον</u>
> 23x (8x Iliad, 15x Odyssey)
> Now as these <u>were speaking</u> things like this to each other

> ὣς ἔφατ᾽, οὐδ᾽ <u>ἀπίθησε</u> [nominative noun/epithet, subject]
> 23x (21x Iliad, 2x Odyssey)
> So he spoke, nor did [subject] <u>disobey</u> him.

> ὣς ἔφαθ᾽, οἳ δ᾽ ἄρα πάντες <u>ἀκὴν ἐγένοντο σιωπῇ·</u>
> 15x (10x Iliad, 5x Odyssey)
> So he spoke, and all of them <u>stayed stricken to silence</u>

> ὣς ἔφαθ᾽, οἳ δ᾽ ἄρα τοῦ μάλα μὲν κλύον ἠδ᾽ ἐπίθοντο
> 13x (7x Iliad, 6x Odyssey)
> So he spoke, and they listened to him with care, and obeyed him.

> ὣς ἔφατ᾽ [nom. sg. participle], τοῦ/τῆς δ᾽ <u>ἔκλυε</u> [nominative
> name/epithet, subject][1]
> 11x (8x Iliad, 3x Odyssey)
> Thus he spoke [doing X], and [subject] <u>heard</u> him

---

[1] Participle is always εὐχόμενος (or -μένη, "praying"), except for one instance in Iliad 1 of δάκρ χέων (weeping, 357) for Achilles addressing Thetis.

ὣς εἰπὼν [or εἰποῦσ’] ὄτρυνε μένος καὶ θυμὸν ἑκάστου
11x (10x *Iliad*, 1x *Odyssey*)
So s/he spoke, and <u>stirred</u> the spirit and strength in each man

ormulas Appearing between Five and Ten Times

ὣς ἔφατ’, ὦρτο δέ [nominative noun/epithet phrase, subject]
8x (7x *Iliad*, 1x *Odyssey*)
So s/he spoke, and there <u>rose up</u> [subject]

ὣς ἄρα φωνήσας [or φωνήσασ’] ἀπέβη [nominative name/
epithet, subject]
8x (5x *Iliad*, 3x *Odyssey*)
So spoke [subject], and <u>went away</u>

αὐτὰρ ἐπεὶ τό γ’ ἄκουσε [nominative noun/epithet, subject]
8x (3x *Iliad*, 5x *Odyssey*)
When (he) had <u>heard</u> this, [subject] . . .

αὐτίκα δ’ [or ἦ ῥα καὶ] ἀμπεπαλὼν προΐει δολιχόσκιον ἔγχος[2]
7x *Iliad*
So he spoke, and balanced the spear far-shadowed, and
<u>threw</u> it

ὣς φάτο [dative phrase, indirect object] ὑφ’ ἵμερον ὦρσε γόοιο
7x (2x *Iliad*, 5x *Odyssey*)
So he spoke, and in [dative] <u>stirred</u> a passion for grieving

ὣς ἔφατο κλαίουσ’ [or κλαίων], ἐπὶ δὲ [nom pl. subject with
verb for "groan"]
7x *Iliad*
So s/he spoke, lamenting, and [subject] groaned in response

ὣς ἔφατ’ [nominative noun, subject], τοῖσιν δ’ ἐπιήνδανε μῦθος.
7x *Odyssey*
So [subject] spoke, and his word <u>pleased</u> all the rest of them

---

[2] This is included in this appendix, although not in any of my data, because although only two
examples of this verse have ἦ ῥα καὶ at the beginning, all the rest directly follow a verse that
concludes a speech.

ἣ μὲν ἄρ' ὣς εἰποῦσ' ἀπέβη [nominative name/epithet, subject]
7x (5x *Iliad*, 2x *Odyssey*)
She spoke thus, [subject], and went away

ἧος ὃ ταῦθ' ὥρμαινε κατὰ φρένα καὶ κατὰ θυμόν[3]
6x (3x *Iliad*, 3x *Odyssey*)
Now as he was pondering this in his heart and his spirit

ὣς φάτο [dative pronoun, possessive dative] θυμὸν ἐνὶ
στήθεσσιν ὄρινε
6x (5x *Iliad*, 1x *Odyssey*)
So he spoke, and stirred up the passion in the breast of
[dative pronoun]

ὣς [verb for "spoke"; nominative name, subject] δὲ διὲκ
[genitive, place] βεβήκει
6x *Odyssey*
So he spoke, but [subject] strode out through [place]

ἤτοι ὅ γ' ὣς εἰπὼν κατ' ἄρ' ἕζετο· τοῖσι δ' ἀνέστη[4]
6x (5x *Iliad*, 1x *Odyssey*)
He spoke thus and sat down again, and among them stood up

Formulas Appearing Three to Five Times

ὣς ἄρα φωνήσας ἡγήσατο, τοὶ δ' ἄμ' ἕποντο
5x (2x *Iliad*, 3x *Odyssey*)
He spoke, and led the way, and the rest of them came on
after him

ὣς ἄρα φωνήσας [or φωνήσασ'] ἡγήσατο [nominative name/
epithet, subject]
5x (1x *Iliad*, 4x *Odyssey*)
So s/he spoke, [subject], and led the way

---

[3] Two of these verses lack a speech immediately preceding them, although all follow a speech i
the general vicinity

[4] Not a single-verse speech concluding formula in the sense that it is a syntactically sel
contained verse, as are all the others in this appendix. It is included here anyway because
generally forms part of a multi-verse passage that is syntactically separate from the vers
immediately preceding and following it.

ὣς φάτο, [genitive pronoun] δ᾽ αὐτοῦ <u>λύτο</u> γούνατα καὶ
    φίλον ἦτορ
    5x (1x *Iliad*, 4x *Odyssey*)
So he spoke, and in [genitive] the knees and the inward heart
    <u>went slack</u>

ὣς φάτο, καί ῥ᾽ <u>ἔμπνευσε</u> μένος [nominative name/epithet,
    subject]
    4x (3x *Iliad*, 1x *Odyssey*)
So [subject] spoke, and <u>breathed into</u> him enormous strength

ὣς ἔφατ᾽, αὐτίκα δὲ χρυσόθρονος <u>ἤλυθεν</u> Ἠώς
    4x *Odyssey* [2 by primary narrator, 2 by Odysseus in Books 9-12]
So s/he spoke, and dawn of the golden throne <u>came</u>

ὣς εἰπὼν <u>ὤτρυνε</u> πάρος μεμαυῖαν Ἀθήνην
    4x (3x *Iliad*, 1x *Odyssey*)
Speaking so he <u>stirred up</u> Athene, who was eager before this

ὣς [verb for "spoke"; nominative name, subject] δὲ <u>χολώσατο</u>
    κηρόθι μᾶλλον
    4x (1x *Iliad*, 3x *Odyssey*)
He spoke, and [subject] in his heart <u>grew</u> still more <u>angry</u>.

ὣς ἄρ᾽ ἐφώνησεν, τῇ δ᾽ <u>ἄπτερος ἔπλετο μῦθος</u>
    4x *Odyssey*
So he spoke, and she had <u>no winged words for an answer</u>

ὣς ἔφαθ᾽, οἱ δ᾽ ἄρα πάντες <u>ἐπήνεον ἠδ᾽ ἐκέλευον</u>
    4x *Odyssey*
So he spoke, and they <u>all approved what he said and urged it</u>

ὣς εἰπὼν [or εἰποῦσ᾽] ἐν χερσὶ τίθει, ὃ δὲ <u>δέξατο</u> χαίρων
    4x (3x *Iliad*, 1x *Odyssey*)
So speaking, s/he put it into his hands, and he gladly
    <u>received</u> it.

ὣς ἔφαθ᾽, οἱ δ᾽ ἄρα πάντες ὀδὰξ ἐν χείλεσι φύντες
Τηλέμαχον <u>θαύμαζον</u>, ὃ θαρσαλέως ἀγόρευε
    3x *Odyssey*
So he spoke, and all of them bit their lips, in <u>amazement</u>
at Telemachos and the daring way he had spoken to them.

ὣς ἔφαθ', οἳ δ' ἄρα πάντες ἐπ' αὐτῷ ἡδὺ <u>γέλασσαν</u>
    3x (1x *Iliad*, 2x *Odyssey*)
So he spoke, and all of them <u>laughed</u> happily at him

ὣς ἔφατ', Ἀργείοισι δ' <u>ἄχος γένετ'</u> εὐξαμένοιο
    3x *Iliad* (all in Books 13 and 14)
He spoke, and <u>sorrow came</u> over the heart of the Argives at
      his vaunting

ὣς εἰπὼν ὃ μὲν αὖτις <u>ἔβη</u> θεὸς ἂμ πόνον ἀνδρῶν
    3x *Iliad*
So he spoke and <u>strode</u> on, a god, through the mortals'
      struggle.

ὣς φάτο, τὸν δ' ἄχεος νεφέλη <u>ἐκάλυψε</u> μέλαινα
    3x (2x *Iliad*, 1x *Odyssey*)
He spoke, and the dark cloud of sorrow <u>closed</u> over him.

ὣς εἰπὼν ὃ μὲν ἦρχ', ὃ δ' ἅμ' <u>ἕσπετο</u> ἰσόθεος φώς
    3x *Iliad*
He spoke, and led the way, and the other <u>followed</u>, a mortal
      like a god.

BIBLIOGRAPHY

I. Editions of Homer, lexica, and other reference works

Chantraine, P. 1990, 1984. *Dictionnaire étymologique de la langue Greque* 1-2, 3-4. Paris.

Cunliffe, R. J. 1988. *A Lexicon of the Homeric Dialect* ed. 2. Norman.

Dunbar, H. 1962. *A Complete Concordance to the Odyssey of Homer.* Rev. B. Marzullo. Hildesheim.

Erbse, H., ed. 1969, 1971, 1974, 1975, 1977, 1983, 1988. *Scholia Graeca in Homeri Iliadem* I, II, III, IV, V, VI, VII. Berlin.

Leaf, W., ed. 1866, 1871. *The Iliad* I, II. London.

Prendergast, G. L. 1962. *A Complete Concordance to the Iliad of Homer.* Rev. B. Marzullo. Hildesheim.

van Thiel, H., ed. 1991. *Homeri Odyssea.* Hildesheim.

———, ed. 1996. *Homeri Ilias.* Hildesheim.

West, M. L., ed. 1998, 2000. *Homeri Ilias* I, II. Stuttgart.

II. Other works

Alexiou, M. 1974. *The Ritual Lament in Greek Tradition.* Cambridge.

Apthorp, M. J. 1999. "Homer's Winged Words and the Papyri: Some Questions of Authenticity." *Zeitschrift für Papyrologie und Epigrafik* 128:15-22.

Arend, W. 1933. *Die typischen Scenen bei Homer.* Problemata 7. Berlin.

Austin, N. 1966. "The Function of Digressions in the Iliad." *Greek, Roman and Byzantine Studies* 7:295-312.

———. 1975 . *Archery at the Dark of the Moon: Poetic Problems in Homer's Odyssey.* Berkeley.

Bakker, E. J. 1997. *Poetry in Speech: Orality and Homeric Discourse.* Ithaca.

Bibliography

Balthes, M. 1983. "Zur Eigenart und Funktion von Gleichnissen im 16. Buch der Ilias." *Antike und Abendland* 29:36-48.

Bassett, S. E. 1938. *The Poetry of Homer.* Berkeley.

Beck, D. 1999. "Speech Introductions and the Character Development of Telemachus." *Classical Journal* 94: 121-141.

Beck, W. 1986. "Choice and Context: Metrical Doublets for Hera." *American Journal of Philology* 107:480-488.

Boedeker, D. D. 1974. *Aphrodite's Entry into Greek Epic.* Leiden.

Bolling, G. M. 1925. *The External Evidence for Interpolation in Homer.* Oxford.

Bowra, C. M. 1930. *Tradition and Design in the Iliad.* Oxford.

Burgess, J. S. 2001. *The Tradition of the Trojan War in Homer & the Epic Cycle.* Baltimore.

Byre, C. S. 1988. "Penelope and the Suitors Before Odysseus: *Odyssey* 18.158-303." *American Journal of Philology* 109:159-173.

Clanchy, M. T. 1979. *From Memory to Written Record: England, 1066-1307.* Cambridge.

Clark, M. E. 1986. "Neoanalysis: A Bibliographical Review." *Classical World* 79:379-391.

Clay, J. S. 1983. *The Wrath of Athena: Gods and Men in the Odyssey.* Princeton.

Collins, D. 1998. *Immortal Armor: The Concept of Alkê in Archaic Greek Poetry.* Lanham.

Combellack, F. M. 1948. "Speakers and Scepters in Homer." *Classical Journal* 43:209-217.

———. 1959. "Milman Parry and Homeric Artistry." *Comparative Literature* 11:193-208.

Crotty, C. 1994. *The Poetics of Supplication: Homer's Iliad and Odyssey.* Ithaca

Danek, G. 1998. *Epos und Zitat: Studien zu den Quellen der Odyssee.* Vienna.

de Jong, I. J. F. 1985. "Fokalisation und die homerischen Gleichnisse." *Mnemosyne* 38:257-280.

———. 1987a. *Narrators and Focalizers: The Presentation of the Story in the Iliad.* Amsterdam.

———. 1987b. "The Voice of Anonymity: tis-Speeches in the *Iliad*." *Eranos* 85:69-84.

———. 2001. *A Narratological Commentary on the Odyssey.* Cambridge.

Dickey, E. 1996. *Greek Forms of Address From Herodotus to Lucian.* Oxford.

)iffey, T. J. 1995. "A Note on Some Meanings of the Term 'Aesthetic'." *British Journal of Aesthetics* 35:61-66.

)onlan, W. 1979. "The Structure of Authority in the *Iliad*." *Arethusa* 12:51-70.

)rew, P. and J. Heritage, eds. 1992. *Talk at Work*. Studies in Interactional Sociolinguistics 8. Cambridge.

)uggan, J. J. 1973. *The Song of Roland: Formulaic Style and Poetic Craft*. Berkeley.

:dwards, M. W. 1966. "Some Features of Homeric Craftsmanship." *Transactions of the American Philological Association* 97:115-179.

———. 1969. "On Some 'Answering' Expressions in Homer." *Classical Philology* 64:81-87.

———. 1970. "Homeric Speech Introductions." *Harvard Studies in Classical Philology* 74:1-36.

———. 1980. "Convention and Individuality in *Iliad* 1." *Harvard Studies in Classical Philology* 84:1-28.

———. 1986a. "Homer and Oral Tradition: The Formula, Part I." *Oral Tradition* 1/2:171-230.

———. 1986b. "The Conventions of a Homeric Funeral." *Studies in Honor of T. B. L. Webster* (eds. J. H. Betts, J. T. Hooker, and J. R. Green) 84-92. Bristol.

———. 1987. *Homer: Poet of the Iliad*. Baltimore.

———. 1988. "Homer and Oral Tradition: The Formula, Part II." *Oral Tradition* 3/1-2:11-60

———. 1990. "Neoanalysis and Beyond." *Classical Antiquity* 9:311-325.

———. 1991. *The Iliad: A Commentary (Volume V: Books 17-20)*. Cambridge.

———. 1992. "Homer and Oral Tradition: The Type-Scene." *Oral Tradition* 7/2:284-330.

———. 1997. "Homeric Style and 'Oral Poetics'." In Morris and Powell 1997:261-283.

mlyn-Jones, C. 1984. "The Reunion of Penelope and Odysseus." *Greece & Rome* 31:1-18.

rbse, H. 1972. *Beiträge zum Verständnis der Odyssee*. Berlin.

eeney, D. 1983. "The Taciturnity of Aeneas." *Classical Quarterly* n.s. 33:204-219.

elson-Rubin, N. 1994. *Regarding Penelope: From Character to Poetics*. Princeton.

enik, B. 1968. *Typical Battle Scenes in the Iliad: Studies in the Narrative Techniques of Homeric Battle Description*. Hermes Einzelschriften, Heft 21. Wiesbaden.

inkelberg, M. 1986. "Is ΚΛΕΟΣ ΑΦΘΙΤΟΝ a Homeric Formula?" *Classical Quarterly* n.s 36:1-5.

Finnegan, R. 1977. *Oral Poetry: Its Nature, Significance, and Social Context.* Cambridge

Foley, H. P. 1978. "'Reverse Similes' and Sex Roles in the *Odyssey.*" *Arethusa* 2:7-26.

———. 1995. "Penelope as Moral Agent." *The Distaff Side* (ed. B. Cohen) 93-115. New York.

Foley, J. M. 1985. *Oral-Formulaic Theory and Research: An Introduction and Annotated Bibliography.* New York.

———. 1991. *Immanent Art.* Bloomington.

———. 1999. *Homer's Traditional Art.* University Park.

Fournier, H. 1946. "Formules homériques de référence avec verbe 'dire'." *Revue de Philologie* 20:29-68.

Friedrich, R. 2002. "'Flaubertian Homer': The *Phrase Juste* in Homeric Diction." *Arion* 10:1-13.

Genette, G. 1980. *Narrative Discourse: An Essay in Method.* Transl. J. E. Lewin. Cornell.

Goffman, E. 1981. *Forms of Talk.* Philadelphia.

Graziosi, B. 2002. *Inventing Homer: The Early Reception of Epic.* Cambridge.

Griffin, J. 1980. *Homer on Life and Death.* Oxford.

———. 1986. "Homeric Words and Speakers." *Journal of Hellenic Studies* 106:36-57.

Gumperz, J. J. and D. Hymes, eds. 1972. *Directions in Sociolinguistics: The Ethnography of Communication.* New York.

Gunn, D. 1970. "Narrative Inconsistency and the Oral Dictated Text in the Homeric Epic." *American Journal of Philology* 91:192-203.

———. 1971. "Thematic Composition and Homeric Authorship." *Harvard Studie in Classical Philology* 75:1-31.

Hainsworth, J. B. 1968. *The Flexibility of the Homeric Formula.* Oxford.

———. 1978. "Good and Bad Formulae." *Homer: Tradition and Invention* (ed. B. Fenik) 41-50. Leiden.

———. 1993. *The Iliad: A Commentary (Volume III: Books 9-12).* Cambridge.

Harriott, R. 1962. "Aristophanes' Audience and the Plays of Euripides." *Bulleti of the Institute of Classical Studies* 9:1-8.

Heath, J. 2001. "Telemachus ΠΕΠΝΥΜΕΝΟΣ: Growing Into an Epithet." *Mnemosyne* 54:129-157.

Heiden, B. 1998a. "The Placement of 'Book Divisions' in the *Iliad.*" *Journal of Hellenic Studies* 118:68-81.

———. 1998b. "The Simile of the Fugitive Homicide, *Iliad* 24.480-84: Analogy, Foiling, and Allusion." *American Journal of Philology* 119:1-10.

Heubeck, A., S. West and J. Hainsworth. 1990a. *A Commentary on Homer's Odyssey Volume I (Introduction and Books I-VIII).* Oxford.

Heubeck, A. and Hoekstra, A. 1990b. *A Commentary on Homer's Odyssey. Volume II (Books IX-XVI).* Oxford.

Higbie, C. 1990. *Measure and Music: Enjambement and Sentence Structure in the Iliad.* Oxford.

———. 1995. *Heroes' Names, Homeric Identities.* New York.

Hoekstra, A. 1965. *Homeric Modifications of Formulaic Prototypes.* Amsterdam.

Holoka, J. P. 1973. "Homeric Originality: A Survey." *Classical World* 66:257-293.

———. 1983. "'Looking Darkly' (ΥΠΟΔΡΑ ΙΔΩΝ): Reflections on Status and Decorum in Homer." *Transactions of the American Philological Association* 113:1-16.

———. 1991. "Homer, Oral Poetry Theory, and Comparative Literature: Major Trends and Controversies in Twentieth-Century Criticism." In Latacz 1991:456-481.

Hölscher, U. 1972. "Die Erkennungsszene im 23. Buch der Odyssee." Reprinted in *Homer: Die Dichtung und ihre Deutung* (ed. J. Latacz) 1991:388-405. Darmstadt.

Hutchby, I. and R. Wooffitt. 1998. *Conversation Analysis.* Cambridge.

Janko, R. 1981. "Equivalent Formulae in the Greek Epos." *Mnemosyne* 34:251-264.

———. 1982. *Homer, Hesiod, and the Hymns: Diachronic Development in Epic Diction.* Cambridge.

Jaworski, A. and N. Coupland, eds. 1999. *The Discourse Reader.* New York.

Jensen, M. S. 1980. *The Homeric Question and the Oral-Formulaic Theory.* Copenhagen.

Jucker, A. H., ed. 1995. *Historical Pragmatics: Pragmatic Developments in the History of English.* Amsterdam.

Kahane, A. 1994. *The Interpretation of Order: A Study in the Poetics of Homeric Repetition.* Oxford.

Kakridis, J. Th. 1949. *Homeric Researches.* Lund.

Katz, M. A. 1991. *Penelope's Renown: Meaning and Indeterminacy in the Odyssey.* Princeton.

Kirk, G. S. 1962. *The Songs of Homer.* Cambridge.

———. 1985. *The Iliad: A Commentary (Volume I: Books 1-4).* Cambridge.

————. 1990. *The Iliad: A Commentary (Volume II: Books 5-8).* Cambridge.

Krarup, P. 1941. "Beobachtungen zur Typik und Technik einiger homerischer Gesprächsformeln." *Classica et mediaevalia* 4:230-247.

Kress, G. and T. van Leeuwen. 1999. "Representation and Interaction: Designing the Position of the Viewer." In Jaworski and Coupland 1999:377-404.

Krischer, T. 1971. *Formale Konventionen der homerischen Epik.* Munich.

Kullmann, W. 1960. *Die Quellen der Ilias.* Wiesbaden.

————. 1984. "Oral Poetry Theory and Neoanalysis in Homeric Research." Reprinted in *Homer: Critical Assessments* Volume 1: The Creation of the Poems (ed. I. J. F. de Jong) 1999:145-160. London.

————. 1991. "Ergebnisse der motivgeschichtlichen Forschung zu Homer (Neoanalyse)." In Latacz 1991:425-455.

Laird, A. 1999. *Powers of Expression, Expressions of Power: Speech Presentation and Latin Literature.* Oxford.

Lang, M. 1989. "Unreal Conditions in Homeric Narrative." *Greek, Roman and Byzantine Studies* 30:5-26.

Latacz, J. 1968. "ἄπτερος μῦθος—ἄπτερος φάτις: ungeflügetle Worte?" *Glotta* 46:27-47.

————, ed. 1991. *Zweihundert Jahre Homer-Forschung: Rückblick und Ausblick.* Stuttgart.

Lateiner, D. 1995. *Sardonic Smile: Nonverbal Behavior in Homeric Epic.* Ann Arbor

Lattimore, R, trans. 1951. *The Iliad of Homer.* Chicago.

————. 1965. *The Odyssey of Homer.* New York.

Lesky, A. 1968. "Homeros" *Paulys Realencyclopädie der classischen Altertumswissenscha* Supplementum Vol. XI (ed. K. Ziegler) 687-845. Stuttgart.

Létoublon, F. 1999. "Epea Pteroenta ('Winged Words')." *Oral Tradition* 14/2: 321-335.

Levine, D. B. 1984. "Odysseus' Smiles: *Odyssey* 20.301, 22.371, 23.111." *Transactions of the American Philological Association* 114:1-9.

Levinson, S. C. 1983. *Pragmatics.* Cambridge.

————. 1992. "Activity Types and Language." In Drew and Heritage 1992:66-10(

Lloyd, M. 2004. "The Politeness of Achilles: Off-Record Conversation Strategies in Homer and the Meaning of *Kertomia*." *Journal of Hellenic Studies* 124:75-89.

Lohmann, D. 1970. *Die Komposition der Reden in der Ilias.* Berlin.

Lord, A. B. 1960. *The Singer of Tales*. Harvard Studies in Comparative Literature 24. Cambridge, MA.

Lord, A. B. and Bynum, D. E. transl. 1974. *Serbo-Croatian Heroic Songs Collected by Milman Parry* Vol. 3: The wedding of Smailagic' Meho, Avdo Mededovic'. Cambridge, MA.

Louden, B. 1993. "Pivotal Contrafactuals in Homeric Epic." *Classical Antiquity* 12:181-198.

———. 1999. *The Odyssey: Structure, Narration, and Meaning*. Baltimore.

McGlew, J. F. 1989. "Royal Power and the Achaean Assembly at *Iliad* 2.84-393." *Classical Antiquity* 8:283-295.

Machacek, G. 1994. "The Occasional Contextual Appropriateness of Formulaic Diction in the Homeric Poems." *American Journal of Philology* 115:321-335.

Mackay, A. 1996. "Time and Timelessness in the Traditions of Early Greek Oral Poetry and Archaic Vase-Painting." *Voice Into Text: Orality and Literacy in Ancient Greece* (ed. I. Worthington) 43-58. Leiden.

Mackie, H. 1996. *Talking Trojan: Speech and Community in the Iliad*. Lanham.

Maquiso, E. G. 1977. *Ulahingan: An Epic of the Southern Philippines*. Dumaguete City.

Martin, R. P. 1989. *The Language of Heroes: Speech and Performance in the Iliad*. Ithaca.

Miller, C. L. 1996. *The Presentation of Speech in Biblical Hebrew Narrative*. Atlanta.

Minchin, E. 2001. *Homer and the Resources of Memory: Some Applications of Cognitive Theory to the Iliad and the Odyssey*. Oxford.

Morris, I. 1986. "The Use and Abuse of Homer." *Classical Antiquity* 5:81-138.

Morris, I. and B. Powell, eds. 1997. *A New Companion to Homer*. Leiden.

Moulton, C. 1977. *Similes in the Homeric Poems*. Hypomnemata 49. Göttingen.

Muellner, L. C. 1976. *The Meaning of Homeric EYXOMAI Through its Formulas*. Innsbrucker Beträge zur Sprachwissenschaft 13. Innsbruck.

Murnaghan, S. 1987. *Disguise and Recognition in the Odyssey*. Princeton.

Nagler, M. N. 1967. "Towards a Generative View of the Oral Formula." *Transactions of the American Philological Association* 98:269-311.

———. 1974. *Spontaneity and Tradition: A Study in the Oral Art of Homer*. Berkeley.

Nagy, G. 1974. *Comparative Studies in Greek and Indic Meter*. Harvard Studies in Comparative Literature 33. Cambridge, MA.

———. 1979. *The Best of the Achaeans*. Baltimore.

———. 1992. "Homeric Questions." *Transactions of the American Philological Association* 122:17-60.

———. 1996. *Homeric Questions.* Austin.

Niles, J. D. 1999. *Homo Narrans: The Poetics And Anthropology Of Oral Literature.* Philadelphia.

Olson, S. D. 1994. "Equivalent Speech-Introduction Formulae in the *Iliad.*" *Mnemosyne* 47:145-151.

———. 1995. *Blood and Iron: Stories and Storytelling in Homer's Odyssey.* Mnemosyne Supp. 145. Leiden.

Page, D. 1955. *The Homeric Odyssey.* Oxford.

———. 1966. *History and the Homeric Iliad.* Berkeley.

Parks, W. 1990. *Verbal Dueling in Heroic Narrative: The Homeric and Old English Traditions.* Princeton.

Parry, M. 1987. *The Making of Homeric Verse: The Collected Papers of Milman Parry.* Ed. A. Parry. Oxford.

Podlecki, A. J. 1971. "Some Odyssean Similes." *Greece & Rome* 18:81-90.

Pope, M. W. M. 1960. "Athena's Development in Homeric Epic." *American Journal of Philology* 81:113-135.

Redfield, J. M. 1994. *Nature and Culture in the Iliad: The Tragedy of Hector.* Durham.

Reece, S. 1993. *The Stranger's Welcome: Oral Theory and the Aesthetics of the Homeric Hospitality Scene.* Ann Arbor.

———. 1994. "The Cretan Odyssey: A Lie Truer than Truth." *American Journal of Philology* 115:157-173.

Reinhardt, K. 1961. *Die Ilias und ihr Dichter.* Ed. U. Hölscher. Göttingen.

Richardson, N. 1993. *The Iliad: A Commentary (Volume VI: Books 21-24).* Cambridge.

Richardson, S. 1990. *The Homeric Narrator.* Nashville.

Riggsby, A. M. 1992. "Homeric Speech Introductions and the Theory of Homeric Composition." *Transactions of the American Philological Association* 122:99-114.

Rimmon-Kenan, S. 1983. *Narrative Fiction: Contemporary Poetics.* London.

Russo, J. A. 1968. "Homer Against His Tradition." *Arion* 7:275-295.

———. 1994. "Homer's Style: Nonformulaic Features of an Oral Aesthetic." *Oral Tradition* 9/2:371-389.

———. 1997. "The Formula." In Morris and Powell 1997:238-260.

Russo, J., M. Fernandez-Galiano and A. Heubeck. 1992. *A Commentary on Homer's Odyssey Volume III (Books XVII-XXIV).* Oxford.

Sacks, H. 1992. *Lectures on Conversation* I, II. Ed. G. Jefferson. Oxford.

Sacks, H., E. A. Schegloff, and G. Jefferson. 1974. "A Simplest Systematics for the Organization of Turn-Taking for Conversation." *Language* 50:696-735.

Schadewaldt, W. 1959. *Von Homers Welt und Werk* ed. 3. Stuttgart.

———. 1966. *Neue Kriterien zur Odyssee-Analyse: Die Wiedererkennung des Odysseus und der Penelope* ed 2. Heidelberg.

Schmitt, R. 1967. *Dichtung und Dichtersprache in indogermanischer Zeit.* Wiesbaden.

Scott, W. C. 1974. *The Oral Nature of the Homeric Simile.* Leiden.

———. 1997. "The Etiquette of Games in *Iliad* 23." *Greek, Roman and Byzantine Studies* 38:213-227.

Scully, S. 1984. "The Language of Achilles: The ΟΧΘΗΣΑΣ Formulas." *Transactions of the American Philological Association* 114:11-27.

Searle, J. 1992. "Conversation." *(On) Searle on Conversation* (J. Searle et al.) 7-29. Amsterdam.

Segal, C. 1971. "Andromache's *Anagnorisis*: Formulaic Artistry in *Iliad* 22.437-476." *Harvard Studies in Classical Philology* 75:33-57.

Shay, J. 1994. *Achilles in Vietnam: Combat Trauma and the Undoing of Character.* New York.

Silverman, D. 1998. *Harvey Sacks: Social Science and Conversation Analysis.* New York.

Stanley, K. 1993. *The Shield of Homer.* Princeton.

Strasser, F. X. 1984. *Zu den Iterata der frühgriechischen Epik.* Königstein.

Taplin, O. 1992. *Homeric Soundings.* Oxford.

Viechnicki, P. 1994. "ἀμείβω: An Interdisciplinary Etymology." *Journal of Indo-European Studies* 22:113-132.

Visser, E. 1988. "Formulae or Single Words? Towards a New Theory of Homeric Verse-Making." *Würzburger Jahrbücher für die Altertumsvissenschaft neue Folge* 14:21-37.

Watkins, C. 1995. *How to Kill a Dragon: Aspects of Indo-European Poetics.* Oxford.

West, M. L., ed. 1997. *Hesiod's Theogony* ed. 2. Oxford.

———. 1990. "Archaische Heldendichtung: Singen und Schreiben." *Der Übergang von der Mündlichkeit zur Literatur bei den Greichen* (eds. W. Kullmann and M. Reichel) 33-50. Tübigen.

West, S. 1989. "Laertes Revisited." *Proceedings of the Cambridge Philological Society* n.s. 35:113-143.

Bibliography

Whallon, W. 1961. "The Homeric Epithets." *Yale Classical Studies* 17:97-142.

Whitman, C. H. 1958. *Homer and the Heroic Tradition.* Cambridge.

Wilamowitz, U. 1916. *Die Ilias und Homer.* Berlin.

Wright, G. and P. Jones, transl. 1997. *Homer: German Scholarship in Translation.* Oxford.

INDEX LOCORUM

Iliad

Odyssey

INDEX OF NAMES AND SUBJECTS

A

Achilles, 32, 45, 50, 86, 200-202, 238-241, 243-244; *aristeia* of, 171, 184, 190, 272; in assembly, 204-228; berserk behavior of, 171-172; and Hector, 184-190; laments for Patroclus, 257-269; and Lycaon, 171-175; and Priam, 135-144; See also vocatives

Athena, 26, 50, 64, 68, 78, 214; and Odysseus, 52-61

athletic games, See funeral games

audience, 17, 18, 22, 24, 37, 39, 78, 274-275; as listeners in group conversation, 194, 203; See also addressee

B

battlefield, 40, 44; one-on-one conversation on, 169, 171; speech as attack on, 166-167; speech and, 165; speech and attack in turns on, 165, 167-168, 169-177; speech conclusions on, 165, 184-185; speech genres on, 150-151; turn sequences for, 166-168, 169-177, 185-186, 189; typical patterns for, 150-153, 165-168, 171-172, 178-179, 183, 184; See also challenge, exhortation, single speeches, vaunt

C

Calchas, 209-210

catalogue, 258

challenge, 149, 150-151, 165-190; variations in pattern of, 168-190; See also vaunt

Chanson de Roland, 246n28

commands, 26, 27

condition, contrary to fact, 75, 121-122, 239

conversation; actions with, 149; average length of, 127; in chariot race (*Iliad* 23), 237-244; competition and, 232, 239-240, 243-244, 272; conflict and, 128-129, 134, 144-145, 149-150, 190, 271-272; differences between *Iliad* and *Odyssey*, 45; emotions and, 49, 71, 83, 88, 90, 106, 107, 135, 144, 159, 209-220; between enemies, 178-190; as exchange, 19-20; as expansion of single speech genres, 154, 164, 169, 190; in literary texts, 22-23; in the *Odyssey*, 51-52; as proportion of direct speech, 2; repair of, 24; representation of, 22, 23; rules for, 21; sequence of elements in, 25-44, 52, 128; silence in, 24, 36, 196, 200-201, 202, 203; social context of, 5, 8, 9, 21, 23, 24, 25, 194, 197, 207; social status and, 50, 149-150, 272; speakers in, 21; turns in, 21, 23, 25, 28, 29, 33, 49, 50, 60, 85, 86, 87-88, 101, 111. 144, 151; as type scene, 2, 3-4, 5, 8-10, 15, 26, 29, 83-84, 88, 90, 126, 136, 144, 149, 184, 272, 275; ubiquity of, 2, 5, 11; See also assembly, battlefield, exhortation, group conversation, initial speeches, one-on-one conversation, replies, single speeches, successive speeches

F

Fenik, Bernard, 10, 31

focalization, 98

Foley, John M., 6

formulas, 2, 3, 5, 9, 10, 52, 56, 59, 63, 70, 72, 100, 134, 184; definition of, 12-13, 30-32; noun-epithet formulas, 12, 14, 67, 129-130, 219; repetition and, 30; See also epithets, reply introductions, speech conclusions, speech frames, speech introductions

funeral games, 41, 45, 149, 230-244, 272; and assembly, 233-234, 244; and battle, 232, 234-235, 244; chariot race (*Iliad* 23), 237-244; conversation not typical in, 232, 237, 244; group sits at, 233; prizes in, 240-243; standing and, 234, 235, 236, 238; turns in, 234-236, 244; as type, 230-232; typical patterns for, 232-237, 239, 244

G

games, See funeral games

gift-giving, 19-20, 94

Greece, archaic, 17-18

group conversation, 9, 29, 37, 45, 149, 191-192, 203-204; behavior with, 192-193, 231-232, 245, 269, 272; formal, 230-231, 251, 269, 272; informal, 202-204; and institutional talk, 231, 249n37, 249n38, 272; See also addressee, assembly, funeral games, lament, speech conclusions, speech introductions

H

Hector, 26, 45, 152-153, 190; and Achilles, 184-190; and Andromache, 128-129; laments for, 246-257, 267; and Patroclus, 178-184

Hecuba, 248-250, 254-255

Hera, 26; and seduction of Zeus, 129-135

Hermes, 136

historical pragmatics, 8, 23; historical linguistics in, 23; pragmatics in, 23

Homeric epics, composition of, 2, 23, 275; unity of, 273-275

Hypnus, 132

Designed and composed by Kristin Murphy Romano
Manufactured by Victor Graphics, Baltimore, MD

The text typeface is Gentium, designed by Victor Gaultney
and distributed by SIL International
The sans serif display typeface is Optima, designed by Hermann Zapf
The sans serif chart typeface is Lucida Sans, designed by Charles Bigelow
and Kris Holmes
The typeface KadmosU is distributed by the American Philological Association.